Jews and New Christians in the Making of the Atlantic World in the 16th–17th Centuries

Studies in Critical Social Sciences Book Series

Haymarket Books is proud to be working with Brill Academic Publishers (www.brill.nl) to republish the *Studies in Critical Social Sciences* book series in paperback editions. This peer-reviewed book series offers insights into our current reality by exploring the content and consequences of power relationships under capitalism, and by considering the spaces of opposition and resistance to these changes that have been defining our new age. Our full catalog of *SCSS* volumes can be viewed at https://www.haymarketbooks.org/series_collections/4-studies-in-critical-social-sciences.

Jews and New Christians in the Making of the Atlantic World in the 16th–17th Centuries

A Survey

Henryk Szlajfer

Haymarket Books
Chicago, IL

First published in 2023 by Brill Academic Publishers, The Netherlands
© 2023 Koninklijke Brill NV, Leiden, The Netherlands

Published in paperback in 2024 by
Haymarket Books
P.O. Box 180165
Chicago, IL 60618
773-583-7884
www.haymarketbooks.org

ISBN: 979-8-88890-345-2

Distributed to the trade in the US through Consortium Book Sales and
Distribution (www.cbsd.com) and internationally through Ingram Publisher
Services International (www.ingramcontent.com).

This book was published with the generous support of Lannan Foundation,
Wallace Action Fund, and the Marguerite Casey Foundation.

Special discounts are available for bulk purchases by organizations and
institutions. Please call 773-583-7884 or email info@haymarketbooks.org for more
information.

Cover design by Jamie Kerry and Ragina Johnson.

Printed in the United States.

Library of Congress Cataloging-in-Publication data is available.

For Professor Tadeusz M. Orłowski, MD, and Janek Ordyński
always present in times of need,
and for Marysia and Helenka as ever

∴

Contents

Preface

In less than thirty years after Columbus' first expedition, Cuba and Hispaniola, the main islands of the Caribbean, had already been inhabited almost exclusively by Spanish conquistadors, their first descendants and incoming settlers from Spain. Even before the conquest of Mexico, the Caribbean Taíno Indians would be ravaged by disease and the labour regime imposed by the conquerors. By the mid-16th century, of the estimated population of just over 50 million Indians of pre-Columbian Latin America[1] no more than 2.5–15 per cent had survived, depending on the region. Two and a half centuries later, colonial Mexico, Brazil and Peru were home to 2.26 million descendants of the European conquistadors and the metropolitan influx of Spaniards and Portuguese (21.5 per cent of the total population) (Newson 2006: 148, 160).[2] With control of the major economic resources and the monopoly of violence secured by local militias and metropolises, this white minority formed the elite of the new societies.

A small part of it consisted of Jews, or more precisely, conversos and New Christians (Catholics whose Jewish ancestors had been baptised voluntarily or under compulsion in Spain and Portugal), and Jews migrating from Amsterdam and other cities of the Republic of the Seven United Provinces (hereafter: the Republic or the United Provinces). Estimates, however, are subject to a considerable margin of error and are probably greatly exaggerated. They suggested that among the more than 2 million Europeans who migrated to the Americas between 1500 and 1760, there were no more than 50–70,000 New Christians and 20,000 Jews, translating into an average annual gross migration of between 270–340 people.[3] Thus, no more than 4.5 per cent of total European migration in the colonial era.

---

1   The figure given for the population of pre-Columbian Latin America reflects the relative consensus among scholars reached at the end of the 20th century. It was contested as being almost three times overstated by Maddison (2001: 233–236).

2   According to other estimates, in 1760 the population of European descent in the Spanish colonies and Brazil could be estimated at 3.39 million (including 390,000 in Brazil) (Pétré-Grenouilleau 2009: 47).

3   The estimate of the number of New Christians is based on the (debatable) assumption that their share among Portuguese emigrants to Latin America corresponded to the share of Jews in the Portuguese population at the end of the 15th century, i.e. 10 per cent (Drescher 2001: 459f). The lower threshold of 50,000 New Christians is due to the adoption of a different estimate of the number of Portuguese emigrants to Latin America (net emigration) than that given by Drescher (Eltis 2000: 9). In contrast, Lewin (1987: 185) estimated the number of New Christians at 40,000, including 10,000 in Brazil.

Estimates for the beginning of colonisation in the 16th century are equally uncertain. The number of conversos and New Christians in all of Spanish America at the end of the 16th century was probably around 6,000, including 2,000 in Mexico and several thousand in Brazil in the early 17th century. Other estimates put the number at 5,000–7,000 in Spanish America in the 1630s (Swetschinski 2004: 64, Studnicki-Gizbert 2007: 44).[4] This was not a small number, measured in relation to, for example, the size of the Sephardic diaspora in northern Europe or the total white population in the New World of the late 16th and early 17th centuries. Aptly, though with some exaggeration, the historian of Amsterdam Jews points out that by the end of the 16th century there was a huge gap between the number of Portuguese New Christians migrating to northern Europe and Italy and the scale of migration within the area controlled by the Iberian states: "Migrations to Spain and the Portuguese and Spanish colonies are measured in the thousands, those to Atlantic and Mediterranean communities in the hundreds" (Swetschinski 2004: 64). Not quite. If one excludes the migrations to the Ottoman Empire after 1492, when the presence of more than 3,000 Sephardic and Balkan Jewish families (about 15,000 people) was recorded in Thessaloniki in 1519 and 8,070 families (about 40,000 people) in Istanbul in 1535, the increase in the number of Jews living in Italian cities from the late 16th century was impressive. In Venice, the number of Jews increased from 900 people to 2,500 between 1552 and 1600 (Israel 2002a: 57, 76, Foa 2000: 163f). By contrast, Amsterdam was home to no more than 650 Portuguese Sephardim in the first decade of the 17th century.

The influx of New Christians into Spanish America would come after 1580, especially in the first decades of the 17th century. The terrible defeat suffered by the Portuguese in 1578 in the battle against the Muslims at Al-Qasr al-Kabir in Morocco, the death of King Sebastian and the extinction of the Aviz dynasty opened the way for Spanish predominance – the Iberian Union was established with Philip II as monarch of both Spain and Portugal. Its creation opened, with some delay, the Portuguese New Christians' access to the markets of Spain and the Spanish colonies. It should be borne in mind, after all, that while Portuguese New Christians appeared in Latin America as early as the beginning of the 16th century, the presence of Amsterdam Jews, mostly of Portuguese origin, dates only from the 1630s. However, the importance of both

---

4 A figure of 2,000–3,000 for New Spain is given by Liebman (1963: 100). This is disputed as "a bit too high" by Baron (1973: 279). Israel (1990a: 317, 319, 330), on the other hand, estimates that in 1641 the Portuguese (without differentiating between 'Old' and 'New' Christians) probably constituted 7 per cent of the white population of New Spain, i.e. 11,000–12,000 people. There were 1,000–1,500 Portuguese living in Ciudad de México in that year.

groups in establishing Latin America and the Atlantic world as an economic area from the 16th century was far greater than the cited estimates would suggest. This was particularly true of the New Christians in the first 150 years of colonisation. Reason enough, it seems, to take an interest.

A consternation, however, arises during the literature review. The role of European Jews and New Christians in shaping the economies of colonial Latin America in the 16th to the 18th centuries is a topic usually ignored even in the best general historical studies of this part of the New World or reduced to a few remarks and/or footnotes (Bakewell 2004, Lockhart and Schwartz 1983, Bethell 1984, Bulmer-Thomas, Coatsworth and Cortés Conde 2006, Elliott 2006, Kamen 2003). Also, in general accounts of Jewish history, the history of the New Christians and Jews in colonial Latin America is treated as a secondary issue (Avni 1992). The underlying theme is the tumultuous changes that, over the course of three centuries, shaped essentially new Jewish communities in Europe, while also shifting the focus of Jewish life towards Central and Eastern Europe.

This is not surprising. The history of the New World as seen by historians tends, in this case, to be at odds with the widespread belief in the overwhelming role of the Jews in the creation of the colonial world. In the perspective of Latin America as a whole, as well as of individual countries, the actions of much more powerful agents other than the Jews stand out. And yet the reflection arises that this is not the only reason. It seems that the complexity of the topic, the fluid boundaries between the convictions, including those of historians, amassed knowledge, and above all the difficulties involved in researching the role of minorities in social processes, tend to result in defensive reactions. These in turn are also expressed in the relegation of the problem to the background, in the minimalisation of its significance. Years ago, R. H. Popkin, an historian of Enlightenment philosophical thought and of Sephardi Jews' attempts at coming to grips with the reconstruction of their religious and social identity destroyed in the 15th–16th century persecutions, observed that "the Jews had been the invisible man of Western history for the last 2,000 years" (quoted in Liebman 1975: 141). He was not the first to admonish the proper place for ethnic and religious minorities. Let us just recall Adam Smith's remark that it was, "the disorder and injustice of the European governments" that in fact contributed to "the peopling and civilisation of America". The result was a long list of exiles making up the New World: "The English puritans, restrained at home (...). The English catholics, treated with much greater injustice (...); the quakers (...). The Portuguese Jews, persecuted by the inquisition, stript of their fortunes, and banished to Brazil" (Smith 1904: 190f).

Of course, the treatment of this subject is different in monographs dealing with the past of the various parts of the Spanish and Portuguese empires, as well as the English, French and Dutch colonies. Here, references are more frequent, especially in areas where this role can be described and where the New Christians and Jews exerted a significant and/or interesting influence. One can even speak of a kind of publishing boom in recent decades. We also have monographs and collective works devoted exclusively or largely to Jewish and New Christian merchants, financiers, trade intermediaries and planters in the Atlantic economy that took shape from the late 15th century.[5]

In this book we will focus on analysis of the role the New Christians and Jews played in the formation of the colonial economy of Latin America in the first two centuries after the conquest and this way also contributed to the emergence of the Atlantic world. This survey is intended as a kind of commentary on selected issues taken up in the literature on the subject. Polish historians have not addressed these issues, apart from a few references.[6] I mention

---

5   By way of example only, as the literature is already vast. A general historical overview, taking into account the literature up to the mid-1960s, can be found in Salo W. Baron's *magnum opus,* as well as in the works of the next generation of historians, notably Jonathan I. Israel and Jonathan Schorsch. The activities of Dutch Jews have been addressed by Yosef Kaplan, Daniel M. Swetschinski and Miriam Bodian, among others. Of importance for the understanding the converso phenomenon are contributions of Benzion Netanyahu, Norman Roth, David S. Gitlitz and Claude B. Stuczynski (from the younger generation). In the study of the Jewish presence in colonial Latin America, the earlier works of Seymour B. Liebman, Boleslao Lewin from Argentina and Günter Böhm from Chile, as well as excerpts from books by the Spanish historians J. Caro Baroja and A. Domínguez Ortiz, are noteworthy. The problem of *judaizantes* in Spanish America and Brazil up to the end of the 17th century has recently been taken up in monographs by Bruno Feitler, Ronaldo Vainfas and Ricardo Escobar Quevedo. Arnold Wiznitzer's book on the Jewish presence in Brazil is still worth reading. Among the classic works on Brazilian New Christians, one should mention contributions by José Antônio Gonsalves de Mello, Anita Waingort Novinsky, and José Gonçalves Salvador (including a controversial book on the participation of New Christians in the slave trade until the mid-17th century). Of note are contributions from Brazilian scholars of the younger generation concerning various aspects of the presence of New Christians both in Brazil and in the Spanish colonies, especially in Rio de la Plata. From more recent contributions, the Jewish presence in Nieuw-Holland, as well as Suriname and the Caribbean, are dealt with by, among others, numerous articles by Wim Klooster, monographs by Robert Cohen, Wieke Vink and Aviva Ben-Ur. Among the collective works published in recent years, see above all the volumes edited by P. Bernardini and N. Fiering and R. L. Kagan and P.D. Morgan, as well as the monographic issues of, for example, *Anais de História de Além-Mar* (dedicated to the theme *Os Judeus e o comércio colonial*), *Journal of Global Slavery* (on various aspects of the Iberian slave trade) and *Jewish History* (special issue on Portuguese New Christian identities, 1516–1700).

6   Research on Gaspar da Gama, a native of Poznań, an important figure who appeared at the beginning of Portuguese colonisation, is modest. The co-founder of Polish historiography

it because this book, first addressed to the Polish reader, was intended as an introduction to a subject far removed from the interests of Polish historiography. With some editorial changes and abbreviations, the book still retains this character. However, it should be emphasised at this point that the birth of the modern European economy in the 16th and 17th centuries, as seen from the perspective of Eastern Europe, has by no means escaped the attention of Polish economic historians. Quite the contrary. Researchers associated with the seminars of Marian Małowist and Witold Kula at the University of Warsaw in the 1960s and 1970s contributed innovative analyses of economic relations between Western and Eastern Europe (Kochanowicz 2006, Sosnowska 2019). In the mid-1960s, the following statement definitely did not belong to the mainstream European historiography: "The first countries of the developing capitalism were setting up sugar or cotton plantations for themselves across the Ocean, and found grain 'plantations' for themselves in Eastern Europe" (Kula 1983: 165). It would take the support of Fernand Braudel, Michael Moïssey Postan, Immanuel Wallerstein and others to appreciate these Eastern European precursors. And at the same time, Polish historians would not pay attention to the role played by Sephardim and conversos if only in the development of Baltic grain and timber trade. They saw the Dutch partners and ships, not the Jewish merchants. This is not the place to dwell on this issue in greater detail. Suffice it to say that for Poland and Eastern Europe, the Jewish diaspora is tantamount to the Ashkenazi, not the Sephardi Jews' presence. The activities and economic interests of those who spoke the "language of Ashkenaz" were only indirectly linked to the development of the Atlantic world. They would appear in limited numbers in the Caribbean and Suriname only in the second half of the 18th century. A rapidly growing comunity, they would be present at and play a role in the consolidation of the Polish semi-periphery, while the numerically smaller group of Sephardim, former New Christians, would participate in the rise of Dutch core capitalism. There were no Ashkenazi Jews among the internationalised great Jewish merchants of the 16th–17th centuries.

However, it is worth starting with a brief declaration of what will not be discussed in this book. In addressing the role of the New Christians and Jews

---

Lelewel (1858: 412f, 168, 581) wrote of him in the 19th century: "Poles travelled always and endlessly, and many out of desire or necessity in the far corners of the world (...). Without a Jew from Poznań, who travelled around India and was baptised Gaspard da Gama, Vasko (sic) de Gama 1498 and Cabral 1500, they would not have had the success in their expeditions that he gained. Amerigo Vespuzzi 1500 wrote down Gaspard's stories". Only one historian of geography and cartography wrote more extensively on this Poznań Jew almost a century ago (Olszewicz 1931: 187f, 203).

in shaping the colonial economy, this work does not look into the debate, ongoing for a century, about Columbus's lineage: was he or was he not a descendant of Spanish conversos who settled in Genoa. He was not, although until a few
years ago it was argued, not very convincingly and indeed echoing the hypothesis put forward almost a century ago by British historian of the marranos,
that Columbus left many traces in his manuscripts, suggesting his supposed
Jewish ancestry (Roth 1959). Thus, references to the Old Testament in his letters, a signature suggesting a Jewish prayer for the dead, etc. have been pointed
out. One could just as well construct elaborate theories by quoting the coincidence mentioned by the explorer in his journal of the first expedition: "after
having turned out all the Jews from all your kingdoms and lordships, in the
same month of January [1492], your Highnesses gave orders to me that with a
sufficient fleet I should go to the said parts of India" (Columbus 1893: 17f). This
was treated as an open question by Dominguez Ortiz (1971: 128f).[7] Nor do we
have in mind the fact that the funding for Columbus's expedition came largely
from conversos, merchants and financiers of Aragon, also royal officials,[8] and
that one of the first to set foot on the soil of the new continent was Luis de
Torres, a newly baptised Jew. On the number of conversos among the 87 members of Columbus's first expedition, there is still a rather sterile dispute. This
includes speculation about the possible influence that the Jewish roots of the
great-grandparents of the *encomendero*, then Dominican and most famous
defender of the Indians, Bartolomé de Las Casas, had on his assessments of
the conquistadors' activities. The same goes for the relationship between the
genealogy and the work of the author of *Don Quixote de la Mancha* or the
intellectual contributions of 16th-century Spanish theologians, philosophers,
religious reformers and counter-reformers with Jewish roots, such as Saints
Teresa and Juan of Avila or Francisco de Vitória of the University of Salamanca
(Clayton 2012: 12f, Orique 2014: 97, Dominguez Ortiz 1971: Chapters 8–9). Nor,

---

7   Even Werner Sombart, the well-known German historian of the turn of the 20th century, who
    asserted that when looking at the portraits of the directors of the Dutch East India Company
    he could easily recognise Jews, distanced himself from this concept. But ... having signalled
    his doubts, he nevertheless resorted to his favourite piece of evidence: "the oldest portaits
    show [Columbus] to have had a Jewish face" (Sombart 1951: 52).
8   In particular, the loan provided by Luís de Santángel, Chief Intendant of the Catholic King
    and Queen, "of the Rothschild family of that time" (Kayserling 1894: 64). These "Rothschilds"
    had already been Christianised for several generations. Santángel obtained the funds to
    finance almost 60 per cent of the cost of the expedition as a loan from an institution founded
    on traditional armed *hermandades* (Ladero Quesada 1992). Columbus's second expedition –
    at least 1,200 sailors and settlers – was financed by the Crown in large part with funds seized
    from Jews expelled in 1492.

finally, do we have in mind the achievements of Muslim and then Portuguese and Jewish oceanographers and astronomers (most notably Abraham Zacuto of the University of Salamanca, then an outcast in Portugal, or his pupil Josef Vecinho), thanks to whom there was a breakthrough in the understanding of space and the creation of maps and instruments to enable oceanic expeditions (marking positions and identifying currents). These are interesting, but on the whole incidental, facts. The exception, bearing in mind the topic at hand, is probably the information that the first Spanish merchant to obtain Queen Isabella's permission in 1502 to trade with the New World tax-free for the Crown was converso Juan Sanchez, grandson of a former royal treasurer. His five caravels delivered grain, honey, horses and other goods to Hispaniola, devastated by the actions of Spanish settlers. This privilege was renewed in 1504 (Seed 2001: 127). So, many caveats.

Here are the issues we intend to address (with varying degrees of detail) in this book: *Jews and New Christians*. We question the overuse of the term 'the role of the Jews'. It blurs the growing differences in that era between the community, culture and economic priorities of Sephardic Jews in the Netherlands (from the second half of the 17th century also English Jews) and the activities of Iberian and Latin American New Christians and the ways in which they participated in wider society. There is no doubt that the activities of all these groups overlapped even in the second half of the 17th century within a network of family and commercial ties. It does, however, raise the question as to whether it is legitimate to treat the New Christians *in toto* as part of a structurally and functionally tight-knit Jewish diaspora whose glue was religion (or a memory of it). It does not seem accurate to diminish the consequences associated with the destruction of Iberian institutional Judaism, in particular the breakdown of the religious community and the blurring of the criteria for the formation of non-Catholic identities. It seems almost impossible to formulate general statements about the religious preferences of converts subjected to the authority of Catholic monarchs. The result of the persecution that went hand in hand with the accentuation of increasingly racialised criteria, which accompanied the economic advancement of part of the New Christian elite, "was to revive New Christians' consciousness, not of their alleged Jewishness, but of a community of interests distinct from those of Old Christians" (Boyajian 1979: 142, also Bodian 1999: 10–17). By contrast, it was a misunderstanding to describe the Lisbon New Christian merchant-bankers, who financed part of the Spanish monarchy's debt in 1627, as "Portuguese Jewish and *converso* (...) financiers" (Munck 1990: 55). We therefore suggest treating the New Christians as a group *sui generis*.

At the same time, we see that the process of differentiation, accelerated by both expulsion and forced baptism, expressed in the phenomenon of the New Christians, was gradual, just as the departure of the New Christians from Judaism was gradual and spread over generations. The separation from and the rupture with Jewish cultural tradition took even longer. This process was accelerated from above at the end of the 16th century by the targeted repression of the New Christians by the Inquisition (especially in Brazil and Portugal, though not bypassing the Spanish colonies). In Spain, the main impact of the newly established Inquisition targeting conversos would come earlier and last from the 1480s to the 1520s-30s. The formation of differing, even opposing, political loyalties, grounded in the increasing differentiation of economic interests between Jews and New Christians, was also an important part of these processes. This was closely linked to the process of nation-state formation initiated in the mercantilist era. 'Cosmopolitanism', which characterised the condition of European merchants participating in the overseas commerce of the early modern era, was increasingly constrained in the process of establishing modern states.

This is one issue. There is another, closely linked to it. The New Christians who were active in the Atlantic world were referred to, especially in the 16th and 17th centuries, as 'Portuguese'. Outside observers, however, often included in the Portuguese *La Nação* not only Jewish Amsterdam merchants, crypto-Jews and New Christians who originated from Portugal, but also Portuguese Old Christians. Should this external view be considered a conclusive criterion? Can other, stronger arguments be adduced for the hypothesis that the Portuguese Nation of the 16th and 17th centuries was diverse, but at the same time represented a community shaped by long-distance trade, despite religious differences? If so, this reinforces the hypothesis that the New Christians constituted a group *sui generis* increasingly integrated within the larger context of *La Nação* networks. At the same time, these *cristãos-novos* were influencing, by their very presence, the evolution of the attitudes and mentality of the Old Christians participating in the Atlantic economy. This interesting issue has recently been raised by Studnicki-Gizbert (2007, 2009) in relation to the years 1492–1640. However, the links between the New Christians and Amsterdam Jews, who were just emerging at the threshold of the 16th century, are more often than not marginalized when discussing the emergence of the Atlantic world. They are a neglected element in the picture painted by the historian: "The Atlantic Jews age was a time when the American Jewish epicenter was (...) in the insular and circum-Caribbean; when for centuries most Atlantic Jews were of Iberian (...) origins; when most hemispheric American Jews lived in slave societies" (Ben-Ur 2020: 12f). Thus, we intend to recall that before these Jews would appear in the Atlantic world, it was the New Christians who in the 16th century were already busy co-creating the New World – with the Caribbean playing a secondary role. And not all of them lived in slave societies, although many participated in the slave trade.

The main directions and forms of Jewish and New Christian activity. Neither the Dutch Jews nor the Portuguese or Spanish New Christians were independent actors in the emerging Atlantic economy, even when they went beyond the established rules of the game (by participating, for example, in large-scale contraband). Above all, they were not the creators of these rules and their guardians. To describe their participation in the development of the Latin American economies of the colonial era as a decisive part of the continent's economic history would simply contradict the source material. Even in the period up to 1650, the period of the apogee of the involvement of New Christians and Jews in international trade: "The fact that Jewish merchants were to be found in all the key centres of capitalism does not mean to say that they created them" (Braudel 1995: 160).

By contrast, in the 16th and much of the 17th century, the New Christians and Jews constituted, together with the Dutch, the Flemish, the merchants of the Italian city-states and the English, the vanguard of European commercial capitalism. In turn, such capitalism "could be a creative force, bringing into existence a *system* of production for exchange" (Sweezy 1978: 42). The New Christians and Jews thus not only participated in ushering in the Golden Age of the Netherlands, but they co-created important elements of the Latin American economies and, more broadly, the Atlantic world. The initiation of the slave trade on a wider scale during this period was a venture organised and controlled until the first half of the 17th century primarily by Portuguese New Christians. In contrast, neither the New Christians nor the Dutch or English Jews would play a major role in the boom in the slave trade from the second half of the 17th century to the end of the 18th century.

At the same time, the family and trade networks they created, important in certain markets and for certain commodities, were not closed or monopolistic, in the sense of excluding Catholic and Protestant merchants. The increasing scale and complexity and diversity of commercial operations in the Atlantic economy of the time meant that achieving such a monopoly in the long term was impossible. This was evidenced, among other things, by the emergence of loose ties involving Jewish, crypto-Jewish, New Christian and Old Christian merchants, non-Jewish trade agents and intermediaries. Indeed, a model example of such ties was the late 16th century collaboration in the marketing of Indian pepper between the powerful New Christian Ximenes d'Aragão family and the influential Milanese merchant Giovanni Battista Rovellasca (Rovelesca).

Jews and New Christians, on the other hand, were unique in some respects among the minorities participating in international trade. Alongside them in this period we find not only the Huguenots and other Protestants, but also Flemings, Basques, Bretons, Scots, Armenians, Greeks, etc. merchant communities probably rivalling the 'Portuguese' group in numbers. What distinguished the latter was not so much the scale of their operations as their degree of internationalisation and their location in the main European and overseas trade centres. One could say that it was the medieval tradition of Jewish Radhanite merchants travelling with goods from the 'court of the King of the Franks' to India and China that was transferred to the new conditions created from the late 15th century. Scattered across the Atlantic world, the Mediterranean, West Africa and Asia, Jews and New Christians operated with the help of their commercial agents and associates (including Old Christians) throughout the world economy of the time. North America was the least penetrated by the 18th century.

The particular importance of the 16th to 17th centuries. As in the Atlantic economy as a whole, in Latin America too, the apogee of the long-distance trade-centred activity of the New Christians and Jews occurred up to the second half of the 17th century, thus the era of the first system of expansion created and dominated by Spain and Portugal. The Netherlands, contesting the dominance of the Iberian powers from the end of the 16th century, found itself in a kind of transitional situation: the first system of expansion had already lost its momentum, while the second – shaped in fierce competition between England, the Spanish empire and the United Provinces – was only in the initial stages of development (Emmer 1993). The 17th century is divided from this point of view into two parts, the era of the transition from "Seville to Amsterdam" (Wallerstein 1974: 199–201) and then from Amsterdam to London. The logic of the activities and expansion of Dutch companies in Asia and the Atlantic already fitted well into the second system, calling into question the methods of organising long-distance trade prevalent in the first system, and also paving the way for the new hegemon, England. The activities of the New Christians and Jews also flourished during this transitional period. The peak of their activity in the Atlantic thus occurred in the first half of the 17th century.

The case of Brazil was to some extent separate. For here the economic activity of the New Christians was evident from at least the middle of the 16th century, not only in long-distance trade, but also in new settlements and the plantation economy and therefore in the production of luxury goods. From the late 17th century, there were also many New Christians participating in the great economic boom associated with the discovery of gold and diamonds in Minas Gerais. In turn, in the 18th century, the experience of the Amsterdam Jews from 1630–1654 in Pernambuco, from the time of 'Dutch Brazil' conquered and controlled by the West India Company (WIC – *Geoctroyeerde West-Indische Compagnie*), would be repeated (with modifications) in Dutch Suriname.

The gradual decline of the role of the New Christians and Sephardic Jews in Latin America and the Atlantic trade was caused by two fundamental factors: (a) the emergence of powers more powerful than the Iberian empires and the Netherlands (England and France) and their growing and differently organised economic elites; this meant the entry as early as the end of the 17th century of a rapidly expanding second system of expansion, which was at the same time a response to the extremely rapid growth of overseas trade, a phenomenon the commercial and financial elites of the New Christians and Sephardic Jews were unable to respond to effectively; (b) the increased activity of the Inquisition in Spanish America and Brazil from the late 16th century and intensified from the mid-17th and early 18th centuries, but also in the Iberian metropolises, symbolised by the successively revealed 'great conspiracies' of Judaising heretics in Ciudad de México, Lima and Cartagena de Indias (hereafter also: Cartagena). To some extent separate from these was the failure, after less than a quarter of a century of existence, of 'Dutch Brazil' (1630–1654), and thus the attempt to move from maritime commercial activities to Dutch and Jewish settlement and trade. The plantation economy in Suriname was merely an extension in the 18th century – and in the long run also unsuccessful – of the earlier Pernambuco experiment.

The balance sheet of the conquest of Latin America and implicitly of the economic role played by Jews and New Christians in the New World was for Adam Smith (1904: 236) ambivalent: "To the natives (...) both of the East and West Indies, all the commercial benefits which can have resulted from those events have been sunk and lost in the dreadful misfortunes which they have occasioned". At the same time, he added justifiably: "These misfortunes, however, seem to have arisen rather from accident than from any thing in the nature of those events themselves". A similar tone would appear in the recent deliberations of historians: "A clear-cut tally sheet of the costs and benefits involved [in European expansion] cannot be drawn up. New crops (...) improved the life of many societies, wheras new pests tormented them" (Osterhammel and Petersson 2005: 45). Does this also concern the mass slavery of Africans? Its origin must be traced to the interaction between European demand for luxury goods and changes in consumption styles and behaviour of settlers-as-economic-agents in the New World. It is debatable whether the transfer from the New World of cassava and maize – crops crucial for sustaining Africa's food supply – balanced the trade in the millions of slaves (Thomas 1998: 133). With some irony, therefore, the German historian wrote at the dawn of the 20th century:

> Around 1830 the total number of slaves in all slave-trading countries amounted to 6,822,759. That the pretty little damsels of Paris and London were able to mobilize this vast black army to satisfy their whims is an intriguing thought.
>
> SOMBART 1967: 145

The two accounts of losses and gains – the one on a macro scale and the one limited to Jews and New Christians – are closely linked, and the attempt to separate them leads, whatever the intention, down a blind alley. Those, therefore, who regard the emergence of Europe in the New World, from a humanitarian or any other point of view, as a calamity and a destruction difficult to imagine, also regard the activity of Jews and New Christians as part of this catastrophe. The opposite is true for those who, without minimising the scale of the destruction and the enormity of the misfortune caused by the appearance of Europeans, will make the reference point the process of the formation of a new, multicultural Latin America and therefore, to emphasise after Smith, "the nature of those events themselves".

It is impossible to reconcile these two points of view, although they are nowadays only symbolic. Instead, it seems sensible to try to understand the interweaving of motivations, conditioning worldviews and circumstances. Only in this way is it possible to come closer to answering the question of why Luis de Carvajal y de la Cueva, descended from the New Christians, governor of Nuevo Reino de León in New Spain in the 1680s and subsequently accused (unjustifiably) of protecting the *judaizantes*, can be described simultaneously as a beneficiary of slavery and as "one of the more enlightened and humane conquistadors" (Temkin 2011, Simpson 1971: 193). Whether he benefited from the slave trade as a royal official in the Cape Verde islands, we do not know. As a later governor, he obtained permission to buy them. On the other hand, the doubts raised do not evade questions about the different styles of colonisation and the creation of Latin America as a strongly differentiated entity. The French and British Caribbean differed, even though both are today subsumed under the general categories of colonial plantation economies and slave societies. The same can be said of the role played by the New Christians in Brazil or the Jews in the British and Dutch Caribbean. As Jews and New Christians, the descendants of the Sephardim were part of the European expansion. Contrary to traditional Jewish historiography, they did not so much passively adapt to their new environment as participate in the creation of new societies, including in the New World, despite persecution. It was often a tragic story, but certainly not one of constant repression and misfortune. A young Jewish historian wrote in his programme article in 1928 that, "it is time to break with the lachrymose theory of pre-Revolutionary woe, and to adopt a view more in accord with historic truth" (Baron 1928: 12).

The history of the New Christians in colonial Latin America was intertwined with the presence of the Iberian Inquisition, and their activity was constantly accompanied by the threat of the tribunal. Likewise, moreover, in the metropolises. It is therefore not surprising that, in Portugal, the dispute over the assessment of the role played by the New Christians and the Inquisition has become an enduring part of historical reflection. Depending on the researcher, responsibility for Portugal's fate, its successes and disasters, was attributed differently. João Lúcio de Azevedo, a prominent Portuguese historian of the early 20th century, would see the New Christians as the main source of misfortune. In contrast, the co-founder of Brazilian historiography João Capistrano de Abreu, states: "I see the misfortunes of Portugal – not in the New Christians – *vae victis* – but in the angelic Holy Office" (quoted in Schwartz 1997: xxviii).[9]

But the point is not only in the tragic intertwining of the history of the New Christians and the Inquisition in the metropolis and colonies and their understandable quest for survival. Jews and New Christians also sought in the New World to preserve their position in the European white elite. These efforts were not fruitless. So we see them as merchants, including slave traders, and co-organisers of contraband, as craftsmen, medics and apothecaries, jewellers and ship carpenters, *senhores de engenho,* we find them among the Brazilian *bandeirantes* who were the terror of the Guarani Indians and the Spanish Jesuits, among those who fought the Indians and held office in Suriname, but also among Caribbean corsairs and pirates, diocesan priests, Inquisition officials and even bishops (one in Latin America, several in the metropolis). They "Judaised" Indians and slaves at times (while perpetuating caste and racial prejudices), and they also filled the secret prisons of the Inquisition. They were burned at the stake.[10] To the amazement of the nobility and mob attending

---

9   Let us note already at this point that the Spanish Inquisition, although established to expose the *judaizantes,* was not confined to fighting them. From the middle of the 16th century, the problem recedes into the background in the metropolis. In the New World, it will appear in the first half of the 17th century, although even here the Inquisition will be mostly preoccupied with other offences against faith and morality (Hordes 1982b).

10   According to Eltis (2000: 71), 32,000 *judaizantes* were burnt at the stake from the late 15th to the early 19th century. This is a mistake. This figure includes all those sentenced

the execution, some met their fate with a confession praising the Inquisition-condemned "dead Law of Moses", as was the case with Isaac de Castro Tartas, a French-born young Jew from 'Dutch Brazil'. Captured in Bahia, the Inquisitors in Lisbon decided to treat him as "a baptized Christian", i.e. heretic (Bodian 2008: 141). He was burned at the stake in 1647. For Azevedo (1922), however, this wretch was an "exalted fanatic", not a Jewish victim.

In all of these roles, the New Christians and Jews were part of the emerging Latin America, its unique, multi-ethnic history and culture. However, let us emphasise the word 'were'. The combination of more than two centuries of repression against the New Christians and the assimilation of a sizeable part of them brought the history of this group to an end in the 18th century. The repression in the first half of this century was merely the last act of the drama. In Portugal, this involved some 2,300 New Christians between 1707 and 1750 (more than 60 per cent of the total condemned by the Inquisition during this period). Even more violent, concentrated between 1720 and 1727, was the repression in Spain – *la última gran persecución*. More than 1,000 *judaizantes*, mostly Portuguese from Seville and Madrid, were convicted during this period. Many were burned. On the other hand, the decisions of the Portuguese reformer Marquis de Pombal in 1768 and 1773–74 to destroy the documents identifying the New Christians (royal *Carta de Lei de 25 de Maio de 1773*) and to abolish the requirement to present a certificate of 'purity of blood' (Novinsky 1987: 147, Israel 2002a: 575, 577, Pulido Serrano 2003: 72, Martins 2008),[11] were formal moves confirming, in fact, the degree to which the integration of the New Christians had advanced:

> When, after an hiatus of some three centuries, authentic Jewish communities sprang up once again on Portuguese soil (...).their membership were all immigrants from Gibraltar and Morocco. Indigenous Portuguese families were conspicuous by their absence.
>
> SARAIVA 2001: 233

---

to death by the Spanish Inquisition and handed over to the secular authorities for execution. Among them were some 17,000 *relaxados en estátua*, i.e. executed symbolically (*in effigie* – in place of the absentee convict, his or her portrait was burned). According to more recent calculations, between 1480 and 1534, i.e. at the apogee of the repression, the Spanish Inquisition sent 2,000 victims to the stake (Kamen 2005: 65).

11 While the political demise of the Marquis de Pombal after the king's death in 1777 enabled the release from prison of many of his opponents, including the arrested Jesuits, it did not result in a reversal of decisions concerning the New Christians.

In Spanish America, the fundamental weakening of the New Christians by the tribunals of the Holy Office can be traced back to the 1630s. In Brazil, on the other hand, after the persecutions of the late 16th century in Bahia and Pernambuco, repression would resume in the early 18th century, mainly in Rio de Janeiro, Minas Gerais and Paraiba, on a scale at least equal to that demonstrated during the investigations and trials in Lima, Ciudad de México and Cartagena de Indias in the first half of the 17th century. In these three capitals, 405 New Christians were imprisoned, while the total number denounced reached 1,650. Care for the purity of the faith was also accompanied in each of these periods by confiscations. In Rio de Janeiro alone, the property confiscated between 1711 and 1720 from a group of 129 of the wealthiest *judaizantes* was estimated to be the equivalent of five tonnes of gold (Novinsky 1998: 303, 306). In contrast, the fate of the Jews in Suriname and the English Caribbean was determined primarily by economic factors. In the case of the French colonies, one can speak of the important role played in limiting their presence by the restrictions imposed by Louis XIV in, among other things, the first article of the *Code Noir* promulgated in 1685. Underlying these were both arguments derived from Catholic doctrine (Jews would be expelled from the islands as "declared enemies of Christianity") and the demands of Christian competitors.

The memory of the New Christians and Sephardic Jews in colonial Latin America was therefore already historical. There is no question of a continuity linking their history with the later, growing presence of Eastern European and Oriental Jews emigrating from the Mediterranean area after the turn of the 20th century. Marked by the activity of the great Jewish and New Christian merchants, the period up to the mid-17th century was a mere century-long flash.

Acknowledgements

I express my gratitude to Daniel Grinberg, Jan Kieniewicz, Marcin Kula and Stanisław Obirek for their scholarly support and comments on the first edition of this book. David Fasenfest deserves more than a short acknowledgement.

Maps

CHAPTER 1

Terminology as Differentiation

The appearance of Jews and New Christians in the colonial economy of Latin America was linked to the catastrophe of the Jewish communities on the Iberian Peninsula at the end of the 15th century. A British historian points out this coincidence:

> this immense process of uprooting culminated not just in the most fundamental restructuring of Jewish life in Europe down to the twentieth century but in a remarkable expansion and strengthening both of Jewish culture internally and, what is most striking, of its role in Europe's economic life and politics.
>
> ISRAEL 1998: 19

The connection between the two developments does not appear to be accidental. It points, on the one hand, to the emergence, after a series of persecutions throughout Western Europe from the late 15th century to the 1570s, to a new and highly differentiated Jewish and New Christian diaspora, and, on the other, through its presence in the main economic centres of Europe, to its role in shaping both the European and Atlantic worlds:

> The transformation in European Jewry's status was rapid, dramatic, and profound (...) for at bottom Jewish readmission was merely a symptom of the more general revolution which convulsed and renewed western life and thought at the close of the sixteenth century.
>
> ISRAEL 1998: 29

At the same time, after the expulsions, the involvement of an elite of dispersed Jews and New Christians in trade and financial operations linking Amsterdam, Lisbon, Oporto, Recife, Salvador, Upper Guinea, Cape Verde and São Tomé, Angola, Cartagena, Goa, Livorno, Thessaloniki (not forgetting Asia) became not only possible, but also a matter of survival. A sizeable group of the Sephardim (Jews, not conversos) emigrating from Spain and Portugal found, in the Mediterranean region, opportunities to survive and continue in their traditional occupations: crafts, petty trade, money lending and other financial services. A minority, already as New Christians or crypto-Jews, and from the

17th century also as Dutch Jews, participated directly in the creation of the Atlantic world.

Let us start with the first issue.

When we write about the role of the Jews, we are referring to the Sephardic Jews of Iberian origin, whose presence in the peninsula probably dates back to the 1st – 3rd centuries AD. In any case, as early as the beginning of the 4th century, the Synod of Elvira (Granada) established regulations against the Jews whom it considered "large and influential" and "not only numerous, but active as well". The aim was, among other things, to limit their contact with Christians and the possibility of proselytism (Soyer 2007a: 27, Dale 1882: 254, 256).[1] The aggressive and alienating language used in the synod documents suggested that such contacts were regarded as a serious threat to the new faith. The memory of Jewish proselytism practised at the beginning of the new era throughout the Greco-Roman world, as well as among the Berbers and Arabs and eventually the Iberians, was probably still vivid. There was a concern that "the Jews gained more by proselytes than they lost by apostates" (Dale 1882: 256, Wexler 1996). More precisely, when we write about Sephardic Jews, we mean those who formed the western diaspora from the 16th century, as distinct from its highly differentiated variant in the Ottoman Empire and North Africa and who defined themselves as a *nação portuguesa e espanhola*. Ashkenazim, who had been settling in increasing numbers in Central and Eastern Europe since the 14th century, were only indirectly involved in these processes.

According to a 19th century Jewish historian, Sephardim "considered themselves a privileged race, the flower and nobility of the Jewish nation". Not without reason, he claimed, with almost uncritical enthusiasm. What distinguished them, even after their expulsion from the Iberian Peninsula, was, in addition to their rich cultural tradition and experience of economic activity in a culturally diverse environment, their "Spanish dignity and distinction" (Graetz 1894: 387f).[2] This was a trait certainly worth noting and played an important

---

1   In the 7th century, the Visigothic Christian rulers Sisebut and Egika launched the forced Christianisation of the Jews and introduced drastic taxation of the resistant (Bradbury 2006: 514–516). This was opposed by the Archbishop of Seville, Isidore (later a saint), but at the same time he accepted its results and treated them as unshakeable. The anti-Jewish findings of the Fourth Synod of Toledo, presided over by Archbishop Isidore, accompanied these measures (Albert 1990) .

2   This trait was also clearly visible among Sephardic women in the Republic in the 16th and 17th centuries, although their place in the family and social life was largely governed by an Iberian and Sephardic tradition of relative isolation at the same time (different for Ashkenazi women) (Bernfeld 2011). For a critical account of the reception in Jewish historiography of the Sephardic experience in the Netherlands, see Kaplan (1999: 213–222).

role in the process of self-identification and economic activity of Sephardic refugees in the new milieu. The strong interdependence of honour, behaviour (*grandeza*) and (noble) origin, is also mentioned by contemporary Portuguese historians (Tavim 2011: 193). This trait was referred to in the 18th century by Voltaire's polemicist, Isaac de Pinto, a Sephardi economist and financier and *homme de lettres* from Amsterdam, when he emphasised the unique position occupied by Portuguese Jews – compared to the Ashkenazim, who would appear in the Republic from the mid-17th century, first as poor and uneducated *tudescos*, then already as more respectable *polacos*. It is not surprising, therefore, that de Pinto informed Voltaire that the Sephardim "jamais ne fe font confondus ai incorporés avec la foule des autres enfants de Jacob" (Pinto 1762: 15, Bodian 1999: 125–131). One idignant Jewish scholar protested, accentuating that de Pinto "commited the grave error of drawing sharp distinctions beween the German and the Portuguese Jews" (Hühner 1905: 119). Perhaps. Pinto himself publicly apologised to the offended Ashkenazim. However, the attitude he demonstrated was also linked to the *Hassliebe* relationship that bound Sephardic Jews to Iberian culture – the self-image of the *nação portuguesa e espanhola* was regarded as an important defining element:

> even those who reached a safe haven in the 'lands of liberty' and decided to live openly as Jews did not necessarily sever themselves from connections with the lands of their Iberian origins. The burden of fear to which they had been subject as members of a discriminated and persecuted community did not erase their longings for their original homes and for the landscapes of their childhood. From Amsterdam, Hamburg, Leghorn, and London their hearts were still drawn to the towns and villages of Spain and Portugal.
>
> KAPLAN 2008: 33f, also SWETSCHINSKI 2004: 175

A century after the expulsions, at the turn of the 16th century, an observer noted that the Sephardim in Thessaloniki spoke Spanish as beautifully as Toledans. One Sephardic emigrant characteristically described his situation in 1627: "a Jew of Portuguese exile" (Tavim 2011: 177). Spanish, gradually replaced in the Ottoman Empire by *judeoespañol*, continued to be the literary language also in Amsterdam, where Portuguese dominated daily life.

However, this "Spanish dignity and distinction" also caused misunderstandings, including reinforcement of a mythologised image of the wealth at the disposal of the Sephardim as a group. There was fascination with descriptions of a wedding reception in a wealthy family of Amsterdam Jews in the 17th century, in which, it was speculated, the combined wealth of the 40 guests could have reached the enormous sum of 40 million florins. The same was true for the description of the entry in 1552 to Istanbul, surrounded by dozens of horsemen, of the heiress to the immense fortune of Grácia Nasci, until then still a New Christian (Roth 1959: 96, Tavim 2011: 178). In any case:

> Because of their love of public display, the Iberian exiles often created the impression of commanding far greater wealth than they really possessed. The contrast between the luxury-loving Portuguese and Spaniards, who had brought with them from their home countries an inordinate appetite for costly garments and conveyances, and the sturdy Calvinist Dutchmen was striking.
>
> BARON 1973: 52[3]

Incidentally, the many Protestant emigrants streaming into the Republic from the Spanish Netherlands, mainly from Brabant, were viewed by contemporaries in a similar way. Besides, the Sephardim were neither the first nor the only ones ostentatiously flaunting their wealth in Europe at the time. The description of the splendour demonstrated by the magnate Jerzy Ossoliński, the Polish envoy to Rome in 1633, is still breathtaking today.

The Amsterdammers of the turn of the 16th and 17th centuries were also astonished by the illegal importation of African slaves by the Sephardim into the land of freedom on the pretext of employing domestic servants. But this was to change. As early as around the 1630s and 1640s, Dutch merchants themselves began to take a prominent place in the slave trade. Still, the presence of Africans in the Netherlands was poorly tolerated and, in economic terms, considered unnecessary. In any case, the ostentatious consumption of members of the Sephardic elite preceded the teachings in Bernard Mandeville's *The Fable of the Bees*:

---

3   The picture of the Sephardic diaspora in both 18th-century Amsterdam and 18th-century Suriname was more complicated. The minority that achieved economic success in the 17th century was only a fragment of a larger, highly polarised whole: "social tensions resulting from the great disparity of wealth that came to characterize the Amsterdam community more strongly than any other" (Swetschinski 2004: 318). In 1780, 65 per cent of Amsterdam's Jews lived from charity. They were mostly Ashkanazi, although of the 2,800 Sephardic members of the community, more than 50 per cent benefited from charity (Cohen 1991: 19, Boxer 1980: 140). Earlier, around 1655, 180 families, i.e. a quarter of Amsterdam's Sephardim, benefited from charity. In 1700 the number of families supported by the municipality and private donors rose to 463 (Bernfeld 2002: 66f).

The root of evil, avarice,
That damn'd ill-natur'd baneful vice,
Was slave to prodigality,
That noble sin; whilst luxury
Employ'd a million of the poor,
And odious pride a million more:
Envy itself, and vanity,
Were ministers of industry;
Their darling folly, fickleness,
In diet, furniture, and dress,
That strange ridic'lous vice, was made
The very wheel that turn'd the trade.

And they probably also shared Mandeville's irony:

Bare virtue can't make nations live
In splendor; they, that would revive
A golden age, must be as free,
For acorns as for honesty.

The Iberian tradition proved, under the new conditions of burgeoning Dutch capitalism, to be an interesting contribution to the analysis of the relationship between luxury consumption and the growth of wealth and the birth of market modernity (Sombart 1951). However, the Calvinist admiration for the high intellectual level of the Sephardic elite and their worldly familiarity was combined, when it came to ostentatious splendour, with strong negative reactions. This explains why, in 1647, the leaders of the Jewish community asked their co-religionists to refrain from wearing overly opulent clothing and to exercise restraint in the display of wealth (Kaplan 2001: 22–25, 31).

However, the earlier attempts to limit the role of the Sephardim in Spain, preceding the expulsions of the late 15th century, and their disintegration through forced Christianisation, had already led to a fundamental diversification of the Jewish community. It is estimated that after the pogroms of 1391 in Seville, Toledo and other cities, baptism (forced, but also in many cases voluntary) was successively extended to more than 100,000 people by 1415, and to 225,000 by 1492 (Gitlitz 2002: 74).[4] The establishment of the Inquisition in

---

4 Baroja (2000: 204f), on the other hand, assumes that the number of so-called new conversos who would appear due to the expulsions was around 240,000. A much higher (600,000–750,000) number of conversos at the end of the 15th century is suggested by other scholars (Roth 2002: 376, Netanyahu 1999: 248). Domínguez Ortiz (1971: 220) regarded the figures

1478 and its activities initially targeting almost exclusively conversos (as prone, it was claimed, to heresy, i.e. Judaising, and also occupying a high position in the economy and social structure) only exacerbated these trends. At the same time, in the 1480s, many Jews who feared persecution emigrated to Portugal and then to other countries in the Mediterranean. In 1492, following decisions by the kings of Spain, a community of over 200,000 Spanish Jews was destroyed (Israel 2009: 32).[5] Those who remained formally ceased to be Jews after being baptised. A few years later, in 1497, there was a forced and rapid Christianisation of both Portuguese Jews and Spanish refugees remaining in Portugal who had refused to be baptised a few years earlier. A total of probably 100,000 people were affected.[6] The decree of the just-crowned King Manuel I, who, unlike his predecessor *O Príncipe Perfeito* (The Perfect Prince) João II, was seen as sympathetic to the Jews, actually caused an earthquake in a country that had hitherto been a relatively peaceful haven for Jewish believers. Anti-Jewish speeches in Portugal were generally met with a harsh response from the Crown. However, it is debatable whether Manuel I's decision – unprecedented in its scale and speed – was, according to a widespread view in historiography, primarily an

---

given by Netanyahu as a "fantasy": if accepted, it would mean that Jews and conversos constituted almost the entire urban population of Spain. The same could be said about the calculations of N. Roth. For a good overview of estimates up to the end of the 20th century see Gitliz (2002: 73–76).

5   This is one of many estimates appearing in the literature. The figure of 300,000, often quoted by Jewish historians, appeared as early as the 16th century, given by Isaac Abrávanel, a commentator on Tora and Prophets and royal advisor until the Great Expulsion. This is disputed, although a figure of 400,000 has also been quoted. The figure of 80,000–90,000 (the population of Spain at the time was over 6 million), on the other hand, appears to be an underestimate. Saraiva (2001: xxxii) gives for the end of the 16th century a figure of 90,000 Jews and 150,000 conversos. The discrepancies are therefore enormous (Roth 2003: appendix B). Also the Muslims persisting in the faith became victims of the expulsion in 1502. The remaining *moriscos* were the Muslim counterparts of the conversos. The response to the uprising of the *moriscos* (1568–1571) was the expulsion of some 300,000 people from the country between 1609 and 1614 (Kamen 2005: 59).

6   A figure quoted by Drescher (2001: 445) with reference to A.H. de Oliveir Marques. This one, however, writes (1976: 167, 287) that "The Jews formed a relatively small group, although precise figures are unavailable", while elsewhere: "In 1542 there were no more than 60,000 New Christians, in 1604 perhaps half that number." At the beginning of the 17th century, they would have represented no more than 1.79 per cent of the total Portuguese population. Soyer (2007: 44), on the other hand, estimated the population of Portuguese Jews at the end of the 15th century at 30,000, while the number of refugees from Spain was at least 30,000. And finally, Azevedo (1922: 43), wrote, probably with exaggeration, of 190,000 Jews residing in Portugal in 1496 (including refugees). The population of Portugal in 1500 was estimated at 0.9 million, in 1527 at 1.215 million and in 1600 at 1.667 million (Freire Costa, Lains and Münch Miranda 2016: 54, 59).

attempt to counteract the effects of the earlier mass migration of Spanish Jews, which had disturbed the previous coexistence between Christians and Jews. Rather, one should speak of a coincidence and a confluence of various factors (including the matrimonial plans of the Portuguese ruler) (Soyer 2007a). In the same year, as if repeating a scenario written in Spain in 1492, Vasco da Gama set off for India.

Despite the Crown's ban on emigration in 1499, a wave of refugees, this time Portuguese, moved, as before from Spain to southern Europe, the Balkans and other areas of the Ottoman Empire, and North Africa. Of the considerable number (possibly several thousand?) of forcibly baptised Jews who found their way to southern France in the first half of the 16th century, many then moved, formally as Christians, to the Spanish Netherlands (above all Antwerp). A few also made their way to the New World, mainly Brazil. Earlier, some 2,000 children taken from their refugee parents from Castile in 1493 were sent by order of João II – previously baptised – to the sparsely populated and small (859 km^2) island of São Tomé off the coast of West Africa (Soyer 2007: 130f).[7] This combined the repression of Castilian Jews, who were unable to pay the tax demanded of emigrants and were in Portugal illegally, with a policy of settlement in a climate-killing territory for Europeans. The São Tomé experiment would later play an important role in the development of Brazil and the slave trade. The island also served as a penal colony, including for criminals convicted in Brazil (Małowist 1969: Chapter 5).[8] However, much of the commercial elite of Portuguese (baptised) Jews remained in Portugal, actively participating in the kingdom's commercial expansion across four continents in the 16th century. But not only that. In the 16th and first half of the 17th centuries, they would form an important part of a network of trade links from the west coast of the New World to Asia in the east.

These rapid changes were accompanied not only by the disintegration of existing communities, but also by the emergence of a veritable mosaic of terminology reflecting this process. A moment's attention needs to be paid to this matter, as the use of generalised terms such as "Sephardic Jews" or "the role of the Jews" in further deliberations could be misleading and make it difficult to assess the actual role played by them.

The result of the gradual but massive Christianisation of Spanish Jews, which began on a wider scale as late as the end of the 14th century, was the

---

7   According to other sources, only 700 children were sent (Gitlitz 2002: 49).
8   As such it was mentioned in the royal *carta de foral* of 1534, the decree establishing Duarte Coelho Pereira *donatário* of the captaincy of Nova Lusitânia (Pernambuco) (Schwartz 2010: 15).

emergence of new terms to refer to this group (in Hebrew *anusim* – 'enslaved', 'forced'): thus, one spoke of *conversos/confesos*, *cristianos nuevos* (as opposed to *cristianos de natureza* – Old Christians) or, offensively, *marranos* (pigs). The latter term, referring, according to the most widely accepted (though not the only) interpretation, to the religiously sanctioned ban on the consumption of pork meat and fats, gradually lost its negative overtones, but only in historical writing. In the vernacular of the era, marrano was synonymous with the term *criptojudio* or, in the terminology of the Inquisition, heretical *judaizante*. Unlike conversos or New Christians, marranos therefore referred to baptised Jews continuing selectivelly Jewish tradition, emotionally attached to Judaism and secretly defining themselves through ritual (often poorly known) as Jews. By contrast, in Portugal, where forced and mass Christianisation appears a few years later, in 1497, Jews baptised by a single act were simply *cristãosnovos* – New Christians (as opposed to *cristãos-velhos* or *cristãos-antiguos* – Old Christian, whose genealogy was not in doubt). In the writings of the visitators of the Holy Office in Brazil, it was precise to write of the "descendants of the New Christians of the Hebrew Nation of Portugal", sometimes, as in São Paulo at the end of the 16th century, of the *judeus cristãos*, and of those suspected of heresy generally as *Nação Hebrea* (Wiznitzer 1960: 33, 40, also Liebman 1984: appendix A).

Thus, in the interpretation of some prominent historians, we have a kind of dichotomous division, depending on the degree of acceptance and internalisation of Catholicism in the long term: on the one hand, conversos and New Christians mostly accepting the new faith, and on the other hand, marranos and crypto-Jews rejecting it, and, of course, Sephardic Jews remaining outside the control of Spain and Portugal and the Inquisition (Schorsch 2009: 16f). In practice, the lines of division and classification thus defined, referred to individual as well as group cases, must be considered fluid. It was pointed out more than half a century ago by a Spanish historian that an important group among conversos were, in addition to sincere Catholics, former Jews or their descendants representing religious syncretism (Baroja 2000: 294f). The Portuguese New Christians were probably still, for the most part, until the mid-16th century, counterparts of the Spanish marranos rather than fully Christianised conversos. According to testimonies from 1524, these New Christians "were every bit as Jewish except in name" (Roth 1959: 31). Perhaps. Only a quarter of a century had passed since the act of forced Christianisation. However, treating these terms as synonymous for the entire colonial era, as Cecil Roth, for example, does in his history of the marranos, seems unwarranted.

The terminological fluidity that is impossible to avoid, but also the need to carefully take into account the time factor and the difficult-to-classify intermediate cases, is reflected in the work of Anita Novinsky, a distinguished researcher on the phenomenon of New Christians and the Inquisition in Brazil and Portugal. This is particularly true of her reinterpretation of the concept of marranos. Far from being devout Catholics, she points out, the Brazilian marranos were in many cases also not religious crypto-Jews: while identifying secretly with the Jewish tradition, they were also "non-religious Jews". She adds that "Marranism among the Portuguese in Brazil was primarily a mental attitude, a sentiment, an outlook on life, rather than a religious observance" (Novinsky 2001b: 226). And these were just two of many difficult to classify cases within a group identifying with a Jewish tradition (or elements of it). One of the most prominent historical anthropologists, hit the nail on the head when writing about "Marrano labyrinths" and emphasising the importance of multivariant syncretism (Wachtel 2013). However, there is no doubt for the Brazilian scholar that "although not all New Christians were Jews, all Marranos certainly were" (Novinsky 2009a: 164, 2001b: 226).

All these terms attempted to describe first the reality created by the gradual Christianisation preceding 1492–97 and the consequent gradual disintegration of the Sephardic community, and then the situation of the Jews who remained in Spain and Portugal and in the colonies after the great expulsions. Despite Christianisation, the intensity of the former Jews' links with Judaism remained an open question. Terms such as *marranos, criptojudios, judaizantes, hombres de la nación*, in fact, expressed the suspicion that baptism was only formal. Public opinion shared such a view through xenophobic reactions against the New Christians, especially in Portugal, while the Inquisition reinforced such a conviction with repression.

However, over time (and the succession of generations), these terms primarily aided ideo-religious mobilisation around (supposedly endangered) Catholic dogmas, while losing touch with reality, just as contact with reality was also lost by the Inquisition in the 17th or 18th century, by multiplying the number of Judaising sinners. The extent to which this was fostered by the mechanism of financing the Inquisition from property confiscated from heretics, as well as by tensions within the economic elites on the peninsula and in the colonies, was and still is a matter of dispute. The Argentine-Jewish historian Lewin's caution is justified when he points out: "Without doubt, the Inquisition was not simply an apparatus of financial drainage. Nor was it composed exclusively of hypocrites and greedheads". In some cases of Inquisition activity in the New World, the link between faith and economic motivations and Spanish or Portuguese *raison d'etat* can be grasped. This was particularly the case with the changes in the main lines of trade of the two empires from the mid-17th century and the accompanying shifts in the focus of Inquisition activity (Lewin 1962: 111, also Green 2012). In a way, the institution followed in the footsteps of the New Christians, who in turn moved with trade and settlers to ever newer centres of economic activity in the colonies (thus also co-creating them). Again, it is not clear whether eliminating the Inquisition's budgetary shortfall played a decisive role in the colonies (Metz 1992: 212, otherwise Liebman 1973: 31 and Baron 1973: 289–291). Monocausal interpretations and explanations will not be of much use here. Religion, economic motivations and the growing importance of ethnic stereotypes, but also the institutional inertia sustaining the invented ever-growing threat from the *judaizantes,* formed a web that was difficult to disentangle over time.

The situation of those who remained was undoubtedly very complicated. Although, as mentioned, cases of crypto-Judaism (marranos) were not uncommon in the first decades after the 1492–97 expulsions, especially in Portugal and Spanish Mallorca, from the mid-16th century most Spanish conversos already remained firmly attached to the Catholic faith: "many, and possibly most, descendants of medieval Spanish Jewry who stayed in the Peninsula (...), were completely Christianized and absorbed into the majority culture" (Israel 1998: 3, also Gitlitz 2002: 41, 43, Drescher 2001: 445). In the narrative of Ashkenazi Jews cultivating examples of martyrdom from, among others, the time of the pogroms accompanying, in German and Bohemian lands, the convocation of the First Crusade, there was sometimes resentment (perhaps even an accusation?) that Spanish Jews were not very willing to accept the role of martyrs for the faith. Such assessments can also be found in parts of Jewish historiography. Indeed, although the persecution in Spain even if only in 1391 created many martyrs, as did the repression directed against crypto-Jewish heretics in the 16th century in the Iberian world, it is striking that "Spanish Jews left a legacy in which martyrdom does not figure prominently" (Bodian 2007: 4).[9] However, from the point of view of the conversos and their descendants, there is even an obvious question: martyrdom for the faith, but which faith? Rejected Judaism or recently embraced Catholicism? The formation of new identities was neither an easy nor a quick process.

Indeed, in the background of the actions of the Spanish Crown and then of the Portuguese Crown, and from 1478 also of the Spanish Inquisition, we find, apart from all the other factors impeding integration through assimilation, the strong influence of the concept of *limpieza de sangre.* This in turn organised thinking about the problem of conversos and New Christians in a

---

9   According to some calculations, in the pogroms of 1391, one third of Spanish Jews were killed, one third were baptised and one third were saved without changing their faith (Ingram 2006: 43).

new way, going beyond the framework of traditional religious conflict. The first important step leading from religiously motivated anti-Judaism to proto-anti-Semitism was taken. At the same time, the concept was seen as an effective "hammer" jointly on the shrinking group of Judaising heretics, as well as on the *anusim* already fully formed by Catholicism. Especially on the latter. A kind of *memento*.

Limpieza de sangre, as a genetic[10] concept of original sin, first appears during the pogrom of conversos in Toledo in 1449, then in Córdoba in 1474, and gradually becomes an increasingly accepted norm, especially after the establishment of the Spanish Inquisition. It finds a place in the rules of religious military orders, the statutes of universities, city councils, guilds and the

---

10   A "racist myth" serving as an instrument of social control, as argued, for example, by Cohen (1992: 47, 54). Analogously, with emphasis on the evolution of traditional Spanish antisemitism towards racism (and references to Nazi racial laws and the extermination of the Jews), Netanyahu (1995: 975–1004, 1999). Such a comparison was also upheld by Cecil Roth when writing about Spanish "racial anti-Semitism", although he changed his position on this years later. More cautiously, Baron wrote about *limpieza de sangre* as an "early manifestation of racism", while Yosef H. Yerushalmi wrote about "proto-racism". The latter did not take the parallels and analogies with modern racism as an agreement to treat late medieval and modern conceptions of race equivalently. Many authors have questioned the link between *limpieza de sangre* and modern racism and anti-Semitism (F. Márquez Villanueva, A. Domínguez Ortiz, N. Roth; for a good review see Hering Torres 2003). By contrast, attempts to interpret the concept as a variant of exclusively religious anti-Judaism have become a thing of the past. Instead, concepts emerged that removed any responsibility from the Inquisition. It was thus claimed, following Américo Castro, that the origins of the doctrine of *limpieza de sangre* should be sought in the religious and ethnic hermeticism of Jewish communities. Earlier, at the end of the 19th century, such a thesis had been defended by Marcelino Menéndez y Pelayo, a classic of Spanish historiography. The appearance after the wave of Christianisation between 1391 and 1415 of a group of marranos was in turn supposed to confirm the thesis of a lack of authenticity and hypocrisy characterising conversos and open the way for the doctrine of the "purity of blood". Nirenberg (2002: 5–7) highlights the birth of an enduring fascination with genealogy in a more nuanced way. He sees it as the result of a 15th-century crisis of identity among Christians and Jews triggered by the emergence of a large group of conversos. This fact fostered the absolutisation of genealogy as a fundamental concept enabling the articulation of particular interests and organising historical memory. Thus Tritle (2015: 190f) would emphasise the emergence of a unique "hermeneutic of the flesh": "In mid-fifteenth-century Castile, the mask of anti-Judaism became attached to anti-judaism and a hermeneutic of the flesh, not only figuratively as it often had in the history of Christian thought, but literally, in the fleshly lineage of baptized Christians who descended from Jews". All these processes were reinforced by the religious fervour of the Church and, from the 1480s, by the Inquisition, which could hardly be overestimated. An important specific factor was also the desire to eliminate part of the new urban elite formed since the 15th century, perceived as dangerous political and economic competition.

regulations of royal offices. The document prepared by the Toledo rebels in 1449, spoke about "conversos descended from the perverse line of the Jews" and as such to be "held as incapable and unworthy to hold public or private office" (Estatuto-Sentecia 2008). Announced a century later in 1547, *El Estatuto de limpieza* prepared by the Spanish Grand Inquisitor and Archbishop of Toledo Juan Martínez Silíceo would be approved in 1555 by Pope Paul IV and ratified by King Philip II the following year (Rawlings 2006: 50–55).[11] As a *limpeça de sangue* it would also appear from the mid-16th century in Portugal and then also in its colonies.

By its very design, this concept not only eliminated conversos and their descendants from public life, but also multiplied the number of the excluded; children of mixed marriages were automatically counted among the 'tainted'. Social advancement without a certificate attesting to a genealogy free of Jewish ancestors was formally impossible and in practice severely hampered. This outcome was a perverse (and in its own way rational) response to the growing importance of conversos in the economic and social life of Spain in the 15th century. This included their continued presence in profitable but unpopular occupations, such as tax farming. The phenomenon of the growing influence of conversos did not escape the Spanish church either. Priests and monks were included among the many descended from baptised Jews, including at least six bishops. However, the hatred towards conversos could no longer be expressed in terms of a clearly defined religious conflict. It required a new justification. Improper 'blood' became the basis for accusations questioning the Catholicism

---

11   In the 15th century, the position of the popes on the "purity of blood" evolved: from condemnation of the concept by Nicholas V in 1449, to de facto acceptance by Alexander VI in 1495, when he approved the 1486 Rule of the Hieronymite Order, which excluded conversos up to the fourth generation from this religious order. Earlier, under the order's general Alonso de Oropesa, who strongly opposed the stigmatisation of conversos, the Hieronymites had rejected *limpieza de sangre*. Subsequent popes in the first half of the 16th century did not present a unified position either. On the other hand, in the Society of Jesus, founded in 1534 and already numbering 3,000 brothers 30 years later, the principle of "purity of blood" was not universally applied almost until the end of the 16th century, and the activities of the order were (co-)shaped by the brothers-conversos (the second general of the Society was converso Diego Laínez Gomez de León). Among the Portuguese Jesuits, however, the principle of "purity of blood" had been introduced earlier, from around 1550. In Spain, where membership of the Dominican Order – at the forefront of prosecuting Judaising heretics – was seen as suitable for noble-born young men, those entering the Jesuit order were seen as "Jews" in the mid-16th century. A break with the practice of tolerance formed under the overwhelming influence of the order's founder Ignatius de Loyola would be formally made in 1593 (Maryks 2009: passim). The principle of *limpieza de sangre* would be maintained in the order until 1946.

of conversos and the credibility of their baptism. All these phenomena accompanied the gradual disintegration of traditional, no longer fully feudal, but not yet modern social structures, motivations and behaviours (Rawlings 2006: 52, Roth 1959: 35f, Lea 1906: 121f).

What is striking about the concept of 'purity of blood', however, is its internal contradiction: the Christianisation of the Jews, to which so much importance was attached, could not, by definition, create true Catholics out of them, since genealogy precluded this possibility. One-fourth, one-eighth, even one-twentieth of Jewish blood is enough to make one an enemy of Christ, proclaimed one learned Spaniard at the end of the 17th century (Hering Torres 2003). A kind of perpetual stigmatisation in which 'Jewish blood' – the particular sin of lack of grace – invalidated baptism. Unlike modern racism, however, this was still a flexible stigmatisation, allowing for the negotiation of status and possibly the obliteration – in social space – of bad origins. At the end of the 16th century the Dominican friar Agustino Salucio, who himself was probably descended from a family of conversos, asked (and not without irony) the question, "who is an Old Christian?" and answered that, "an 'Old Christian' was the person who converted to Christianity before the 'New Christian'" (quoted in Ingram 2006: 16). He himself was an author of a memorandum proposing far-reaching changes to the concept of *limpieza de sangre*.

Although *limpieza de sangre* anticipated the racist arguments, it linked the inheritance of Jewish characteristics mainly to the ideas of Aristotle and religion. According to Francisco Márquez Villanueva, "the conversos did not carry in any moment an indelible biological stigma" (quoted in Hering Torras 2003: 4). With one caveat, however: such an assessment applied only to the early period. But even then, it did not apply to the group of Jews on Mallorca (Spanish: *chuetas*, Catalan: *xuetes*), who were Christianised several times over several centuries and not entirely successfully (Herzog 2003: Chapter 6). Contreras (1996: 67f), on the other hand, points out that the 'rule of law' (baptism and admission to the Catholic community) was, when it came to conversos, replaced by political domination exercised by the centres of power using the instruments available to them (including the principle of 'purity of blood'). The consequences were also felt by the Holy See under Philip II:

> Even Pius V, one of the least tolerant of the sixteenth-century popes, was amazed by the king's intransigence. When, in 1570, he suggested to Philip the appointment of his favorite, Francisco de Reinoso, as archdeacon of the Cathedral of Toledo, the king refused because of Reinoso's *converso* ancestry. The Pope could not understand why a man of outstanding virtue and learning should be disqualified merely because of his Jewish

origin. Pius finally prevailed upon the king to appoint Reinoso to the bishopric of Córdoba.

BARON 1973: 164[12]

It is estimated that the actions of the Spanish Inquisition probably affected 6–12 per cent of conversos at the height of the repression in the 1530s. If these calculations are reliable, they would suggest that the application of the *limpieza de sangre* principle – by then already de facto incorporated into the legal system – did not imply a desire to eradicate them altogether (Alpert 2001: 17, Pulido Serrano 2003: 46, Cohen 1992).[13] This despite the intentions behind the establishment of the Inquisition and the very principle of the 'purity of blood'. One must also bear in mind the barriers posed by the limited effectiveness of the Iberian bureaucracy and the scale of the problem. However, there is no doubt that the repression that affected one in ten converso sowed fear and terrorised the entire group. No one could feel safe in such conditions.

However, by the 1570s "it is correct to speak of a mass crypto-Jewish sub-culture in Portugal", albeit already limited to 30–50,000 people (Israel 1998: 20). This was favoured by the late establishment of the Holy Office in that country. It is therefore not surprising that the Portuguese Inquisition, especially after the establishment of the Iberian Union in 1581, went on the offensive towards the end of the century. Above all, it carefully recorded the extent to which New Christians were 'contaminated' with Jewish blood. Thus, in its documents we

---

12   In fact, Francisco de Reinoso was only appointed Bishop of Córdoba in 1597, and not by Pius V (who died in 1572), but by Pope Clement VIII, who was critical of Philip II of Spain. The Jesuit Diogo de Areda, a close associate of the Portuguese Grand Inquisitor, was aware of the contradictions into which the principle of *limpieza* de *sangre* entangled the universal message of Catholicism. Thus, writing in 1625 on the methods of combating *do judaismo neste Reyno de Portugal,* he pointed out that persecution on the basis of Jewish ancestry alone was "unjust and contrary to [the principle of] church unity" (quoted in Stuczynski 2014: 53).

13   During the first half century of the Inquisition's activity, repression affected 30–50,000 conversos (Pulido Serrano 2003, Baroja 2000: 204f). Kamen (2005: 76), on the other hand, suggests that from the mid-16th century *limpieza de sangre* "was never widely practised in Spain or attained legal approval". It had previously played a role in Toledo and some cities in southern Spain. This is not a universally shared opinion. But certainly, the implementation of the principle was a staggered and regionally differentiated process. While downplaying the importance of the *limpieza de sangre* and of *raza* and religion, Kamen has at the same time emphasised the importance of power and control as factors fundamental to understanding the phenomenon of the Inquisition. In contrast, Netanyahu upholds the hypothesis that the political objective of the Inquisition was the total elimination of the marranos from Spain. And, last but not least, the Inquisition's financial needs as an incentive for repression should not be overlooked (Novinsky 2009a: 209).

find the standard notations of "part XN", or more precisely "one-half XN" or "one-eighth XN" (*XN*, i.e. New Christian) (Pieroni 2001: 245). But also, in the case of Portugal, one can speak of a non-eliminationist approach, especially when it came to Brazil. According to Anita Novinsky's calculations based on the Inquisition data contained in *Rol dos Culpados* (The Book of the Guilty), during the colonial era the Inquisitors indicted 1,076 Brazilians, of whom over 600 were convicted on charges of Judaising (several sent to the stake). The repression was particularly intense at the end of the 16th and then in the first half of the 18th century (Novinsky 2006: 5, Bogaciovas 2006: 134–136). As in the case of the Spanish Inquisition, there was a small yet sufficient number to sow uncertainty and fear among New Christians regardless of their 'guilt'.

The non-eliminationist approach of the Inquisition for a time was, it has been suggested, clearly motivated by economic considerations, while at the same time the activities of Portuguese Inquisitors in the metropolis from the mid-16th century were often characterised as harsher, compared to the Spanish. Especially when it came to heresy and New Christians. In any case, when, in the wake of the riots against New Christians in 1671, the regent, Duke Pedro II decided to expel from Portugal all those accused of 'Judaising' and to confiscate their property (*Lei do Extermínio*), the Inquisition came out against such a move. Not without reason. The removal of suspects would have led to a questioning of the legitimacy enabling further action, while the absence of heretics (and their estates) would have meant a weakening of the economic basis of the institution's existence. Earlier, during the reign of João IV, the argument regarding the important role of confiscations in financing the activities of the Inquisition appeared in a letter of the Holy Office addressed to the king. The reason for this was the decision to exclude from the confiscations New Christians investing in a newly created monopolistic company in control – theoretically at least – of carrying out Atlantic trade (this project was also supported by the Jesuits). After the king's death, in 1657, the Inquisition got what it wanted – the restoration of confiscations without exceptions (Novinsky 1991: 175f, Saraiva 2001: 214).

Attempts by representatives of the New Christian merchants – aided by the Jesuits – and the Holy See to settle the dispute over the *Lei do Extermínio* failed. A proposal for an amnesty for the *judaizantes* was rejected and, as a consequence, the New Christians' offer to allocate 500,000 cruzados to revitalise trade with India and to provide, through the Pope, assistance to Poland, which had been fighting the Turks since 1672, hung in limbo. Under pressure from the Inquisition, the Cortes and protests directed against those who "want to be a Jew, a heretic, a sodomite and marry three times", Pedro II, who had initially favoured compromise, relented. In the meantime, many merchants arrested by the Inquisition died in prison, while mass confiscations carried out brought in funds to the tune of 500,000 cruzados. The decisions against the New Christians, announced in 1683, ruled out the possibility of mass emigration; they were also preceded by further arrests (Hanson 1981: 78, 91–99, Alden 1996: 128).

Let us note, however, that the efforts to secure inflow of financial resources were also justified by the scale of the expenses incurred by the Holy Office. The *Visitação* of the Inquisition to Brazil in 1591–95, as well as earlier visits to the Azores and Madeira, entailed enormous costs. Almost 65 per cent of the entire deficit of the Portuguese Holy Office in 1594 was caused by the visitation to Brazil. As a consequence, the planned visitation to Cape Verde and São Tomé had to be cancelled. This was probably a difficult decision, for in these very islands and the territory of Upper Guinea linked to them through trade, the presence of Judaising New Christians – white and mulatto – was already very much in evidence in the 16th century. The rapidly growing deficit, however, could not be ignored. In this case, writes the historian, the principle of purity of faith had to give way to the need for order and purity in the accounts (Green 2012b: 13, 2015: 24).

Despite the aforementioned turbulence in policy towards the New Christians and conversos, however, there is no doubt that in both countries the period from the late 17th to the 1720s-1730s was a time of increased, and on the whole, effective repression. After the blows dealt in the metropolis and colonies during this period, the New Christians as a group *sui generis* did not recover again. In Brazil, the New Christians in Rio de Janeiro and Minas Gerais, the new economic centres of the colony, were hit particularly hard. At the same time, *limpieza de sangre* underwent fundamental transformations, reflecting not so much a struggle for the souls of the descendants of those once baptised, but increasingly anti-Semitic, ethnic stereotypes (whether these were also proto-racist is open to debate).

Before this, however, life went on with its own rhythm in Brazil and the Portuguese metropolis. Despite the threat posed by the Inquisition and its informers, formal and informal relationships between New and Old Christian couples were not uncommon. Among the Lisbon merchants, this process was already well advanced by the end of the 16th century. Mixed marriages were also not surprising among the New Christian emigrants from Portugal who arrived in London in the early 18th century. In Brazil, according to the findings of Angela Maria Vieira Maia (1995), the majority of marriages concluded by the end of the 16th century in Bahia and Pernambuco by New Christians were mixed. This was especially true for families belonging to the commercial elite and planters. Mixed marriages also occurred among the elite of colonial officials. Brazil was much more liberal in this respect than the metropolis, not least because of the strongly felt lack of white women. Living conditions in the colony also played an important role, especially during the first period of its formation: "Brazil did not offer an environment conducive to philosophical discourse" (Novinsky 1972: 65, see also Salvador 1976: passim, Studnicki-Gizbert 2007: 24, Kaplan 1994, Schwartz 1985: 266).

At the root of such risky decisions, challenging the 'purity of blood', as well as the endogamous relationships favoured by tradition (not only Jewish), we find pursuit of the rational maximisation of other benefits, including enhancement of social status. Here we are dealing with strategies similar to those that emphasised the importance of the family as a factor in strengthening a sense of security and stability in the wider, hostile environment. Mixed marriages can be seen as a part of risk-reducing activities and, at the same time, as strategies that fostered new contacts, in particular the strengthening of network arrangements both economically and socially, which also included circles of aristocracy (Roitman 2011: 13f). The result was, on the one hand, a softening within the elite of the divisions between New and Old Christians, while, on the other, the Inquisition multiplied the number of suspects. Unmasked descendants from mixed marriages enlarged the group of stigmatized *XN*s, although wealth, family colligations and political connections could in some cases weaken the vigilance of the inquisitors.

In general, however, the inquisitors did not use microscopes and fine scalpels in their fight against the *judaizantes*, especially during periods of mass repression. At the beginning of the 17th century, in order to establish a list of New Christians required to contribute to the huge sums as payment for the amnesty, their number was estimated at 24,000–30,000 (6,000 families). By contrast, in 1624, the Portuguese Inquisition presented a shocking calculation, which showed that the number of New Christians (with varying degrees of 'Jewish blood') should be estimated at 200,000 families, i.e. around 1 million people. This would therefore represent more than half of the Portuguese population (Saraiva 2001: 132).[14] These calculations, intended to terrify the Madrid

---

14   Jakób Sobieski, father of the future Polish king, who travelled to Portugal at the beginning of the 17th century, among other places, wrote: "the Jews (*sic*) a harsh thing there (…) and though it burned them, were driven away, yet a force of secret Jews was found among them" (Sobieski 1833: 107). According to an Englishman who visited Portugal in 1693, "the New Christians and Jews (*sic*)" made up one third of the population, thus less than the Inquisition estimated, but still at a level questioned by historians. Let us note, however, that when an attempt was made in 1663 to create a new prestigious fraternity, the *Confraría da Nobleza,* most candidates were unable to prove an unblemished Old Christian 'blood' (Azevedo 1922: 342, Hanson 1981: 73).

court, probably played a role in exacerbating the repression. This occurred primarily in Portugal itself and, with some delay, in the Spanish colonies, where the victims of the fight against heresy were mainly 'Portuguese'. In turn, the rise of anti-Jewish sentiments intensified from the late 17th century, although they did not yet take the form of a developed (anti-Semitic) ideology among the Iberian inquisitors (Graizbord 2006: 359).

However, the influence of the *limpieza de sangre* was not limited to the New Christians (the Jews, as 'incapable of heresy', were of no interest to the Inquisition, and after 1492 and 1497, the issue became irrelevant since they formally ceased to exist in the Iberian Peninsula). We find it – as well as a growing tradition of negative attitudes towards the 'other' during the Reconquista – also at the root of the *sistema de castas* introduced by the Spanish in Latin America. It was, indeed, a kind of bio-ethno-politics organising a particular kind of stratification in the multicultural societies created – out of necessity, not choice, spontaneously, not according to a planned intention.

The obsession with genealogy (and 'honour' belonging only to white Catholics, preferably of noble origin) became an immanent feature of the societies of the Iberian colonies, the other side of the process of racial mixing. In Jorge Juan and Antonio de Ulloa's (1964: 27) account of their journey to Latin America in the first half of the 18th century, we find in their remarks on the population of Cartagena a succinct description of the results of the mixing of whites and blacks: thus, we have the Mulattoes, then the Tercerones, the Quarterones and finally the Quinterones. The children of Whites and Quinterones are called Spaniards and "consider themselves as free from all taint of the Negro race". The terminology used and the number of cases of racial mixing considered in each region may have varied, while the general principle remained constant: "In general, it was the colour of the skin that determined social position" (Rosenblat 1954: 179). Only in special circumstances was a process of social 'whitening', a change of 'racial' status by rich mulattoes or mestizos, possible.

This obsession was reinforced by the fact that on the Iberian Peninsula, genealogy, as an important element of the social gradation system, was by no means limited to the study of the proportion of Jewish or Muslim 'blood', although this issue undoubtedly occupied a prominent place in the late 15th and early 16th centuries. Basque elites in particular proudly perceived their status as a unique group untainted by admixtures of the 'blood' of others. They traced their lineage back to distant antiquity and then to Visigothic Christians never subjugated to Muslims in the north of the peninsula. Incidentally, this myth of uncontaminated ancestry was conducive to maintaining solidarity among Basques in Latin America as well, and to preserving the positions they had acquired (e.g., in the elite of mining entrepreneurs and the Potosí city council in the late 16th century). Castilians and others were, despite their protests, treated by the Basques as representing 'tainted blood'.

In fact, argued Américo Castro, in turn, the importance attached to genealogy as an organising criterion for the system of social gradation did not appear in Spain until after the 13th century. "Spanishness" was not and is therefore not a genetic trait; there is not, as he answered critics bitingly, a straight line connecting "Seneca with Unamuno". It is only from this period onwards that one can speak, he argued, of a progressive crisis of *convivencia,* a complex relationship of cooperation and conflict between three religions and social groups: Christians, Muslims and Jews. It was this relationship that shaped the identity of Spaniards in the Middle Ages (Wolf 2009).[15] Its product was also, in the 11th century, El Cid. This Christian conqueror of Valencia had previously fought side-by-side with the Muslim ruler of Zaragoza in order to then – at the head of Christian-Muslim troops – resist an Almoravid invasion carrying 'unadulterated' Islam. He would be mythologised in a later era and encased in a kind of national-Spanish cocoon.

In turn, the situation of the Sephardim in Spain during this period, and in the following two centuries, differed considerably from that of the Jews in other countries of Western Europe. Pogroms, which appeared in the run-up to the First Crusade, and recurred with almost lethal regularity in times of epidemics and other cataclysms, fortunately did not become a permanent part of the Spanish Jewish experience until the end of the 14th century. An anomaly of sorts. Although the anti-Jewish decisions of the 1215 Lateran Council were (belatedly) enshrined in Castile by Alfonso X in the collection of laws *Las Siete Partidas*, they did not come into force until the mid-14th century. The enthusiasm of Pope Innocent III in combating Jews resembling "fratricidal Cain", did not extend to the Spaniards at this time (Klener 1998: IXF). The situation of the Jews in Portugal can be similarly characterised, perhaps with the only difference: the earlier end of the Reconquista than in Spain probably prevented the emergence of a numerically significant group of conversos and attempts at a top-down ideo-religious unification. This otherness fostered the empowerment of Portuguese Jews.

---

15 The well-known medievalist Claudio Sánchez-Albornoz firmly rejected the hypothesis of a major Jewish and Muslim contribution to the formation of the Spanish nation: "he treated Castro as a Spanish apostate who deliberately and viciously aimed to challenge the true culture of Spain" (Ingram 2006: 28). He himself used downright anti-Semitic stereotypes in describing the Sephardim.

The place of *convivencia* is finally taken in the early 16th century by the political project of Spanishness as a hegemonic idea in the state that had victoriously ended the Reconquista. From the unification of Castile and Aragon onwards, it was consistently implemented by Ferdinand II. Spanishness became not so much a complement to the previous multicultural tradition, but an alternative project, an expression of the Catholic exclusivism forming Spaniards that appealed to religious-ethnic criteria (Wolf 2009, Netanyahu 1995: 55, Kubiaczyk 2012). The myth of 'purity of blood', which led to the negation of any constructive influence of Islam and Judaism, established during the conflict with conversos before and after 1492, as well as with *moriscos* in the 16th century, survived the following centuries. It was also well enough known outside Spain to be reflected, for example, in the poetry of Lord Byron. In the first song of his poem *Don Juan,* he writes thus, and not without irony, about the origins of his Seville-born hero (*Of all the Spanish towns is none more pretty*):

> His father's name was Jose—Don, of course,—
>   A true Hidalgo, free from every stain
> Of Moor or Hebrew blood, he traced his source
>   Through the most Gothic gentlemen of Spain;
> A better cavalier ne'er mounted horse,
>   Or, being mounted, e'er got down again
>   CANTO I

Notably, in Chile at the beginning of the 20th century, Nicolás Palacios, lamenting the 'national decline', would develop, in line with racist theories popular at the time, the concept of the *raza chilena* as a mixture of warrior Goths and Mapuche Indians – in contrast to other Latin American countries where tainted 'Latin blood' was prevalent. In an already different context, the Visigoth heritage will appear in the works of the aforementioned critic of *convivencia,* Sánchez-Albornoz. According to this medievalist and anti-Francoist politician, it was this experience, preceding the Muslim conquest of the peninsula, that created the basis for national unity and the foundation of 'Spanishness' (pro-Francoist historians shared this view) (Ingram 2009: 343f). While such a view cannot be reduced to the concept of 'purity of blood', there is no doubt that the tradition associated with *limpieza de sangre* and the exclusion of 'others' weighed on all discussions of Spanish identity. The process of racial mixing in the 13 British colonies and then in the United States was viewed differently. Here, the complex variants of *mestizaje* (race mixing) present in the Iberian colonies, and the possibilities of social 'whitening' were replaced by the White-Black dichotomy. It reflected the persistence of prevailing racist notions among whites of what the 'somatic norm' was as a fundamental criterion of stratification in multiracial societies (Hoetink 1973: Chapter 6). The interdependence of 'race' and 'class' was quite radically reduced in the British colonies and then in the USA to race relations.

Perceptions of the New Christians and their status in the New World were thus largely determined by the confrontations with an expansive Christianity – combined with Iberian imperial ideas – with the growing diversity and complexity of the newly emerging societies. Imposed new hierarchies were therefore codified and mythologised. In these newly created gradation systems and stratification structures, Jews and New Christians perceived their place as identical to the status of the elite – by virtue of skin colour, while ignoring differences in their distinctive religion and genealogy. While this status was contested on more than one occasion, these attempts were largely unsuccessful. The handicap of genealogy was compensated for by skin colour. Briefly, they were inferior according to certain criteria, but at the same time it became impossible to exclude them from *la nobleza blanca*. Although in colonial Bahia, New Christians and "coloureds" were classed together as "forbidden races", at the same time, being white and Catholic implied honesty and integrity. A white New Christian girl was a 'virtuous girl' (Russell-Wood 1992: iv154, also Schorsch 2009: 5f, Chapter 1, 2004: Chapters 7 and 8, Baron 1973: 271f).

Lost on the grounds of religious principles, the struggle for equality or even tolerance in the Catholic world did not end in total defeat for Jews and New Christians on the grounds of racial dogma. Against all odds, they persisted in the colonies as members of the white elite. Racial dogmas were to take on deadly significance in Europe in a different era, in the 20th century, in the process of redefining social hierarchies with the help of racial categories. At the end of this process, the *Einsatzgruppen* and the guards of the *Vernichtungslagern* would appear as ultimate arbiters of the "Jewishness" of the converts.

'The Portuguese'

With regard to the emigrants who from the 1490s successively left Spain and Portugal heading towards France, the Netherlands and Hamburg, the matter was no less complicated, but in a different way. Many, whose ancestors had previously been baptised, returned to Judaism in Amsterdam. They thus became proud, no longer persecuted *homens (gente) da nação,* Sephardic Jews, while still remaining part of the wider Portuguese diaspora. This also applied to emigrants in some Italian cities, including at various times Pisa, Florence, Livorno, Ferrara and Venice.

The situation was different in Antwerp, the destination for many emigrating New Christians. In this "rendezvous of European commerce" (Pirenne 1914: 512) there was already from the end of the 15th century a thriving Portuguese community numbering in the 16th century probably around 500–1,000 people, i.e. 100–200 families. It was largely made up of New Christians residing here with the encouragement of the municipal authorities, mostly wealthy merchants trading in Asian spices, diamonds, and sugar from Madeira and the island of São Tomé. As they accumulated capital, their trading activities were increasingly complemented by financial operations. The group of New Christians attending the annual meetings of the 'Portuguese nation' included 85 married and 17 unmarried men in 1570 (Pohl 1967: 352). However, unlike the later evolution of similar communities in southern France and in some German and Italian cities, in Antwerp the activities of the 'Portuguese people' were not associated either in the late 16th or 17th century with attempts to return to Judaism. Here the 'Portuguese' continued to act – out of precaution or choice – as New Christians, just as in Spain and Portugal or the Iberian colonies. A traveller who ended up in Antwerp in the mid-16th century noted that there were no Jews in the city at all (Foa 2000: 170).

In the 16th century, therefore, Antwerp was undoubtedly the 'Mecca' of New Christian merchants, a place where vast fortunes were made for the time, but it never became the 'Mecca' of Portuguese New Christians returning to the faith of their forefathers. In the first half of the 16th century, however, this did not protect even the most powerful New Christian merchants from repression – by the royal authorities and by the Inquisition specially established for the Netherlands (the attention of both institutions, however, was focused mainly on Anabaptists). Moreover, the Emperor, preoccupied with building up Spanish power and involved in wars with France and the Ottoman Empire, among others, was primarily interested in the fortunes of the New Christians, and less so in their consciences.[1]

When citing cases of returns to Judaism within organised forms of Jewish life – such as in Amsterdam – it should be borne in mind, after all, that the emigrants who headed towards Northern Europe had mostly stayed with Catholicism for good (Cohen 1992: 68, Israel 2009: 3f, 2002a: 14, 71). Moreover, in many cases such returns to Judaism for the generations of the second half of the 16th and early 17th centuries were not easy. Religious self-awareness of the descendants of the converts, knowledge of Jewish Scripture, traditions, rituals etc. was generally poor: "Roman Catholics without faith and Jews without knowledge but wishing to be Jews" (Schorsch 2009: 65). The holy books were mostly unknown or known at second-hand as condemnable texts quoted by Catholic priests. The founding of a Jewish community in Amsterdam therefore owed much to the activity of the Sephardim in Italy of the late 16th century. It was the publisher in Ferrara that printed translations of the Hebrew holy books (Cohen 1992: 76). The first *Biblia de Ferrara* in Ladino (*Judeoespañol*) appears as early as 1553. In contrast, the organisational structure of the Jewish community in Amsterdam was adopted from Venice. The dominant role was played by the council of elders (*Mahamad*), operating on the basis of annual co-optation. Its members (*parnasim*) were mainly drawn from among important merchants and financiers, not rabbis (Israel 2002: 77f, 80, 88f). An eminent scholar of the problem wondered whether the word "return" was appropriate in this context, or whether one should rather speak of the phenomenon of the creation of "new Jews" in the Republic (Kaplan 1994). There were also other factors impeding the return of Iberian exiles to Judaism:

---

1 The repressed were defended in the 1530s by Popes Clement VII and Paul III, whose stance towards the Jews was not hostile. This was made possible, among other things, by the support given by high papal officials, who were lavishly rewarded by the attorneys of the arrested merchants (Nelson Novoa 2008: 175–177). During this period, such repression affected Diogo Mendes, a trading and financial partner of the kings of Portugal and England who headed an informal consortium of Portuguese merchants who traded Asian spices in Antwerp. He was accused of Judaising, supporting the illegal migration of New Christians into the Levant and monopolising the spice trade. His arrest was met with protest primarily from João III and his wife, Charles V's sister. In letters to the emperor, which even extolled the integrity of Diogo Mendes to the skies, they at the same time defended their own income from pepper sales threatened by Spanish seizures (Salomon and Leone Leoni 1998). After reaching a settlement with the emperor and paying 50,000 ducats as an interest-free loan, Diogo Mendes was freed. After his death, Charles V renewed his accusations. This caused the remaining family to flee the Netherlands. The vast Mendes estate was by then managed by Diogo's widowed sister-in-law, Beatriz de Luna. After rejecting Catholicism, she was known as Doña Grácia Nasci (Leone Leoni 2005: 20f, Mateus and Mendes Pinto 2011).

> the bonds linking the Portuguese of Amsterdam to the Iberian Peninsula were stronger than those attaching them to the sixteenth-century rabbinic tradition. (...) the Iberian origins of the majority of the community's members made it impossible for them to disavow those still living in exclusively Catholic countries (...) it is difficult to comprehend how those who immigrated to Holland reconciled being both Portuguese and Jewish. The link between both identities was fluid and ambiguous and was, at times, even conflicting.
>
> FEITLER 2009: 129, 132

The converso or New Christian raised in the Catholic culture of Spain and Portugal constructed a somewhat imaginary world after emigrating to the Republic. The community they created "did not grow up and develop in an organic way with each generation passing on the heritage of its ancestors. Among the Sephardi Jews of the seventeenth century, one might speak of an *invented tradition* with a traditional community emerging *ex nihilo* under new conditions in new times" (Kaplan 1999: 228). Religious orthodoxy was thus mixed with innovative economic activities, and the element that gave cohesion to the community of "new Jews" was very much an Iberian tradition, especially its Portuguese variant. Portuguese, not Dutch, was the main means of communication. This multifaceted distinctiveness of 'the Portuguese', seen in the broader context of the history of the Sephardic diaspora scattered across Europe, has been the subject of intense research for years (Bodian 2008, Kaplan 1992, 2008).

A frequent phenomenon in religious life, but also in the moral sphere, was the phenomenon of a double (or split) consciousness (*o homem dividido*, according to Anita Novinsky's apt term). Present among the marranos and among the new emigrants to Amsterdam, it did not bypass those New Christians who were already outside Judaism (or on the border between Judaism and Catholicism) and who sought a place for themselves in the Catholic New World. This was well illustrated by the peculiar theological *bricolage* noted by historians – the raising of prayers to the "holy Moses" (Novinsky 1972: Chapter 5). This also often led to tragedy, when preserved elements of Jewish tradition, taken out of their now new Christian context, were presented as evidence of 'Judaising' in the denunciations of Inquisition informants. Sometimes it was only in the course of interrogation that suspects learned from the inquisitors that some of their behaviour and customs in fact confirmed the offence of worshipping the "dead Law of Moses" (as the Inquisition termed the Jewish faith). Incidentally, any zeal in the New Christians' adherence to Catholic customs could also have raised suspicion and warranted an Inquisitorial investigation.

The consumption of pork meat and the use of pig fat were not unquestionable proof of 'purity of blood' in 16th and 17th century Portugal or Bahia (Salvador 1978: 87). Other examples of marranos adopting elements of Christian customs and religious behaviour include the intertwining of hands during prayer or praying while kneeling (Liebman 1975: 156). "Split consciousness" encouraged the breaking of traditions.

Despite enormous initial difficulties, the "new Jews" became a reality. Amsterdam was transforming itself into a centre for the reconstruction of Sephardic religious and cultural life. It was also becoming a unique example of the co-founding of economic modernity, largely at odds with previous European Jewish history. Not on the margins of mainstream economic life as a forced combination of Jewish poverty with petty trade, usury and other financial operations of the elite, but in its internationally important financial and commercial centre. The Amsterdam Jews in no way resembled – when it came to their place in the wider society and economy – a model case of the "speculative pariah-capitalism" (Weber 1974: 271). And at the same time, the new community that was created was also constantly confronted with the enormity of poverty. But it was not only social and economic polarisation that was a problem. The community taking shape in Amsterdam in the 17th century would also become a seedbed of rebellion against the tradition of rabbinical Judaism – witness the dissident ideas of Uriel da Costa as early as the 1620s, followed by those of Juan de Prado and Baruch Spinoza.

However, in this clash it was orthodoxy that prevailed. Critics and doubters were marginalised, cursed (*herem*) and, like de Prado and Spinoza, excluded from the community (Israel 2002c: 137ff). All of this simultaneously contributed to the suicide of Uriel da Costa, who, according to his account, was humiliated by the punishment of lashes administered in the synagogue. This religious ferment can be interpreted in many ways, including as a symptom of the maturity of the new diaspora in the second half of the 17th century. An alternative interpretation is also possible: the harsh reaction of the *parnasim* and rabbis to this ferment expressed rather hidden concerns about the sustainability of the Jewish institutions and customs created in Amsterdam, under the influence of the Venetian rabbis and the Iberian cultural and religious tradition. The community founded in Amsterdam was not a harbinger of the Enlightenment, a precursor of the Haskalah initiated in the second half of the 18th century by the German *maskilim*. At the cultural and religious level, "the values brought from the Iberian Peninsula served most [of Sephardim] as a means of bolstering the authority and legitimacy of the Jewish tradition" (Kaplan 1999: 225). The first article of the 1639 community statutes (*haskamot*) proclaimed: "The *Mahamad* [council] shall have authority over everything"

(Bodian 1999: 111). Uncertainty was exacerbated by the millenarian sentiment prevalent at the time. The strength of expectations of a breakthrough was evidenced by the enthusiastic reception in the 1660s by many of the wordly Jews of Amsterdam and Hamburg to the message of the 'messiah' from Smyrna, Sabbatai Zevi. Among his followers would appear the wealthy merchant and community leader in Amsterdam, Abraham (Tomé) Pereyra, who had arrived from Spain, as well as João de Yllan, a prominent merchant adventurer in Amsterdam, active in the 1650s in Curaçao, among other places. These sentiments resonated with Antonio de Montezinos's (Aharon Levi) earlier revelations in 1644 about his discovery among the Indians in New Granada of the Rubenites, one of the 'ten tribes of Israel', who had disappeared back in the 8th century BC. This revelation, received with attention by the leaders of the "new Jews", was consonant with the mood of expectation of change intended to lead, once the dispersion was complete, to the unification of the Jewish people. Efforts to allow Jews to stay in England under Cromwell were part of this process. The Smyrna 'messiah' had already spoken of a return to the Land of Israel (Israel 2009: 267–271, 259–261, Schorsch 2009: Chapter 9).

In Western Europe, these Portuguese Jews were defined simply as 'Portuguese', just as the Sephardim arriving in Italian cities in the 16th century were either *levantini*, those coming from the (Ottoman) east, or *ponentini*, those coming from the west. In Antwerp, baptised emigrants settling from 1511 were referred to, to avoid persecution, as *mercadores da nação portuguesa* (merchants of the Portuguese nation). Similarly, in Bordeaux, where they also settled as Christians or 'Portuguese merchants' with the encouragement of the king and the municipal authorities as a group able to help restore the splendour of the city and region after the devastating Hundred Years' War. Portuguese became the *lingua franca* of trade in northern Europe and the Mediterranean. The term 'Portuguese' and the phrase *la gente de negócios de Portugal* were also in common use in Spanish America and Spain itself as synonyms of "merchant". However, unlike in Brazil and the Spanish colonies, the diaspora in the Netherlands no longer had any reason to appear to the outside world as New Christians. This was also reflected in Dutch documents of the period, where terms such as *Joodsche Natie* or *Portugeesch Natie* appeared interchangeably. Many Jews saw themselves as *os da nação* (those of this nation), but not all linked Jewish (self-)identification with religion. Religious indifferentism was not an alien phenomenon to Jews in the Republic at the time.

It should also be borne in mind that not all New Christians arriving in the United Provinces returned to their ancestral religion and fully identified with the Jewish community. Some did not make such a choice, remaining 'Jews without Judaism' or even returning to Catholicism after a time, risking an uncertain future in Spain or Portugal. These were by no means isolated cases (Kaplan 1994, 2008, 1992: 82f, also Graizbord 2004). Caution or forethought was partly justified when it came to maintaining contacts with New Christians in Spain and Portugal and in the New World, often families and/or trading partners. In a word, many "preferred an unobtrusive private Judaism without being drawn into the obligations and collective practices of an organized community. This resulted (...) in a continuing quarrel about the rite of circumcision and the status of formal prayer with a *minyan*, in the presence of at least ten adult men" (Israel 2002a: 92).

However, even in the Netherlands, unique in terms of the extent of freedoms already achieved by Jews, the elimination of discriminatory regulations was a staggered process. Resistance, especially from Calvinist ministers, radical Protestants and parts of the economic elite, especially merchants, was extremely strong. This would also prove to be the case between 1630 and 1654 in 'Dutch Brazil'. The laws enacted in the Republic were sometimes more liberal, one observer noted, than the behaviour of the Dutch themselves. However, progress was already enormous at the beginning of the 17th century.[2] In the Europe of the Counter-Reformation, the United Provinces of the Free Netherlands became for two hundred years the least intolerant country in Europe (Boxer 1965: 141). Belatedly, but from the late 17th century, England – and its Caribbean colonies – would become a similar place for the Sephardim. For the initially few fleeing 'Dutch Brazil' after the defeat of the Dutch in 1654, the English colonies and New Amsterdam in North America would also play the role of a safe haven. What is striking, however, is the modest scale of these migrations, especially to England. We are talking about hundreds rather than thousands of migrants; in the 18th century, the number of Ashkenazi Jews arriving on the British Isles from Eastern Europe far exceeded the Sephardic population (Endelman 2002: 38).

The role played by Portuguese Jews in Western Europe and by the New Christians in Brazil and the Spanish colonies, including their links with the New Christians in the Iberian Peninsula, raises the question almost

---

2 The breakthrough came with a memorandum (*Remonstrantie*) by Hugo Grotius in 1616, and the actions of the city councils of Amsterdam, Rotterdam and Haarlem. Grotius proposed to put the 'Portuguese' on an equal footing with the Dutch in much economic activity, especially in wholesale trade (less profitable than retail trade) and the liberal professions (doctors), and religious tolerance (with restrictions) for Amsterdam Jews. However, as late as the mid-17th century, Sephardic purchased Amsterdam citizenship rights (*poortersrecht*) could not be inherited. In 1606, only seven Portuguese (six merchants and one tailor) were allowed to purchase Amsterdam citizenship (Koen 1970: 29, Swetschinski 2004: 20f). Full political rights for Jews would not be mentioned until 1796, in the era of the French Revolution (Huussen 2002).

automatically: why exactly 'Portuguese Jews' and 'Portuguese New Christians'? The short answer would be: largely due to a combination of several factors, of varying importance, more pronounced than in Spain. Firstly, the strongly marked distinctiveness of the Jewish community in the period prior to forced Christianisation; secondly, the intensity and scale of the persecution in Portugal itself (the dramatic year 1497 and the massacre of several thousand already baptised Jews in Lisbon in 1506), which represented a dramatic break with the previous tradition of Christian-Jewish relations; thirdly, the relatively late arrival of the Inquisition; fourthly, the impediments to emigration, which, contrary to the intentions of the court, in practice sustained the influence of the Judaising New Christians in the metropolis; fifthly, the monarchy's relative lack of interest in Brazil until the 1540s (and the Inquisition even later). The successive issuing and revoking of emigration bans allowed the overseas territory to be regarded as a de facto place of exile for the New Christians (alongside other undesirable elements), and by them as a place of escape. Not insignificant was also the limited amnesty negotiated in 1544 with the Holy See by the influential *XN* s. Duly paid, it was intended for heretics who had already been condemned, but also with the aim to further postpone the decision to initiate the Inquisition, already taken by the Pope. This was in fact a desperate move after the failure of earlier efforts to permanently block the decision to establish a Holy Office in Portugal. The cancellation, a few years later, of some important provisions of the amnesty concerning, for example, the prohibition of confiscation of property and the use of non-inquisitorial investigative procedures, was an important factor in the subsequent waves of emigration.

A few comments on this subject, therefore, are required.

From the perspective of the almost two centuries that had elapsed since the destruction of Jewish communities in the Iberian Peninsula, Baruch Spinoza pointed to the different effects of the Christianisation and expulsion of Spanish and Portuguese Jews. In Spain, it may be recalled, the first wave of the mass 'creation' of conversos and their subsequent gradual and selective integration had already been initiated after the pogroms of 1391. In 1492, the opportunities for Christianisation and (limited) social advancement with the simultaneous removal from Spain of rejectionists faithful to Judaism resulted once again in a relatively strong religious and social integration into the Catholic environment of many Christianised Jews. Spinoza (1891: 55f) wrote of them:

> When the king of Spain formerly compelled the Jews to embrace the State religion or to go into exile, a large number of Jews accepted Catholicism. Now, as these renegades were admitted to all the native privileges of Spaniards, and deemed worthy of filling all honourable offices, it came to

pass that they straightway became so intermingled with the Spaniards as to leave of themselves no relic or remembrance.

The expelled Jews headed mainly towards the city-states of Italy, North Africa (especially Morocco) and the Ottoman Empire (where they then took control of trade in the Balkans relatively quickly). Many of the baptised rejectionists, probably around 30,000, ended up in Portugal. Formally this was conditional consent, with no right to stay longer than six months. In practice, many tried to ignore these restrictions. But, immediately after the expulsions of 1492, only 600 families, i.e. around 2,400–3,000 people, were granted permission to settle in Portugal for a rather high fee. This group included, in addition to rich Jews, blacksmiths, tinsmiths, enamelers, armourers and goldsmiths who were in demand in Portugal (they paid only half the fee). After a few years, the presence of only 150 families of Castilian refugees (600–750 people) was mentioned (Soyer 2007a: 111, 116–122, 2008, Saraiva 2001: 4).

In contrast, the forced Christianisation in 1497 of thousands of Jews in Lisbon – *os baptizados em pé* (literally: 'standing up', 'collectively') in the gardens of Lisbon's Eastaus Palace, then also in other cities – was preceded by a decree in December 1496 – first on the expulsion of all Jews and Muslims from Portugal, and then, in order to speed up conversion, with a decree of March 1497. The latter provided for the removal from the recalcitrant Jewish parents of children aged 14 and under and their transfer to Catholic families. Even for the conditions of the time, this was a move that horrified not only Jews. The subsequent decision of forced conversion in lieu of expulsion, which was also taken with a view to avoiding the losses that the removal of Jews would have caused, halted this process (Soyer 2007a: 187–194, 210–212). All these measures provoked passive resistance; a relatively widespread, secretive persistence in Judaism became a reality. Indeed, contrary to the expectations of Manuel I, when deciding to forcibly Christianise, he simultaneously announced the introduction of a 20-year period of tolerance for possible heretics; he assumed that over a period of two decades the integration of the New Christians into Catholic society would take place. In 1512, this deadline was extended by a further 16 years. In brief, by eliminating Judaism, a source of religious incongruity and division, Portugal would at the same time preserve, according to the monarch's idea, the Jews, already important in many respects, as good Christians. Other moves, in turn, were intended to weaken the in-group solidarity of former, formally, Jews by supporting mixed marriages. This included the ban on marriages between New Christian couples introduced between 1497 and 1507 (Levine Melammed 2004: 71). It should also be kept in mind that this was not only about the integration of the Jewish elite, but of most of the Jews with strong ties to the Portuguese province: they were present there as small merchants, craftsmen and (a few) as peasants. In short, the role played by the Jews explained to a large extent the top-down, coercive nature of the conversion, as well as the reasons for the King's prohibitions on emigration, accompanied at the same time by conciliatory gestures towards the New Christians.

The attack on the New Christians in Lisbon in April 1506 reinforced both the resistance on their part and the tendency to (illegal) emigration. The scale of this pogrom was enormous, with between 1,000 and 4,000 victims. Its backdrop was the plague in Lisbon, and its pretext was the doubts loudly expressed in the Dominican church by a New Christian about the authenticity of the miracle of healing that had been proclaimed. Portuguese Catholics murdering the New Christians were soon joined by sailors from foreign ships moored in the harbour. Equally bloody was the repression ordered by the monarch: some 500 alleged and actual perpetrators (including the Dominicans who incited the aggression) were executed on the gallows and at the stake. One important motive for such a harsh response from the king was precisely the concern regarding future relations with the New Christians (Soyer 2007b: 237). However, it is possible at this point to speak of a breakdown in the project of the evolutionary and voluntary integration of the New Christians into Catholic society. With the exception of the cooperation between New Christian elites and Old Christian trading partners, the differences separating most New and Old Christians were petrified instead of diminishing. Their elimination implied violence, and its tool would become the Inquisition from the 1540s. A descendant of Portuguese emigrants described the new situation of the Jews in Portugal as follows: "for they always, though converted, lived apart, inasmuch as they were considered unworthy of any civic honours" (Spinoza 1891: 56). Despite the simplifications contained in his description of the differences separating Spanish and Portuguese Jews (Kaplan 2008: 55), Spinoza in fact indicated that the preservation of Jewish identity and the essence of 'Jewishness' were not a work of divine Providence (Myers 1998: 7f).

France, the southern Netherlands, and Italian cities became destinations for the new emigration, as well as Brazil for much of the 16th century and the islands off the coast of West Africa. But the New Christians who remained, especially those who belonged to the economic elite, gradually found a place for themselves in Portuguese society. Or at least they made attempts to do so. This was all the more so because Christianisation was also associated with the formal lifting of the traditional restrictions on the participation in the professional life or the assumption of office that had previously excluded Jews. This was a factor that enabled the New Christian elite to spread their wings from the beginning of the 16th century. An example is the family of "maestro João de Paz", Jewish refugees from Spain, who quite quickly became part of the elite in the northern province of Entre-Douro-e-Minho. "Maestro de Paz" was not only a royal physician and surgeon, but also an astrologer, collector of customs duties and tax farmer of the Crown. The career of his son Duarte de Paz had been – until then – brilliant. This young officer, diplomat and merchant, who had distinguished himself in battles in the Maghreb, was accepted into the prestigious religious military Order of Christ created by the Pope after the destruction of the Templar Order. The grand masters of this order were actually Portuguese monarchs (*ex officio* from 1551). This promotion was to strengthen his position in Rome as a participant in the negotiations for the establishment of an Inquisition in Portugal. His two brothers also received *hábitos* in other military orders. Duarte de Paz, an extremely controversial figure, although formally representing the monarchy, in fact played an important role in Pope Clement VII's blocking of King João III's plans to create an Inquisition as early as 1531–33. It would not come into being until 1536. At the same time Pope Paul III, responding to the dramatic appeals of the New Christians, would attempt to limit the scale of the persecution (Ryś 2023: 208–215).[3]

In any case, the liberalisation of attitudes towards the New Christians decreed in 1507, which allowed them freedom of travel, unfettered business and social advancement, played an important role, despite the resentment surrounding them. The growth in trade and monetary circulation associated with overseas expansion and domestic market development resulted in the weakening and, in the long term, the breakdown of the time-honoured ways of doing business. The role played by the New Christians in this process also made them even the ideal culprit responsible for the misery caused by increased taxes and prices, monetary speculation, etc. (Baroja 2000: 213–215).

Before this, however, the "result of [1507] decree was a release of New Christian energies". Many welcomed the decree "not as an opportunity for

---

3 An analysis of Duarte de Paz's several years of activity in Rome leads to the conclusion that this "cool-headed [man], far removed from any extravagance, cunning, calculating, bold, and eloquent, initiated into all the trickery of diplomacy" probably got lost: "[he] entwined the threads of his intrigues so intricately that to this day it is impossible to ascertain exactly whom he deceived, whether the king or the Marranos" (Graetz 1894: 512f). Historians' opinions on Duarte de Paz are still divided: for some he was "a cunning bastard", for others "a leader of the New Christians in the struggle against the establishment of the Inquisition in Portugal" (Nelson Novoa 2007: 273f). In any case, his activity in Rome even infuriated João III, who was pushing for the establishment of the Inquisition. He survived a failed assassination attempt (which the king's agents were suspected of). Moreover, it appeared that Duarte de Paz "had misappropriated for his own use part of the money entrusted to him" (Graetz 1894: 518, Nelson Novoa 2014).

leaving Portugal to embrace Judaism in the Ottoman realms, but as a sign of the monarch's trust in the permanence and sincerity of their Christian affiliation" (Rivkin 2003: 172). For almost three decades, until the establishment of the Inquisition, this arrangement appeared, despite the limited progress in integrating most of the New Christians, to be relatively sustainable and mutually beneficial. It was not without success when it came to the elite of the New Christians, especially in long-distance trade and finance. Thus, we find them in a narrow group of *homens de negócios* operating at the interface with the state, among merchant-bankers (*mercadores-banqueiros*), rather than ordinary retail merchants, who enjoyed less prestige, not to mention peddlars. As a result, "between 1497 and 1535 the New Christians secured their dominant economic position in the mercantile community and gradually supplanted its Old Christian elements" (Saraiva 2001: 25). After a century, according to the findings of an American historian, between 1640 and 1656, there were 23 New Christians (70 per cent) among the 33 Lisbon *mercadores-banqueiros* (Smith 1974: 255). However, this staggering success of the *XN* s was the germ of divisions and conflicts. It would contribute both to the growing hostility towards the New Christians and to a syndrome linking 'modernity', 'commerce' and 'bourgeoisie' with ethnic criteria. The persecution of the Portuguese Inquisition, which intensified from the second half of the 16th century, would be an important element in this explosive link.

Attempts at integration of the commercial and financial elite were also reflected in matrimonial strategies. The flexible treatment of the tradition of endogamous marriages and the acceptance of mixed unions (also reaching for partners from outside *La Nação*) appearedin the elite group of Lisbon merchant-bankers, mostly New Christians, of the late 16th and first half of the 17th century. We are talking about the 28 families that made up the seven extended merchant-banker houses. Although mixed unions were already not uncommon in the 15th century, by the 16th century such matrimonial strategies were no longer surprising: they expressed, on the one hand, an increasing willingness to assimilate and a desire to be among the aristocracy, and, on the other hand, widened the possibilities for profitable commercial operations and facilitated entry into the elite circle of court financiers and *asentistas*. The questioning of endogamous unions consequently confirmed the distinctiveness of the New Christian elite, its *sui generis* character and, above all, weakened its links with the Jewish tradition (if such were still cultivated) (Boyajian 1979, Almeida 1997, Lea 1906: 127f). How far one could go in being flexible on the issue of endogamy and the differences separating New and Old Christians was also shown by the actions of Emperor Charles v. In the 1540s, this arch-Catholic monarch, hoping for a major boost to his treasury from the New

Christian trading house of the Mendes of Antwerp, acted as a matchmaker of sorts. Namely, he attempted to arrange the marriage of the still underage daughter of Beatriz de Luna (later Doña Grácia Nasci), who managed the vast estate after the death of her husband and brother-in-law Diogo Mendes, with a Spanish aristocrat, his protégé and possibly illegitimate son. This marriage did not materialise, although the emperor pressured – possibly even blackmailed – Mendes (Salomon and Leone Leoni 1998: 154f, Birnbaum 2003: Chapter 3).

All in all, it was a schizophrenic situation from the point of view of the elite New Christians, when a growing sense of economic power and utility and attempts at integration collided with discrimination and exclusion. It is worth paying a moment's attention to this issue.

According to a Brazilian historian, already in the first half of the 16th century, through the accumulation of the debts of the Crown in the hands of the "bourgeois *da etnia hebréia*", Portugal "transforms itself from a compulsion not of choice into a client of the Portuguese Sephardim" (Salvador 1981: 6). Indeed, part of the Portuguese Crown's debts were in the hands of the New Christian *homens de negócios*, just as the Fuggers, Welsers and Italian (mainly Genoese) bankers exerted an overwhelming influence on Spanish finance in the 16th and early 17th centuries. In the Europe of the time such interdependence was not surprising. Debt management was the daily (and bitter) bread of the monarchs. However, in the case of the New Christians, who were to some extent replacing foreign lenders in Portugal (who were treated with even greater distrust), it was a decidedly asymmetrical relationship. It could just as well be argued that this "bourgeoisie *da etnia hebréia*" had been held hostage for more than a century and a half by the Portuguese, and for more than half a century by the Spanish Crown. It was the Crown that set the rules of the game, while the Inquisition controlled, repressed and looted the New Christian merchants with confiscations. Another Brazilian historian would claim otherwise:

> Without thoroughly banishing the Jews, as Spain had done, or open war on religious dissenters, as the French monarchy did against Protestants, Portugal punished, plundered, and usurped the rights of its crypto-Jewish mercantile bourgeoisie. The denial of civil rights to an economically powerful community was established as a political principle. The revenge of the aristocracy on the bourgeoisie dramatically marked the evolution of the Brazilian and Portuguese societies.
>
> ALENCASTRO 1993: 163f

It would be difficult to find a better exemplification of the asymmetry inherent in the Crown's relations with the New Christian merchants than the extortionate contributions collected on several occasions in the 16th and early 17th centuries by the Iberian monarchies from the New Christians. Interest-free loans with extended repayment periods were also demanded (a thing difficult to imagine when dealing with Christian bankers). This kind of phenomenon did not, of course, appear in the Crown's relations with the Fuggers and Genoese (unless we consider as such the decisions of the monarchs to suspend debt repayment on several occasions until the mid-17th century). Compensation was the temporary relaxation of the Inquisition, the right to migrate to the colonies and other privileges ensuring (piecemeal and temporary) equal treatment. In moments of crisis, such forced payments were an important supplement, a kind of financial drip, to the treasury's revenues. All in all, it was still better than in France, where in 1182 Philip Augustus simply seized the property of the Jews and drove them out of France, which was repeated in 1306 by the next monarch again plundering the Jews, who had previously been brought back to France.

However, as time went on, the policies of the Portuguese crown caused a backlash among the younger generation of the commercial and financial elite of the Portuguese New Christians:

> These men knew very well that the monarchy relied upon them alone to prop up the unprofitable royal monopoly [in the trade in Asian pepper and other spices]. By 1618 their forced loans and other contributions to support the royal monopoly equaled and perhaps surpassed the annual pardon contributions of 1606–10.
>
> BOYAJIAN 1993: 102[4]

On the other hand, Gonçalves Salvador's proposed monocausal approach to the question of the sources of Portugal's economic weakness must be considered limited and misleading. The core issue, i.e. the problem of the sources of the weakness of the Portuguese bourgeoisie and domestic production, is

---

4 It was about Portuguese merchants being forced to buy – at 50 per cent inflated prices – Asian pepper, which was a royal monopoly. Protests in 1618 resulted in repression. Despite the arrest of several prominent merchants, the compromise finally reached provided for a reduction in the purchase price to close to the market price. In the following years, however, Portuguese merchants reduced their involvement in the Asian pepper trade. This is assessed as one important reason for the weakening of Portugal's position in Asia (Veen 2000). In return for the amnesty declared in 1605, the New Christians had to pay a huge contribution, the repayment of which was spread over six years. By 1610, some 1.55 million cruzados (more than 91 per cent of the designated amount) had been paid. The sum of the contribution was calculated as the equivalent of the lost benefits, i.e. the revenue that, had it not been for the amnesty, the inquisitorial confiscations would have brought (Graizbord 2004: 22).

relegated to the background in this scholar's approach. A fact obvious to a Portuguese historian also disappears from Salvador's view: "The most profitable undertakings always belonged [in the 16th century] to the Crown, the nobles or the foreigners" (Marques 1976: 293). The latter formed not only a numerous (around 7,000 'souls') but also an extremely influential group in mid-16th century Lisbon. Their role would increase immeasurably after Portugal's independence in 1640. Not surprisingly, since the position of Portuguese New Christian merchants and financiers was constantly undermined by the repression of the Inquisition. At the same time, considerable capital was squandered in expenditure designed to emphasise the aristocratic lifestyle of the rich merchants. Consequently, Portugal's finances in the 16th century become, due to the internal weakness of the economy and the narrow tax base, largely hostage to the income generated in overseas trade. Just by way of illustration: whereas in 1580–88 Crown revenues generated by taxation of the domestic economy (including the sale of salt and fisheries) covered more than 42 per cent of expenditure, by 1607 their share had declined to 36 per cent. The share of revenues from overseas trade and the colonies increased correspondingly (Veen 2000: appendix1.1., Costa Freire, Lains and Münch Miranda 2016: 97).

However, the decades that separated the traumatic events of the late 15th century from the economic success of the first half of the 17th century were a period of fundamental change in the former Jewish community, indeed its gradual disappearance. The place left by the Jewish community was taken by New Christians, who could only partly be counted as *judaizantes*. Socially discriminated against and persecuted by the Inquisition, they sought to assimilate into an environment hostile to such projects. Many, to refer to the terminology of Albert O. Hirschman (1970), unable to hold on for equal treatment (*voice*), chose, after attempts to conform (*loyalty*), to resign and emigrate (*exit*). However, this did not involve a rejection of the new faith. Incidentally, the Pombal decrees of the mid-18th century, which abolished the division between New and Old Christians, only highlighted the de facto dominance of Catholicism. These processes, however, remained outside Spinoza's field of interest. The perspective of the Republic, where it was the New Christians who created the 'new Jews', was not conducive to noticing them, but it was conducive to preserving the memory of the drama of 1497.

The events at the turn of the 16th century had momentous and far-reaching effects far beyond Portugal. In the period separating forced Christianisation from the commencement of the Portuguese Inquisition in the 1540s, there was rapid learning by the New Christians of the principles of the long-distance trade revolution that had already begun and the acquisition of new skills. According to Rivkin (2003: 176), "as a class, they had gained these skills *after* their forced conversion and *because* of their conversion. (...) *Professing Jews were excluded totally from settling in the areas of commercial, financial, and inustrial innovation*". In short, they were exemplary students of the Genoese, who dominated overseas trade at the time. However, they did not start this education with a primer; on the contrary, even as Jews, and therefore before 1497, they already had quite considerable experience in such trade. Some acquired new skills if only by participating in the trade with Portuguese islands in the Atlantic and in exchanges with West Africa, others in trade with Northern Europe. According to Portuguese historians, the role of Jews in the long-distance commerce of the 15th century was widely recognised. Between 1466 and 1491, at least 32 Portuguese Jews were active in various international markets. The experience accumulated from the beginning of the 16th century, however, was decisive: it was symbolised by the New Christians' combination of commercial expansion in the Atlantic with the assimilation of the modern techniques of Italian merchant-bankers (Almeida 1997, Boyajian 1979: 131). In contrast, the trade in which Spanish conversos participated until the conquest of the New World was mostly concentrated in local markets, mainly in parts of the Mediterranean. The great merchants from among the conversos and the few international networks, among others, would appear quite late (Casado Alonso 1997).

The dispersion of Portuguese New Christians and crypto-Jews not only accelerated the learning process, but also created the possibilities for effective action in the new conditions that emerged with the beginning of the colonisation of the New World and the opening of the sea route to India. Moreover, the fact that most male Jews were already literate increased their market value and competitive advantage. Such literacy also characterised many New Christian women, actively participating in their spouses' businesses and sometimes running them themselves.[5] Increasingly complex business transactions generally required a written form, knowledge of the law and modern accounting.

Thus, a sizeable pool of "human capital" seeking security and stability emerged in Western Europe at the beginning of the 16th century. Alongside

---

5   At the beginning of the 17th century, illiterate men accounted for only 1 per cent of the New Christian male migrants to Amsterdam. Illiteracy among women reached 30 per cent, but this was still a far lower rate than among women in general (Swetschinski 2004: 88). It is therefore not surprising that, for example, many widows successfully continued the economic activities of their deceased spouses, also in technically complex fields (Bernfeld 2011). Among the male conversos in colonial Mexico who found themselves the focus of the Inquisition, 90 per cent claimed to be able to read, while 83 per cent also claimed to be able to write. Among women, these rates were 68 per cent and 50 per cent respectively, well above the average for all women in Mexico (Hordes 2005: 44).

the craftsmen, entrepreneurs with links to local markets, medics and apothecaries, publishers and printers, there appeared above all merchants already
experienced in long-distance trade, international commercial and financial
intermediaries, now outside the Portuguese empire, but by no means cut off
by an impenetrable wall from relatives and friends who remained in Portugal.
This was a resource ideally suited to the conditions necessary to sustain the
accelerated development of commercial capitalism in the 16th century. And
the essence of such capitalism was expressed precisely by long-distance trade,
the financial instruments associated with it and, above all, a specific form of
capital accumulation through the maximisation of profit margins (Braudel
1982: 319, 443, Małowist 1976: 232). At the same time, the scale of money circulation began to outstrip the capacity of traditional bureaucratic-ideological
control during this period, and it undermined scholastic concepts of usury and
fair profit. Selective access to information on new products and markets (early
modern imperfect competition) was also an important feature of this capitalism. This strengthened the position of those who chose to take risks and at the
same time had the capacity to transform information into economic decisions.
In short, *La Nação* can also be seen as the world's commercial information
gathering and distribution system of the time.

These processes were facilitated, as already mentioned, by the late establishment of the Portuguese Inquisition. It undertook its activities formally
from 1536, but de facto in the 1540s, while in the colonies the first pyre was
lit in 1543. In Goa, a Judaising medic was burnt after a diocesan court verdict
(an Inquisition tribunal was established later, in 1560). The Inquisition only
became particularly active in Portugal (to a lesser extent in Brazil) from the
1570s. The relative freedom of movement of Portuguese New Christians up to
this time, including Judaising Christians, was reflected both in contacts with
the Netherlands, the Mediterranean area and, above all, with Brazil and, with
some delay, the Spanish colonies. We also find New Christians in Portuguese
feitorias (trading post) in West Africa, Cape Verde and São Tomé. A few reached
India. All this despite formal prohibitions against emigration to the colonies.
These appeared as early as 1499, were revoked in 1507, reintroduced in 1521 and
confirmed in 1531. An amnesty in 1533 briefly eased the previous restrictions;
investigations against *XN*s were also closed. Another amnesty in 1577 sus-
pended the ban on emigration and halted the confiscation of property, at the
same time involving the payment of 250,000 cruzados by the New Christians
to King Sebastián (this made it possible to finance much of the cost of the disastrous war in Morocco). In 1601, in connection with negotiations for the lifting
of restrictions on the movement of the New Christians, there is once again
a royal assurance that in future no one will refer to them as Jews or as New

Christians. The first such assurance was given in a decree of 1502, followed by a decree in 1577. The former read: "We forbid every individual and all persons to call a man who has become a Christian 'Marrano' or a woman 'Marrana'" (Saraiva 2001: 198, xv, also Kayserling 1894: 130). This was a fiction, but one that well reflected the bargaining dimension of Portuguese legislative politics. Its oscillations clearly reflected the contradiction between the "repressive fury" and the "desire to profit from the economic activity of the New Christians". Incidentally, settlement bans in the colonies were sometimes treated liberally in the case of merchants who were not required to prove their 'purity of blood'. An example is Angola, where a New Christian doctor was repressed in 1626, leaving merchants alone (Alencastro 1993: 162f, Schorsch 2009: 52, Azevedo 1922: 233).

Moves alternately easing restrictions and then restricting the mobility of the New Christians also appeared in subsequent years. Thus, laws introduced in 1580 and 1587 once again prohibited them from leaving the kingdom. In 1601, this law was repealed, reconfirmed in 1603 and repealed in 1612 by reinstating the 1587 ban. In practice, effective ways were found to circumvent these restrictions: from bribery to the fabrication of "good" birth certificates and documents, not forgetting the sluggishness and inefficiency of officials in both Iberian monarchies. The later governor of the border province of New Spain, the aforementioned Portuguese New Christian Luis de Carvajal, reached Mexico via the Canary Islands thanks to the fact that the official in charge of document control in Las Palmas forgot to insist on the 'purity of blood' certificate required of travellers to the colony since the mid-16th century (Temkin 2011: 27f). Whether such a failure occurred as a result of an appropriate financial incentive, we do not know. A number of New Christians (how many, it is difficult to say) probably took advantage of a loophole in Spanish regulations that allowed soldiers, sailors and domestic servants to travel to the New World without the appropriate certificate. On the other hand, when Luis de Carvajal is ordered a few years later to establish a settlement colony in the northern frontier province of New Spain and to pacify the warlike Chichimeca Indians living there, the relevant edict of Philip II will have explicitly instructed officials not to check the information (re: genealogy) concerning the settler candidates (Hordes 2005: 75). This reinforces the hypothesis of a significant proportion of conversos, including marranos, among the settlers in Nuevo Reino de León.

Unsurprisingly, those who migrated towards first France, then Antwerp and Hamburg, or finally the United Provinces and the American colonies, were largely Portuguese New Christians. Hence also the common designation of Jews and New Christians on the two continents, both faithful Jews and

Catholics – 'Portuguese'. Also in the English colonies, for example in Barbados in the second half of the 17th century, 'Portuguese' actually meant a Portuguese Jew, usually connected in some way to the diaspora in the United Provinces. It was not a neutral term. Between 1580 and 1640, and thus during the period of the Iberian Union, "the word 'Portuguese' became in the Spanish empire an epithet, a synonym for 'Jew', despite the fact that Catholic Portuguese greatly resented the term and felt it unjust" (Lockhart and Schwartz 1983: 225, also Böhm 1963: 38, Davis 1909: 1). The problem was that a sizeable part of the Portuguese commercial elite was by this period already 'marked' by relationships with the New Christians, mainly through mixed marriages. And according to the *limpieza de sangre*, the descendants of such marriages – even in 1/16 XN – lost their status as Old Christians. It cannot be ruled out, therefore, that the epithet applied to the majority of the merchant elite – in the mid-17th century, among 364 Lisbon merchants, 78 per cent were New Christians (Studnicki-Gizbert 2007: 10, 24f; Pijning 2001: 492, Schwartz 1991: 754). However, in a particular sense, as discussed below, equating 'Portuguese' with 'Jew' was indeed 'unfair'.

It was not only in Northern Europe that the 'Portuguese' emerged. When the Count-Duke de Olivares (Gaspar de Guzmán Pimental), who was in many ways favourable to the New Christians, gained influence at the court of Madrid from the 1620s as Philip IV's minister, projects to attract some of the important 'Portuguese' merchants and financiers residing outside the kingdom[6] became the order of the day. This was an extension of earlier initiatives related to the activities at the court of Philip III between 1598 and 1618 of the influential (until removed from favour, inter alia, due to the scale of corruption) minister and *privanza* Duke de Lerma (Francisco Gómez de Sandoval y Rojas). These mainly concerned the preparation of a broad amnesty and, earlier, the lifting of certain restrictions on the mobility of New Christians. This involved the already mentioned huge compensation to the royal treasury of 1.7 million cruzados. This was *grosso modo* equivalent to the deficit of the Crown's finances in the crisis year of 1598 (Carrasco Vázquez 2005: 6).

The measures taken by Olivares in 1627 and the following years were not limited to a simple continuation of his predecessor's policy (already challenged in his time, around 1610, due to resistance from the Inquisition). What

---

6   The Count-Duke de Olivares was the great-grandson of converso Lope Conchillos, secretary to the Catholic Monarchs. His acceptance into the prestigious religious military Order of Alcántara meant that he was regarded as untainted by bad descent (Alpert 2001: 46). Created in the 12th century, the Order of Alcántara was one of the first to start applying the principle of *limpieza de sangre*.

was new was, above all, the admission of New Christians to profitable *asientos*, i.e. contracts for providing various supplies (especially for the army, navy and court) and the leasing of monopolies – not only in the slave trade as before. The opportunity was also created for 'Portuguese' residing in Western Europe to return and not be discriminated against by buying clemency for acts under the jurisdiction of the Spanish Inquisition. Few took advantage of this high-risk opportunity. In contrast, some of the merchant-financial elite of the New Christians of Portugal, taking advantage of the earlier unification of the two kingdoms at the end of the 16th century, had already begun moving to Seville, Madrid and Cadiz (Kaplan 2008: 39–43). The moves of both favourites and ministers of the Spanish kings accelerate this process:

> Between the state bankruptcy of 1627 and the dismissal of the Conde-Duque de Olivares in 1643, the Portuguese became such important bankers and tax farmers as to create a second [next to Amsterdam] New Christian diaspora centred in Spain and branching out to the colonies of the Portuguese diaspora in Spanish America, Antwerp, France, and Italy.
>
> SWETSCHINSKI 2004: 61[7]

This experiment of including influential New Christians in debates about the state of Spanish finances and placing control of certain financial institutions in their hands was also part of an earlier process of migration of merchants and artisans from Portugal that had begun and intensified after 1627. The scale of the repression targeted by the Portuguese Inquisition for several years already against the New Christians made Spain, paradoxically, the place where security was sought. This, in turn, caused concern in Spain itself and reinforced accusations that the migrating New Christians were responsible for the high prices and other economic troubles and, as *judaizantes,* were also a threat to the Catholic nation. Observers at the time also cited greatly exaggerated

---

7 The great Portuguese merchant-bankers, who from 1627 would join in the financing of the Spanish debt (and in the *asiento* contracts), would also take up the issue of the status of the New Christians concerning themselves earlier. Among other things, they proposed that amnesties, promulgated from time to time, should be replaced by changes in regulations discriminating against New Christians. However, created by Olivares in 1622, *La Junta Grande de Reformación* proposed only some liberalisation of attitudes towards conversos, including the rejection, in the absence of additional evidence, of anonyms questioning "purity of blood". In contrast, in 1627 and 1629, amnesties are promulgated by Philip IV allowing New Christians to settle in Castile, protection of some of their property from the Inquisition, limited access to offices and titles of nobility in Portugal and participation in trade with Spanish America, including the right of settlement (Alpert 2001: 54f., Studnicki-Gizbert 2007: chapter 6).

numbers of Portuguese emigrants: 70,000 were said to have arrived in Castile, 40,000 of them in Madrid, and "none of them cultivate the land, work physically, farm (...) or have an artisan's workshop". It was also maintained that a quarter of Seville's population was Portuguese (probably confusing their concentration in certain neighbourhoods and/or their participation in the economic elite with their presence throughout the city). Certainly, however, the extent of Portuguese migration was considerable. And also fuelling tensions was the realisation that migrants prosecuted for the crime of heresy committed in Portugal were not prosecuted in Spain (Azevedo 1922: 205, 463 appendix 9).[8] In any case, the repression of the Portuguese Inquisition and some liberalisation of Spanish policy towards converts made Seville and Madrid attractive places of settlement and capital investment.

But in Spain, too, the situation for the New Christians could hardly be described as secure and stable. The resistance offered by the aristocracy was too strong. Most aristocrats despised the merchants and financiers, whom they identified with usury, speculation, disrespect for religious and national values and having dubious genealogy. And was not just the aristocracy. The "party of political conservatism" (of a kind), opposed to the "party of commercial experimentation" favoured by Count-Duke de Olivares, was formed by an extremely diverse informal coalition of aristocrats, members of the guilds (*consulados*) in Seville, Lima and Ciudad de México, royal officials, inquisitors, playwrights, priests and monks (Studnicki-Gizbert 2005: 154). These groups blocked the implementation of the project accepted by the Cortes of Aragon in 1626 to recognise commercial activity as compatible with the status and honour of nobility (Molas Ribalta 1987: 97). Nor did the Inquisition give up its search for heretics among the financial and mercantile elite. In 1632, the Portuguese merchant-banker João Nunes Saravia (in Spain he acted as Juan Núñez), for some years already an '*asentista* of His Majesty the King', as a *judaizante,* was secretly arrested together with his brother by the Inquisition of Toledo (for this inquisition exercised 'guardianship' over the royal court). The pretext was the denunciation of a New Christian woman, while one of the important reasons

---

8   In 1642, according to a census carried out by the parishes, Seville had more than 31,000 families (about 147,000 inhabitants). The Portuguese group was estimated at 3,808 families (almost 18,000 people, or 12.2 per cent of the total population). Among them were probably about 2,000 merchants. Other foreigners (2,029 families) were predominantly Flemish (Luxán Melendez 1993: 127–130). Critics attacked the liberal attitude towards crimes of heresy committed by the Portuguese before migration to Spain, claiming that by washing its hands of the matter Madrid was becoming, following the example of Amsterdam and Geneva, a city that protected heretics (Graizbord 2004: 23).

was his involvement in contraband that undermined the Spanish embargo on trade with the Republic after 1621. After torture and several years' detention and a humiliating forced public confession of guilt, he was sentenced to a fine of 20,000 ducats. He was bankrupt – the losses of both brothers were estimated at a huge sum of 300,000 ducats. This was not an isolated case. Another notable *asentista*, the merchant-banker Garcia de Yllán – also the author of interesting proposals on the empowerment of merchants and the role of trade in the Spanish empire – avoided an inquisitorial investigation by moving in advance to Italy (Sánchez Durán 2015). Moreover, this repression came at the height of de Olivares's influence, which showed the actual balance of power in the Spanish political class: the strength of the "party of political conservatism" forced the minister of Philip IV to make complicated manoeuvres and combine concessions to the New Christians with the acceptance of targeted repression. On the other hand, however, it should be borne in mind that in 1632 Nunes Saravia's position among the royal lenders was already severely weakened. The time when, in 1625, he negotiated with Olivares on behalf of the New Christian bankers about the terms of their cooperation with the court was already history. By not defending him, therefore, Count-Duke did not cause any harm to the Crown's financial credibility (Boyajian 1983: 118f, Alpert 2001, Carrasco Vázquez 2004: 262–264, 280f). Incidentally, earlier, the name of Nunes Saravia (also as Savaria) appeared in the investigation of the smuggling of counterfeit coins into Spain and in connection with the 1620 murder of Madrid's English informer on the matter.

The experiment of incorporating the 'Portuguese' into Spanish finance also caused serious friction among the New Christian elite operating between Lisbon and Seville and Madrid, which would come out in full force during Portugal's independence in 1640. For the 'party of political conservatism', Portugal's breakaway was clearly evidence of the treacherous attitude of the New Christians *in toto*. In the New World, on the other hand, the Inquisition in Lima, Ciudad de México and Cartagena would lead in the 1630s and 1640s, but also in the earlier visitations to Brazil, to the reduction of influence and, in the long term, to the elimination of the 'Portuguese' from Spanish America and their weakening in Brazil. And the deep and prolonged financial crisis of the Spanish Crown in the 1640s would also undercut their influence in the metropolis, prompting many of them to emigrate.

We have mentioned that the term 'Portuguese' was commonly applied not only to the New Christians or the Jews of Amsterdam. It also included Portuguese Old Christians, who were seen as 'Jews'. In total, this applied in the early 17th century to 9,000 merchants scattered all over the world, many already born outside Portugal (Studnicki-Gizbert 2002: 95, 2007: 11). Such an interpretation was only partly justified. First of all, *La Nação* organising part of the international trade of the time cannot be reduced to its New Christian, let alone its crypto-Jewish, component. Treating religion or Jewish origin as an exhaustively defining element of *La Nação* was a distorting reflection of the Inquisition's activities. At the beginning of the 17th century

> the Portuguese Nation numbered in the thousands, a constellation of over three dozen Portuguese expatriate communities established in all the major ports and cities of the Atlantic world. It extended from Amsterdam to Buenos Aires and from Lima to Luanda. (...) This was a nation built on maritime trade. Despite the mobility and dispersion (...) and the composite nature of its religious culture, the Nation maintained its collective integrity.
>
> STUDNICKI-GIZBERT 2007: 11

While it was the overseas trade that would constitute the most dynamic part of *La Nação's* activity – probably more than half of the Portuguese dispersed around the world were New Christians – members of the 'Nation' were not limited to the dynamic group of 9,000 merchants already mentioned. At the beginning of the 17th century, *La Nação* numbered no less than 20,000 'souls', most of whom were merchant-serving shipowners, ship pilots, sailors, carpenters, craftsmen and dock workers (Studnicki-Gizbert 2007: 10,41f). At the same time, it was a 'Nation' defining itself in part in opposition to the groups associated with the court, who controlled trade with Asia – "the enterprise of the king, a few favored contractors of pepper, and privileged fidalgos dealing in spices" (Boyajian 1993: 14). The time of the New Christians on the *Carreira da Índia* and in the profitable intra-Asian trade would come later. This would occur from the second half of the 16th century, partly as a consequence of the crisis of the royal monopoly and partly as a result of the New Christians focusing their attention on other luxury goods (especially diamonds, other precious stones and porcelain). During this phase, their role in the Asian trade would increase, not least through the opening of the route from Manila via Acapulco to the New World markets. However, before this happens, the New Christians would first appear as second-class participants in the global quest for wealth:

> Without the known gold and silver of Mexico and Peru or the spices of Indonesia, Brazil attracted a different kind of European. The military nobility went off to become *conquistadores* in the eastern seas. Those attracted to Brazil were mere merchants.
>
> CURTIN 1990: 49

In any case, having previously had limited access to Asian trade, the New Christian members of *La Nação* concentrated their energies in other areas and in the redistribution of incoming luxury goods in Europe. There follows at the same time a reinforcement in the 17th century of the stereotype that identified the merchant with the Jew, the crypto-Jew or the foreigner (Smith 1974: 233). In fact, as a whole,

> the merchants of the Nation were far from a religiously homogeneous group. They included a large minority of Old Christians, and the greater part of the remaining New Christians were, in fact, of mixed New and Old Christian ancestry. This pattern of religious heterogeneity certainly held true for Portuguese merchants working in the Spanish Atlantic.
>
> STUDNICKI-GIZBERT 2007: 71

In brief, it was not only the converts who formed a group *sui generis*. A much larger group was also the 'Portuguese' operating as *La Nação*. In their day-to-day activities, "the division between Old Christians and New was meaningless", although the intensity of contacts was, as part of a preference for transactions between members of *La Nação*, strongly correlated with kinship (and indirectly with religion) (Studnicki-Gizbert 2007: 25, 2009: 94f).

This complicates consideration of the 'role of the Jews' in the Atlantic economy up to the mid-17th century. Segmentation occurring together with elements of group in-group solidarity formed a whole that was impossible to describe solely in terms of religious and/or communal loyalties. In some cases, especially when referring to the Amsterdam segment of *La Nação*, where it was not the New Christians, but the Sephardic Jews who dominated, the question of the religious identity of the majority seemed uncontroversial. This is different for the Iberian Peninsula, Latin America and West Africa, although some historians tend to view the 'Nation' in these areas in religious terms as well. According to Israel (2002a: Chapter 3), in Mexico until the 1640s one can speak of an overlap between the merchant community of the Portuguese and an illegal religious community formed by crypto-Jews. The latter was supported by marranos from France and Jews from Italian cities. It is debatable, however, whether the relationship between the two communities was really as close as Israel claims. Portuguese Old Christians were not uncommon in Mexico, and not all New Christians were crypto-Jews. Also, counting some influential New Christian merchants in Europe and the New World as crypto-Jews is questionable, reflecting a tendency "to maximize the Jewishness of the New Christians" (Schorsch 2006, also Pulido Serrano 2011).

Looking beyond the mid-17th century, the factors contributing to the growing differences between the Jewish diaspora and the New Christians became more important. These, together with the mercantilist practices of the emerging modern European states, would contribute to the breakdown of *La Nação's* (relatively weak) in-group solidarity and the emergence of proto-nationalist loyalties in the separate diasporas. Although cosmopolitanism was not disappearing, it was weakening. The clash in Rouen in 1633 between the marranos, who guarded their 'otherness' in relations with the Christian bourgeoisie, and the New Christians, who sought integration into Catholic society, can be seen as one of the important indirect harbingers of these processes (Brunelle 2003, Alpert 2001: 64–71). The result of this clash was a weakening of the marranos. In Nantes, on the other hand, crypto-Jewish activity had already disappeared by the beginning of the 17th century (Bodian 1999: 143).

Moreover, from the end of the 17th century, in the main centres of residence of the 'Portuguese' in France, the phenomenon of the reconstruction of Jewish life as part of French society would appear with increasing intensity – without the previously imposed from above condition of religious unification (Christianisation). Louis xv, issuing a decree in 1723 that restored the rights taken away from the 'Portuguese' by Louis xiv, was thus able to write, "the Jews (...) known and established in our kingdom as Portuguese, or else New Christians" (Benbassa 1999: 50). The processes of differentiation were also reflected in the conflict that would emerge between the New Christians in Portugal and the Jews of Amsterdam as a follow-up of the tension in Dutch-Portuguese relations after Lisbon's independence in 1640. This was already a clash of (emerging) separate political loyalties.

CHAPTER 3

Sombart's Fantasies: Jews, the Netherlands, and the Colonisation of the New World

> Historians already refer to the 'age' of the Fuggers and the 'age' of the Genoese: it is not entirely unrealistic in the present state of scholarship to talk of an 'age' of great Jewish merchants, beginning in the decade of the 1590s and lasting until 1621 or possibly even 1650. Their age was one of intellectual brilliance.
>
> BRAUDEL 1982: 823

However, this challenging comment proposed by Fernand Braudel, referring primarily to the 'Portuguese' settled in the United Provinces, should not be overinterpreted. And Braudel's unique language present in many passages of his *magnum opus* may favour such overinterpretations. When he points to "the parallelism between the economic situation and the vicissitudes of the Jewish people", we know that this claim is verifiable, while when he writes about the fate and/or destiny of civilisations, we enter the realm of unverifiable convictions (Braudel 1982: 821–824).

Henri Pirenne, a great figure of European historiography at the beginning of the 20th century, sketching the stages of European development and the corresponding types of economic leadership, described the period of the 16th and early 17th centuries as marked largely by the ascendancy on the scale of prestige and wealth of the parvenu. We already see nouveau riche in France, the German lands, the Italian cities, and the United Provinces. And "[t]he Antwerp exchange is a pandemonium where bankers, deep-sea sailors, stock-jobbers, dealers in futures, millionaire merchants, jostle each otherand sharpers and adventurers to whom all means of money-getting, even assassination, are acceptable" (Pirenne 1914: 512–514). Pirenne does not mention the Jews, the marranos or the New Christians among these new captains of trade and the money economy, although they were probably the ones who most strongly approved of the idea that "liberty is the soul of commerce".

In contrast to Pirenne, Braudel, however, was right that "the age of great Jewish merchants" was an important episode of the "long 16th century" (ca. 1450–1640). However, it is not his work that we focus on here.

As already mentioned, consideration of the role of Sephardic Jews and New Christians in the colonisation of Latin America often revolves between mythology and sound research by historians, who in turn cannot always provide conclusive or easily appealing answers. Particularly on issues that continue to arouse, such as the modern slave trade, disputes and controversies far beyond the academy. In the study of the 'role of the Jews', therefore, we are confronted with two extremes of varying importance, however. The first is to overestimate – for many, sometimes strongly opposing, reasons – the activity and importance of the Jews, variously defined, in the overseas expansion of Europe. This will apply both to the early stages of Portuguese and Spanish colonisation, then to Dutch expansion and the burgeoning Atlantic trade, and finally to the spectacular development of the Caribbean and British colonies in North America. The second, opposing, view is founded on the assumption that the Portuguese New Christians acted as fully integrated members of the community of Portuguese and Spanish settlers and international merchants, while the role of the Amsterdam Jews was relatively limited. The goals they wished to achieve were fully compatible, if not identical, with those assumed and realised by Portuguese and Spaniards. Such a dichotomous view can also be found in Jewish historiography:

> The study of the economic history of the Jews was in the past largely a matter of hit-and-miss: according to the climate of prevailing pro- or anti-Semitism, it was argued whether offensively or defensively that the Jewish role in economic development had been all-embracing, or that after all it was insignificant.
>
> ROTH 1961: 131

In this chapter we comment briefly on one variant of the first approach, leading to an overestimation and mythologisation of the "role of the Jews". We will return to the second approach, which is far less emotionally loaded, later in the discussion of more specific issues.

The role played by the Jews in the birth of the modern Netherlands, but also in the colonisation of the New World, attracted the interest of Werner Sombart in the early 20th century. This once revered economic historian and co-founder of historical sociology, an ambivalent anti-Semite who at one point wanted to be regarded as a precursor of Hitler's 'National Socialism', is today almost completely forgotten (wrongly). We are referring to his most frequently cited *Judenbuch* (Sombart 1951), in which, among others, he identified Judaism as an alternative to Protestantism in explaining the origins of capitalism and market modernity. It was not only a polemic against Max Weber's 'Protestant hypothesis'. To a large extent, the theses and interpretations put forward by Sombart set the tone and direction of the discussion on the 'role of the Jews', which still echo today, albeit often without any mention of Sombart himself.

So first about the Netherlands:

> It is indeed surprising that the parallelism has not before been observed
> between Jewish wanderings and settlement on the one hand, and the
> economic vicissitudes of the different peoples and states on the other.
> Israel passes over Europe like the sun: at its coming new life bursts forth;
> at its going all falls into decay.
>
>   SOMBART 1951: 35f

The point, however, is not so much in the parallel but, as Sombart goes on
to argue, in the causal relationship. If so, what is missing from his considerations is the reference that such a view was put forward earlier, in the middle of the 17th century, by the famous Amsterdam rabbi Menasseh ben Israel
from Madeira (or by birth Manoel Dias Soeiro from Lisbon, according to other
sources) in his *Humble Addresses* addressed to Oliver Cromwell. This view was
repeated in the second half of the 19th century by the Jewish historian Heinrich
Graetz. Here he wrote that in the period before the influx of Portuguese Jews,
the Netherlands "had been one of the poorest states, and the bitter, destructive
wars had made the land still poorer". In such a situation, the capital of Jewish
merchants and financial intermediaries even played a key role in building the
economic power of the Netherlands: "The Dutch were now enabled to lay the
foundations of their prosperity. The capital of the fugitive Jews made it possible
to find great transmarine companies and fit out trading expeditions, in which
they participated" (Graetz 1894: 667f). A picture as dramatic as it was false.

Sombart, however, goes much further than the Jewish historian in claiming
that Spain and Portugal were deprived of their reserves of bullion primarily as
a result of the wandering of rich Jews, to the benefit of the Netherlands and
England.[1] An analogous thesis was propounded in Spain, along with other variants of the conspiracy theory, as early as the turn of the 16th and 17th centuries
(Studnicki-Gizbert 2007: 92f). And further:

> Just as the expedition of Columbus would have been impossible had the
> rich Jews left Spain a generation earlier, so the great India Companies
> might never have been founded and the great banks which were

---

[1] Certainly, bullion and coins moved out of Spain in large part with the Spanish armies to the
     Channel region, the rebellious Netherlands, and the Mediterranean. Under Philip II, Spain's
     costly military potential consisted of 200,000 mainly mercenary infantry, some 30,000 cav-
     alry and a fleet of dozens of battle ships. The planned landing in England in 1588 was to
     involve 34,000 troops (Kamen 2003: 325, 327).

established in the 17th century might not so quickly have attained their stability (...) had the Jews been expelled from Spain a century later than was actually the case.

SOMBART 1951: 185

Thus, in both of the variants mentioned by Sombart (one hundred years earlier or one hundred years later), the critical variable is 'the Jews' (and their capital). A curious example of counterfactual speculation indeed. It could just as well be argued that if it had not been for Lord-Protector Cromwell's insistence on the readmission of a small group of Sephardic Jews into England, the status of the island as a maritime and colonial power and subsequently as a pioneer of industrialisation and modern growth would have come into question. Such a view, however, poorly justified in the light of England's historical experience, found a place in Sombart's (1951: 38) treatise: "The economic development of the country (...) the growth of capitalism, ran parallel with the influx of Jews, mostly of Spanish and Portuguese origin". Incidentally, the first political battle on the readmission of Jews fought by Cromwell in 1654–1655 was formally, though not actually, lost. Moreover, despite the removal of some barriers, the influx of Sephardim into England in the following decades was not impressive.

Contrary to Graetz-Sombart's imagination-stirring thesis, the birth of the power of the Netherlands, like that of its great chartered companies, the East India Company (*Vereenigde Oostindische Compagnie* -VOC) in 1602 and the West India Company (*Geoctrooieerde Westindische Compagnie* – WIC) in 1621, was not the result of the presence and activity of the 'Portuguese'. This was clearly indicated by a German historian in an immediate well-argued response to Sombart's *Judenbuch* (Wätjen 1913) – and ignored. After decades other historians returned to the topic to find that in the VOC's founding capital of approximately 6.5 million guilders, Jewish participation was minimal: it probably did not exceed 20,000 guilders (0.3 per cent) invested by a dozen Jewish merchants. Among the 1,143 investors in the Amsterdam branch of the VOC were two Jews, who invested a total of 4,800 guilders. There was not a single Jew among the 81 most important investors (total contributions of approximately 1.57 million guilders). It would not be until the 18th century, already in the midst of a clear decline in the international role of the Netherlands, that this share would rise to 25 per cent of the VOC capital (Baron 1973: 42f, Israel 1995: 346). As for the West India Company, its creation was received by both Jews in the Netherlands and their trading partners, the New Christians, in Brazil and Portugal with mixed, rather negative feelings and greater doubts than in the case of the VOC. In contrast, the few Ashkenazi Jews emigrating from the east belonged to the poor strata of Dutch society and did not play a major role in the economic development of the United Provinces during this period.

The growth of Dutch power was certainly supported from the beginning of the 17th century by the growing role of the 'Portuguese' in international commodity trade, the nascent modern banking system and stock-exchange and certain crafts that had remained outside the control of the powerful guilds. The already vast experience accumulated by Dutch merchants and merchant fleets in the European trade, especially with Portugal and the North Sea and Baltic regions, was at some point, especially during the Twelve Years'Truce of 1609–1621, reinforced by the know-how of the already former New Christians in intercontinental, but also Mediterranean, trade. The same, though with more emphasis, can be said of the earlier and incomparably larger emigration (mostly Protestants) from the Spanish Netherlands. In the first two-three decades of the 17th century, almost a third of the population of Amsterdam's more than 100,000 inhabitants were emigrants from the southern Netherlands and their descendants (Boxer 1965: 32). This emigration was even instrumental in creating the economic, including commercial, potential of the Republic, paving the way for the Dutch to participate in the growing *rich trade* (i.e. in luxury goods). Part of this process was the Flemish support, active in southern Europe, for the expansion of the Republic's merchants in the Mediterranean. An equally important group in the emerging Dutch economic elite were the growing native regent-merchants. This is, at any rate, what emerges from an analysis of the composition of the Dutch merchant elite from the late 16th century (Israel 1995: 309, 344).

However, it is important to note the chronology of these processes. Before the first Portuguese Jews appeared in Amsterdam at the end of the 16th century, it is the growing economic power of the then Spanish Netherlands in the 16th century that became one of the factors contributing to the rebellion initiated in 1566–68. The small Netherlands, in terms of population (the Dutch population was estimated at 1.5 million in 1600), had already been on a growth path for several decades. The spectacular economic growth of the country in the 16th century was combined with increasing prosperity and the "spiritual emancipation" of the bourgeoisie of Antwerp and other cities (Wee 1971: 53). And this did not apply only to the south, Brabant and Flanders. The economic growth of the seven northern provinces that would form the bastion of anti-Spanish resistance after 1579, with a centre in Amsterdam, was equally impressive, clearly accelerating from 1580 onwards. The most striking indicators documenting these changes were the rapid development from the 1570s to the 1580s of shipbuilding, textile manufacturing, urbanisation, the then unique increase in nominal and real wages going hand in hand with demographic growth, and changes in the production profile and level of agricultural productivity. All this was made possible, among other things, by the steady supply of grain from the Baltic region (Greenfeld 2001: Chapter 2, Wallerstein 2011: Chapter 2). The famous *fluitschip*, an innovative combination of modern shipbuilding technology and economic calculation, would appear just at the end of the 16th century. It provided the Dutch with a competitive advantage at sea and consequently a dominant position in trade with the Baltic and North Sea regions (but also an important role in trade with Portugal). The near monopoly position of the Dutch in the grain trade from Gdańsk at the end of the 16th century provided them with access to Iberian and North African markets, especially in years of crop failure. The increase in the number of ships and tonnage of the Dutch fleet from the late 16th century was even unprecedented.

Also present in this process, in still very limited numbers, were New Christian merchants, encouraged by the revolting provinces to trade, but, understandably, only through the territory of the northern Netherlands. This was reflected, for example, in the trade privileges and *sauvegardes* of 1581, 1588 and 1592 largely analogous to those granted to Dutch merchants and foreigners from countries not in conflict with the United Provinces (Roitman 2011: 232–234). However, it does not appear that the presence of this small group of 'Portuguese' and their contacts could have been instrumental in launching the Dutch economic miracle or in (co-)financing the commercial and military global offensive against the Iberian empires undertaken by the United Provinces between 1590 and 1609 (Emmer 2003). Let us again consider the following facts:

Firstly, the initially small community of 'Portuguese' in Amsterdam can only be spoken of from the 1590s. In the first decade of the 17th century, the number of Jews reached 600–650, while the influx of Portuguese immigrants between 1598 and 1619 can be estimated in the tens, not the hundreds (Swetschinski 2004: 71, 76, 80, 83, 91). According to other data, around 1605 the still informal Jewish community numbered between 200 and 600 people, in 1631–35 between 1,000 and 1,500 people (Amsterdam's total population was estimated at around 137,000 in this period, whereas earlier, in 1600, it was estimated at 60,000), and in 1655 it rose to 1,800 people (Nusteling 2002: 59f).[2]

---

2 400 Jewish families in Amsterdam in 1650 with 300 houses were mentioned by Rabbi Menasseh ben Israel (1901: 88). According to other data, there were approximately 800 Sephardim living in Amsterdam in 1626 and in 1655 — 1200 (Boxer). At the end of the 18th century, the presence of 2,800 descendants of 'Portuguese' and 20,000 Ashkenazim, i.e. a total of about 10 per cent of Amsterdam's population, was recorded in the city (Cohen 1991: 19).

The second fact worth recalling, which concerned the place of the Sephardim in the new merchant elite, was probably of far greater significance. The capital raised by the VOC in 1602, indeed without the participation of the 'Portuguese', amounted to 6.5 million guilders, while the value of the cargo of pepper, cinnamon, sugar, silver bullion and jewellery intercepted by the English on the route from Portugal in 1603 on six ships leased by 15 Jewish merchants from Amsterdam and sailing under the Emden flag was estimated in London at over £28,000 (about 300,000 guilders) (Israel 1990a: 421, 2002a: 95f). A huge sum, but it was only less than 5 per cent of the VOC's capital. This, or similar capital, was held by some individual Dutch merchants descended either from the Protestants of Antwerp or Germany, or from among the native Protestant regent-merchants. Among the richest ten citizens of Amsterdam in 1631, the first three had estates of between 400,000 and 500,000 guilders each. There were no Sephardim among them (Israel 1995: 348). It has been estimated that in the first two decades of the 17th century, the group of 66 major Jewish merchants in Amsterdam did not match the wealth, scale and intensity of commercial operations of the elite of Protestant merchants (Koen 1970: 26f).

Certainly, however, these early contacts formed the seeds of the close cooperation that would bear fruit in the following decades and enable the 'Portuguese', in Israel's assessment, "to play a more significant role". At the same time, the period from the appearance of the first Sephardim in Amsterdam (ca. 1595) until 1648, he argues, were years when "[t]he community was of some, but by no means fundamental, importance in the working of the Dutch economy". Only after the end of the Thirty Years' War and the opening of Iberian ports to Dutch merchants, during the years of the Golden Age of the Republic, would the Amsterdam Jews emerge "as one of the vital components in the imposing edifice of Holland's global commerce" (Israel 1990a: 418). However, this assessment is disputed for the early years of the 17th century. At that time Amsterdam Jewish merchants "attracted more business activities to the city than the East India Company, mainly because of their sugar trade" (Vlessing 1995: 243). And in the case of Holland's forceful entry at the turn of the 16th and 17th centuries into Mediterranean commerce "the spread of the *marranos* throughout the Mediterranean [prepared] the way for the Dutch and [marked] the beginning of the age of Amsterdam in world history" (Braudel 1995: 640). In short, it was not the migration of Jews that created the space of freedom in the Netherlands and the foundations of its economic power. The growth, accelerated in the second half of the 16th century and in the decades to come, and the political and religious determination of the Dutch Protestants in the following decades combined to create such a space. And its successful defence opened the road leading to the religious and economic prosperity of the Amsterdam Jews. Not the other way around. In brief, "the emergence of Dutch capitalism clearly owes almost nothing to the Jewish emmigrants" (Swetschinski 2004: 163). At the same time,

> the Dutch Republic's general primacy in international trade, shipping and finance from the 1590s down to around 1730 enabled the Jews living in the Netherlands, and the Dutch colonies, simply by virtue of operating within the Dutch *entrepot,* and close to the Amsterdam stock exchange or in contact with the Dutch East and West India Companies, to exert greater influence on world trade and finance than would have been conceivable anywhere else.
>
> ISRAEL 2002b: 10f

Finally, let us note that the fallacy of the "Sombart-Graetz theory" is even more powerfully demonstrated by the contrasting fates of the small community of Jews in the Netherlands (and earlier in Hamburg), on the one hand, and on the other by the vast majority of Sephardic Jews expelled from Spain and emigrating from Portugal. Indeed, many of them found their place in the traditional political and socio-economic environment of North Africa, also in Italian cities and above all in the Ottoman Empire. Some 60,000 Sephardim reached the latter after 1492, to the satisfaction of Sultan Bayezid II. Earlier, around 1454, one of the Jewish refugees wrote with enthusiasm:

> I, Isaac Zarfati, from a French stock, born in Germany, where I sat at the feet of my teachers, I proclaim to you that Turkey is a land wherein nothing is lacking. (...) Here every man may dwell at peace under his own vine and his own fig-tree. In Christendom, on the contrary, ye dare not clothe your children in red or in blue, according to your taste, without exposing them to insult and yourselves to extortion.
>
> GRAETZ 1894: 272f

Certainly, compared to Catholic Europe at the time, the Ottoman Empire seemed to many Jews an example of limited, bearable discrimination. Stability at the price of wearing a distinctive yellow turban or being forbidden to ride on horseback seemed a favourable option. However, the rapidly developing centres of trade and commerce in Ottoman Thessaloniki, Istanbul or Safed did not develop into the seeds of modernity. Just by way of example: the production and distribution of woollen goods in Thessaloniki, which remained under full Sephardic control, would be in crisis by the end of the 16th century due to English competition. The backwardness of the empire was not conducive to economic innovation (Klooster 2001: 123). The same was true of the Ashkenazim in the Polish–Lithuanian Commmonwealth, who by the end of the 17th century formed the largest Jewish community in Europe, and a new centre of Jewish handicraft: "In Poland-Lithuana the Jewish artisan class grew by leaps and bounds, and long before the partitions of Poland [at the end of the 18th century] Jewish craftsmen far outnumbered their non-Jewish rivals in many localities" (Baron 1967: 67). However, they were an important, relatively autonomous segment of the semiperipheral economy and society, not rebels against backwardness. On the other hand, despite Sombart's assertions (1951: 38), England's growing power from the 16th century was scarcely due to the presence of Jews in its trade and manufacturing. Neither at the time of Cromwell nor after the end of the Glorious Revolution can one speak in relation to England of an 'age of great Jewish merchants' (Trivellato 2009a: 114, Israel 2002a: 34f). These contradictions have already been pointed out more than once (Brentano 1916, Schipper 1918: 131). In short, the 'Sun of Israel' shone with different intensity in different parts of the world and in different eras, reinforcing different economic options. The emergence of divergent developmental paths in Europe did not contradict the observation that "Sephardim and Ashkenazim should have re-entered, gained ground, reached the peak of their importance, and then declined, hand in hand, as it were *pari passu*" (Israel 1998: 223).

It would, however, be a mistake to diminish the importance of these Eastern European and Ottoman Jewish communities in the wider context of the European economy of the period. The Jewish presence in both of these powerful states facilitated economic contacts in the Mediterranean, as well as with northern Europe, while at the same time expanding through trade the field of action of both traditional (such as the Italian cities) and emerging economic powers (such as the Netherlands). The Sephardic diasporas in the Italian states and the Ottoman Empire, initially without strong contacts, began to co-shape the relations linking the emerging Atlantic world with the Mediterranean and Eastern areas from the end of the 16th century. The diaspora of 'Portuguese', formed from the end of the 16th century in Amsterdam, owed much to the network of transnational trade contacts, as well as to the social and religious ties created jointly by the Jews of the empire and Venice (and other Italian cities). In particular, it was able to take advantage of the already available "experience, techniques, intellectual apparatus, and organization structures" characteristic of already established intercontinental trade networks (Israel 2002a: 68, 93).

Thus, without diminishing the contribution of the Sephardim, like the Protestant emigrants from Antwerp, to the economic power of the Netherlands, their role as an active actor in the Atlantic world already in the 16th century was strengthened in the 17th century thanks to and through the United Provinces. It is another matter that the emerging opportunity was seized by the 'Portuguese'. When one thinks about the Netherlands and the Jews of Amsterdam in the 17th century, and of the Atlantic trade of Portugal and Spain in the 16th and early 17th centuries, the thesis that "the Jews followed the trade, and not the trade the Jews" (Jacobs 1919: 256) seems overly cautious and partly misleading. They certainly did not play the role of passive followers in the growing international trade. This will be discussed further.

However, the results of their actions, apart from the revival of Jewish life in the Netherlands already as an integral part of the emerging European modernity (an achievement in itself), can hardly be considered a clear success. Having grown with the Republic, from the end of the 17th century, they had to give way to stronger players in a world of increasingly competitive Atlantic commerce. For admittedly different reasons, but also in the Jewish world, they ceded the palm of primacy to expansive Ashkenazi communities in Central and Eastern Europe. Assessing the results of this change is extremely difficult. And last but not least, the quality of Jewish religious life created in 17th century Amsterdam was questionable both to classical Jewish historiography and to modern historians. According to Graetz (1894: 682), "It was a misfortune for the Amsterdam community that its first spiritual guides (...) were possessed of only mediocre talents, in some degree lacked mental poise" (see also Israel 2009: Chapter 2).

By contrast, Sombart (1951: 50f) begins his argument on the 'role of the Jews' in the colonisation of Latin America surprisingly and not without irony:

> The very discovery of America is most intimately bound up with the Jews in an extraordinary fashion. It is as though the New World came into the horizon by their aid and for them alone, as though Columbus and the rest were but managing directors for Israel. It is in this light that Jews, proud of their past, now regard the story of that discovery, as set forth in the latest research.

Let us leave aside his detailed reflections and the way in which he interprets, for example, the works of the turn-of-the-century Jewish historian Meyer Kayserling, as well as his numerous factual errors. What is striking, however, is the unintended paradox: it is not difficult to see, as one reads the subsequent pages on colonisation, that the initial irony turns into even an enthusiastic, uncritical and often extreme acceptance of the thesis of the overwhelming influence of Sephardic Jews on the economy of colonial Latin America. This was for different reasons, however, than had been the case in traditional Jewish historiography before and after Sombar. This, like other national histories, was largely apologetic. The establishment of slave sugar plantations on the island of São Tomé, the beginnings of Brazil and the development of its economy, where Jews became the "ruling caste" and controlled all major plantations, the mastery of the gemstone trade, the transfer of sugar cane cultivation and sugar production technology to English Barbados, where they also ruled indivisibly, similarly in Jamaica, not to mention Suriname or the French colonies – this is the picture sketched by Sombart of a colonial Latin America created and economically dominated by Jews. Facts are mixed with fiction, individual Jewish planters become groups ruling over entire economies, accusations accompanying the competitive struggle between Jews and Christians appear as an objective description of the situation and a conclusive argument. Gone along the way is the irony about Columbus and other explorers as "managing directors for Israel". Gone are the Spaniards and Portuguese and the empires they created, not to mention the English, who had nothing to do with the Jews, the Puritan "new merchants" (competitors of the traditional city merchants) who dominated, among other things, the plantation economies of the Caribbean and the tobacco cultivation and trade in the North. This leaves only the Jews as the *spiritus movens* of the colonisation of the Americas, its strike force. In a twofold sense: as exercising control over economic resources (the 'ruling caste') and embodying, through Judaism, the 'spirit of capitalism'. Such a depiction must inevitably have aroused resistance, and from many opposing camps. Azevedo, already quoted above, who was critical of the role of the New Christians, saw Sombart as even "passionately attached" to the Jews. He pointed out, aptly, that he hastily recognised Tomé de Souza, the first governor of Brazil, as a descendant of the Jews, while at the same time emphasising, incorrectly, that the Portuguese New Christians had played no role in the development of the sugar plantations (Saraiva 2001: 307 appendix 3).

A critical analysis of every detail of the picture outlined by Sombart does not seem to be an interesting challenge (see however Wätjen 1913, Szlajfer 2010). One point, however, is worth noting.

The question of whether, when considering the role of Jews in Latin America, one should nevertheless be tempted to make a distinction between New Christians and marranos, crypto-Jews and Jews *tout court* is not considered. For an obvious reason: in Sombart's view, they were all Jews. Incidentally, but for other reasons, Jewish historians of the time would argue similarly. In his view, even the departure of a Jew from Judaism and the community changes nothing; it is a misleading appearance – "even descendants of such, seeing that historically they remain Jews" (Sombart 1951: 30). This is determined by 'racial' characteristics and their effect is the adaptability that characterises Jews.

Adopting a different position, he concludes, makes "the contribution of the Jews to the fabric of modern economic life will (...) appear smaller than it was in reality" (Sombart 1951: 33).

However, having clarified in quantitative terms the problem of Jewish participation also in the colonisation of Latin America and its leading economic sectors ("they dominated"), a few years later Sombart will complicate – whether intentionally is another matter – this fundamental finding. This will occur when he addresses the broader issue of the role played by migration and "strangers" – not just Jews – in the colonisation of the Americas. Thus, he will conclude that only the combination of "a certain fitness", a trait which "must be in the blood", with the status of the immigrant uprooted from his native environment, "in Jews and Gentiles alike", thus also among Protestants and Catholics, creates the chance for the emergence of a "developed capitalist spirit" (Sombart 1915: 302, 307). Elsewhere he put it even more strongly: "Everywhere the immigrants were foremost in building up the capitalist fabric; more especially, the growth of banking and of industries in all lands owes much to them" (Sombart 1915: 295f). Indeed, even if we leave out the Jewish migrants, according to Sombart "a wandering race since the Babylonian captivity", it would be difficult to ignore the role played by the French Huguenots. These had been leaving France since the 16th century, but migration would particularly intensify after the revocation of the Edict of Nantes in 1685. The majority of at least 200,000 refugees would move to the United Provinces, Prussia and England, and then also to the American colonies.

Such an approach, which weakens the previously accentuated link between Jews and capitalism, implies the possibility of a number of complex intermediate cases making quantitative analysis of the 'Jewish share' extremely difficult. How should one interpret, for example, the situation of an immigrant who combines the "fitness" of a "genetic Huguenot" with the fitness and entrepreneurial spirit of a Jew acquired through mimicry? And how should one interpret the case of a mestizo, not to mention a mulatto, the fruit of the union of an immigrant "genetic Jew" with an Indian woman? Such questions can be multiplied, but, in the perspective proposed by Sombart, they no longer make much sense. The answer will be known in advance. They will all be Jews and certainly they will be prisoners of the "Jewish spirit". Compared to racist theories, this was, we might add, a breakthrough and progress. At the end of his life, although he praised the salutary role played by the Nazi *Führer*, he noted that "the Jewish spirit is by no means bound to the Jew as a person", and he informed enthusiasts of the Aryan race that "the German spirit in a Negro is quite as much within the realm of possibility as the Negro spirit within a German" (Sombart 1937: 178, 175). Finally, let us add that in the second edition of his *Der moderna Kapitalismus,* Sombart, referring to the problem of "leadership" and "entrepreneurship" in particular economic epochs, no longer mentions Jews at all. This was not, he seems to suggest, necessary or intellectualy exciting. Thus, when he mentions *Frühkapitalismus*, which preceded the developed, industrial *Hochkapitalismus*, he indicates that the "entrepreneurs" characteristic of this period came from among an extremely diverse group of enterprising individuals: nobles, adventurers, merchants, craftsmen, as well as 'energetic princes' and royal officials. A quarter of a century after the first edition of *Der moderne Kapitalismus* in 1902, Sombart actually returned to his original account of the role of the Jews. At the time, he wrote that they had indeed played an important role in the "birth of the capitalist spirit", but, he stressed, "their influence in this area [*in dieser Richtung*] should not be overestimated" (Sombart 1902: 390, 1928: 11).[3]

In any case, returning to the issue raised above, for Sombart, but also for those scholars – often far from Sombart's view of the "role of the Jews" in the history of Europe and colonisation – who regard the distinction between Jews, crypto-Jews and New Christians as irrelevant or even a fiction, the doubts signalled were not problems worth addressing. Let us therefore leave them with this conviction. It is worth remembering, however, that his reflections on the Jews met with a crushing comment from one of the leading economists and historians of Wilhelmine Germany. He described them not only as "frivolous" and arrogant in places, but above all as "one of the most dreadful occurrences in the field of German science" (Brentano 1916: 159).

---

3   This and other threads of Sombart's reflections on the role of the Jews in the birth of capitalism were critically analysed from a Marxist perspective by Abram Leon (1950, 61–65), a young Belgian left-wing Zionist and then Trotskyist who was murdered in Auschwitz-Birkenau in 1944.

CHAPTER 4

More about the New Christians

The ideas developed by Sombart in his *Judenbuch* were an extreme example, but the perception of the problem he proposed therein has by no means gone away. It also echoes in some works devoted to the Black slave trade in the 16th and 17th centuries (Salvador 1981).[1] This was a specific period. It was during this time that the hitherto slave trade carried out by Portuguese, Arab and African merchants was transformed into an Atlantic venture. Although its scale was still small in the 16th century, the New and Old Christian *negreiros* paved the way for other strong players: the English. the French and the Dutch.

Before addressing this issue, however, a few additional remarks about the New Christians as a group *sui generis* are in order. For it was they who would take an active part in shaping the economies of the New World in the first century of colonisation. Still present in the following century, they would gradually give way in the Caribbean and in Suriname to Jews from Amsterdam. This is for many reasons even crucial. Neither in the Iberian Peninsula nor subsequently in the Spanish and Portuguese colonies did the Sephardim and their descendants act as Jews or Jewish communities. Their presence was primarily a phenomenon of New Christians and conversos. And let's repeat, the problem of how to treat Iberian converts is one of the most complicated and has been intensively debated for decades. Reaching a consensus on this issue is, however, a task for the future. Nota bene, also in the world of Ashkenazi Jews, which was destroyed during the Holocaust, this issue is not only a matter of historical reflection. Threatening in the eyes of many Christians and poorly understood, the phenomenon of baptized and assimilated Jews, which emerged in the Polish lands in all acuity from the late 19th century, is often part of the nationalist narrative even today, in a world without Jews. But that's another story.

In Cecil Roth's (1959) classic, the problem was resolved by identifying the New Christians and the marranos (the latter being defined as crypto-Jews). Such an approach had appeared earlier in the considerations of Lea (1906), an historian of the Inquisition, writing about the inauthenticity of the Catholicism of many conversos. Their economic activity was then reinforced by Sephardic

---

1 Without going into detail, his predilection for anti-Semitic terminology (Semites, Hebrews, Hebrew ethnics, blood descendants, Abrahamic blood–*sangue abraâmico*, etc. as opposed to Catholic-Roman ethnics or Aryans) and a bio-ethnic approach is objectionable.

Jews *tout court*, thus mainly the Portuguese Jews of Amsterdam and, from the second half of the 17th century, also to some extent English Jews. Within such a framework, therefore, the question of conversos and New Christians as a group *sui generis* could not arise, although the problem of apostates often occupied the attention of Jewish theologians of medieval and early modern times. However, the reductionism that led to the minimisation of the specificity of the New Christians raised objections. These grew *pari passu* with the expansion of knowledge, for example, of the process of Christianisation of the Jews in Spain in the 15th century, and as the documents of the Inquisition tribunals were reanalysed by new generations of historians.

In contrast to Cecil Roth, a well-known Spanish historian argued that conversos should be treated as a group distinct from Catholics and Jews, having the characteristics of a "social class" (Dominguez Ortiz 1971). Although the degree of differentiation of conversos made it impossible to treat them, in sociological terms, as a class, other factors justified Dominguez Ortiz's view of Jews and conversos as fundamentally different groups. By this we mean the perception of the group, self-identification as well as the specificity of religious experience of its members. At the same time, we are dealing with a group created from above: "there was no precedent in the history of Western Christianity (...) for distinguishing newly baptized individuals as an entire social class and across the generations in order to underscore their supposedly essential difference, as was the case in Iberia with *judeoconversos* and *moriscos*" (Graizbord 2013: 17). Arguments pointing to the authenticity of the religious transformation of the majority of conversos in the century before 1492 were also presented by an American historian: " Conversos very definitely considered themselves not only Christians but Spaniards, and to some extent at least the two were seen not only as inseparable but as the ultimate definition of what a Christian was, i.e., to be a Spaniard was to be the paragon of Christianity". He also pointed to the growing conflict in the 15th century between the ideological conversos and the rapidly diminishing Jewish community:

> Conversos themselves, at least those whose conversion was motivated exclusively by religious zeal and conviction, were the worst enemies of Jews. (...) An important element of the anti-Jewish activity and attitude of the conversos was the production of manuals or guides for the Inquisition, intended to enable the Inquisitors to 'detect' (...) supposed 'Jewish practices' of those whom they wished to condemn as heretics.
>
> ROTH 2002: 161, 188f

This group included, in no small number, members of the hitherto Jewish intellectual and economic elite, to mention the well-known Rabbi Solomon ha-Levi of Burgos. After his conversion in 1391, he became Bishop of Cartagena and then of Burgos as Pablo de Santa Maria. In turn, the faithful Jews, who felt increasingly isolated, did not remain passive, referring with increasing resentment to the *anusim*, i.e. Sephardim "forced" into Catholicism. In response to imposed Christianisation, and rising repression, a radicalisation of the interpretation of rabbinic law and frequent use of excommunication appeared. And at the same time, in everyday life, contacts between Jews and conversos were not severed. Festivals or family celebrations were shared by both, and the same doctors, midwives etc. continued to be called in times of need. However, this only made it possible to survive, not to avert an impending disaster. Indeed, one of the tasks of the just created Inquisition was to firmly counteract such contacts, to force separation (Levine Melammed 204: 35f, Gitlitz 2002: 38). This result was achieved. Against the backdrop of these dramatic disputes and the process of disintegration of the Sephardic communities in Barcelona, Toledo and Burgos, which had hitherto enjoyed authority, we find both an existential and intellectual crisis. The time of the golden (Arab-Muslim) and then silver (Christian) age of Iberian Jewry was already history in the 15th century (Lévy and Cohen 1992, Zając 2014: 42f).[2]

On the other hand, however, the traditional view proposed by Cecil Roth could not be decisively rejected. The time required for the formation of a New Christian group was probably longer than two to three generations: the transformation itself not only complicated but also not predetermined. The testimonies of 15th-century intellectual representatives of conversos already confirming a permanent break with Judaism and a commitment to Catholicism did not always and not at every moment necessarily reflect the situation of the group as a whole, especially in the initial phase of the transition. In any case, the process initiated on a wider scale with the pogroms at the end of the 14th century was accelerated in Spain in the 15th century. It would culminate in 1492: Spanish Jews had to make a choice – baptism or exile. In Portugal,

---

2   The rights of the Jews were radically restricted by the document *Ordenamiento sobre encer-ramiento de los judios e los moros,* promulgated in 1412 by the Regent of Castile Catalina. Its co-author was the converso bishop Pablo de Santa Maria (Netanyahu 1995: 168–191). Among other things, it contained a ban on contacts and conversation between Catholics and Jews, but at the same time allowed usury (*sic*) to continue. While the *Ordenamiento* was selectively enforced, it undoubtedly induced thousands of Castilian Jews to accept baptism (Lea 1906: 115–117, 122, 124).

already without the right to choose, forced Christianisation became a reality five years later.

The bringing in of New Christians into the picture means that the Jew vs. Gentile dichotomy is no longer sufficient when explaining the traditionally understood 'role of Jews' and Jewish exodus. Not only does a differentiation of Jewish diasporas depending on their place of settlement take place, but individuals and groups formally not belonging to the diaspora, *meshummadim* (apostates, "destroyed", as opposed to *anusim,* "forced") emerge. The latter by choice and/or as a result of a curse, as was the case in Amsterdam or Hamburg. As already mentioned, also "new Jews" travelling in the 17th century to the 'countries of idolatry', Spain and Portugal, were subject to criticism in the communities of Amsterdam, Hamburg and Livorno. Apart from drastic cases of exclusion from the community, this was usually combined with a restriction of religious rights and other mild forms of *herem*. This primacy of religious principles often led to losses in trade, given the importance of the contacts of the "new Jews" with Iberian partners.

In short, there is a need for change and a fundamental reinterpretation. But how to set its boundaries? What criteria to apply? In quantitative terms, it is simply impossible. The available sources only indicate that in the 16th century, "many" baptised Sephardim never returned to the Jewish religion and tradition, and "many" also were in fact marranos, crypto-Jews. The question of the proportion between the two groups is still debated (probably with no chance of resolution). There were also some 'Portuguese', rather few in number, who made the long journey leading first to a return to Judaism in the early 17th century and then another return, this time to Catholicism (Kaplan 1994, Schorsch 2009). Both in Europe and in Brazil.

Netanyahu's (1995: 993–995) discussion of conversos and the genesis of the Spanish Inquisition, like his earlier publication on the marranos, is inconclusive. On the one hand, he argues passionately that most of the New Christians had already been exiles from Judaism, in the literal sense, for several generations in the 15th century, an example of a genuine break; on the other hand, there is the thesis that stresses the impossibility of an irrevocable departure from Jewishness despite the change of religion. He writes of the descendants of the Spanish Sephardim: "while the convert abandoned his people, his peoplehood did not abandon him". His peoplehood survived even in the process of assimilation, with the result that "the converso could still be recognised – even several generations after his ancestor's conversion". He reiterated, in fact, the conviction of Isaac Abrávanel, a commentator on Scripture in the time of Ferdinand and Isabella, that the descendants of conversos would eventually find their place in the Jewish community, that "conversos would return" at the time of the coming of the Messiah and the redemption. At the same time, the ambivalent behaviour of the conversos, including the self-irony that characterised many of them, only confirmed their Christianisation *sui generis*. Simply, conversos were the product of circumstance and human action, and weakness: "A mouth they have, but speak not; eyes they have, but see not; Ears they have, but hear not" (Psalm 115). They were masks. Netanyahu, while not dismissing the possibility of reconciliation in the distant future, nevertheless emphasised, unlike Abrávanel (Ben-Shalom 2009: 287–289), the authenticity of the Catholicism of conversos. This in turn reinforced in his argument the importance of non-religious distinctions. If the Jewish law (*halakhah*) of medieval times defined the Jew – according to some interpretations – as embodying the unity of faith and non-religious characteristics, the departure from religion resulted in an accentuation of the importance of the latter, hitherto treated as secondary. These, in turn, provided the premise for a possible 'return' to the community abandoned by the ancestors.

All in all, the policy referring to the *limpieza de sangre* introduced a completely new point of reference into the way conversos were perceived. Paradoxically, it was close to the conditions determining the possibility of return, present in the interpretations of Jewish law quoted above. The point, however, was not in the paradox, but in the perverse even abuse of the concept of 'return' and its premises. Ethnicity and genealogy, variously defined, which had previously coexisted with the tendencies towards exodus from Judaism and assimilation, had not formed an impenetrable barrier and did not constitute a condition *sine qua non*. The ambiguity, the acceptance of a relatively much wider space for interpretation, the many question marks, all offered the possibility of a nuanced, flexible view and resolution of the problem.

From the end of the 15th century, ethnicity and genealogy became, under pressure from the mob and competitors, alongside theological interpretations and then the Inquisition, non-negotiable factors. Jews who searched for middle-of-the-road solutions were confronted with an environment hostile to compromise. The room for manoeuvre was hence fundamentally narrowed. The revolt in Toledo combined with the pogrom against conversos in 1449 also found ideological expression in the adoption of the *Sentencia-Estatuto*, and this document, together with the *Ordenamiento* by Doña Catalina promulgated in 1412, effectively paved the way for the stigmatisation of conversos. As a member of a distinct group, the converso inevitably retained links to the Jewish past, even to their distant ancestors. The possibility of choice and rupture, which, while having many shades, had hitherto been somewhat guaranteed by the universal Church and its doctrine, was transformed into the inevitability of inauthentic assimilation. Guarding this already permanent otherness of conversos, which separates them from the Old Christians, are an ideology and institutions founded on the hypothesis of a pernicious assumption concerning conversos' dubious Catholicism and the principle of *limpieza de sangre* (Netanyahu 1995: 367–385). Any assertion of attachment to the Church must – because of the genealogy, i.e. non-religious characteristics – be treated as suspect. In place of the Jew, there can only be a poor copy of the good Catholic. After almost two centuries, this essentially inquisitorial mindset was challenged in a dramatic letter to the Pope by the Jesuit Antonio Vieira.

This justification for the activity of the Inquisition had nothing to do with the aforementioned medieval *halakhic* interpretations, which continued to treat an apostate from the female line as a Jew, albeit a sinful one. *Halakhah*, despite many interpretive disputes, accepted at the same time the authenticity of the conversion of non-Jews to Judaism (Katz 1962: 68). By contrast, the prevailing opinion among Spanish rabbis in the 15th century was that the way back to Judaism was closed to conversos. By adhering to the new faith and thus making an ideological choice, they became Christians and therefore non-Jews. The question of their 'blood' was irrelevant here (Netanyahu 1995: 927f). Such an uncompromising stance reflected, putting other factors aside, the enormous tension in relations between conversos and unyieldingly faithful Jews during this period, which went hand in hand with an immediate threat to the very existence of the latter.

The converso, a good Catholic and at the same time imprisoned by his origins, was therefore the embodiment of a contradiction that was irresolvable in the eyes of many, and not only religious dogmatists. This issue was viewed differently by scholars who adhered to traditional interpretations and were not keen to put too much stress on the distinctiveness of conversos. This was the case, for example, with an eminent Israeli historian, Yitzhak Baer, who wrote that "conversos and Jews were one people, united by bonds of religion, destiny and messianic hope" (quoted in Roth 2002: 363). If this did not even apply to the elites, who, according to Baer, betrayed, the concept of "one people" certainly included those conversos who retained some connection to Judaism. Thus, in line with this view, there were many crypto-Jews among the conversos, and, in this sense, the activity of the Inquisition was not reduced to the chasing of a chimera. Martyrdom was, in a way, inscribed in the Jewish destiny. And at the same time, in this view, one can see an attempt to create a link between the exiles and the vision of a new unification of the Jewish people. The fate of the conversos thus became part of a narrative concerning the already contemporary transformation of the diaspora into a nation (Bodian 1999: x).

There is no need to continue the discussion on this topic. Let us merely note that it seems difficult today to maintain a position that treats conversos as crypto-Jews. The issue, moreover, is not limited to scholarly debate. Netanyahu's *magnum opus* demonstrates that the dispute is as much about the worldviews, passions, and convictions of historians themselves as it is about their hopes and ideological choices. One is dealing here with the peculiar proselytising implicit in such a position, directed towards Jewish people lost to Christianity as a result of historical circumstances. This was aptly put by a Brazilian scholar when he wrote about the "internal movement" of the Amsterdam community directed towards the New Christians living in the Iberian Peninsula, with the aim of converting them and possibly moving them to the 'lands of Judaism', including Amsterdam. Proselytism focused on Brazilian New Christians in Nieuw-Holland between 1630 and 1654 was similarly seen "as an internal movement within the Nation, not as an example of universal missionary élan" (Feitler 2009: 133). The latter was by this time a thing of the past (Katz 1962: 143–148).

In contemporary historiography, the approach proposed by Netanyahu is no longer questioned *in toto*; on the contrary, it is possible to speak on the one hand of attempts to follow it and, on the other, of new hypotheses questioning the universality of crypto-Jewish attitudes. N. Roth, who discerns in the crypto-Jew a "romantic myth", undoubtedly belongs to the first group of researchers. He writes: "It must be understood once and for all: conversos were not 'crypto-Jews'; they were Christians, who chose completely to separate themselves from the Jewish people, and not just from the Jewish 'faith'" (2002: 364). And this is also how they were perceived by Jews who refused to convert. Alpert (2001: 29f), on the other hand, emphasises the presence of numerous crypto-Jews among the 1492 converts and suggests that they made up a considerable part of the Inquisition's victims by the 1530s. This brings us back to the question of the proportions between the different groups of conversos, which is in fact impossible to resolve. Instead, we share the opinion of Bodian (1999: 175) that "[n]o serious scholar today would argue that cryptojudaizing was entirely a fabrication of the Inquisition". And, last but not least, of the many positions presented in the literature, it is worth noting Ellis Rivkin's hypothesis concerning the New Christians. Those who rejected the option of returning to Judaism and leaving Portugal or Brazil, he argues, often treated their religious identity as negotiable, prioritising security and the prospects of economic advancement over their ancestral faith. Such a choice was reinforced by strong intangible motivations. The descendants of those en masse baptised in 1497 were thus neither sincere Catholics nor conspiratorial crypto-Jews, but "crypto-individualists" (quoted in Novinsky 2001: 217.

Other authors who have addressed this specific group also emphasise the contradictions that such an attitude implied. Certainly, they were to a large extent the result of enforced baptism or the memory of such – and not only – symbolic violence passed on to the next generation. By definition, as it were, this led to a violation of the moral order, especially the duty of loyalty sanctified by tradition. The consequence was the emergence of cynical attitudes, although they were probably not predominant. A converso who rejected both Judaism and Christianity was not only an individualist, he also refused "to play by the conventionalisms of a corrupt and oppressive system" in which he lived (Faur 1992: 49–52). In any case, "in large part [Rivkin's] description corresponds to the situation in Brazil, especially with regard to wealthy businessmen and contractors", although generalising this description may make it difficult to understand the diverse variants of marrano attitudes (Novinsky 2001: 217). Another historian would see in the conversos a phenomenon of pan-European significance. Namely, he suggested, they "were (...) the first socioreligious population group of Europe in which a religious individualism began to spread already in the course of the 16th century as a result of external circumstances, and not from an inherent impulse within the core of the religion itself" (Greyerz 2008: 217).

The case of the famous Don Josef Nasci, Duke of Naxos (formerly New Christian João Micas), related to Beatriz de Luna-Doña Grácia Nasci (both also spelled 'Nasi'), confirmed such a statement. As we know, after the death of her husband and brother-in-law Diogo Mendes, it was she who headed the powerful family trading and financial empire. The story of Don Josef Nasci, who in his youth befriended the later Emperor Maximilian II, is indicative. He fought as a cavalry officer and was then active in family interests in Portugal, Antwerp and Italian cities, developed in the 1560s, following in the footsteps of Grácia Nasci, widespread economic and political activity as a Jew in Turkey: "He was the prototype of the ideal entrepreneur, for his identity was rooted in his economic function. And though not every Jewish entrepreneur of the 17th century was an embodiment of this ideal, there was not one who did not approximate it" (Rivkin 2003: 190, also Tavim 2011). His network of commercial agents included the Polish city of Lvov in the time of Sigismund Augustus, where he obtained permission to trade in wine, the Mediterranean, the Iberian Peninsula and northern Europe. Simply, the "Fugger of the East" (Braudel 1995: 698) Nor did he break off political contacts with Portugal, although the nature of these is still unclear. Like Doña Grácia Nasci, Don Josef Nasci, carried out a wide-ranging campaign to help Sephardic migrants in the Mediterranean.

Another emblematic, equally colourful figure representing, through a multiplicity of demonstrated loyalties, a growing individualism was Samuel Pallache (1550–1616). This Moroccan Jew's role was that of merchant, international mediator and diplomat, who contributed to the anti-Spanish alliance between Morocco and the United Provinces, informer to both the Sultan and the Court of Madrid and anti-Spanish corsair. He was at the same time the diplomatic agent of the King of Morocco in the Republic. As an alleged pirate he was put on trial in England (and declared not quilty, but not without the intervention of the States-General). However, the results of Pallache's engagement in Jewish community life in the United Provinces, exalted by many, were in fact unclear: "there are important reasons for believing that [as a Spanish Jew] Samuel Pallache was never fully integrated into the predominantly Portuguese Jewish community" (Garcia-Arenal and Wiegers 2003: 63f). In short, a downright walking contradiction. The same can be said of the New Christians who never returned to the religion of their forefathers and, moreover, were active in an environment that even forced them to distance themselves from any links with Judaism. The aforementioned Duarte de Paz, after the failure of his mission to Rome to prevent the establishment of the Inquisition in Portugal, left the Eternal City in 1538 disillusioned and in protest converted to Judaism. Conflict with the New Christians, who accused him of embezzlement and threatened persecution in Christian countries, in turn caused him to settle in the Ottoman Empire at the end of his life and embrace Islam (Novoa 2007).[3]

The individualisation of attitudes to religion would also appear among those who, while becoming "new Jews" in the Netherlands, at the same time did not regard religious identity as decisive in economic activity. They precisely separated the spheres of the *sacred* and the *profane* (already understood in a Christian way). Thus, when writing about the emigration of New Christians towards France as well as Antwerp triggered by the establishment of the Inquisition in Portugal, the historian notes that, except in rare cases, "it becomes well-nigh impossible, except in rare cases, to determine whether a given individual's emigration was prompted by inquisitorial persecution or inspired by prospects of commercial gain" (Swetschinski 2004: 60). Indeed. Trying to read individual motivations centuries later seems a rather risky undertaking, although the Sephardim's choice of settlement sites in northern Europe suggested the importance of economic motivations. However, was it the only one? It does not seem justified to minimise the role of faith or fear of the terror of the Inquisition as factors prompting emigration. All the more so given that in the first half of the 17th century, a period of increased migration of New Christians, "the number of immigrants from Portugal does, to some

---

3   After his departure, other representatives of the New Christians would appear in Rome. Their contacts and money facilitated a papal letter in 1542 in defence of the New Christians in Lamego, northern Portugal. It contained a crushing criticism of the local Inquisition tribunal, its bias and the greed of the Inquisitors (Mateus and Novoa 2008).

degree, correspond with the figures of inquisitorial victims". In contrast, there is no doubt that the emerging circles of the Portuguese diaspora, with varying degrees of acceptance of Judaism, were "held together by common ties to Portugal" (Swetschinski 2004: 70, 59). Let us also add Seville, although in this case the 'Portuguese' would appear in greater numbers in the first half of the 17th century.

A few more words on the ways in which the history of the New Christians has been documented.

In research on New Christians in Brazil, one of the methods employed is onomastics. It was used intensively by Salvador (1976), among others, in his monographs on the role of the New Christians. However, other researchers have pointed out that, in fact, the New Christians used traditional Portuguese names. No predilection for particularly distinctive names can be noted. Moreover, there were frequent cases even of brothers using different surnames, depending on the circumstances, which necessitated a distinction between surnames 'inside' and 'outside' the family. Incidentally, such a distinction appeared in an answer given by an alumna at a Jesuit college in Bahia in the 17th century (Novinsky 2006). The pretext for the change may have been marriage, migration, and the security requirement for commercial transactions with partners from Spain, Portugal, or the Iberian colonies. The organiser in the 17th century of the Jewish settlement in the then Dutch Cayenne and later in Suriname, David Cohen Nassi, was probably born in Portugal as Christovão de Tavora, and in the Netherlands used the name José Nuñes da Fonseca in dealings with his family in Portugal and trading partners (Stern 1992: 143). In brief, only in-depth genealogical studies could provide an answer about the history of the New Christians, a torturous task and in many cases impossible.

In addition, and perhaps above all, the relationship between genealogy and the religious identity of the individual whose activity is of interest is not clear. A problem, implied by *limpieza de sangre*, concerns the identification of every New Christian as a Jew or the tendency among even prominent historians "to maximise the Jewishness of New Christians" (Schorsch 2006). Another aspect of this problem, related to the economic history of the Sephardim settling in the Republic, is pointed out by a historian of Amsterdam Jews: "In this case, Jewishness obscures the fact that, as *conversos*, the Portuguese had already been members of European society and stood outside the main traditions of Jewish history" (Swetschinski 2004: 103). Indeed, the New Christians settling in Amsterdam did not represent, in economic terms, an historical continuity, a narrative traditionally emphasising exclusion. On the contrary, one can speak of a rupture. This will find expression in the unique character of the community created in Amsterdam by the "new Jews", above all in the economic activities of its members that directly contributed to the rise of market modernity. Furthermore, the regulations and statutes describing in detail the conduct of the members of the Amsterdam community in matters of faith did not touch their economic activity (Kaplan 1992: 88). This sphere of social life had already freed itself in Amsterdam from the hegemony of Jewish law. In short, "the economic history of Amsterdam's Portuguese Jews will tell us more about Jewish history than vice versa" (Swetschinski 2004: 103).

However, the most serious challenge is to prejudge the 'Jewishness' of the New Christians and their religious choices on the basis of documents produced by the Inquisition. We are talking about an institution whose informants Novinsky (2009: 161) described – exaggeratingly – as "Gestapo informers of the time". In turn, the institution itself was described by Rabbi Saul Levi Morteira, Spinoza's teacher who subsequently participated in his exclusion from the community, as "a cruel and unjust beast, tyrannical and without pity" (Faur 1992: 42). However, in the absence of other comprehensive documentation, the source for the history of the New Christians in the colonies is precisely the records of the Holy Office. However, an Inquisition scholar aptly noted that these sources have a unique characteristic: "unless considerable care is exercised they will only confirm our presuppositions and appear to demonstrate (...) either that most of the New Christians denounced to the Inquisition were crypto-Jews (...) or that they were the innocent victims" (Rowland 2001: 126, also Rivkin 1957). Thus, it has been argued that while there is no doubt about the authenticity of the surviving Inquisition records, their reliability is suspect. These documents are *autênticas mas não são verdadeiras*. The Portuguese Inquisition, according to the critical views of some 18th century authors, was a "factory producing marranos" (Saraiva 2001, also Marques 1976: 287).[4]

The descriptions in surviving records of the Inquisition of investigations ending in *auto de fé* and sometimes burning at the stake (usually, however, with a confession of guilt, 'coming to terms with the Church' and social exclusion) only tell us that the problem existed and that the search for *judaizantes* was both a task to be performed and an obsession. Such a characterisation fits well,

---

4 Jesuit Antonio Vieira used such a comparison as early as the 17th century: "Just as coins are stamped in the Royal Mint so in this miserable kingdom we have factories for minting Jews" (quoted in Novinsky 1991: 179). I.S. Révah, on the other hand, maintained that the marranos were not a marginal phenomenon, and he also questioned Saraiva's hypothesis that the Inquisition's target was the emerging Portuguese middle class. In his view, most of the victims came from the lower classes (Saraiva 2001: appendixes). This was different in the colonies, where repression affected the XNs mainly from the middle class (Studnicki-Gizbert 2007: 169).

it seems, especially with the Portuguese Inquisition of the late 16th to mid-18th centuries. But in its case, too, one should keep things in proportion. Although the first visiting inquisitor of the Santo Officio in Brazil dealt extensively with Judaising heretics, he also spent a great deal of time investigating the widespread millenarian cult of *Santidade*. This mixture of Christianity and Indian and African beliefs was in the 1580s popular among Indians and black slaves. The followers of this cult received support, probably with a view to securing a supply of Indian labour, from an Old Christian, the owner of *engenho* Jaguaripe in Bahia (Azevedo 1922: 227, Metcalf 1999). Until the first *Visitação*, among 223 cases of inquisitorial investigations in Brazil in the 16th century only 17 concerned Judaisers (Marcocci and Paiva 2013: 118). Nota bene, the Spanish Inquisition, after a period of fierce prosecution at home until the 1530s, then concentrated in the metropolis and colonies until the end of the 16th century on tracking down and punishing blasphemers, sodomites, bigamists and (a few) Protestants. To this must be added a growing concern about corruption. The tribunal established in 1610 in Cartagena de Indias, the main port for the supply of slaves to Spanish America, also addressed this problem (Navarrete Peláez 2007, 2002). The massed attack of the Inquisition on the New Christians in Spanish America would come in the 1630s to the 1640s, preceded from the turn of the 16th century by migrations of the 'Portuguese' to Spain and its colonies facilitated by the establishment of the Iberian Union.

The search for Judaising heretics was not frowned upon in public opinion at the time. On the contrary, the Spanish Inquisition was the result of "a movement that reflected the will, the feelings and the attitudes of the majority of Spain's Christian population" (Netanyahu 1995: 925). By contrast, when asked whether the Spanish Inquisition was popular, a Spanish historian would answer that it definitely wasn't (Dominguez Ortiz 1999: 326). A Polish-Jewish historian, on the other hand, wrote in an interwar textbook for high schools, without hiding his emotions:

> The Christian people (...) did not see the poor marranos who, in the darkness of the suburban streets, bloodily earned their daily bread with the work of their hands, they saw only those rich 'Jews' who ate the fruits of their labour; the Castilian official saw the influential 'Jews' in the highest positions, and the poor parish priest saw the 'Jewish bishops'. All the anger and hatred towards the Jews now shifted to the marranos.
>
> BAŁABAN 1925: 221f

Indeed, the entire state-corporate structure of Iberian and colonial societies supported hostile behaviour towards conversos and New Christians, epitomised in part by the Inquisition. All three 'classes' represented in the Portuguese Cortes (clergy, nobility, people) were united in their hatred of the New Christians. On this issue, the aggressively disposed vanguard was mainly made up of representatives of the 'people'. It is therefore not surprising that, according to some estimates, informers of the Inquisition made up 2 per cent of the population of 16th century Spain and about 10 per cent of 17th century Brazil. Without this mass support, the effectiveness of a small group of Inquisitors would have been severely limited (Stuczynski 2011: 249; Mark and Silva Horta 2011: 165).

If anything was objectionable, as during the wave of repression that began in the 1580s and lasted almost half a century, it was the arrogant behaviour of some Inquisitors, as well as instances of enriched officials of the Holy Office. The fundamental objective – the fight against conversos – was not in question. The *familiares*, the secular arm of the Inquisition, obliged to track down heresy as well as, in times of need, to defend the Inquisitors in arms, made no secret of their status. On the contrary, it was regarded as an honour (and a confirmation of 'purity of blood'). Similarly in Portugal, where in the 16th and 17th centuries the number of *familiares* exceeded 1,000 (limited in the second half of the 17th century by Pedro II to 601, who were entitled to privileges costly to the crown). In both countries, *familiares* were generally drawn from the noble elite, although they included – as the *Suprema* (Supreme and General Council of the Inquisition) warned against in Spain – shopkeepers and butchers. In Córdoba and Granada, New Christian judges were also recorded among *familiares* in the late 16th and early 17th centuries. In Brazil, between 1613 and 1820, 66 *comissários* (commissioners) and 663 *familiares* were nominated in Pernambuco, the centre of the sugar economy, with the strongest increase occurring after 1690. However, in 1720, as in Portugal, the number of those who could count on royal privileges was limited to 60 in Brazil (Marques 1976: 289, Hanson 1981: 79, Wadsworth 2007: 38).

Envy, the desire for revenge and therefore denunciations (even years later) from commercial competitors, abandoned spouses or slaves played an important role in the activity of the Inquisition. However, these hardly laudable motivations were often reinforced by a sense of religious duty, loyalty and fear. The latter should not be underestimated. As an important motive, it appeared with great frequency among those enjoying the privilege of a 'grace period' during the visitations of the inquisitors to Pernambuco in 1594–95 and to Bahia in 1618 (Aufderheide 1973). The value of this kind of testimony, like that extracted during the investigation, was in many cases questionable. The accused had been tortured, reads the record of one investigation by the Inquisition in Mexico, and confessed at the second turn of the wheel. The same was true of a surgeon and also a slave trader in Cartagena (Liebman 1963: 102, Schorsch 2009: 128). In contrast, the coercion of a 13-year-old child by Inquisitors in Mexico to testify against 108 people, including his family, was not a routine act (Lea 1922: 230).

The use or threat of torture – part of the formally sanctioned investigation procedure – led many suspects to seek a compromise with their persecutors. The Inquisitors expected confirmation of practising forbidden Judaism, the surrender of accomplices and the identification of as many other *judaizantes* as possible. Such behaviour often made it possible to negotiate a sentence and, above all, to avoid the stake. Many of the testimonies provided by informers about the secret cultivation of Jewish customs are considered by some historians of the Inquisition to be downright absurd. Take, for example, the accusation of blasphemy against a New Christian merchant. In a dispute with an indebted customer, he exclaimed when asked if "his account books are the Gospel" that they were "more important than the Gospel". He ended up with a mild fine, having to attend mass with his mouth gagged and donating a candle to the church. The lack of smoke from the chimneys on Friday night was also cited by the tribunals as clear evidence of Judaising. In some cases, yes. Often, however, this lack of smoke was a product of fantasy (Roth 2002: 217–219, 268, 354). The Portuguese Inquistion imprisoned from the end of the 1530s an Old Christian, a knight of the Order of Christ and appellate judge (*desembargador*), under the pretext that he had asked for advice from New Christians when preparing the Portuguese translation of the Old Testament. Years later, in a letter to the Pope, king João III referred to those responsible for this scandal as "plebeian idiots and simpletons" (*idiotas plebeios e simprizes*) (Marcocci and Paiva 2013: 33f).

These are doubts that call into question many of the verdicts made by the Inquisition tribunals. It should also be borne in mind that, in Brazil, the first decision of the Visiting Inquisitor – who appeared in 1591 – was to promulgate, in accordance with procedure, the decrees of 'grace period' (*edito da graça*) and 'confession of faith' (*edito da fé*). In addition to promising leniency to suspects who came forward of their own volition within 30 days, these acts included information about the obligation of the inhabitants of the city and the surrounding area to report offences against the church and the faith. There is also an instruction describing behaviour and symbolism indicative of the crime of Judaising (Abreu 1922: 39–45). A kind of handbook for informers *in spe*. It was aptly observed by a Portuguese historian that the task of the visitator was not to give absolution and mercy; the visitation was in fact a kind of police operation geared to gathering evidence of guilt. Thus, neighbours and friends were denounced, under various pretexts. The first victim in Bahia would be the XN accused of denying Mary's virginity (Azevedo 1922: 225f, Wiznitzer 1960: 13f).

However, reservations about the wisdom of the Inquisition's actions were not often formulated in Portugal, especially when it came to New Christians. It is all the more noteworthy that they were strongly expressed around the middle of the 17th century by the well-known Jesuit Father António Vieira. He judged the activities of the Portuguese Inquisition to be decidedly negative and the testimonies extracted during the investigations to be unreliable. Several centuries later, some historians would agree with this assessment. The price of this criticism, like the defence of the Indians against the colonists in Brazil, was high – more than two years of repression (including imprisonment) for the critical Father. He was only saved from such oppression by the intervention of Pope Clement X (Novinsky 1991, Alden 2003).[5] Certainly, however, his report on the Portuguese Inquisition contributed to the Pope's suspension of this institution for several years. The claim of Father Vieira's almost complete isolation among the Portuguese Jesuits is also disputed (Stuczynski 2014: 44f). For other, more pragmatic reasons, among the defenders of the *judaizantes* we sometimes also find their Old Christian trading partners. In several cases their testimony saved the accused, such as in Oporto in 1618. Also "fidalgos in Asia protected some New Christians from the Inquisition because they were their associates in profitable trading ventures" (Boyajian 1993: 175, Ebert 2008: 67f). However, the fact remains that after a hiatus of several years, the Inquisition in Portugal resumed its activities, while António Vieira moved to Brazil and would never return to Portugal.

Instructive, however, is above all the case of a well-known and prominent merchant in Lima, Manuel Bautista Peréz, related to Diogo Rodrigues de Lisboa. This Lisbon merchant-banker was active in the trade of Asian spices, but also in the slave trade and, probably, in the sale of arms to African rulers. As a *negativo* (i.e. a detainee stubbornly refusing to admit to heresy), Bautista Peréz was sentenced to be burnt alive at the stake in the great Lima trial of the 'Portuguese' in 1639. Among the 73 defendants were 63 suspected Judaisers; 11 were sentenced to the stake by the tribunal. Despite several years of imprisonment and torture, this Portuguese New Christian did not admit to practising Judaism, although some witnesses considered his behaviour and contacts with other *judaizantes* 'suspicious'. Indeed, Bautista Peréz's residence, named by Lima inhabitants *Casa de Pilatos* and 'the synagogue' by the Inquisitors, was not only an architectural achievement but also a place of interesting discussions. This influential merchant combined slave trading, mining and

---

5 Enemies of this rebellious Jesuit were also spreading rumours that his maternal grandmother was a New Christian. However, in fact the Jesuit's paternal grandmother was a mulatta (Dutra 2003).

ownership of two plantations with diverse intellectual interests: "He had a collection of 125 paintings and a library of 135 titles in 155 volumes. By the criteria of his period, this was a collection of rare abundance and exceptional quality" (Wachtel 2013: 55, also Pérez 1991, Mark and Silva Horta 2011: 122). At the same time, Bautista Pérez's teaching of the Catholic faith to his own children was intense, while donations to the Church, membership in religious confraternities and other deeds cemented the image of a devout Catholic. Moreover, although Portuguese, Bautista Pérez spoke mainly Spanish, demonstrating his attachment to the House of Habsburg.

However, this and other evidence cited during the trial, including by the seven friars and two chaplains called as witnesses by Pérez, did not convince the tribunal. While condemning Pérez as a *negativo* and treating him as a "rabbi or *capitán grande*" of Peruvian *judaizantes*, the tribunal at the same time considered, as if in passing, that the drinking of a beverage made from African kola or the taking of snuff indicated that the accused practised Jewish customs. In the atmosphere of colonial Peru, taking into account the mentality of the time and the conspiracy theories developed by some friars and Inquisitors, combining kola and tobacco with Jewish customs was not considered an aberration. On the contrary, it pointed to the supposedly common roots of Indians and Jews, and the apparent synthesis of strands of Jewish, African and Indian tradition (Silverblatt 2000: 532–536, Lewin 1960: 65). It was a theory as good as the aforementioned revelations of Montezinos. He was not alone, either in Europe or in Latin America. In the early 17th century Brazilian Indians as alleged descendants of the crew of King Solomon's lost fleet were mentioned by Ambrósio Fernandes Brandão, author of the *Diálogos das grandezas do Brasil* (Wiznitzer 1960: 27f).

Analysing this admittedly complicated case, an historian of marranos religiosity thus wonder whether Manuel Bautista Pérez was "a Jewish martyr or a Christian martyr. The answer, in his case, is not obvious, but it is not implausible to suppose that he was the victim of a dual sincerity – straddling two different standards while experiencing doubts and uncertainty about both of them" (Wachtel 2001: 154, 2013: 69, also Pérez 1991, Maldavky 2000). Other historians have no such doubts, mentioning Pérez simply as one of the leaders of the "Judaising groups" in the New World (Israel 2002a: 29, Alpert 2001: 140) or one who actually stressed the importance of solidarity among members of the Nation and gave it verbal expression (Quevedo 2008: 238), We should add that the context in which the conviction of Bautista Pérez took place may have indicated that the main objective of the Inquisitors was to strike not so much at a powerful merchant and (dubious) *judaizante,* but at a whole group of resident

Portuguese (including Old Christians) in the Viceroyalty. We will return to this issue in Chapter 11.

It can be assumed that those victims who were less resistant to the investigative method of the Inquisition, *judaizantes* or not, admitted the sin of heresy in desperation while hoping to avoid torture and the stake. "Testify or die" – this rule known to most actual or fictional *judaizantes* – was not a theory. Wearing the disgraceful *sambenito* for a period of time or the prohibition of carrying weapons, jewellery and riding horses (we are talking about mild punishments) discriminated but did not kill. The same applied to the punishment of wearing the *sambenito* for life or confinement in a monastery. Centuries later, they would be counted among the *judaizantes,* confirming the verdict of the Inquisition tribunal. The myth of crypto-Jews secretly and *en masse* cultivating the forbidden faith was widespread – also among scholars. On the other hand, however, to dismiss the documents of the Inquisition *in toto* would be unwise (Gitlitz 2002: 77–80), even if disclosing and eliminating the "structurally determined" false evidence they contained is not a simple task (Rivkin 1957).

Nor, of course, can we dismiss the numerous testimonies of attachment to Judaism given by crypto-Jews who subsequently escaped the reach of the Inquisition, while the less fortunate found themselves in its hands. Such cases include the activity of the *esnoga* (synagogue, understood as 'meetings') organised at the end of the 16th century on a plantation near the Matoim River in Bahia by the New Christian Heitor Antunes and his wife Ana Rodrigues. This wealthy merchant, tax farmer and *engenho* owner, ennobled even before his arrival in Brazil, held a high position among the white elite and also enjoyed the confidence of Governor Mem de Sá. The couple's wide-ranging and not very carefully concealed activities were assisted by their daughter Beatriz Antunes, otherwise married to an Old Christian *engenho* owner. Incidentally, Beatriz Antunes' sisters also associated themselves with Old Christian partners. After the death of Heitor Antunes, Ana Rodrigues took over his role. The widely known activities of the *esnoga* did not attract the attention of the church for years, until in 1593 when the widow and her daughters were accused of Judaising by the first Inquisition visitor to Brazil. The fate of the accused women was indeed tragic (Assis 2004, Schorsch 2009: 232–244).

With less flair and more discretion, similar practices to *esnoga* Matoim were also repeated elsewhere. The commitment to Jewish tradition was also evidenced by more than one investigation and more than one trial. During interrogations, some XNs took up a dangerous dispute with their persecutors in defence of their religion. Imprisoned by the Inquisition in 1626, a young Portuguese surgeon from Chile, Francisco Maldonado de Silva, who was burnt alive at the stake in Lima in 1639, not only did not reject his ancestral faith in prison but is said to have induced two prisoners to convert to Judaism (Bodian 2007: Chapter 5, Wachtel 2013: Chapter 2). The dramatic fate of Luis de Carvajal "el Mozo" in late 16th century Mexico, grandson of the governor of Nuevo Reino de León in New Spain, as well as his mother and three sisters, was not an isolated incident. Rather, their tragedy was a foreshadowing of the coming misfortunes that would culminate in Spanish America in the 1630s and 1640s. These martyrs for the faith were paying the ultimate price: burning at the stake.[6] What united the New Christians who found, happily, refuge in Antwerp or Amsterdam and conversos who, suspected of being Judaised, became victims of the Inquisition, was a particular attitude to Christianity and baptism. For both of these groups, "Christianity was merely a means to escape Christian violence" (Faur 1992: 47).

We assume, therefore, that the break with the faith and the Jewish tradition in the broadest sense was a tendency that characterised most of the New Christians, and that it resulted in an attempt to integrate fully into the Catholic world. When, in 1605, the need arose to collect from XN s a huge sum as payment for the amnesty, "from the very beginning some New Christians considering themselves devout Catholics saw no reason why they should pay for a favour which, they claimed, did not apply to them at all" (Pulido Serrano 2006: 367f). Such opinions were widespread, especially in Lisbon. Some New Christians petitioned the king for exemption from payment, while others questioned the legitimacy of the New Christians negotiating the terms of the amnesty. These were not, on balance, successful endeavours. The majority paid. Protests also emerged in Castile. In short, the goal of much – if not most – of the New Christian elite was assimilation, honorary titles and nobility and other privileges pledged to the Old Christians, not the underground cultivation of the ancestral religion.

This direction of the evolution of social status desired by many New Christians was well illustrated in the 16th century by the example of the Ximenes d'Aragão family. The co-creator of its power was Fernão Ximenes, who was active in Antwerp. In addition to Baltic grain, which, as a benefactor of Ferdinando I, the grand duke of Tuscany, he supplied at the end of the 16th century to a principality affected by crop failure, his trading house participated above all in the spice, slave and sugar trades. The ruler of Tuscany granted Fernão Ximenes a noble title, which opened the way for the integration of the

---

6   According to an Inquisition official's report, when being led to the stake, Carvajal reportedly took up at the last moment the cross and confessed his sin. By way of mercy before being burned, he was garroted. The credibility of this report is disputed (Bodian 2007: 76, Costigan 2010: 76f).

Tuscan branch of this family into the aristocracy of Florence (earlier, in 1586–88, Ximenes' virtuous origin had been confirmed by Pope Sixtus V). In turn, for his services to the church, "Simone Ximenes and his siblings" were honoured by the Pope in a special way: he became a member of the papal family including the right to use the Pope's family name, Peretti. Almost at the same time, another member of the family, António Fernandes Ximenes, who did business in Goa, was accused of Judaising (Thomas 1998: 117, Fischer 2011, Alessandrini and Bastos Mateus 2015: 39f). In the late 16th and early 17th centuries, many Ximenes bought their place among the European aristocracy. Several of them invested at least 600,000 cruzados in Spanish *juros* (bonds) and certain amounts in real estate providing annuities to finance an adequate lifestyle. In total, the Ximenes froze over 1.5 million cruzados in ordinaries (Boyajian 1993: 173f). Not without a note of malice, a Polish-Jewish historian wrote: "the rich [converts] colluded with the aristocracy and gilded with their wealth the faded coats of arms of the decrepit nobility" (Bałaban 1925: 220).[7]

What we have here, therefore, are almost model cases of New Christians participating in the commercial networks created by *La Nação,* but on the other hand already far removed from any links with Judaism. The example of another member of the Ximenes family, who at the beginning of the 17th century was Archdeacon of Braga Cathedral and author of an 'anti-rabbinical' text, shows just how far removed. It is also worth mentioning the case of the XN Gramaxo family of the late 16th and early 17th centuries, some of whose members in Europe and the New World sought to integrate into the Christian environment. Although the Gramaxo did not match the wealth or influence of the Ximenes, they held a prominent place among Iberian merchants thanks to their trade in slaves, textiles and pearls. Resident in Cartagena, Jorge Fernándes Gramaxo, according to Vila Vilar "the archetype of the American *negreiro*", obtained naturalisation and the right to reside legally in this strategically important Spanish port, held office and at the same time organised the illegal slave trade on a huge scale, unavailable to most New Christians. His accumulated capital enabled him to take over, without recourse to credit, legal and (more often) illegal slave transports. He confirmed his links with Catholicism by founding a Franciscan monastery in Cartagena. After his death, he was buried there in a Franciscan habit (Roitman 2009: 133, Vila Vilar 1979: 165–170, 1977, Restrepo 2011: 227–235). Another Portuguese slave trader Diogo da Veiga

---

7 Since an aristocratic title often became a commodity, the honour belonging to an aristocrat by birth required confirmation in a *limpieza de sangre* certificate. This created a wonderful field for abuse by *linajudos,* professional creators of 'proper' genealogies (Soria Mesa 2010).

(Spanish: Diego de Vega) would also achieve considerable success in the early 17th century, becoming a *vecino* (citizen) and politician in Buenos Aires.

The tendency expressed in the reduction of the number of New Christians was evident in the 16th century. According to the findings of Oliveira Marques, already quoted, if in the first half of the 16th century there were 60,000 New Christians in Portugal, in 1604 about 30,000 people (6,000 families) were considered New Christians. We also assume that this was not only a complex process, but also a long one – measured by generations. In some cases, however, this process, if supported – for various reasons – by local aristocrats, proceeded surprisingly quickly (Diago Hernando 2014). In brief, the religious identities of the New Christians of the 16th century cannot be treated as immutable. If at the beginning of the century the presence of crypto-Jews was still strongly marked, from the middle of the 16th century, after the departure of the generation that had first-hand knowledge of customs and sacred books, a substantial increase in the number of authentic Catholics must be assumed. From the mid-17th century, there is already a definite weakening of Portuguese *marranos and* New Christians (Gitlitz 2002: 36ff). Repression in Brazil and Portugal in the first half of the 18th century would complete the work of destruction.

It can also be suggested that the increased mobility and opportunities that emerged for New Christians due to the formation of the Iberian Union in 1581 were a strong incentive for ambivalent behaviour. The growing repression of the Inquisition was also not without influence; this was the other side of the coin of the new economic opportunities opening up. The long-term outcome of this process was as follows:

> When the Iberian Inquisitorial period came to an end and freedom of religion was introduced in Latin America after the wars of independence, former New Christians did not reemerge as Jews, Protestants, or marranists. Roman Catholicism remained the overwhelming locus of communal religious identity, whatever the genealogical composition of the inhabitants.
>
> DRESCHER 2001: 454f

At the same time, however, against their own will, for almost three centuries the New Christians did not, as a group, acquire the status of full members of the Catholic community. They were primarily the suspected and stigmatised descendants of Jews. Neither were the new Latin American states, which were gradually removing formal obstacles to equality, able to eradicate with a stroke of the pen the hostility entrenched in popular myths and Christian dogma. This was symbolised by two concepts that were important for the Catholic, as well as for the Lutheran perception of the Jews, which were closely inter-twined: the devil and the Jew (Trachtenberg 1943, Elkin 2014: 18–20). Coming to terms with this legacy took time. In Argentina, which opened its borders relatively early to foreigners, including Protestant Anglicans, tolerance was still understood to apply only to Christian churches in the mid-19th century. The formal parting with the legacy of the Inquisition and the de facto acceptance of Judaism occurred in 1860 (Lewin 1960: 100).

The attainment of a position in colonial society by the New Christians that ensured equal treatment was a matter of circumstance, not a rule related, for example, to wealth. Despite the role they played in Brazil's economy, from the early 17th century onwards, no one who had even a drop of Black or Jewish blood in their veins, or who was married to such a person, could be a member of the elite, charitable brotherhood of Santa Casa da Misericórdia in Bahia. This also applied to the Third Order (Tertiaries) of Franciscans, established in the 1630s, as well as to the less prestigious Secular Order of Carmelites. In individual cases involving influential New Christians, this restriction became the subject of discreet negotiations. These were aimed at making possible the miracle of the transformation of the New into the Old Christian according to orders' own interpretations of the meaning of "purity of blood" (Russell-Wood 1968: 135–138, 1992: V64, V88, Flory and Smith 1978: 586f). However, these were indeed exceptions. Imposed 'otherness' appears in this period as an immanent mark of the New Christians. For the priest who preached at the *auto da fé* in Coimbra in 1625, it was clear that the New Christians "are present in the church, [but] their thoughts are in the synagogue, they have Jesús on their lips, and the [Jewish] Messiah in their hearts" (quoted in Oliwa 2012: 80). The Inquisitors, on the other hand, believed in the guilt of the conversos, not in their conversion. None were isolated in this. Written in relation to the Bahia of the 17th century, Novinsky (1972: 162) noted that, treated by Catholics as a Jew, by Jews as a Catholic, the New Christian had little choice, so he remained "a New Christian by the grace of God", and so Catholic *sui generis*.

However, the rigidity of the gradation system and the exclusion associated with it emerged late in Brazil. In the case of Pernambuco

> The formal exclusion of New Christians from ecclesiastical offices and honourable institutions did not become widespread until the first decade of the seventeenth century. By that time, many New Christian families had already gained ecclesiastical offices, entered the military orders, and intermarried with Old Christian families.
>
> WADSWORTH 2007: 76

Changes for the worse occured gradually from the end of the 16th century. In 1591, the first *visitador* of the Inquisition began to operate for several years in Bahia and then in Pernambuco. However, the *Vista,* defined as a substitute for a permanent tribunal, was a suboptimal solution. For various reasons that are still unclear today, a permanent tribunal of the Inquisition was not established in Brazil. The steps taken in this regard in 1621–23 by Philip IV were unsuccessful (Marcocci and Paiva 2013: 220–222). It is possible that, the strong autonomy of local elites, especially in Rio de Janeiro and Pernambuco, also stood in the way. In the first capitaincy, the long reign of the Correira de Sá family (1574–1661) may have been an impediment to the establishment of an institution beyond family control (Lang 1979: 60f). Some historians (Novinsky 1998: 304, Lockhart and Schwartz 1983: 226) suggest that the establishment of the tribunal in Brazil may have been blocked by the king himself, appreciating the economic importance of Brazilian New Christians. Such an argument had appeared already in the early 18th century in Germany (Kohut 1896: 126). Let us further note that among those who opposed the idea of establishing a tribunal in Brazil was also, for unclear reasons, the Portuguese Grand Inquisitor. It cannot be ruled out that financial constraints played a major role in this case (Wadsworth 2007: 24).

At the same time, we find examples in the Iberian New World of non-compliance with rules that were discriminatory for *XN* s – without entering into doctrinal disputes. These reinforce the hypothesis about the key role played by the Inquisition in reinforcing anti-Jewish stereotypes and petrifying the status of *XN* s. This is emphasised by Marques (1976: 287f) when he writes that by "discriminating against [New Christians] and accusing them of Judaism, the Inquisition created a true ghetto and kept it alive, instead of extinguishing it. The integration of the New Christians was thus artificially stopped, and their caste maintained for two hundred years". In mentioning examples of non-compliance with discriminatory regulations, we have in mind the history of some of the merchant-New Christians in La Plata, mainly in Buenos Aires. Namely those who had settled permanently in this colony in the first half of the 17th century. They were the opposite of the *peruleiros*, mostly from Brazil temporarily residing in La Plata in transit to the Potosí mines. This group, however, should not be confused with the Spanish *peruleros* present at the same time in Peru.

But also in Buenos Aires, there were demands in the early 17th century for the establishment of a tribunal of the Inquisition, a topic well discussed by historians (Medina 1945, Gelman 1987: passim, Saguier 1985: 47f, 1985, Böhm 1998: 50–52, Lea 1922: 337f, Quiroga and Saporiti 2009). These were put forward by that part of the elite – the *beneméritos* – that came from among the descendants of the conquistadors who had conquered Paraguay and La Plata. This group was associated with local, mainly Paraguayan, livestock and agriculture. Due to the nature of the production and economic resources (large ownership and partly slave labour of the Indians), limited links with the market and little monetary turnover, one can speak of the dominance of the quasi-natural economy in the area. The core of the *beneméritos* was formed in Buenos Aires by a few dozen of the former *encomenderos* who came from Paraguay to refound the city in 1580. It was therefore a party hostile to the opening up to the world, and its supporters regarded as a threat the merchants (including the Portuguese), some of them smugglers and slave traders, and the creoles associated with them, present in Buenos Aires. The opponents were all those linked to the money economy and international trade, who defined themselves as *confederados*. This group would be led by the Spaniard Juan de Vergara, supported by the New Christian Diogo da Veiga. Clashes between the two factions intensified between 1610 and 1617. After the separation of La Plata from the Paraguayan *gobernación* in 1617 and the appointment of a new governor favouring the *confederados,* the council (*cabildo*) of the city came under the control of this faction (it also included two New Christians). As an Argentine historian noted, if the *cabildo* under the *beneméritos* could be called the *Junta de Encomenderos*, the victory of the *confederados* marked its transformation into the *Consulado de Comercio*.

However, the conflict with the 'Portuguese' merchants, who played an important role among the *confederados*, was to be presented primarily as a religious clash. It gave ideological coherence to the *beneméritos*, although the inter-group quarrels and bribery led to an alliance between some of its members and the *confederados*. In any case, to take up the fight against the "Portuguese New Christians, formerly Jews" was a matter of extreme urgency, claimed in a 1619 memorial to the king Manuel de Frias, one of the leaders of the losing *beneméritos*. At stake were the security of the colonies and the role of the 'Portuguese' in the economy: "they are extremely rich and powerful, very well versed in all kinds of goods and slaves". Furthermore, argued the former vice-governor of Santa Fé and Buenos Aires, the presence of these *personas ynfectas* also in Chile was poorly controlled by Lima's Inquisition, which reinforced the need for a tribunal in Buenos Aires. In parallel, the *Suprema* was also making efforts to establish a tribunal for La Plata (Medina 1945: 204–211).

An Inquisition tribunal was never established in Buenos Aires. The cost of such an endeavour seems to have been a foregone conclusion. Not only in the case of La Plata. Disputes with monarchs over the maintenance of confiscations *ex ante* (i.e. already at the start of an Inquisitorial investigation), rarely led to a positive financial outcome. However, this did not mean that the Holy Office was absent. The Inquisition also operated through *comissários* and authorised bishops. In Brazil, the first *comissário* started to operate apparently as early as 1579, although the first official appointment was delayed until 1611 (Lewin 1960: 29, 37–39, Wadsworth 2007: passim, Marcocci and Paiva 2013: 526). In contrast, the problem of the 'Portuguese' settled in Buenos Aires was solved in a different way, outside of Santo Officio and in fact against it, by "structural assimilation":

> a middleman minority, such as the Portuguese immigrants in early seventeenth century Buenos Aires, did learn the native language (Spanish), did invest in the land market, did marry local creole women, and did involve themselves in the local politics. Moreover, unlike the Portuguese in Vercruz, Cartagena, and Lima, the Portuguese migrants to Buenos Aires did not experience any kind of religious persecution. Given this economic and social mobility, we can understand why the Portuguese minority in seventeenth-century Buenos Aires was assimilated so rapidly.
>
> SAGUIER 1985a: 49, 1985b

Let us summarise. In the highly stratified, multicultural societies of the New World, the New Christian achieved a status belonging to the elite: he was a member of a white minority, and in the Spanish colonies – also outside the *sistema de castas*. Achieving such a position was a key element of New Christian self-identification. In the case of the poor, this was impossible; in La Plata, the New Christian pauper was often counted, as a dubious white, among the *castas* in the 17th century. Thus as whites, Jews "could not belong to the lower strata", as Jews, however, "they could not belong to the white apex" (Cohen 1991: 157). This specific variant of status incongruence was challenged by the asymmetrical relations of Jews and converts with non-Whites:

> Sephardic writers come across as full participants in the anti-Black discourse that had spread through much of Europe by the seventeenth century. Writing as outsiders (…), many Sephardic authors sense a need to distance themselves and their people from Blacks, this other Other.
>
> SCHORSCH 2005: 128

It is not surprising, therefore, that the regulations adopted in Suriname in 1711 stipulated that the punishment for the interracial sexual contact with white women ("unnatural whoring") was the death penalty for an African man, flogging and banishment for a white single women, while for a married woman also the branding. Two years later, these regulations were also applied to a Jewish woman and an Indian slave (Vink 2010: 221f).

Jews were not isolated in their attitudes and their actions were not simply a reaction to a discrimination and insecurity in contacts with the Catholic elite. The behaviour separating them from non-whites demonstrated the specific ways in which European values and norms appeared in the New World: a racial dichotomy. Skin colour enabled Jews and *XN*s to internalise such a division, while at the same time providing an argument that would eliminate even a chance of any kind of solidarity with non-whites. As in other racially divided societies, community of faith and universal values gave way before differences in melanin levels. Slave society was founded on a well-understood context: "once in the colony, Jewish settlers by definition became part of the community of white colonizers. Their white skin and free status set them apart from slaves, the free blacks, and the coloured people" (Vink 2010: 47, also Ben-Ur 2020: 14–17). Thus, when the issue of mulattoes professing Judaism (*mulatten yoden* or *couleurlingen*) came up in 18th-century Suriname, the Jewish community would find a special place for them in religious observance and institutions. Alongside the *jehidim*, white members of the community, there were racially mixed, restricted *congregantes*. As in 17th-century Amsterdam (Cohen 1991: Chapter 7, Hondius 2008: passim).

CHAPTER 5

The Iberian Atlantic: an Overview

The time of Braudel's "great Jewish merchants" from the late 16th to the mid-17th century was synchronous with the gradual decline of the Iberian system of expansion, The rise of Spain as a great power in the mid-16th century ran parallel not with the commercial expansion of (the nonexistent) Amsterdam Jews, but with the the the acivities of New Christians and conversos. The rapidly growing importance of silver mines in Potosi and Zacatecas was part of this process. In Portuguese America, this was when the first slave sugar plantations expanded to form a flourishing slave economy and society, "one of the most ambitious experiments in social engineering of the early modern era" (Osterhammel and Petersson 2005: 47). And the "Black Atlantic" ceased to be only an experiment, becoming transformed into the booming Middle Passage. The first slaves, brought not from Portugal or Spain (*esclavos ladinos*) but already directly from Africa, known in Spanish as *bozales* and in Portuguese as *boçais* ('muzzled', in the sense of 'savages'), would appear in the Caribbean in the second decade of the 16th century. They were seen by the settlers, in contrast to the *esclavos ladinos,* as inherently gentle. But it was they who would mutiny in December 1521 on Hispaniola, at a plantation owned by Cristóbal Columbus' son, the first organised rebellion in the New World by African slaves.

In the European economy, the 16th century was a period of fundamental yet diametrically opposed transformations.

Above all, Spain's growing importance in European politics since the end of the Reconquista was evident. American bullion fueled these developments. The involvement in European affairs went hand in hand with Madrid's attempt at empire building, embracing at first an insignificant Caribbean outpost and then, from 1519, a vast colonial area (see Map 1). At the same time, the smaller Portugal, in contrast to Spain marginally involved in Mediterranean politics (Morocco being the exception), expanded and strengthened its presence in West Africa that had begun as early as the 15th century; its ships and merchants then reached India, the Spice Islands and the Maldives and finally Japan. Brazil was formally a colony, but it was only from the late 1530s that Lisbon began to take a closer interest in it. The establishment of *La France Antarctique* in 1555 in the region of what later became Rio de Janeiro was a threat to Lisbon's interests. The expulsion in 1567 of the French, partly Huguenots, accelerated colonisation and the development of the plantation economy (Kula 1987: 17). Half a century later the French swept briefly to the north: between 1612 and 1615,

France Equinoxiale appeared in what is now Maranhão. The Atlantic became the Iberian *Mar Océano,* as underlined by title given to Columbus: *Almirante Mayor del Mar Océano.* This picture would be muddled from the turn of the 16th and 17th centuries by the aggressive entry of the Dutch.

MAP 1   Latin America in the first half of the 17th century
             SOURCE: AUTHOR

From the mid-16th century, Atlantic trade entered a phase of growth, feeding the Iberian metropolises with bullion, as well as a whole range of luxury goods belonging to the *rich trade*. However, by the 1630s, at least 80 per cent of imports from the New World to Spain was bullion. Between 1550 and 1629, the value of silver produced in Potosí was over 370 million pesos, while in Zacatecas it was 90 million. Gold production during this period was over 33 million pesos (Fisher 1997: 59, 97, Bakewell 2004: 188). As in the Late Middle Ages, long-distance trade was thus dominated by luxury goods. In the 16th century, it was Asian pepper, silk, diamonds and porcelain, as well as American gold and silver, and cocoa and cochineal, that kept the European expansion in motion. The distance measured in sailing days, the small tonnage of the ships and the enormous risks of the voyage, determined which goods could be profitably transported. Although it took less time to cross the Atlantic than a voyage to Asia (almost two years with return voyage), a round trip from Lisbon to Pernambuco with the necessary port stops could take up to a year (Russell-Wood 1993: 35). It has been noted, however, that a round trip from Gdańsk (Danzig) to Lisbon took as long as one from Lisbon to Brazil (Ebert 2008: 115). It was thus profitable to trade in goods of very high unit value, and both continents can be seen as depots for such goods during this period. In the same way, moreover, as Africa with its gold, ivory and *melegueta* pepper. The situation was different in the Baltic region, from where grain and timber for shipbuilding were imported, or in the North Sea, where herring fishing dominated. Trade in these commodities counted as strategically important *moedernegotie* in the northern Netherlands. Nor should we forget salt from Portugal, which was of strategic importance for Dutch fisheries. These hard-to-overestimate instances of *staple* (or *bulk*) *trade*, however, do not change the predominant profile of the emerging Atlantic trade. Moreover, it was the *rich trade*, not *moedernegotie*, that would become the most important factor explaining the rapid growth of Dutch commerce from the 1690s onwards (Israel 1995: 316f).

What changed as a result of entry into the Pacific and Atlantic was the expansion of trade in new luxury goods and radical changes in volume. The latter were made possible by the boom in the Iberian and Dutch shipbuilding and the gradual increase in ship tonnage. The diet of the European courts, aristocracy and wealthy merchants was thus enriched at this time by sugar and cocoa, while the production of fine textiles is facilitated by dye extracted from Brazilian wood (*pau-brasil*), cochineal and indigo carried from India. New patterns of consumption were also emerging, encouraging the development of new lines of production. This novel idea presented at the dawn of the 20th century by Werner Sombart would reappear decades later as an assertion that "the slave and sugar trade (along with the importation of other 'colonial' goods) was essential to European industrial development precisely because it stimulated and ultimately reshaped the entire pattern of Western consumer demand" (Austen and Smith 1992: 184). And bad habits were enriched by tobacco (originally called the 'sacred herb'). It was tobacco indeed that was to be the first of the new products to become an object of mass consumption in the second half of the 17th century. Already between 1622 and 1638 there had been a spectacular increase in tobacco imports into England, from £61,000 to £2 million per year (Nater 2006: 95, Brenner 2003: 113). And it was in England that the pamphlet, *A Counter-blaste to Tobacco,* aimed at this new addiction, would appear as early as 1604. Its author, King James I, criticised the taking over of the "barbarous and beastly manners of the wild, godless and slavish Indians" (Blackburn 2010: 149). Sugar, on the other hand, would remain a luxury commodity until the 18th century.

Due, among other things, to the dramatic increase in the scale of production, however, this traditional structure of exchange led to revolutionary developments in one sphere: the declining phase of the Iberian system of expansion coincides with the rapid growth of the slave trade. Above all, slavery became the crucial factor linking the demand for luxury goods, the production of commodities of increasingly popular consumption (such as tobacco and then sugar) and gradually also raw materials (such as cotton). Given the almost symbiotic relationship between sugar and slavery, an eminent historian notes: "it is hard to argue that the benefit to European diets was worth the investment in lives and treasure that it finally cost" (Curtin 1990: 206). See Chapters 9 and 10 for more on this topic.

As a consequence of Iberian expansion, new economic institutions were gradually taking shape in Latin America itself, enabling the control of resources, especially labour. The early colonial *encomienda* and *repartimiento* (in New Spain) and the *mita* (taken over from the Incas and then, through the rejection in practice of *reciprocidad,* deformed), from the end of the 16th century began to give way to other forms of control over land and Indians. The huge disparity between the small number of European immigrants and the Indian population – despite their decimation – was accompanied by a growing labour deficit. Europeans, even the poor, did not migrate overseas in search of just any work, but of opportunities to get rich quick.

The increasing demand for Indian labour, as white settlement progressed and production increased, and the continuing demographic catastrophe, forced changes in labour relations, though not always their improvement. Positive changes were noticeable in silver mining. In Potosí, from as early as the 1570s, many Indians forced into mines as low-paid *mitayos* also worked during their rest time as better-paid contract labourers (*mingas*). By 1600, half of the miners were already the more productive *mingas*. This was especially true for Indians with sought-after skills. The situation of the unskilled *mitayos* deteriorated. A much more rapid transition to contract labour occurred in the silver mines of northern Zacatecas, Mexico (Bakewell 1988: 19, 165f, Semo 1973: 145f). These changes were also accompanied by the elimination of African slaves from mining. In agriculture and livestock farming, that is the main spheres of production of colonial economies, the direction of change was no longer so favourable, although the move away from *repartimiento*, a system of disposing of labour resources that encouraged over-exploitation and waste, was an advance. Key to this were the labour relations shaped within the framework of Spanish large-scale property, the haciendas, also to some extent the livestock *estancias*. Above all, the owners of the haciendas sought to limit labour mobility. Peonage (labour for debt), widespread under various local names, was emerging on a wider scale. In Peru, Bolivia and Ecuador *yanaconaje* was gaining in importance (Mörner 1975: 31–35). From the end of the 16th century, however, it no longer had much in common with the Inca institution and social group of the *yana*. In practice, *yanaconaje* became a variant of peonage and even outright serfdom.

In particular, the populating of *Terra da Santa Cruz*, later named Brazil, took place initially at a slow pace. Unlike India and the Asian archipelagos, ventures involving the Crown, aristocracy and wealthy merchants, it was not a particularly attractive territory, rather a place for the persecuted or those seeking the chance to improve their status. It will be described later as 'paradise on earth' (especially by Jesuits and New Christians), sometimes as 'eternal hell'. However, positive views prevailed (Schwartz 1989: 25, Costigan 2010). Although *feitorias* scattered in Africa and Asia were also not settler colonies, they were nevertheless valuable. In Goa, the most densely populated colony, the number of Portuguese was estimated at 2,500 in 1524, and by 1540 the population of European origin (including from mixed unions) had risen to around 10,000. Whites on the west coast of Africa could be counted in the hundreds in the 16th and early 17th centuries. In Angola in 1621 there were 400 Portuguese and in 1660 just under 3,302. In the Cape Verde, which had been previously colonised, the presence of more than 1,600 whites was recorded in 1582, while on São Tomé in 1620–21 it was 800 (Russell-Wood 1993: 6of, Silva 2011a: 124, 125).[1]

Brazil at this time was not regarded as a particularly valuable territory. In the mid-16th century, there were probably no more than 15,000 white emigrants

---

1   No more than a few hundred Portuguese officers and soldiers participated in the battles in Ndongo (Angola) at the turn of the 16th and 17th centuries, supported, however, by thousands of African warriors (*guerra preta* or *quimbares*).

living here, although this estimate seems to be greatly inflated. The presence of 9,405 white settlers and 1,640 African slaves is mentioned, more realistically, in relation to 1546, while the sometimes quoted figure of 3,000–4,000 may refer to an earlier period, the mid-1530s. After a few decades, in 1584, the number of whites reached 25,000, increasing in the mid-17th century to around 50,000 (Marcilio1984: 45, Augeron and Vidal 2007: 35, Russell-Wood 1993: 61). In this early phase of its presence in Brazil, the Portuguese metropolis sought to replicate the model of commercial empire already tried and tested in Africa and Asia. Only the transfer from Madeira of sugarcane cultivation and probably from São Tomé of the know-how indispensable for the organisation of modern slave plantations would radically change the situation. This also involved a weakening of the royal monopoly and enabled individual investors to take greater initiative – through the granted *sesmarias*. The transformation of Brazil into a settler colony was also taking place. But this too would take time. The acceleration of the colony's demographic growth in the last two decades of the 16th century, however, was evident, as was the increasing migration from the metropolis (its peak, however, would be in the 18th century).

Along with sugar, Black slaves would appear – with considerable delay – in Brazil, completing the already initiated importation of Africans to Spanish America. Compared to New Spain or the Viceroyalty of Peru, where 45,000 slaves arrived, they were still few in number; by 1580, only 13,000 had reached the entire territory of then known Brazil. Planters continued to experiment with the Indian labour available locally (often de facto slaves). This was all the more so because the Indian slave was considerably cheaper during this period. Counting by sugar equivalent, in 1574 an African cost 357 kg, while an Indian cost 143 kg. According to other, similar, estimates, a Black slave was three times as expensive during this period (Eltis 2000: 9, Barrett and Schwartz 1975: 544).

A boom in the importation of African slaves would begin in the following decades and by the 1630s they too would become the main labour resource for the plantations. Important factors favouring this change were rising sugar prices, prompting increased production and the opening up of Angola's vast human resources from the 1570s. If in the decade 1561–70 Angolan slaves accounted for 13.28 per cent of all those transported from Africa, in the decade 1581–80 this share rose to 54.85 per cent (Eltis and Richardson 2008: table 1.7). From the planters' point of view, the availability of African slaves coming from highly developed cultures of sedentary agriculture and handicrafts, more readily adapting to the demanding regularity of plantation agriculture, was particularly beneficial. The resistance of the Indians, the smallpox epidemics decimating them in the 1560s, especially in the sugar economy area and the prohibition of their slavery introduced by King Sebastian in 1570 (renewed under the Iberian Union) all helped to reinforce this new trend (Klein 1986: 41f, Pons 1985: 250). Indian slavery, however, did not disappear overnight. It was not only a complex but also a turbulent process. An attempt to enforce a royal ban in the early 17th century caused riots in Bahia; white Rio de Janeiro was also on the brink of revolt. And *bandeirantes* experienced in the capture of Indian slaves, who hailed mainly from the region of Santos and São Paulo (then the capitaincy of São Vicente), would appear in greater numbers in the first half of the 17th century (Schwartz 1968: 40f).[2] In any case, in the description of the *engenho* Sergipe, one of the largest at the time, belonging de facto to the governor Mem de Sá, we find that Indians constituted – not only in the early 1570s but still in 1591 – the majority of the workforce (out of 147 slaves, only 23 were Black or mulatto). By contrast, the 1635 description of Sergipe no longer mentions Indian slaves (Barrett and Schwartz 1975: 544).

And the protective umbrella over the emerging Atlantic system was extended by the ships of both Iberian states, albeit to an unequal degree. The monopoly of trade guarded by the Spanish armada and the voyages of Portuguese merchants were only disrupted during this period by English and French privateers as well as by the seekers of El Dorado. Sometimes they inflicted painful blows, such as during Francis Drake's raid on the west coast of Latin America (1578) or by attacking Cadiz twice (1587, 1596), the second centre of trade with the New World after Seville. However, the Spanish system of protected convoys (*Flota de Indias*) introduced in 1543 worked well on the Atlantic route (*Carrera de Indias*). In turn, to prevent a repeat of the raid carried out by Drake, in 1581, the Spaniards embarked on an extremely ambitious project to fortify the Straits of Magellan. This would end in complete failure. A few years later the ships of another English corsair, Thomas Cavendish, forced their entry into the Pacific amidst a blockade. The Portuguese, on the other hand, were not following in the footsteps of the Spanish. As a rule, their ships sailed the Atlantic without special protection, although the sugar they transported was already becoming a prized booty in the second half of the 16th century. Attempts to establish monopolistic trading companies on the Spanish model also failed. Originally

---

2 Among the *bandeirantes* were also some New Christians. These included the famous Antônio Raposo Tavares, who took several thousand Indians captive in 1628 and removed the Spaniards (including the Jesuits) from much of the southern territory of present-day Brazil. His expedition of some 900 whites and *mamelucos* (supported by more than 2,000 Indians), included more than 50 New Christians. The ferocity with which this *bandeirante* fought the Spanish Jesuits was probably also due to the memory of the persecution suffered by his family in Portugal. His stepmother who raised him was accused of being a Judaiser and spent six years in prison. Raposo Tavares' mother was also an XN (Bogaciovas 2006: 120–122, Salvador 1976: 145f.).

designed back in 1619 with the Atlantic trade in mind and only established in 1628, the *Companhia de Navegação e Comércio da India* failed to play a serious role and was abolished in 1633 (Oliveira 2001). Only after suffering huge losses at the hands of the Dutch following the expiry of the truce in 1621 did the king of Portugal in 1649 reach for the system of monopolistic companies and protected convoys, tried and tested by the Spaniards, but costly for merchants and planters.

This is one side of the developments, demonstrating the dynamic and successful process of establishing overseas empires as an administrative structure, a system of transoceanic trade and the exploitation of available resources. The other is the not so spectacular (but with consequences that are difficult to overestimate) shifting the centre of economic gravity in Europe. This was a protracted process, lasting more than a century. The Mediterranean economies and Levantine trade were still seen as crucial in the second half of the 16th century and the profits made in trade with the East were the solid foundations of the fortunes made by Italian and Spanish merchants, not forgetting Antwerp. From the end of the 16th century, the new English trading companies, the Levant Company and the East India Company, increasingly interested in direct imports from the East, joined the game vigorously in the area. In terms of their composition and modes of operation, however, they did not represent a breakthrough in English merchant practice; rather, they were continuations of the traditional elite company of Merchant Adventurers. The new model of the English merchant and investor (also a planter) would emerge in the first half of the 17th century in North America and the Caribbean (Brenner 2003).

During the same period, the Dutch also forcefully entered the Levant trade. The number of Dutch ships operating in the Mediterranean increased from four to 400 between 1590–94 (the extent of this increase, however, is debated). Dutch merchants did not operate alone, cooperating with both Jewish and/or crypto-Jewish *levantini* in Italy and New Christians in Antwerp, Lisbon and Seville. Their activities were also supported by the Flemish residing both in the Republic and in Spain and the Mediterranean. This was facilitated by the fact that the Dutch turn to the Mediterranean was probably in part caused by Flemish emigrants arriving in the Republic from the Spanish Netherlands, already experienced in trade in the Mediterranean. Above all, however, together with the New Christians, the Dutch provided a supply of grain from the North, mainly from the Baltic region, in years of crop failure. They also did not shy away from corsairing and at the same time were increasingly flexible when it came to the commodity structure of their trade. Already in the first decade of the 17th century, they gradually moved away from an almost exclusive concentration on trade in grain, wood and herring to become suppliers of more refined and valuable products (pepper and other spices, dyes, as well as munitions) (Israel 1989: 97–100, Engels 1997: 47f).

For the Netherlands, a fast-growing maritime and commercial power, gaining a strong foothold in the Mediterranean was part of a policy to diversify its existing overseas trade. Another important direction was the growing Atlantic trade, especially with West Africa (gold and ivory were imported, but not yet slaves), Brazil, the Caribbean and the coast of New Granada. The gradual closure, after the establishment of the Iberian Union in 1581, of the ports of Portugal to Dutch and other foreign merchants (especially from the late 1590s), and therefore also the obstruction of access, even indirectly, to Latin American markets, only accelerated this process. And a matter of paramount importance, therefore, was integration of expansion in the Mediterranean and the growing interest in the Atlantic into the commercial and military offensive in Asia against the Portuguese. The creation in 1602 of the East India Company (VOC) was a decisive step, as it would turn out, in the struggle for direct access to the riches of India and other Asian territories. The hitherto indirect access, through Portuguese ports, would be made much more difficult by the late 1590s. This already posed a threat to the interests of Dutch merchants. It can also partly explain the fact that already in the period 1595–1601, luxury goods were transported from Asia by 65 Dutch ships. In the period 1601/2 -1620, on the other hand, 137 ships left Lisbon for Asia and 56 returned. During this period, the VOC sent 193 ships (but with less tonnage), 90 returned (Veen 2000: annexes 3.1 a and c, and 8.1). It can be assumed that, even in the absence of a threat from Portugal and Spain to the Dutch trade in Asian goods conducted via Lisbon or Antwerp, Amsterdam merchants would have challenged the two powers one way or another. The prospect of huge profits was too tempting (Parthesius 2010: 34, Israel 1995: 321).

Wondering why it was the Netherlands and not England at the end of the 16th and first half of the 17th century that showed more activity in overseas trade simultaneously in several parts of the globe, especially in the Atlantic, Braudel writes:

> Holland, by her proximity to the Catholic provinces of the Netherlands and by her penistence in forcing the coffers of Spain, had better access than England to the Peninsula and the American treasure upon which her commerce depended. For without the pieces of eight patiently extracted from Spain, Dutch shipping could not have sailed the seven seas.
>
> BRAUDEL 1995: 635

Let us merely note at this point that these "American treasures", like luxury goods from Asia, did not so much create Dutch commercial power as give an impetus to the trade of the United Provinces with the Iberian Peninsula from the end of the 16th century that can hardly be overestimated. Indeed, this trade was already firmly established from the end of the 15th century in the exchange of grain and timber from the Baltic region and Dutch manufacturing (woollen goods and ships) for Portuguese salt. By the end of the 16th century, the Netherlands' main competitor in this strategically important trade, the Hanseatic League, had been defeated. It should also be borne in mind that it was exchange within Europe that determined the commercial power of the Republic in the 16th-17th centuries (Ebert 2003: 52f, 2003).

In contrast, from the second half of the 17th century onwards, the situation of the Dutch would change dramatically, when English merchants in the Atlantic, backed by naval power and state subsidies, would begin to push them more and more effectively into the background. This was, however, a long-term process. The opening of Spanish ports to Dutch ships from the mid-17th century strengthened the merchants of the United Provinces in particular: "By 1650, every Spanish port from San Sebastián to Barcelona, then still in rebellion, was filled with Dutch shipping almost to the exclusion of any other, much of it being chartered, and in some cases owned, by Dutch Jews". The same took place in Portugal: "In the three years 1643–1645, Dutch ships accounted for over half the total of non-Portuguese vessels entering the port of Lisbon" (Israel 1990a: 407, 1996: 152). On the other hand, the increasingly close cooperation at this time between Portugal and England limited the room for manoeuvre of Dutch merchants. The result of the four Anglo-Dutch naval wars fought from 1652 would be to break the power of the Republic in the early 18th century. At the same time, English trade would become one of the important elements of the industrial revolution from the mid-18th century. This was a unique phenomenon: Dutch or French trade had never played such a revolutionary role. According to a Dutch historian's figurative phrase, in contrast to England, the economic history of these countries is "a killing field for anyone who wanted to combine industrialisation with overseas trade" (Emmer 2006b: 164).

Symptoms of twilight therefore appeared in the second half of the 16th century, and the weakening of Spain's position in the Mediterranean was an important, but not the only, sign of this.

However, before the final transfer of the dynamic centre of the European economy from the Mediterranean to Northern Europe and the Atlantic became evident, Antwerp first emerged as the new centre of European trade and finance (including the distribution of Asian pepper and silver from Peru and Mexico). New Christians were also active here, albeit internally divided between those in favour of integration into the Christian world (by far the majority) and the (few) crypto-Jews. The next step leads first to Hamburg and other German cities and then to the future (from 1579) rebellious United Provinces, where Amsterdam gradually takes over the role of Antwerp. On a smaller scale, the role of such a centre was played by southern France and England at this time.

The time for the latter had not yet arrived despite the smashing of the *Grande y Felicisima Armada* by the ships of Elizabeth I in 1588. Beaten in a single battle, the Spanish fleet still reigned supreme in the Atlantic and it was Madrid (from 1581, together with Lisbon) that continued to control the most important routes until at least the second half of the 17th century. Even in the following century, the deterrent power of the Spanish fleet was quite considerable, especially when assisted – not gratuitously – by the French fleet. Losses in silver shipments from the New World were more a consequence of storms and errors in navigation than of the effectiveness of attacks by the English or the Dutch. Only three times did silver transported in convoy fall prey to Spain's competitors. The first time was in 1628 by the Dutch admiral Piet Hein in the service of the WIC, who seized silver, gold and other goods with a huge value of more than 11.5 million guilders (almost 2.5 times the VOC's gross annual revenue) in Matanzas Bay near Havana. Further, less successful, attacks took place in 1657 and 1702 – not many during over 200 years of silver and gold shipments in armed convoys. This indeed proved the high efficiency of the Spanish protection system developed in the 1560s by the fleet commander Pedro Menéndez de Avilés (Walton 1994: 188–190, Ebert 2008: 174).

If one judges by the number of ships leaving Seville for the New World, Spanish trade with the colonies was entering a boom phase in the late 16th and early 17th centuries. From the 1570s, trade with the American colonies grew steadily and in the record-breaking year of 1608, more than 200 ships sailed from Seville to the Atlantic, compared to an average of 130 in the last decade of the 16th century or only 60–70 in the 1670s. The increase in volume was even greater due to the arrival of ships of greater tonnage and capacity. At the same time, the production of silver in the Viceroyalty of Peru and New Spain increased rapidly thanks to technical innovations, reaching a maximum in the first quarter of the 17th century (Fisher 1997: 57f). Sugar production in Brazil also increased by leaps and bounds from the mid-16th century.

However, these were symptoms not so much of the vitality of the Spanish metropolis as of a disease that had been gradually growing for some time. The foundations on which the Spanish empire of Philip II's time rested were not strong, and the wars fought, even the victorious ones, were draining Spain's human and material resources. The structural crisis of the Spanish economy and society would become evident in the mid-17th century. The epidemics of 1595–1602 and 1647–1652 and the associated demographic losses weakened the country's economic potential. During the plague epidemic of 1649, Seville lost, compared to 1597, more than half its population. By the end of the 17th century, the number of Spaniards was already 20 per cent less than a century earlier. Almost constant wars from the 1560s to the late 1650s led the kingdom – after a series of bankruptcies under Philip II and complicated negotiations to restructure and eliminate part of its debt – to financial collapse. Spain's debt rose from 36 million ducats in the 1550s to 85 million by the end of the century and to 180 million ducats in 1667 (Findlay and O'Rourke 2007: 185, Davis 1973: Chapter 9).

In the first half of the 17th century, this growing crisis in the state's finances would contribute to a fundamental weakening of the Crown's previous main lenders, first the Fuggers and then the Genoese banks. At the same time, this opened the way more widely for merchants and merchant credit from Northern Europe. During the financial collapse of 1626, the importance of an informal consortium of Portuguese New Christians, some already settled for years in Madrid and Seville, also became apparent. The names of Duarte Fernandes, Nuno Dias Mendes de Brito, Manuel de Paz, Simão Soares or João Nunes Saravia would appear in the following decades – although not always in the same composition – at important moments for Spain and Portugal related to economic decisions. Their offer of a substantial loan in exchange for *asiento* contracts was accepted by Philip IV after negotiations. It was also part of the Crown's broader strategy seeking to weaken the dominant position of the Genoese. This intention was realised: whereas in 1621–26 the Genoese share of loans to the royal treasury was 73 per cent, in 1627–39 it was reduced to 44 per cent; in turn, the share of the 'Portuguese', previously zero, reached 27 per cent in the second period (Boyajian 1993: 211–213, Álvarez Nogal 2003: 25f, 1997: 23, 27). This was not, however, a sustainable trend. The thesis that Portuguese bankers of Jewish origin played a decisive role in the provision of capital until the end of the century (Kamen 2003: 422) is therefore untenable. In fact, after the break-up of the Iberian Union in 1640, the Portuguese share steadily declined over the next quarter of a century (6 per cent in 1665).

As the financial problems increased, a reduction in competitiveness and a collapse of the Basque shipbuilding industry (to the benefit of shipyards in the Netherlands and the colonies, mainly in Havana and Guayaquil), the iron and other metals industries (in favour of Sweden) and in the main non-agricultural sector, the textile industry, was also evident. An important factor in these processes was the gradual elimination of Spanish producers from their markets, as well as a reduction in demand for Spanish ships. Producers from the Spanish

Netherlands, the Republic and England making finished products (mostly luxury goods) from Spanish wool would take over – legally and illegally – a part of the market of Spain, Portugal and the colonies (Davis 1973: Chapter 9, Elliott 2006: 109–111, Wallerstein 1974: Chapter 4). From the last quarter of the 16th century, the Spaniards ceased not only to act as an effective "guardian of the Mediterranean" against the expansion of merchants from England and the Republic (the advance of the Ottoman Empire was stopped at Lepanto in 1571), but also failed to defend Seville against its competitors:

> Abandoned by Genoese capitalism, the export trade from Seville found other sponsors. Firms in the Netherlands (...)were to advance their own goods and to wait for payment until the Indies fleets returned with silver. In other words, the merchants of Seville now became merely commission agents: they saw goods pass through and took their percentage (...). From now on, their capital was to go into buying land and villages, *juros*, or settling entails. (...). In this way Seville was conquered, eaten away from the inside by the obscure gnawing of termites, and all to the advantage of Holland.
>
> BRAUDEL 1995: 638

This description appeals to the imagination. Certainly, from the end of the 16th century Atlantic trade was no longer a monopoly of the Iberian states, rather a "shared monopoly", and the Atlantic a European sea (Vila Vilar 2005: 296). Also, the 'price revolution' in Europe, already initiated in the second decade of the 16th century and lasting until the middle of the 17th century, entered a new phase: after 1560 reinforced by the rapidly increasing influx of bullion from the New World (Munro 2008). It was, at the same time, one of the key mechanisms for the reallocation of financial resources across Europe, as well as for widening the gap between the Iberian Peninsula and the northern part of the continent. This is well reflected in a saying by a Spanish jurist and theologian in 1600: "if there is a shortage of gold and silver coin in Spain, it is because they are here; the reason for her misery is her wealth" (quoted in Wallerstein 1974: 195). Spanish silver *reales de a ocho* (a coin of 8 reales containing 20.3–25.5 grams of silver), also known as pesos or piastres, Portuguese gold cruzados and later silver and gold escudos attested to both the wealth of the colonies and the crisis of the metropolis, ending up one way or another in Antwerp, Amsterdam, Hamburg or the Italian cities. A similar mechanism would emerge in Portugal's relations with Britain following the discovery of gold deposits in Brazil's Minas Gerais at the end of the 17th century. Briefly, 'The facade of the [Spanish] mercantilist monopoly survived in all its splendour, but its structure was weakened' (Fisher 1997: 58). Large-scale contraband only exacerbated these tendencies.

The next step was an attempt by the Netherlands to reject the intermediation of Seville and Lisbon, and take up the Atlantic game on its own. By choice, but also by necessity after the experience of the increasingly effective blockade from the 1590 to 1609 (with brief interruptions) of access for Dutch ships to Iberian and New World ports. First, in the late 16th and early 17th centuries, the Republic challenged Portuguese power in Asia when the VOC was established in 1601. However, by 1609, i.e. the Truce Agreement, this commercial and military offensive did not yet produce a decisive settlement, although the strengthening of the Dutch merchants' position in Asian trade was already becoming apparent. It was only a matter of time before they would achieve hegemony. The confrontation in the Atlantic, on the other hand, was generally peaceful until 1621, even though the Dutch (but also English and French) corsairs waged an unspeakable war against the Portuguese and Spanish. On the approach to the ports of southern Europe, on the other hand, such war was also waged by *moriscos* expelled from Spain after the crushing of the uprising, and Berber pirates. As in the Mediterranean at the end of the 16th century, in the Atlantic too the Dutch appeared in the period leading up to the signing of the 1609 truce with Spain and Portugal "like so many heavy insects crashing against the windowpanes – for their entry was neither gentle nor discreet" (Braudel 1995: 634). Indeed, many Spanish and Portuguese windowpanes were broken, but the essential goal of creating in the Atlantic – through legal and illegal trade rather than settlement and colonies – an alternative to the Iberian empires, was not achieved. In the rapidly expanding trade with Brazil, the merchants of the Republic had to recognise, during the truce (until 1621), the dominance of the Portuguese on the Atlantic route; this was expressed, among other things, in the maintenance of the near-monopoly position of Portuguese ports in the Brazilian Atlantic commerce.

This clash, which was peaceful until 1621, highlighted in passing, as it were, the importance of the New Christian merchants, especially in the Brazilian sugar and timber trade and in the increasingly important African slave trade. The twelve-year ceasefire in the wars with the Iberian powers made it easier for the Dutch, including Amsterdam's Jews, to establish, by necessity rather than choice, a system of indirect access to the resources of the Spanish and Portuguese New World. Direct access to the colonies was still formally closed to them, hence the growing importance of co-operation with the trade networks established by the Portuguese New Christians. For these, firmly entrenched in the trade of the colonies and metropolises, sought on the one hand to preserve their cooperation with the Netherlands (an important, even strategic partner in European trade) and on the other, facilitated the expansion of the reach and scale of the United Provinces' merchants in the Atlantic. All the more so since Portuguese activity in the area was not constrained by the rigid regulations that characterised the activities of the Spaniards. This more flexible and partly competitive system favoured the Dutch and Amsterdam Jews, even if they were forced to transact business under a foreign flag, share profits or act as 'junior partners' of the Portuguese New Christians (see Chapter 8).

A break with the policy of peaceful confrontation in the Atlantic would occur after 1621. In Africa, Brazil and the Caribbean, the armed promoter of Dutch trade, the West India Company, would confront the Iberian powers. The implementation of the long-postponed decision of the States-General (*Staten Generaal*) to create the WIC would initiate a change in the methods of Atlantic trade and thus also affect the role of the New Christians in the area. At the same time, this was a controversial decision, if one considers the exponential growth of Dutch trade in the Atlantic by 1621, also in comparison to trade with Asia and the Mediterranean. Earlier, widely accepted estimates showed a substantial advantage of trade with Asia over Atlantic trade (a 2:1 ratio) (Emmer 2006: 163). According to new findings presented by the Dutch historian:

> In 1611, the Mediterranean merchants estimated the value of their trade at 4 million florins, which equaled that of the VOC trade with Asia. Before 1620, income from the Asian trade was between three to four million guilders. (...) the returns of the Dutch commerce in the Atlantic region totaled between 4 and 7.5 million florins per year.
>
> ENTHOVEN 2003b: 46f

This was only the beginning. In 1636, already in the new situation created by the WIC's control of northeastern Brazil and over sugar exports from Pernambuco, the value of imports from the Atlantic area to the Republic rose to 17.5 million florins (more than 31 per cent of all imports to the United Provinces). In the same year, the value of imports supplied by the VOC from Asia amounted to 8 million florins. However, such a high share of the Atlantic area in Dutch trade could not be maintained in the second half of the 17th century. If in the boom phase this trade involved 200–250 ships per year, by 1700 it was already only 100 (Enthoven 2003a: 437, 439).

But it was not only the Dutch who were active in weakening the Iberian Atlantic. After the boom in Spanish shipping in 1608, the following decades saw a sharp reduction in the number of merchant ships sailing in convoys on the *Carrera de Indias*: 125 in 1618 and only 72 in 1628 (Studnicki-Gizbert 2007: 91). Not only foreign goods, but also foreign flags increasingly appeared in New World ports. Despite repeated prohibitions. Ships leased by Dutch and Amsterdam Jews reached the New World and Portuguese ports legally or illegally under the flags of Portugal, Hamburg or Emden. Cut off from Portuguese salt in Europe, the Dutch acquired this strategically important commodity, like tobacco, for a time in the Spanish Caribbean, above all on the coast of present-day Venezuela.

Moreover, in the areas peripheral to the *Carrera de Indias,* the role of contraband was even more accentuated and difficult to overestimate. The economic importance of La Plata from the end of the 16th century was determined primarily by the role it played in the illicit trade linking the Atlantic economic area with the Andean silver mines. This was primarily the trade between the largest *audiencia* of Charcas (present-day Bolivia, part of Paraguay and La Plata) and southern Brazil. Much of the smuggling also went through the commercial centres of Cartagena, Acapulco, Veracruz, Puerto Belo and the ports of the Caribbean. Slave ships in particular were a useful instrument for contraband on a large scale: alongside undeclared surplus slaves, undeclared English and Dutch goods were also imported under various pretexts. In order to stop this illegal trade, the Spanish Crown sometimes took downright desperate measures. In 1602, this led to the depopulation of a part of Hispaniola, which had often been haunted by Dutch ships. Settlers' homes were burnt down, and people and cattle dispersed. In 1605, on the other hand, Spanish galleons defeated Dutch smugglers off the coast of what is now Venezuela and, at the same time, to punish settlers who were not very willing to obey the law, the Crown imposed a 10-year ban on tobacco cultivation (Sluiter 1948, Israel 1990a: 200f). Acapulco, in turn, was the centre of both legal and illegal trade with Asia. The scale of the latter reached, depending on the estimate, between 10 and 50 per cent of official transactions (Hoberman 1977: 492).

Meanwhile, in colonial Latin America, the process of formation and solidification of local elites, already increasingly Creole, was accelerating. The Spanish Crown may have countered (only partially successfully) the feudalisation of the New World in the first decades of colonisation and taken measures to weaken the influence of an elite group of some 600 *encomenderos* in New Spain and 500 in the Viceroyalty of Peru, but it could not inhibit the development of local elites of land, mining and trade at all (Elliott 2006: 40, Simpson 1982). The mentality and behaviour of the *encomenderos* and then the *hacendados* can also be seen as a formative factor in the new elite's sense of its own distinctiveness. In its absence, "the Indies would have remained a very subordinate, colonial society in both social and psychological terms" (Mörner 2002: 64). Similarly, in Portuguese Brazil, although here the birth of the new elite proceeded without dramatic upheaval and conflict with the metropolis, as occurred in the mid-16th century in the Spanish New World (especially in Peru), namely the violent resistance that the *encomenderos* put up after Emperor Charles v promulgated the *Leyes Nuevas* targeting them in 1542. A greater threat was posed to the Portuguese colony until the 1560s by French attempts to penetrate the Brazilian coast and Indian attacks on the still few Portuguese settlements, than by divisions between the Crown and the emerging local elites.

It was also not insignificant that the autonomy of the Portuguese aristocracy and the Cortes was much reduced in favour of the Crown back in the late 15th century. This also had consequences in Brazil. The control of the metropolis was strongly emphasised, which was also reflected in the titularity: after the discouraging experiment with the *donatarios,* Brazil was governed from 1549 by governors rather than viceroyalties, as in the Spanish New World and the Portuguese East (Mauro 1987: 45, Marques 1976: 365). The first viceroy would appear in Brazil briefly in 1640–1641 and then in 1720, combining this formal title with the admittedly important post of governor of Bahia. However, this did not imply far-reaching centralisation. The time of the Iberian Union changed nothing in this respect. In practice, the Brazilian colony was a collaborative effort between the 'king-merchant', *donatarios*, governors and other senior officials, merchants and planters, an endeavour that provided the local elite with a considerable margin of freedom: "there was no equivalent in Spanish America to São Paulo, a city that expelled [in 1640] Jesuits on its own authority.. Colonial administration in Brazil was but a shadow of its Spanish neighbor" (Lang 1979: 71,73, also Cardim 2004). Nota bene, although the reason for the removal of the Jesuits was their conflict with the São Paulo council, which defended – also against the metropolis – the practice of enslavement of Indians, at the same time the Jesuits of Paraguay, threatened by the *paulistas,* often referred to them as "Jewish bandits" (Boxer 1962: 33). However, the presence of the New Christians in São Paulo and their influence on the formation of the identity of the *paulistas* was often mythologised. A reflection of this myth was also the suggestion of the dominance of New Christian ancestors in the *quatrocentana* group (families with four centuries of ties to São Paulo) (critically, Falbel 1999, Bogaciovas 2006). And finally, the autonomy of the local authorities was also strengthened by passing on to them, out of necessity rather than choice, expenses associated with defence and the construction of fortifications. On the other hand, in this dynamic game between the metropolis and local authorities at the time of the Iberian Union, it was the metropolis that gained the upper hand in the north, reserving for itself – after the expulsion of the French – direct control over Maranhão and Grão Para. The dominance of the metropolis in intellectual life was also conspicuous. Brazil did not live to see a university in colonial times and the first printing press of its own did not appear in Rio de Janeiro until 1808 (in Ciudad de México it was in 1538) (Schwartz 1989: passim).

The problem, however, was how to embed the profession of merchant, especially those active in overseas trade, as well as other economic activities related to settlement, into the hierarchies of prestige in corporatist Iberian societies. As in other feudal and late feudal societies, the status of the merchant was regarded as unattractive in Portugal and Spain (Sampaio 2014). Indeed, tradition placed them below the useful yet low-rated seven 'mechnical' professions (peasants, hunters, soldiers, sailors, surgeons, weavers and blacksmiths). The exceptions were the *homens de negócios* (their elite were *mercadores-banqueiros*) who controlled overseas trade and, from the late 16th century, participated as lenders and contractors in the important royal *asientos* (also New Christians would be among the *asentistas*). The presence of members of aristocratic families in the elite group of *homens de negócios* was not surprising. However, Portuguese aristocrats did not regard the fact of descending to the level of a rich merchant and assuming his role as disgraceful. The latter, on the other hand, reached for nobility and *hábitos* of religious military orders at some point and saw this as confirmation of the position they had achieved. This was one of the main routes to social advancement within a social order they accepted based on corporate-state loyalties (Marques 1976: 180f, Sánchez 2015).

They were not reformers seeking to change established hierarchies. They were thinking of accommodation, not revolution. But even these limited aspirations of a small group nevertheless caused tensions in the metropolises. In societies still strongly bound to feudal systems of hierarchy and prestige, such ambitions were seen as absurd and unacceptable; moreover, when it came to the merchant-New Christians, it was claimed that this group came from a religious and cultural tradition that was alien to those values (Boxer 1962: 106f, Baroja 2000: 9). With many exceptions, as the example of the Ximenes family and others proved. We should add, however, that the sale of honourable titles was not exclusively associated with the New Christians. The projects for the creation of the four trading companies contemplated during the time of the Count-Duke de Olivares also included the idea of combining shares in them with such a practice. In Aragon, it was envisaged that 550 hidalgo titles, 25 baron titles and 25 coats of military orders would be sold (Molas Ribalta 1987: 98). By the end of the 18th century, the trade in titles had become an open transaction (Prado, Jr. 1969: 488).

It should be borne in mind, however, that it was only after the proclamation of independence at the beginning of the 19th century that Brazilian elites gained under Emperor Pedro II wider access to the non-hereditary titles of nobility. During the colonial era, relatively few Brazilian creoles were ennobled, although a royal instruction given in 1548 to the colony's first governor Tomé de Souza authorised him to grant patents of nobility for military merits "either aboard ships of my fleet or on land" (Schwartz 2010: 51, 1985: 273–275, Raminelli 2014, Gonçalves 2007: 44f, 55). The policy of the Spanish crown in the New World was different: it was not uncommon to confer not only nobility but also aristocratic titles. In the 17th century, 422 Spaniards received titles in the colonies – with no traditional privileges except *mayorazgo* – while 409 did so in the 18th century (Carmagnani 2011: 65). Thus, in Brazil, prestige was primarily guaranteed by the status of *senhor de engenho*. Without formalised decisions, instead, thanks to their political influence, lifestyle and wealth, the major owners of the *engenhos* formed a colonial aristocracy de facto, the *nobreza de terra* ('nobility of the land'). The colonisation at the end of the 16th century of the areas north of Pernambuco and Itamaracá, above all Paraiba, was in part a response to the aspirations of both the new immigrants and the Portuguese already settled in Pernambuco: new lands meant new opportunities to obtain *sesmarias* and achieve *senhor de engenho* status. Only such an outcome was seen as a promotion and an escape from misery. In Mexico, a change in social position was generally determined by a shift, as in the metropolis, from trade to land ownership, although the income associated with it was often not particularly high. The negative consequences of freezing capital into prestige land purchases and financing the annuities necessary for a hidalgo-worthy, honourable lifestyle were obvious. By contrast, in Asia, where Portuguese expansion did not emerge as an attempt at larger-scale settlement, trade, including petty trade, was popular. In Brazil, too, retail trade was, in areas already intensively colonised, the last line of defence against the degradation of the white man to the role of plebeian (Kieniewicz 1976: 89–92, Małowist 1976: 284–286, Prado Jr. 1981: 94).

In the economic sphere, the response to the drain on the resources of the colonies by the metropolises was the emergence of various means of capturing some of the financial surpluses drawn down by Madrid or Lisbon; the relatively independent position of the creoles in the colonial (especially local) administration was also strengthened by various means. The large-scale spoiling of silver coinage at the royal mint established in Potosí in 1575 was only a particularly glaring example of such activities, which intensified in the first decades of the 17th century. So much so that, at one point, they began to refuse to accept coins minted in Potosí – until Madrid clarified the situation. The main culprits were beheaded. A matter of particular interest (and criticism) was, of course, the monopoly on trade imposed by both metropolises (this mainly affected Spain) and other moves restricting the freedom of action of the *criollos*. Again, in Brazil, disputes and conflicts of this kind, while serious, were handled much more smoothly.

Not only contraband and other forms of circumventing monopolistic restrictions were used in this game of redistributing the wealth created in the New World. Developing – though poorly controlled by Madrid – trade with Asia also served this purpose. Judging by estimates of the value of the silver transported from Acapulco to Manila, serious deals were involved here. At the apogee of the Manila Galleons trade, in the total transfers of bullion from New Spain to Manila, the share of private remittances rose from 18 per cent in 1581–1590 to 34 per cent in 1621–1630. And this concerns legal remittances only. Imports of silk and brocade from Asia, but also of textiles of varying quality (from luxury to cheap goods for the lower classes), posed a threat to Spanish manufacturers and merchants (Gasch-Tomáas 2019: 72, Hoberman 1977: 493). The development, despite prohibitions, of intra-American trade served the same purpose – to weaken dependence on the metropolis. Also, the expansion of *La Nação* during the Iberian Union in Spanish America necessarily undermined the rules of the Spanish (and Portuguese) monopoly. An autonomus chapter in these developments was the growing intra-Asian trade, on the route Cochin (Malabar Coast)–Macao–Manila in which conversos (mainly Portuguese New Christian) were heavily involved (Sousa 2019).

The local economic elites were also strengthened by taking over for defence purposes a part of the revenue from silver and excise duties and taxes, after payment of *quinta real* (royal fifth). Such measures were justified, for example, in Lima in the early 17th century by the threat posed by the appearance of Dutch ships off the coast of the viceroyalty. In the second half of the century, Lima's defence expenditure matched the value of the silver exported to Spain. Moreover, between 1591 and 1660, an increasing proportion of silver production that remained in private hands was accumulated in the colonies, private (legal) exports of bullion declining (Fisher 1997: 59, Bradley 2001: 654, Veen 2000: appendix). The entry of the colonies from the late 16th and early 17th centuries into demographic growth was quite impressive. Rising demand was met with difficulties by legal imports. The supply gap would be filled by contraband (also driven by the settlers themselves). By the beginning of the 17th century the scale of contraband was so great and the influence of those caught up in smuggling so strong that, in parallel with the repressive measures taken, in 1606 Philip III declared an amnesty for smugglers and others involved in the illicit trade in Hispaniola, Cuba and Venezuela (Klooster 2009a: 114). The development of local textile manufacturing and handicrafts was also a response to the widening supply gap.

These processes would culminate from the middle of the 17th century, when Spain's economic decline would already be evident. In Latin America, when we compare its development with that of Europe at this time, there would be trends that Ruggiero Romano described as *conjonctures opposées*: a clearly marked separation of fundamental trends concerning demographic development, the growth of agricultural, mining and craft production, settlement, monetary circulation. Against the background of European stagnation (England and the Netherlands being the exceptions), the New World emerged as a region of growth and important economic and social transformations. This was also aided by the introduction of new crops imported from Europe and Asia and the creation of new economic resources (such as livestock farming). This was an important part of the wider changes referred to as the *Columbian* and *Magellan Exchanges*. The European crisis of the 17th century contributed to changes in the colonies that strengthened local markets and production and accelerated the formation of new social groups (e.g. the relatively small group of *encomenderos,* who had aristocratic aspirations, were replaced by the much more numerous *hacendados*). There is also a certain loosening of economic ties with the Iberian metropolises. In the case of Spanish America, the decline in silver production in the main mining centre of Potosí from the 1620s would play an important role. At the same time, it should be noted that the crisis in silver production was much weaker than the crisis in bullion transfers to Spain. Also, contraband would contribute to weaken and then permanently challenge the Spanish monopoly in Atlantic trade. The "Latin Americanisation" of the Creole elite gradually became a reality in the 17th century (Romano 1992: passim, Fisher 1997: 97, Bakewell 2004: 225–230, Pietschmann 2010: 357–360).

Converts became an important factor in these above sketched processes. Above all, from the beginning of the 17th century there was a gradual shift by the New Christians, hitherto heavily involved in trade with Asia, in the focus of their interests to Europe and the Atlantic. The offensive of the Dutch VOC in the East and the intensifying competition from other Europeans combined began to bear fruit. The superiority of European competitors in Asian markets became evident around the middle of the 17th century. The Jews of Amsterdam also became active participants and beneficiaries of these processes from the early 17th century. Between 1590 and 1650, the globally dispersed 'Portuguese' would form a unique infrastructure of trade and financial contacts linking northern Europe with the Atlantic world and the Iberian Peninsula, as well as with Asia: "The leading New Christian merchants were major players in all of the overseas endeavours, and they probably were the only Portuguese merchant families represented in all of these regions at once" (Boyajian 1993: xiii, Studnicki-Gizbert 2005: 156). This is also the time of Braudel's Jewish "great merchants", as a new factor in *La Nação* activities. They were assisted by the scattered descendants of Sephardic emigrants in the Mediterranean, as well as conversos in Spain.

The tensions and instability as a consequence of such contradictory tendencies were almost inevitable and could not end well for the New Christians. This was particularly evident in the failure of their "risky gambit to gain political influence" in Spain in 1627 and the following years at the royal court under the Count-Duke de Olivares. The success was muted, although the careers of some of the New Christians who settled in Spain were spectacular. We have in mind, for example, Marcos Fernández Monsanto, who belonged to a group of Portuguese *homens de negocios,* engaged in financial operations with the court, while from 1632–43 he and his brother took over the customs office (*Almojarifazgo General*) of Seville and the Indies. This extremely popular philanthropist in Seville ended up bankrupt (Álvarez Nogal 1997: 31, 102f, Aguado de los Reyes 2005: 147f). This and similar careers, however, did not lead to a lasting improvement in the position and change in the formal status of the New Christians as a group. And the growing structural crisis in Spain and the empire was not only inconducive to solving this problem, but left a contrast between internal stagnation and the global reach of the Jewish "great merchants" (Studnicki-Gizbert 2007: 160f, Boyajian 1983).

Olivares' forced departure in 1643 only accelerated the decline of the Portuguese New Christians in Spain and in Spanish America. The Inquisition contributed in the 1630s and 1640s to this outcome, especially in the colonies. But also in Spain itself, the 'Portuguese' predominated among the heretics condemned to the stake. This was a response not only of the Holy Office, but also of the traditional elites to the policy of selective openness to New Christians, in part a delayed reaction to Portugal's breakaway from Madrid's control in 1640. It saw in this anti-Spanish revolt the hand of the New Christians, just as it did in the (unsuccessful) Catalan revolt launched at the same time.

Before this, however, the 'Portuguese', taking advantage of contacts with New Christians in Antwerp, southern France and Italian cities, would seek a place for themselves in the Mediterranean and, increasingly, the Atlantic world for most of the 16th century. The Jews of Amsterdam would come later.

Back to Long-Distance Trade: Networks

By the 1590s, the descendants of persecuted Spanish and Portuguese Jews were gradually finding new fields and forms of activity. This was not so much as a result of a deliberate collective strategy, but as an outcome of individual-ised reactions to the liquidation of previous communities. Family and circles of friends would become the main points of reference. Religious motivations, now under attack, were still present, but significantly weakened. They only appeared as an increasingly selective memory and tradition reduced to the level of the closest circle. Their guardians in the family were generally women. They also constituted, for example, in Brazil in the first half of the 18th century, the majority of the victims of the Inquisition (Assis 2004, Gorenstein 2005: 112). So, it is no longer just the absence of the state, but also of religion as an insti-tution: synagogues and schools, learned rabbis and their books, charitable activities, praise, prohibitions and injunctions. In such circumstances the Old Testament reappeared in a quite new role as an oppositional reading: "The Book of Esther, in particular, describing the vicissitudes of a secret Jewess, and her divinely inspired victory over the anti-Jewish agitator Haman, frequently served as a source of hope and comfort to the clandestine Iberian Judaizers in their darkest moments" (Baron 1973: 169). Paradoxically, however, along with the Old Testament and oral tradition, one of the sources enabling XNs to familiarise themselves with elements of Jewish tradition would be the pub-licly promulgated Inquisitorial *editos da fé e da graça,* which included detailed information on the indications of heresy and apostasy. Addressed to (poten-tial) sinners they were also intended to make it easier for willing delators to identify *judaizantes* (Studnicki-Gizbert 2007: 71f, Gitlitz 2002: 40).[1] Institutions would only reappear in the process of creating "new Jews" in the United Provinces from the early 17th century onwards, and then only in those parts of the Atlantic world that were controlled by Dutch and English Protestants. The small communities of Sephardic Jews scattered on the Senegambian coast at

---

1   Forced Christianisation was accompanied by the confiscation of the property of Jewish com-munities. This also applied to Hebrew books. Their possession was punished. The medieval "violent war against Talmud" (Trachtenberg 1943: 179) entered into a new stage. Some of the collections confiscated in Portugal were sold in Morocco and even in India, where Jewish communities existed (Soyer 2007: 207–209).

the beginning of the 17th century, openly practising their ancestral faith, were an exception confirming the rule.

After all, before the emergence of institutions under the protective umbrella of Protestantism, there remained a crypto-Jewish "faith of remembrance" (Wachtel 2013). In colonial Latin America, this faith would be the only and at the same time gradually fading link between the past and the colonial reality. The second strong impetus would be the acceleration of Europe's overseas expansion. Until the end of the 15th century, however, this was still limited to the exploration of parts of the West African coast, the colonisation of the Azores and Madeira, the Canary Islands and the islands of Cape Verde and São Tomé, and the reinvigoration of the Levantine trade from the 12th century. This, through Muslim controlled territories, included, until the 11th-12th centuries, limited contacts with the East.

Sephardic Jews participated in both of these great economic ventures preceding the expulsions and the 16th-century Atlantic boom, although they did not play a leading role in them. The time had now past when European Jews had maintained limited contacts between the post-Roman periphery of Western Europe and the civilisations of the East in the 8th-11th centuries, together with Christian Syrians. The western Mediterranean was at this time a "Musulman lake", and the "ancient Roman sea had become the frontier between Islam and Christianity" (Pirenne 2001: 162f). Alongside the Syrians, Jewish merchants were the only ones acceptable to Christian and Muslim rulers for small-scale trade: "It was through them that the Occidental world still kept in touch with the Orient" (Pirenne 2001: 162, 258). This was a simplification. Alongside Syrians and Jews, contacts with the Islamic world were maintained by Italian and Byzantine merchants (Holo 2009: 191f, 197). Jews were visible also in intra-European trade. The Carolingians treated the activity of Jewish merchants, money lenders and craftsmen, with approval (Benbasse 1999: Chapter 1, Lea 1906: 80–82). This was particularly true of the community at Narbonne, near the Gulf of Lyon, which played an exposed role in sustaining Mediterranean trade: "Charlemagne took little notice of the decrees enacted against the Jews by the Christian legislators and, with minor concessions to Church laws and principles, granted the Jews of Narbonne basic freedoms and the full protection of his government" (Netanyahu 1995: 60). Discriminatory moves would emerge after the end of the Carolingian dynasty, although there had already been growing resistance from the Church against the overly liberal treatment of the Jews. A description of the main route taken by Jewish Radhanite merchants, left by a Persian high official, dates from the mid-9th century. We are therefore talking about merchants who, according to many historians, originated from southern France or from parts of Italy controlled by the Franks, who speak Arabic and Persian and Rumr (=Greek), and Ifranjr (=probably Latin) and Andalusi (=Spanish) and Slavic. They travel from east to west and from the west to the east, by land and by sea. They market slaves from the west and maidservants and boys, and silk cloth, and rabbit hides (...) and sable furs (...) and swords. They sail from Firanja [*land of Franks*] in the western sea and leave from Farama [*Pelusium*] and transport their goods on the backs [*of camels*] to Qulzum [*Suez*], whereas there is between (these two places a distance of) 25 parasangs (about 150 kilometers); then they sail in the eastern sea [*Red Sea*], from Qulzum to al-Jar [*port of Medina*] and to Judda [*port of Mecca*], then pass on to Sind and to Hind and to China. They transport from China aloe wood, cinnamon and more (goods that they regularly) transport from those areas; they then return to Qulzum and then transport them to Farama, then they set sail in the western sea; sometimes they turn to Constantinople with their merchandise and sell it to the Byzantines; sometimes they travel with it to the king of Firanja and sell it there.

   GIL 2004: 618 new translation, italics added

Ibn Hurdadbeh also describes two other routes frequented by Jewish Radhanite merchants on their way to Asia, including through central and eastern Europe (probably via Prague and Przemyśl) to the Khazar empire. These evocative descriptions of long-distance travels by Jewish merchants are linked today by some scholars to the activities of Oriental Jews, the largest concentration at the time being in and around Baghdad. According to Israeli medievalists, European Jews, due to their small numbers as well as their limited resources, could not play the role ascribed to them. The situation was different for Oriental merchants (Gil 2004: 636f, Toch 2013: 197f, 2008: 184). Other hypotheses have also emerged in this long debate which goes back to the 19th century, such as treating Radhanite merchants as the equivalent of merchant adventurers rather than as a hegemonic group systematically controlling much of the Mediterranean trade. The dispute is far from over.

   Without going into the details of this debate, suffice it to say that the breaking of the relative isolation of Christian Europe by the Crusaders in the late 11th and 12th centuries pushed the few Jewish merchants engaged in long-distance trade into the background. With the exception of Barcelona and Mallorca, where their presence was still evident, "the revival of Mediterranean commerce in the eleventh century made it possible to dispense with them as intermediaries with the Levant" (Pirenne 1937: 132).[2] The mass slaughter of Jews alongside Muslims by Crusaders who conquered Jerusalem in 1099 facilitated this process. Their place was taken by the Genoese and Venetians, also by the Catalans; the former also reached from the 13th century through their colony at Kaffa in the Crimea to Central Asia and China (with some Jewish and Armenian participation) (Małowist 2010: Chapter 4). Also, the development of shipping between the Mediterranean and Northern Europe undermined the importance of trade conducted via land routes. When the first Venetian galley called at Antwerp in 1314, the sea route thus opened up undercut the importance of the traditional Champagne fairs, although this was not the only factor determining their fate (Baron 1967: 100f, Kuliszer 1962: 242f, Abu-Lughod 1989: 70f).

As a result of all these circumstances, Jewish merchants would be seen primarily as individuals and small communities scattered across Europe, operating in local and partly regional markets, limited in their scale of operation and view of the world. It is striking that Jews were absent from the Hanseatic League operating from the 13th century in German cities, the North Sea and Baltic region, whose activity would peak in the 15th century. They would only appear in the Hanseatic League area in the 16th century as New Christian merchants together with Protestants emigrating from Antwerp. Their destination would mainly be Hamburg. Incidentally, the same Hamburg whose councillors restricted the activities of local Ashkenazi Jews. At the same time, not without pressure from Christian competitors, the presence of Jews in a wide range of urban occupations would be effectively curtailed after the end of the Carolingian dynasty. Diversity gave way to niche activities, and the preponderance of moneychangers, peddlars, usurers and pawnbrokers in contacts with the Christian populace. This was not an activity imposed on the Jews. Instead, the problem was one of the skewed occupational structure of post-Roman European societies, a result of the backwardness of their material culture, which "meant first of all [that it] was primitive and purely rural" (Sombart 1916: 41). The gap in the economic structure was eliminated by bringing in the Jews, not without the encouragement of the Church and the royal courts (Roscher 1875). With roots in the early Middle Ages, "the story of the pregnant relationship between Jews, Commerce and Money" (Toch 2013: 177) was perpetuated subsequently as a natural role ascribed to the Jews. Let us note, however, that the situation in the

---

2   The cooperation in Mamluk Egypt between Muslim Karimi merchants and Jews is mentioned by Abu-Lughod (1989: 227–230). She is referring to a unique Muslim trading company with a loose structure, whose merchants traded from China to Egypt, mainly in spices. Its members also included a small number of Oriental Jewish merchants (Abulafia 1987: 437–443).

Iberian Peninsula still deviated from this European norm until the 12th century. The place occupied by Jews at the time of the Reconquista between Islam and Christianity made it possible for Sephardic communities to maintain a much more diverse occupational structure. Witness the presence of Jewish goldsmiths, enamelers, dyers, blacksmiths, armourers and other crafts, medics, advisors, geographers and cartographers, and navigators. In Portugal, we also find Jews in agriculture – also as estate and vineyard owners, and olive and fig growers (Soyer 2007a: 72f).

By contrast, we know little about Jewish participation in Portuguese expansion along the African coast in the 15th century. Małowist (1969: 169f), in his study of the origins of the Portuguese presence in Africa, mentions that wealthy Jews, favoured by the then King Alfonso V, probably participated in the trade with West Africa in the second half of the 15th century and owned Black slaves in Lisbon; he also points out that in the speeches of some representatives to the Cortes in 1472 and 1473 "it was stated with indignation that foreigners and Jews were driving the Portuguese out of the [ivory] trade". Portuguese scholars, on the other hand, report that Alfonso V provided Jewish merchants with the opportunity to trade with newly discovered territories, as well as the right to build ships. Already during the first years of the reign of João II, in 1481 and 1482, complaints reached the court about Jewish and Genoese merchants trading sugar and honey from Madeira. They were accused of causing a drastic increase in prices for these goods in Lisbon (Almeida 1997). On the other hand, references to the involvement of Portuguese Jews in the slave trade during this period are quite scarce; more is known about the activities in this sphere of the Florentine merchant and banker Bartolomeo Marchionni in Lisbon (Quevedo 2008: 212).

The slave trade was, moreover, a specific enterprise at the time. If one excludes the shipments directed to Portugal and Spain from 1441 onwards, the trade in Africans was primarily a means to obtain gold, not an end in itself. The Portuguese, as intermediaries, supplied slaves from Benin to Muslim merchants and African rulers on the Gold Coast in exchange for gold. This was the case of the majority of the 81,000 slaves sold between 1450 and 1500 (Alencastro 1993: 166f).[3] The *feitoria* and, from 1481, the fort of Elmina played a key role as entrepôt in this enterprise. In these operations, the slave was treated as proxy money and a commodity which could be exchanged against gold, rather than as a productive resource or an object of missionary activity (Blackburn

---

3   According to Curtin (1969: 116), 33,500 slaves were exported from Africa during this period (including 8,500 to Madeira, São Tomé and other Atlantic islands).

2010: 106). The story of the forced Jewish settlement of African islands and the modern plantation-oriented slave trade begins later, after 1492.

In short, continuity was largely broken as far as the participation of European Jews in long-distance trade up to the 11th-12th centuries was concerned. The return to this role would take place under different conditions: the breakdown of Sephardic communities, dispersion and the expansion of Europe initiated by the voyages of Columbus and Vasco da Gama. And in the eastern Mediterranean at this time, the Jews would resume their role as an important trading partner thanks to the Ottoman Empire. At least until the first half of the 17th century they would act as intermediaries in the Levantine trade in Muslim-controlled areas. Already by the end of the 16th century, Jewish merchants from Istanbul controlled two-thirds of the commerce between Venice and the Ottoman metropolis. The High Porte kept the overly expansive Italian merchants in the Adriatic, Aegean, and Balkans at bay with their help (Israel 2002a: 62).

This was the role played by, among others, the aforementioned Don Josef Nasci during this period. At one point, together with Doña Grácia Nasci, who also resided in Istanbul, he even challenged the merchants of Ancona by blocking (unsuccessfully) their activities. This was in response to the persecution of the Jews initiated by Pope Paul IV. Unlike his predecessors, Paul III and Julius III, who encouraged Jews to settle in this economic centre, Paul IV embodied the mentality of the Counter-Reformers. The burning alive of 25 Portuguese Jews in this city on his orders in 1555 and other targeted moves against Sephardic refugees in Italy meant that the main wave of Jewish migration turned towards the Ottoman Empire in the following years. The Counter-Reformation, as well as the escalating confrontation with the Grand Porta combined to cause a sharp retreat from the policies of Italian rulers and city councils hitherto neutral or sympathetic to Jewish migrants. The defeat of the Turkish armada at Lepanto in the Ionian Sea in 1571 was instrumental in halting, in the long term, these negative trends. Changes for the better would occur from the 1580s.[4] During this period, the cooperation of economically strengthened Jews from the Ottoman Empire (mainly from Thessaloniki) and Venice

---

4 Tuscany would return in 1593 to the policy of openness towards Jewish and Muslim merchants initiated in 1551 and subsequently interrupted. The laws adopted (*Livornina*) guaranteed religious freedoms in the port of Livorno to merchants of all nationalities: Jews (*hebrei*), *leuantini, e' ponentini*, Turks, Armenians, Persians, Greeks and others. However, heretics, i.e. New Christians maintaining links with Judaism were still treated as criminals. In 1622, among the 10,545 inhabitants of Livorno we find 711 Jews (*nazione ebrea*), mainly merchants (Israel 2002a: 63f, 67f, 74f; Levi 2005: 191f, Engels 1997: 40, 42, Trivellato 2009b).

would take a new form of intercontinental trade network. In any case, it is only after the end of the 17th century that the role of Sephardic Jews in the crafts, finance and trade of the empire would be challenged to some extent by Greek and Armenian competitors, among others.

In the Spanish New World, the presence and activity of conversos was not particularly pronounced in the first half of the 16th century. On the one hand, this was a result of the restrictions on mobility, the prohibitions on emigration to the colonies (issued in 1501 and the much stricter ones of 1518–22). On the other hand, it was due to the low level of development of the new economies. And gold and silver, after the conquest of Mexico and Peru, were a royal monopoly and a source of income for a small group of Spanish merchants and mining entrepreneurs. It was carefully protected by the *Casa de la Contratación de las Indias*, which had been created as early as 1503 in Seville and modelled on the Portuguese Casa da India. From the late 16th century, this protection was not always effective, as evidenced by the considerable scale of the illegal silver trade. The appearance, nevertheless, by the mid-16th century of a certain number of Spanish conversos, both in Hernán Cortés' expedition and subsequently in colonised Mexico, was partly the result of decisions taken at the royal court and not just bureaucratic inertia. With the Crown's approval, some conversos close to the court, despite being related to families whose names appeared in 1510 in the Sevillean *Padrón de Conversos* (the list of conversos composed by the Inquisition), held important positions in the new colonial administration, as well as in the conquest itself. A number of them reached the Caribbean in 1514, subsequently participating in an expedition to Mexico (Uchmany 2001: 187–189). Pedro Arias (Pedrarias) Dávila held a special place in the early colonisation of parts of what is now Central America and northern Venezuela and Colombia. He came from a family of conversos already firmly established among the Spanish aristocracy, the princes of the Church and at the royal court since 1411. Dávila himself was a respected commander (including having troops from Segovia and Toledo subordinate to him during the battles of Oran) and a high official, though after 1492 a brutal and notorious conquistador. In 1513 he was appointed the first ruler ('captain') of Castilla del Oro (today's Panama, Nicaragua, Costa Rica and parts of Colombia) (Roth 2002: 120–124, Dominguez Ortiz 1971: 131).

This period of "royal favorites", as the historian writes, ends with the increasingly restrictive laws implemented in 1522 (formally adopted in 1518), which mandated the removal of all settlers of Jewish or Muslim backgrounds from the conquered territories. Charles V's idea of creating an 'ideal society' in the colonies was incompatible with tolerance for otherness, especially for those marked by tainted blood. Here, however, the informal rule of noble disobedience *obedezco pero no cumplo* worked. These rules were largely ignored, but this already entailed increasing risks for those hiding their origins (Uchmany 2001: 190–192). Individual conversos also found their way into the conquered Inca state and participated in expeditions to Chile; their numbers increasing in the following decades. One letter addressed in 1570 to the Grand Inquisitor notes that conversos easily arrived in Chile and Peru, no one bothered them, and "with respect to the few Spaniards in these parts, there are two times as many converts as in Spain" (Böhm 2001: 205, 1963: Chapter 2).

Despite the limited presence of *conversos*, the first victim of the Inquisition's persecution in Latin America was precisely one of them, Hernando Alonso, a blacksmith and boat-builder, a participant in the battles against the Indians, rewarded by being granted *an encomienda* for his wartime merits (among other things, he participated in the dramatic battle of the Spanish withdrawal from Tenochtitlán – *La Noche Triste*). This enterprising *encomendero* took up mining and cattle breeding and by 1528 was a de facto monopolist when it came to supplying Ciudad de México (raised on the ruins of Tenochtitlán) with meat. He was burned at the stake in Cuba in 1528. Alonso's accusation of Judaising was probably a pretext concealing the underlying motive of the New Spain rulers of the time, hostile to Cortés. The aim was to strike at people loyal to the conqueror of Mexico and indebted to him for social and material advancement (Schulamith 2011, Hordes 2005: 30–33). A relative of the unfortunate Alonso was involved in pearl fishing in the Caribbean and even became mayor of a small town. He was also murdered in 1528, and the perpetrator was convinced that by killing a descendant of Jews he was not committing a sin (Uchmany 2001: 190f). A massive influx of Portuguese New Christians into Spanish America would not occur until the 1680s, after the formation of the Iberian Union. It was with reference to them that the ruthless, terror-sowing Inquisitor Francisco Estrada y Escobedo, operating in Mexico, wrote in 1646 with pathos about the heretics hiding under the mask of Catholics: "New Spain seethed with Jews" (Israel 2002a: 97). And the Inquisitorial tribunal had already been involved in the systematic destruction of the *judaizantes* in Mexico since 1642. Nota bene, this Inquisitor would be accused a dozen years later by the Royal Inspector and *Suprema* of, among other things, appropriating money and jewellery confiscated from the 'Portuguese' during the repression of 1642–49 (Greenleaf 1988: 418),

The more serious economic ventures involving the New Christians during this period can be spoken of primarily in relation to Brazil. Although there were prohibitions on emigration, liberalised after the pogrom against the New Christians in Lisbon in 1506, in practice Brazil was kept open for several decades due to the lack of particular interest in this new land by the Portuguese political and commercial elite. India came first. This gave a specific colour to the early migration to Brazil, both during the 'Royal Monopoly' era (until the 1530s), when all decisions concerning the new land were pledged to the Crown, and during the 'Private Monopoly' era (from 1534), when the burden of colonisation fell mainly on private investors and *donatarios* managing captaincies. It was they who had the right to grant land – *sesmarias* – in the name of the king (Augeron and Vidal 2007). In the words of the Governor-general of Brazil, Mem de Sá, in a 1560 letter to the regent, Queen Catarina, "Your Majesty should remember that you people this land with convicts and criminals". Earlier, the *donatario* of the capitaincy of Pernambuco, Duarte Coelho Pereira, wrote in 1546 about the influx of criminals, "poor and naked", as a phenomenon that only brings harm: "they are worse here than the plague". Nevertheless, in 1549 Governor Tomé de Souza brought 400 *degredados* to Bahia (the number is disputed). Although they had a bad reputation, outside the main areas of colonisation they were in demand as settlers and soldiers (Schwartz 2010: 92, 23, 1989: 21).[5] This was especially true in the southern capitals.

However, as early as 1503, the first group of New Christian merchant-settlers appeared in the new colony, organised by Fernão de Noronha (or Loronha, while an Italian commercial agent in Lisbon wrote of him as 'Firnando dalla Rogua'). This well-known Lisbon merchant had converted to Catholicism a few years before the fateful year of 1497, and was ennobled for his merits in 1506. The main purpose of the group he organised was to settle and trade in the valuable *pau-brasil*. They were the first white settlers in the new territory (if one excludes a few criminals put ashore by Cabral or castaways). In the contract with the king, in fact an agreement in which new territory would be leased to a private investor, de Noronha committed himself to the gradual settlement of part of the northeastern coast of Brazil and the establishment of a trading post. This contract was extended, with changes, until 1513–1515 (Norton 2007, Johnson 1999). This was an important precedent. Due to the limited resources at the Crown's disposal and only limited interest shown, the formation of Brazil

---

5   The ways in which the *degredados* were described in accounts of the period varied (Kula 1970: 104–106). In more recent literature, the stereotype of the 16th-century *degredado* as a criminal is not sustained. Some people convicted of crimes against the faith became officials in colonial Brazil (a royal instruction given to the first governor Tomé de Souza provided for this possibility) (Coates 2001: 78, Silva 2007: 42f). According to Eltis (2002: 72), 2,000 *degredados* were exiled to Brazil by 1580, and around 5,000 between 1580 and 1640. The region of their concentration at the beginning of the 17th century would become the newly occupied and administratively retained Maranhão. The majority of *degredados*, around 18,000, would appear in the colony between 1640 -1755. In total, 75,500 convicts were sent to all Portuguese colonies over the three centuries (Silva 2011a: 117).

was initiated as a private enterprise. The "royal monopoly" found expression in the subsequent years above all in the exclusive rights to and control over *pau brasil* trade as an income-generating source and the creation of administrative and power structures (including the appointment of *donatarios*). Here, the king's trusted men, sometimes not belonging to the hereditary nobility (such as the *donatario* Duarte Coelho Pereira, a highly distinguished commander), as well as impoverished noblemen, appear (Augeron and Vidal 2007: 31f).

However, the story of Fernão de Noronha does not end with this Brazilian venture. Instead, the subsequent fate of the group of merchant-settlers is not further known. It has been suggested that in the following years, together with disembarked insubordinate sailors and undesirable elements (*degredados*) sent from the metropolis, they may have formed the nucleus of a group of whites (soon to be *mestizos-mamelucos*). They found their place among the Indians and subsequently also facilitated trade contacts between them and the settlers and merchants arriving from Portugal.[6] Whether this was actually the case, we do not know. Anyhow, the first two criminals had already been put ashore by Cabral (they were joined by two fugitives from the admiral's ships). One of them survived until the arrival of the next Portuguese ships and acted as an intermediary and interpreter with the Indians (Metcalf 2005: 34, 38). By contrast, a few decades later, it was the New Christians brought from Madeira and probably from São Tomé who contributed to the rapid development of slave sugar plantations in Brazil. Simply, it was not criminals who made Brazil, although the presence of *degredados* was noticeable in the relatively small community of the colony's first white inhabitants.

The situation was different in the Portuguese islands along the coast of West Africa, which had been occupied since the 15th century. Two thousand children taken by force in Lisbon from Jewish parents, refugees from Castile, were sent to São Tomé in 1493, it should be recalled. Around 600 probably survived the following years (Soyer 2007a: 131). They formed over time a unique community, partly – culturally and religiously – Creole, partly racially mixed. Things were similar, moreover, among the Old Christians. This was a process largely facilitated from the beginning of colonisation in the 1480s by the Portuguese Crown. The shortage of white women resulted in single white settlers looking for with African slave women, while the liberation of mulatto children and their black mothers took place in 1515 (Małowist 1969: 400). Alongside the whites, mulatto New Christians also appeared.

---

6   Salvador (1976: 215f) speculates that thanks to this group, some Hebrew words found their way into the Tupi Indian language. According to Green (2007: 77), "such a theory probably owes more to overwork than to accuracy".

Some of them were among the *lançados* (the 'cast out ones') also known as *tangomãos* ('tattooed'), an interesting group of cultural, religious and economic frontiersmen (the former term was more commonly used by Portuguese officials). Formally outlawed but extremely useful in trade, including the slave trade, and gradually acculturated, they lived among African communities as settlers and middlemen uncontrolled by Portuguese authorities. On a much smaller scale, whites and *mamelucos* who settled among the Indians played *a* similar role during the initial phase of Brazilian colonisation. However, these were individual cases. One such figure was Diogo Álvares Correia, a Portuguese sailor washed up from a wrecked ship onto the shore in 1509. As a Caramurú ('man of fire' or 'wielder of fire' because of the firearms he possessed), he then lived for several decades, married to the daughter of an Indian chief, among the Tupinambá Indians in the Bahia region, performing the extremely useful role of intermediary with the Portuguese. The role of intermediaries was also played by the *degredados* Vasco Fernandes Lucena in the 1530s, working in Pernambuco with the founder of that captaincy, or João Ramalho, who was active from 1512 in the area of present-day São Paulo and Santos. Also, the French, who competed with the Portuguese for Brazilian timber and influence among the Indians, made frequent and skilful use of their own, often Norman, trade intermediaries (and interpreters) living among the Indians – the *truchements* (Metcalf 2005: 62).

The phenomenon of the *lançados*, however, was not limited to the first contacts with West Africa, in practice Upper Guinea (an area stretching from present-day Senegal to Sierra Leone). Such outcasts, although they originated initially mainly from the Cape Verde, are found from the late 16th century at almost every point of contact between Portuguese and Africans. They got involved with Black women, established their own settlements on the coast, maintained trade contacts with the islands bypassing the formally empowered Portuguese *feitorias* and "not surprisingly a number were New Christians (...) whose chances for advancement in Portuguese service were limited" (Thornton 1998: 60f). One such case was that of a New Christian from the Portuguese Alentejo, João Ferreira, known as 'Ganagoga'. Married to the daughter of an African local ruler, he developed trading activities on the Senegal River in the 1590s (Silva 2011a: 196). Going further than Thornton, other scholars link the phenomenon of the *lançados* primarily to the New Christians. They argue that these merchant adventurers were "mostly New Christians and controlled the slave trade from the early 16th century, and supplied foreign ships docked on the coast" (Quevedo 2008: 212, also Mark and Silva Horta 2011: Chapter 2). However, it is difficult to talk about proportions when data are lacking. In any case, it is clear from the available descriptions that even in the early 17th century the

New Christian *lançados* still counted in the Portuguese-African trade in Upper Guinea. The mulatto descendants of the Portuguese would also appear in the Congo and later in Angola as *pombeiros* or *pumbeiros* (intermediaries ensuring the supply of slaves in collaboration with African partners). They would also make a major contribution in the late 18th century to the growth of the slave trade precisely from Angola (Thomas 1998: 299, Metcalf 2005: 169). By contrast, we know little about their relationship with the New Christians.

The influx of New Christians into West Africa from Portugal and at the beginning of the 17th century also from the Netherlands, which was illegal but de facto tolerated for lack of counteraction, also continued. In this case, it was no longer just about the *lançados*, people from the cultural, religious and racial borderlands somewhat created by conditions in the *feitorias* and the African environment. We are talking about the Portuguese New Christians operating openly as a Jewish community who appeared on the Senegambian coast, south of present-day Dakar, settling in Joal and Portudal (Porto d'Ale). Some of them had previously resided in the Republic and had already reached Africa as practising Jews. Their mulatto descendants also declared themselves as Jews.

Residing in several settlements, probably dozens of families in total, these Portuguese Jews maintained close contacts with both African, Muslim rulers and the Jews of Amsterdam. The figure given by the Jesuit Baltazar Barreira of 100 Jews in 1606 in Portudal alone was greatly exaggerated (Green 2007). Their main partners in Amsterdam were the two influential Sephardim Diogo Nunes Belmonte (after emigrating from Madeira he took the names Jacob Israel) and Diogo Dias Querido (after settling in Amsterdam he took the name David), but the trade contacts of these communities also reached Portugal, Morocco, Livorno and Brazil. Supplies to African rulers of prized short swords (*terçados*) made in Amsterdam and Italian cities and assembled in Portugal and other cold weapons reinforced their importance and also played a role in the development of the slave trade. In turn, religious services (and copies of the Torah in Spanish) were provided to the settlers by an Amsterdam Jew associated with Nunes Belmonte, who combined trade – including the representation of Dutch merchants' interests – with knowledge of Judaism. This activity was later continued by his son and the religious practices facilitated by the construction of two houses of worship.

The protection afforded to useful Jewish commercial intermediaries by Muslim rulers was an essential factor in allowing such an anomaly to persist. These in turn appealed to the principles of market competition and tolerance. The gradual blending of merchant-settlers into the local environment was also remarkable. They were both 'Jewish *lançados*' and increasingly mulattoes. However, this racial distinction did not mean discrimination in African conditions, unlike in Amsterdam. After the occupation in 1630 of Pernambuco by the WIC, some settlers moved to 'Dutch Brazil'. All these factors meant that by the second half of the 17th century the Joal and Portudal communities had practically disappeared (Mark and Silva Horta 2011: 20f, Chapter 4, Green 2007: 175–183).

With even greater intensity, albeit with no chance of openly practising the Jewish religion, similar processes emerged in the Cape Verde, especially in the colonial capital Ribeiro Grande. At the end of the 16th century, in 1582, we find a fairly numerous colony of whites on these islands, numbering 1,608 people (Silva 2011a: 124). Already since the beginning of the 16th century, not only New Christian tax collectors had been appearing here, but also, increasingly, merchants serving the transit trade between Brazil and Lisbon, including slave traders. It was here, in an archipelago more than 650 km from the African coast – a place of exile but also of escape for *XN*s discriminated against in the metropolis – that the outlines of the Atlantic trade network took shape in the first decades of the 16th century (Green 2007: passim). In Madeira, on the other hand, the New Christians were present relatively early, in the mid-15th century. They participated in the development of sugar production, most often as merchants and experts taking care of the mill facilities, and alongside the Italians as owners of sugar mills and sugar cane plantations. However, until the mid-16th century, the economy of Madeira, especially the sugar trade, was mainly dominated by the Genoese and Florentines.

The dispersal of the New Christians to the islands, which, at least until the mid-16th century, played an important role in sugar production and then in the gradually developing Atlantic trade (mainly in slaves), had momentous consequences. This can be seen as one element in the networks that the New Christians formed across the Atlantic (and together with the Jews also beyond it, mainly in the Mediterranean). Their scale and methods of operation were crucial for understanding the economic role of the New Christians and the (few) Jews in this period, especially in the long-distance trade. The following description of the role of Portugal in the 16th century is in fact also a tribute to the networks the New Christians created: "Very few of the commodities arriving on the wharves of Lisbon remained in Portugal. But they did enable Portugal to become a major player in a global network of commodity exchanges and trade networks reaching from Danzig to the Zambezi and Mato Grosso to Manila" (Russell-Wood 1993: 129). However, this description also helps to understand the limits of *La Nação*'s influence, a question sometimes overlooked in the analysis, but worth bearing in mind.

In the emerging Atlantic economy, it is first Spain and Portugal, then the Netherlands and then increasingly England and France who were imposing – more or less successfully – the rules of the game, dictating the directions of development and the structure of intercontinental exchange. Mercantilism reigned, although, depending on the country, with varying degrees of intensity and effectiveness. The consequences of mercantilist actions also varied from country to country. In practice, mercantilism was not only an expression of building commercial power and taking care of a country's balance of trade, but also – in the long term and for some monarchies only – the creation of a modern state and the realisation of the concept of *raison d'etat* (Szlajfer 2012: Chapter 2). Royal monopolies rented to merchant-bankers, rationing and tax privileges, but also trade wars, privateering and contraband as a response to restrictions on access to markets were only elements of the practices in overseas trade at the time. But not the only ones. In short, the mercantilism of the European powers formed the basic framework of Atlantic trade. It was constantly challenged, but at least until the mid-17th century provided the Iberian monarchies with a degree of control over the economies of the colonies and a share in the benefits of trade. In the case of Portugal's policy towards Brazil, one eminent historian has no doubt that what was being referred to was a textbook case of mercantilism and bullionism (Russell-Wood 2002: 108).

Unlike the Spaniards, the Portuguese, the Dutch, the French or the English, the Jews and New Christians scattered across Europe did not, because they could not, play an independent role in the process or in the economies of the individual colonies, much less a political role. They were, on the other hand, a useful and, at one point, extremely important part of European expansion. In a relatively short period of time, they became, in the 16th and 17th centuries, a kind of forerunner of 'capitalism' (in the Braudelian sense), albeit a very specific one. In the mercantilist era of the birth of modern states and the emergence of modern patriotism, the New Christians, who combined "specialized economic competence and political powerlessness", were indeed "exemplary non-patriots". Economically active, they "remained aloof from theological divisions and political rivalries" (Muller 2010: 7, Sutcliffe 2009: 28). And in any case, they made efforts not to appear as a party (or victim) in these disputes. While it is true that in this early period of the formation of mercantilist ideas and practices, the 'cosmopolitanism' of the trade was a common phenomenon, certainly the great New Christian merchants (and, from the early 17th century onwards, also the Jewish merchants of Amsterdam or Livorno) moved much more easily in such an environment. The need, forced to a large extent by dispersion, to operate flexibly in many markets and in a diverse environment using an extensive network of contacts was thus turned into a virtue and, in practical terms, into a competitive advantage. The Flemish operated in a similar way in European markets, but also in Brazil.

It should also be kept in mind that this specific internationalism, expressed in the concentration on long-distance trade and related financial operations, was not only a consequence of the dispersion and the "natural", supposedly, predispositions of the Sephardim. Incidentally, these "natural" characteristics of the Jews were dwelt upon by Sombart, though he was not the only one. A well-known Portuguese historian of the early 20th century, who viewed the role of the New Christians decidedly negatively, would write that usury *foi sempre predilecto do povo hebraico* (Azevedo 1922: 2). This internationalism arose primarily from the combination of the new situation in which the Sephardim found themselves after the expulsions, with the effects of the discriminatory policies of the guilds and cities imposed on them. In the 17th century,

> At Hamburg, the rules imposed by the Senate excluded the Jews from practically every form of activity other than overseas trade (...). Even at Amsterdam, guild restrictions excluded Jews from most crafts and forms of shop-keeping and those crafts they were allowed to practice, such as diamond-processing, tobacco-spinning, and chocolate-making, were, generally speaking, closely connected with colonial trade.
>
> ISRAEL 1989

Furthermore, in 1632, the mayor of Amsterdam de facto closed the way for Jews to become members of guilds. Of the dozens operating in the city, only a few were open to them, including medics, apothecaries, booksellers and brokers (with restrictions). Moreover, Jews were not allowed to broker transactions between Christians (Israel 1990a: 425, Koen 1970: 28, 37f). The fact was that there was a strong involvement of "new Jews" in the development of printing. "To set up a printing house is a sacred work" – this statement by the Jewish publisher of the first book in Portugal in 1487, became a practice first in Italy, then in Amsterdam. A prominent printer was, among others, the Amsterdam rabbi Menasseh ben Israel from 1627 (Swetschinski 2004: 149–154). Widening access of the "new Jews" to new crafts and domestic trade would occur from the mid-17th century, weakening their involvement in long-distance trade.

Before this, however, in the *Humble Addresses* submitted to Cromwell in 1655, rabbi Menasseh ben Israel cited the following, by now well known, arguments justifying the economic benefits that would accrue to England from the admission, after more than four centuries of absence, of a nation "dispersed throughout the whole World": firstly, Jews maintaining contacts and being able to negotiate "where-ever they are (...) and having perfect knowledge of all kinds

of Moneys, Diamants, Cochinil, Indigo, Wines, Oyle, and other Commodities";
secondly, "holding correspondence with their friends and kinds-folk, whose
language they understand". In other words, Menasseh ben Israel sought to
convince the Lord Protector that information, especially reliable and timely
information, was a prerequisite for effective action – and for multiplying capital. The Sephardic diaspora had such information. He went on to point out
that "they do abundantly enrich the Lands and Countries of strangers, where
they live". He cited the example of Livorno, which, thanks to Jewish activity,
had transformed itself from "a very ignoble and inconsiderable City" into
a flourishing centre of commerce. He was exaggerating, but that is not the
main point here. And finally, he added, the Jews in Holland and Italy trade
not only with their own capital, "but also with the riches of many others of
their own Nation, friends, kinds-men and acquaintance, which notwithstand-
ing live in Spain, and fend unto them their moneys and goods". They do so as a
safeguard "from danger that might happen unto them, in case they should fall
under the yoke of the Inquisition" (Menasseh 1901: 82f, also Wolf 1901).[7] The
last-mentioned issue involved the emigration of some of the New Christian
merchant-financiers from Spain a few years after the fall of de Olivares in 1643
(most of the Portuguese remained). Sometimes emigration was preceded by
the transfer of capital and goods. A strong incentive to leave was the forced
bankruptcy of the Portuguese *asentistas* in 1647. Of the 30 bankers affected
by Philip IV's decree, 27 were Portuguese. The frozen obligations to the New
Christians exceeded the enormous sum of 11 million ducats. This was a very
specific financial reserve at the King's disposal during the crisis of 1647. The
Genoese *asentistas* – with the exception of three – were not affected by the
decree. It is not surprising, therefore, that the place of the Portuguese would be
taken – in accordance with the Crown's intentions – by the Genoese again, but
already investing on a much smaller scale (Boyajian 1983: 154f, Israel 1990: 400–
403, Álvarez Nogal 1997: 39–42).

For a number of reasons, these arguments by the respected Menasseh ben
Israel appealed to the Lord Protector, while at the same time worrying the
authorities of the Republic, who feared an exodus of "new Jews" to England.
Ideological motives stemming from a Puritan reading of Scripture, including
the religious fervour characterising Cromwell himself and present in the revolutionary New Model Army, certainly played an important role. In addition,

---

7 Earlier, in 1638, the Venetian rabbi Simeon Luzzatto submitted the *Dicurso circa il stato de
   gl'Hebrei* to the doge. In it, he outlined, among other things, the benefits in trade and taxes
   that the Republic had derived from the presence of the Jews, emphasises their loyalty and
   international contacts serving the city.

Cromwell considered it English raison d'etat to include the Jews in his projected expansion in the Spanish Caribbean. It is possible that the next step would have been expansion in Spanish South America as well. Combining the forces of English Puritans and Jewish merchants in this offensive to break the Spanish monopoly seemed a rational (and exciting) solution. The mood that emerged during this period was evidenced, for example, by the proposal made to Cromwell in 1655 by Simón (Jahacob) de Cáceres. This prominent Sephardic merchant residing in London, and Cromwell's informant on West Indies affairs (mainly Jamaica), proposed in his memorandum that the Jews organise and finance an armed expedition of four frigates and 1,000 soldiers and conquer Chile. The aim would also be to disorganise Spanish trade on the west coast of the New World. Although with Jewish participation, the expedition would have been an English venture and under English command (Böhm 1963: Chapter 3, 121f). This plan, never executed, nevertheless fitted well within the prevailing atmosphere in the Lord Protector's circle. More than half a century later, a well-known English publisher and politician, in remarks on "the race of people called Jews", would confirm the main thesis of *Humble Adresses*:

> They are, indeed, so disseminated through all the trading parts of the World, that they are become the Instruments by which the most distant Nations converse with one another, and by which Mankind are knit together in a general Correspondence: they are like the Pegs and Nails in a great Building, which, though they are but little valued in themselves, are absolutely necessary to keep the whole Frame together.
>
> ADDISON 1761: 569

The opinions cited thus referred to the characteristic ways in which Jews and New Christians conducted long-distance trade based on an extensive informal network. Indeed, such a mode of operation could hardly be considered unique. In the 16th or 17th centuries, the use of informal trade networks was the modus operandi of all ethnic and religious minorities involved in international trade without exception. They would also appear among new groups seeking their place in the world of trade and enterprise. This was true of the 'new merchants' in England and North America of the time of parliamentary opposition. Already in the run-up to the Civil War of the mid-17th century, their elite was closely connected: trade, networks of interests and family ties and the growing power of Puritanism formed a compact whole (Studnicki-Gizbert 2007, Trivellato 2009a, Brenner 2003: 113f). Nor should we forget the trade networks created by Asians. The essence of such trade is presented by the historian of *La Nação:*

Operating in a zone of informality outside the purview of the state, these networks were similarly informal in their structure and functioning. The networks created by Portuguese merchants resembled nothing so formally organized or functionally determined as a "machine". Contrary to more formally organised commercial institutions, such as the joint-stock company or the modern corporation, the Portuguese trading network was decentralised in form and function. It was knit together through the commercial links that extended from and between the different merchant houses. Each of the Portuguese merchant houses that participated in the network was a quasi-autonomous unit: it controlled its own pool of capital and it was responsible for the success or failure of its commercial ventures. At the same time, however, there was a clear need for collaboration among the members of a trading house and between houses.

STUDNICKI-GIZBERT 2007: 93f

A network understood in this way could only have played a key role in the era before more powerful, otherwise organised participants in long-distance trade entered the game. We are referring here to the trading companies gradually formed from the early 17th century – with state support:

The first real corporations – the Dutch and English East India Companies, West India Companies, and so on (...) were new in several ways. They were anonymous (...). They separated ownership from control (...). They were permanent: if one or more partners did want out, there was no need to renegotiate the whole arrangement. Finally, they were legal entities separate from any one owner, and they had unlimited life.

POMERANZ AND TOPIK 2013: 186

These companies were, also because of the degree of formal institutionalisation, very much the opposite of the network trade, which involved merchant houses or smaller merchants in usually one-off (though recurrent) contracts. A joint venture may have meant several merchants sharing in the outlay of chartering or purchasing a vessel and goods. Such one-off and highly diversified ventures were characteristic not only of the New Christians, but also of the Dutch. In order to distinguish them from VOC activity, they were called 'pre-companies' (*vóórcompagnieën*), while the risk-reducing sharing between several merchants in a one-off, short-term investment was referred to as *partenrederij* (Postma 1992a: 9f, Boxer 1965). The capital involved in such a venture could, however, be considerable, reaching tens of thousands of guilders (hundreds of thousands in today's dollars). The contrast between trading networks and trading companies, however, did not imply a sharp contrast between amorphous, poorly structured entities and formally empowered, institutionalised agents of international trade. Such a sharply delineated dichotomy pitting custom against formal institution did not in fact exist. Also, trade networks as specific merchant coalitions were formed on the basis of legal rules that, together with oral tradition, provided merchants with "shared norms and expectations" (Trivellato 2009b: 163, also Greif 1993).

The VOC and the WIC were also perceived, with exaggeration, as a major threat to the ventures and traditional networks established by the New Christians and Jews, as well as the Dutch Protestants. Arguably, in the longer term, their monopolistic (formally, though not always actually) position in the turnover of luxury goods and their innovative structure contributed to some extent to the relative marginalisation of Portuguese New Christians and Amsterdam Jews in long-distance trade. This was, however, a staggered process. In the case of the VOC, until as late as the mid-1620s the Portuguese network-based, family-owned trade was still competing effectively with the Dutch corporation, especially in the intra-Asian market. Between 1600–50, Portuguese merchants supplied, according to some estimates, an average of 16–17 tonnes of silver per year to Asia, outside the *Estado da Índia* structures. By contrast, only 8 tonnes were supplied annually on average through the VOC and the English East India Company between 1601–25. The change comes in 1626–50, when deliveries through both companies reached 19 tonnes. Thus, it is only from the second half of the 17th century that one can speak of a clearly marked predominance of corporate trade (Studnicki-Gizbert 2000). It would also be difficult to defend the thesis that the WIC corporation displaced individual merchants *in toto* from lucrative ventures on the Atlantic. Closer to reality would be the claim that from the 1620s onwards, a dynamic co-existence took shape in the area, sometimes leading to conflict, but more often to cooperation. As early as 1638, the WIC monopoly was reduced in favour of the Company's private shareholders, while in 1647–48 there was a loosening of the monopolistic rigours of the slave trade – 45–50 per cent of the turnover was controlled by private, mainly Calvinist, merchants. Around the mid-17th century, the number of private ships operating in the Atlantic was almost five times the size of the WIC fleet (Antunes and Silva 2011: 56f, 2012: 7, Enthoven 2003b: 391f). In contrast, WIC's involvement in the slave trade in Dutch Brazil proved to be a financial disaster. In 1674, the company was disbanded but as soon as 1675 was reactivated, with the task of sustaining trade with Africa.

Certainly, however, a factor of paramount importance that led to the relative marginalisation of the networks formed by the New Christians and Jews was the enormous growth of trade in Europe, Asia and the Atlantic from the second half of the 17th century (Romano 1992: Chapter 4, Findlay and O'Rourke 2007). This rapidly growing exchange seems to have far outstripped the organisational capacity and human resources of *La Nação*. Merchant houses and informal networks, which had played an important role in accelerating the pace of overseas trade from the late 15th century, were no longer an appropriate institutional response under the new conditions. However, they would still play a significant regional role in the early 18th century, especially in the Dutch and English Caribbean. In brief, trade based on New Christian and Jewish networks was certainly a pioneering enterprise, an important part of the beginnings of modernity, but not the embodiment of its maturity. It confirmed "the image of Jews as simultaneously avant-garde and retrograde" (Karp 2010: 27). This thesis therefore accentuated the fact that there was a timeframe of the 'Jewish moment' in modern economic history. The first half of the 18th century would see the completion of the transformation of this 'moment' into its opposite: the failure to keep up and the relative absence of a Jewish presence in certain modern economic processes related to manufacturing and the build-up of internal markets (Israel 2009: Chapter 10, Emmer 2001: 512f). However, this process was misleadingly generalised by Max Weber by treating it as a manifestation of Jewish traditionalism and "pariah-capitalism".

Almost simultaneously with the Dutch and English trading companies, a broader institutional infrastructure for international commercial and financial operations (banks and financial intermediation, commodity exchanges, risk insurance arbitrage) was gradually emerging; new, anonymous forms of capital mobilisation (stock market trading) were also emerging. On the one hand, Amsterdam and English Jews gradually reduced their involvement in long-distance trade under pressure from stronger competitors and new circumstances; on the other hand, some found from the end of the 17th century a new field of activity in these very institutions and economic spheres that were gaining in importance. It is from this period that the Jews of Amsterdam would begin to play, among other things, a significant role in the trading of VOC and WIC shares and English securities (Israel 2002a: 454). This would be the most brilliant period in the history of the "new Jews", who were further strengthened after 1647 by the emigration of New Christian merchant-financiers from Spain and Antwerp. There was a shift from commodity trade to extensive financial services as an indispensable part of local and international commercial transactions. In addition to participation in the increasingly important financial sphere, army supplies and other transactions with the royal courts became a substitute for the reduced participation in overseas trade (however, these "court Jews" would not survive as a meaningful factor after the middle of the 18th century). Jewellery making became increasingly important, as well as the continued prominence of Amsterdam Jews in the diamond and pearl trade. Changes of this nature also extended to the New Christians in Portugal (Swetschinski 2004: 138–148).

Before this happened, however, for more than a century, trade networks would make it possible for the New Christians and then also Jews to return to overseas operations and participation in the Atlantic economy shaped by the Iberian mercantilist trade system. Their modus operandi has been the subject of lively debates for years. This concern in particular the already noted issue of combining formal (legal regulations) and informal (reputation and pledge) actions and procedures that build trust and enhance credibility. A colourful picture was drawn by Duarte Gomes Solis, a New Christian merchant active in Goa in the late 16th and early 17th centuries and later, already in Lisbon, author of mercantilist treatises:

> In the *Rua Nova* of Lisbon [the main shopping street once Jewish now mainly New Christian], without getting off their bobtail mules, these merchants, the most trusted financiers of Europe, scribble on scraps of paper letters of credit honoured in all European cities, payable in local coin
>
> SARAIVA 2001: 196[8]

"I may lack money and luck," wrote the Lisbon-based New Christian merchant, "but, thanks to God, I have my reputation and the good opinion [of others]". Gomes Solis, in turn, added: "trade is based on credit, and credit is based on truth". Trust and reputation, key variables in the analysis of networked trade between highly differentiated diasporas, were not a given from above, in particular they were not assigned as self-evident to specific religious and/or ethnic communities (quoted in Studnicki-Gizbert 2007: 84, see also Wachtel 2011: 178, Trivellato 2009b: 12–14). Instead, they were the product of the complex and multi-directional interactions created by the practice of overseas trade – an activity capable of yielding huge profits but also risky. It is no exaggeration to say that the trade of the time was an occupation for people ready for anything. Let us just mention that the mortality rate among the crews operating

---

8   The right to ride a mule with bridle and saddle was a privilege not available to Jews in the 15th century. In 1464, it was granted as an exception to the king's advisor Isaac Abrávanel (Schorsch 2004: 39). Gomes Solis was the author of projects to improve the situation of merchants. He also raised the need to equalise the status of New and Old Christians and to also allow *casta Hebrea*, i.e. European Jews and XNs together, into Iberian trade (Coelho 1995, Wachtel 2011).

the *Carreira da Índia* was still enormous in the early 17th century. The conditions for transporting slaves across the Atlantic were terrible (the scarcity of drinking water increased the mortality rate), but for the white crews, the sea voyage was also a gamble. From the first Dutch expedition to Asia in 1595, only 87 out of 249 crew members returned after three years. The average mortality rate on slave ships in the late 16th and early 17th centuries was around 23 per cent, although it ranged from 6.5 per cent to over 33 per cent on a case-by-case basis and reached 27–30 per cent in the 16th century. A reduction in mortality would occur from the 17th century (Parthesius 2010: 34, Newson and Minchin 2007: 10, Almeida Mendes 2008a: 73, Curtin 1969: 277–279).

An important part of these interactions was the formation of the attitudes and skills of young family members in an elaborate system of preparation for the role of international merchant and heir to the family fortune. Their mobility, like that of small merchants aspiring to wealth, was, given the means of transport of the time, almost unbelievable. Spatial mobility, moreover, was an inherent characteristic of most Portuguese merchants: "It was not surprising to hear about Portuguese parents changing houses with their brothers and sisters, children and servants up to five or even six times during their lifetime" (Studnicki-Gizbert 2009: 81f). If the Portuguese empire can be described, according to A.J.R. Russell-Wood's apt phrase, as a "world on the move", this applies all the more to *La Nação*. Mobility was an essential condition for the 'Nation' to maintain its unique network of intercontinental trade links and information contacts.

At the same time, trust, which went hand in hand with the widespread dissemination and expansion of the functions of already known financial instruments (such as bills of exchange of various kinds), made it possible to at least partially reduce risk. A similar role was fulfilled by a network of commercial agents and intermediaries scattered in various parts of the world. Among such agents, we not infrequently find, in addition to family members, also ship captains. The direct link between the merchandise and the merchant-investor was no longer regarded as necessary and natural, especially in the case of the important great *comerciantes do grosso trato* standing at the head of the merchant houses. These, in turn, were often included in the elite group of *homens de negócios*. However, sometimes, even great merchants still mustered on ships as captains (for example, one of Diogo Nunes Belmonte's major partners in the slave trade).

Also closely linked to the workings of the network is the concept of so-called '*port Jews*', proposed in the late 1990s in parallel by Lois Dubin and David Sorokin. This distinct type of diaspora would be defined by its focus on long-distance trade and the specific ties formed in ports serving overseas ventures.

It would therefore be a group that formed a natural part of the formation and expansion of commercial capitalism. It has also been pointed out (with some exaggeration) that almost all Jewish communities in the New World – with the exception of Suriname – "were founded by port Jews" (Dubin 2006: 119).

Regardless of how we define the 'port Jew' in relation to other types of Jewish communities, without also entering at this point into a consideration of the notion of the 'Jewish community' in Iberian Latin America (as opposed to the Anglo-Saxon colonies in North America), the 'port Jew' was in a way a natural offshoot of the preeminent role played on both sides of the Atlantic by port cities and overseas trade in the 16th and 17th centuries. Alongside these came a flexibility of approach to matters of faith and the breaking down of cultural barriers (although this was not the general rule, as the rise of anti-Jewish sentiment in Hamburg proved) and a cosmopolitanism that shaped the economic *Weltanschauung* of port communities. The latter also reflected a particular kind of homogenisation of behaviour, a focus on international trade, the increasing importance of calculus and economic calculation in assessing success and/or failure, in sum, as 17th-century, also Jewish, critics of modernity in its then embryonic form pointed out, the emergence of a materialist 'Babylon' threatening traditional values (Schorsch 2009: 53f). In the economies of 16th-century Europe, which were affected by the price revolution and the shock of the huge influx of silver bullion and coins, the scholastic account of economic processes must have broken down. This was stated, for example, in the first half of the 16th century by Cristóbal Villalón, the author of literary dialogues as well as economic works, writing about "making money with money" (Almedia 1997: 9). He pointed out that the hitherto merchant, who performed a useful role by satisfying himself with a decent, socially acceptable percentage, was giving way to an unscrupulous player – in the market for goods and money. In the 18th century, such a new *Weltanschauung* would appear above all in connection with stock exchanges and the growing scale of financial operations. This is reflected in the entry 'Presbyterian' in Voltaire's Philosophical Dictionary (1901), who noted that at the Royal Exchange of London "the Jew, the Mohammedan, and the Christian bargain with one another as if they were of the same religion and bestow the name of infidel on bankrupts only".

Finally, let us emphasise once again that trust and reputation, "commercial proficiency and rectitude", while firmly rooted in religious and family loyalties, were not entirely determined by ethnicity, religion or kinship. Also "[m]embership in the Sephardic diaspora at large (…) facilitated but did not ensure bonds of trust among those involved in long-distance trade" (Trivellato 2009b: 9). These notions also referred to relationships beyond the circle of New

Christians and Jews, and thus to commercial operations involving adherents of other religions in common action alongside Old Christians. Ties implying community, if we understand by them family and circles of friends and, in the case of crypto-Jews and "new Jews" from Amsterdam or Jews from Italian cities, also a common faith, were located in broader intercultural context. In short, "[t]he number of kin may be counted; their significance cannot" (Swetschinski 1981: 65). However, in researching *La Nação* networks there has been a tendency to absolutise the importance not only of religion, but also of kinship, at the expense of the broader notion of trust.

Interdependence (Studnicki-Gizbert 2002), as it is referred to here, took various forms, but certainly without this element, which implied a certain degree of openness of ethnic and/or religious communities, the networks created by *La Nação* would have been far less effective. This was also true of the growing group of Jewish merchants in Amsterdam from the early 17th century. With varying degrees of intensity, their commercial and financial operations in Europe and the Atlantic area were conducted jointly not only with their New Christian relatives, but also with their Catholic and Protestant partners.[9] They were no exception in this. In Jamaica at the end of the 17th century, the successes achieved by Sephardic merchants in large-scale contraband trade were the result of a confluence of two factors: "High levels of trustworthiness within the Jewish community provided a competitive advantage which stimulated envy and retaliation but also allowed the Sephardim to combine with the Christian elite to capture rent-seeking opportunities and obtain political protections" (Zahedieh 2018: 26). Sociality, group solidarity and openness were not only true in such high-risk ventures. The 'Portuguese' who traded French linen from Rouen,

> obtained the cloths from French associates who had direct relations with local weavers. In Arequipa [Peru] some of the linen was passed to native

---

9   The example of three wealthy Sephardic merchants from Amsterdam in the first half of the 17th century was interesting (Roitman 2011: passim). Bento (Baruch) Osorio took an active part in the life of the Jewish community, Manoel Rodrigues Vega was religiously indifferent and saw his links with Judaism primarily as economically important, and finally Manoel Carvalho, who would only emerge in the life of the Jewish community after several years in Amsterdam. All of them collaborated with the Gentiles, and to a much greater extent than the average for Amsterdam's group of Jewish merchants as a whole. Among the more than 16,000 contracts concerning Atlantic trade signed in 1598–1674 by Jewish and New Christian merchants, more than 27 per cent were cross-cultural, mainly with Protestants (Antunes and Silva 2011: 50, 57f).

Andean merchants and *curaças*, who organised its sale among Andean consumers.

STUDNICKI-GIZBERT 2009: 95, 97[10]

In such intercultural contacts there was no room for the all-too-frequent application of double standards when dealing with Gentile trade partners. And this despite the fact that, compared to the Middle Ages, there was a hardening of religious and social barriers blocking contact between Christians and Jews from the 16th century (Katz 1962: Chapter 13). The effectiveness and sustainability of trade contacts required the continuous protection of a certain minimum common institutional infrastructure: standards of weights and measures, the value of money, the certainty of bills of exchange and insurance contracts or, within the limits of reasonable risk, the certainty of trade. These issues were raised, among others, by Rabbi Menasseh ben Israel. The circulation of millions of ducats between Madrid and Antwerp in the first half of the 17th century through New Christian bankers would have been impossible in the absence of such an infrastructure. Thus, it was a matter of universalising merchant practices and customs to stabilise risky international trade. All the more so because "colonial trade was attended with high risks. The commerce was based on a long chain of promises, promises to provide goods, promises to deliver, promises to pay" (Zahedieh 1999: 158). A scholar of Sephardic-Christian trade relations would therefore point to the importance of "routines that generated, if not trust, at least firm expectations about behaviour" (Trivellato 2009b: 4).

Deviations from these rules did occur, of course, but they were treated precisely as regrettable breaches of the rules of the game, which were crucial to the cohesion of the larger system. Although important players, such as Manoel Carvalho of Amsterdam, sometimes got away with cheating on ship and cargo insurance, these were exceptions to the rule. The reaction to deviations from good merchant practices were temporary exclusions from the community or even excommunications (Roitman 2011: 206–208, Strum 2013b: 41). Also, gossip was part of the system of punishment for negative behaviour. In any case, the issue of trust was of crucial importance. In the Atlantic sugar trade, among the trade intermediaries and lower-level agents in the ports we find a number, larger than has been assumed so far, of Catholics and/or Protestants acting for and on behalf of Amsterdam Jews and Portuguese New Christians (Strum 2013b: passim, 2013a).

---

10   *Kurakas* – regional traders and intermediaries and at the same time leaders of Indian communities. Some derived their ancestry from Inca nobility.

Part of the process of setting-up this minimum institutional infrastructure was also the spread of various forms of cargo and ship insurance. The establishment of an efficient and discreet risk insurance chamber (*Kamer van Assurantie en Averij*) in Amsterdam in 1598, as well as the corresponding dispute settlement procedures, fostered the spread of this instrument, which had already been known for at least two centuries. The growing interest in insurance was a response to two challenges: the increasing emergence of intercultural relationships in commercial activities in the first half of the 17th century and the growing scale and complexity of trade (Ebert 2011, Go 2009: 95–116). Also, the increased activity of privateers and pirates encouraged a commensurate rise in risk mitigation.

Finally, note that the networks also contained elements of an informal hierarchy, depending on the resources at the disposal of the particular merchant houses and their advantage in particular markets. This also applied to relationships with local small producers and retail distributors. Vertical integration allowed for the stabilisation of the network as a whole, not to mention the reduction of transaction costs. The latter were interpreted as perhaps the most important contribution of Jewish and New Christian merchants to the growth of the European economy (Studnicki-Gizbert 2009: 107–111, Klooster 2001: 127–129). In the case of the distribution channels of large merchant houses, the capture of at least part of the monopoly rents also came into play. Often, New Christians appeared at both ends of this vertical structure: on the one hand, as big merchants operating on international markets, and on the other as small shopkeepers and peddlars.

The importance of the trade networks created up to the mid-17th century by the New Christians, and from the turn of the 16th century also with the participation of Amsterdam Jews, would become most visible in the trade of two key colonial commodities: sugar and slaves. The first would dominate the Brazilian economy until the end of the 17th century. The second, on the other hand, although linked from the 1570s primarily to the Brazilian plantations and then to the Caribbean, would first appear in Spanish America. The slave trade remained mainly in the New Christians' hands, without the noticeable participation of Amsterdam Jews.

CHAPTER 7

Brazilian Sugar and the New Christians: Networks and Production

Let us return once more to Fernão de Noronha, a well-known New Christian elite merchant. The 1503 expedition in six ships to the new territory discovered by Cabral was not his first important venture. A year earlier, Noronha had bought a license to trade in the Rios dos Escravos area (Benin coast) from Bartolomeo Marchionni, a Florentine merchant-banker already resident in Lisbon for years and trusted by the king. Spices and ivory and slaves were involved. It was a lucrative venture (Norton 2007: 186f, Thomas 1998: 38f, 105, Wiznitzer 1960: 7–9, Metcalf 2005: 60). Marchionni had already been trading in these goods since the 1480s under a license purchased from the Crown for the substantial sum of 40,000 cruzados. It was he who supplied almost half of the slaves sold in Portugal between 1493–95. Since the end of the 15th century he had also traded sugar with Italian merchants from Madeira, subsequently engaging in trade with India. His ships also took part in the expeditions of Vasco da Gama and Pedro Álvares Cabral. Noronha also invested twice in the trade with India (Thomas 1998: 86, Silva 1987: 293, 328, 330).

Fernão de Noronha, whose activities would cover the Benin coast and India in the early 16th century, as well as Brazil and, as a transit point, the Cape Verde, forms one of the first New Christian trade networks in the Atlantic area. Marchionni too, although already heavily involved in trade with India, continued to collaborate in Noronha's ventures in Brazil. Other Italian merchants were also involved. One of the ships serving their joint activities brought 30 Indian slaves, parrots, jaguar skins and Brazilian wood in 1511. The latter in particular was a profitable venture: Noronha's annual turnover of 50,000 ducats from the sale of 1,200 tonnes of wood included a profit of 10,000 ducats, i.e. 20 per cent usually expected from sea ventures (Johnson 1999: 486). Before long, other partners, including members of his extended family, would participate in his ventures or supported by him. In 1504, he would also provide surety to a group of New Christian merchants who were seeking, successfully, a contract for tax farming in the Cape Verde. Among them was his nephew. Then, from 1510 to 1516, this contract was taken over by António Rodrigues Mascarenhas, son of the New Christian Lisbon merchant and slave trader João Rodrigues Mascarenhas. This important partner of Noronha, a "Marrano upstart (...), the farmer of taxes", was infamous and "through him all the Marranos incurred hatred" (Graetz 1894: 486). He was killed after a dramatic battle in a pogrom against the New Christians in Lisbon in 1506.

The example of Fernão de Noronha shows the formation and activity of a trade network, also with associates outside *La Nação*, far ahead of the boom initiated in the last decades of the 16th century in trade with Brazil. Its symbols would become sugar, slaves and, from the end of the 16th century, also tobacco. In the 16th century, however, such networks primarily served the Mediterranean trade and facilitated Northern Europe's contacts with the area. It is here, in trade with Catholic and Protestant merchants, that the great fortunes of the New Christians, such as the Ximenes families of Antwerp and Lisbon, were also made. These descendants of Spanish Jews, who emigrated to Portugal, were already present in the Mediterranean trade. At the beginning of the 1690s, Fernão Ximenes ensured, with his partners, the supply of grain to crop failure-stricken Tuscany at a high profit (Swetschinski 2004: 107, Braudel 1995: 673). Such networks played an equally important role in the second half of the 16th century in the trade of Northern Europe with Portugal, also plagued by bad harvests and dependent on grain from the Baltic region. These, in turn, were provided, as well as supplies of wood for masts, by the Dutch cooperating with the Portuguese on their *fluitschepen*.

From the beginning of the 17th century, the great Amsterdam Jewish merchants Manoel Carvalho and Bento (Baruch) Osorio joined this trade. The former arrived in the Netherlands from Brazil and, between 1606 and 1608, took control of the grain trade that the Amsterdam Jews had been conducting with partners in Livorno and Venice. Still, the focus of his business was Brazilian sugar imported through a relative from Oporto. This grandson of Pedro Álvares Madeira, co-owner of the Camarajibe plantation, one of the first in Pernambuco, was regarded in Amsterdam as an expert on trade with Brazil. At the same time, although he arrived in Amsterdam in 1603, he did not maintain links with the emerging Jewish community until 1616 and, like Manoel Rodrigues Vega, did not change his name to a Jewish one (Roitman 2011: 43–45, 105f). In contrast, Osorio, probably the richest Jewish merchant in Amsterdam in the first half of the 17th century, was heavily involved in the Portuguese salt trade – for the Netherlands and other areas of Northern Europe. Between 1615–17, he chartered more than 200 ships for this purpose, acting as a factor for the Lisbon merchant Andrea Lopes Pinto, the *asiento* contract holder for Brazilian salt and timber (Israel 1990a: 423, Ebert 2008: 72). The two Amsterdam merchants mentioned here were not exceptions, however. There were also smaller networks serving both Mediterranean and Northern European trade, as well as exchanges with Africa. The importance of the trade with West Africa would increase from the 1520s, firstly because of imported gold and skins, then because of the growing slave trade.

At the same time, a new route to the Indies was also emerging. However, access to the *Carreira da Índia,* dominated by the Crown and the court bureaucracy, aristocracy and royal favourites, as well as to the intra-Indian trade organised under the *Estado da Índia,* was difficult for the New Christians for several decades. Weakly present on the route to India until the 1580s, the New Christians therefore sought their opportunity for much of the 16th century also in the then relatively marginal – except for silver – Atlantic trade. This included the gradually growing importance of the slave trade. At the same time, as Portuguese, they were privileged in this venture because of the control that Portuguese ships, forts and trading posts had over access to West Africa and its human resources.

The New World, on the other hand, has not yet received much attention. This presented an opportunity for enterprising individuals, including conversos and New Christians. However, the initiative for settlement and trade with Brazil – both remaining entirely in private hands – required also, as the Noronha example indicated, the support of the royal court and the important merchant-financiers. Involvement of the Crown was essential given the considerable margin of risk and the high cost of the initial investments. Support was, however, provided mainly in the form of *sesmarias*, which were distributed on behalf of the Crown by the *donatarios*. Thus, it involved grants of land and the right to exploit it, sometimes the provision of tools and tax reliefs. The most popular was exemption from paying *dizimo* for several, usually 10, years. The size of the plots of land allocated to settlers from the 1540s in Bahia on the fertile Recôncavo, in the area adjacent to the bay of Todos los Santos, can be estimated at an average of 72–74 km². The area of the entire Recôncavo was 12,500 km².

On the *sesmaria* set aside in the name of the king, the largest plantation and *engenho* was created on the Sergipe River in 1560. It was first owned by the absentee son of Brazilian Governor Mem de Sá and was actually at the disposal of the Governor himself. After his death, it passed into the hands of his daughter and her husband Fernando de Noronha, Count of Linhares. The legality of this operation was contested, but unsuccessfully (Barrett and Schwartz 1975: 534f, Schwartz 1985: appendix). *Engenho* Sergipe, however, was an exception both because of the scale of production and the number of slaves and the noble birth of the owners. After a wave of initial endowments favouring well-heeled *fidalgos* and influential foreign merchant-financiers at court, the majority of *sesmarias* were given to Portuguese who did not belong to the wealthy, ancestral nobility, or financial elite. It was on them that sugar cane plantations and sugar mills would later be established (Ferraz 2008: 64–66). This created, given the fact of the selective granting of noble titles, problems of self-identification for the new land elite. We should add that there were also foreign Catholics among the less wealthy beneficiaries.

The importance of capital transfers from the Portuguese metropolis was probably limited, and in any case can hardly be considered decisive. Credit, on the other hand, provided by religious orders and charitable institutions mainly to Old Christians, would appear relatively late, on a wider scale only in the second half of the 17th century. Thus, alongside Crown assistance, in the early period of the expansion of the sugar economy, up to the 1670s-80s, and probably also in the first half of the 17th century, the role of merchant credit provided to plantation owners on pledge of the sugar harvest and production "was an essential element in the early growth of the industry" (Schwartz 2004b: 176).

It was almost as a rule expensive credit, though not usurious. However, the merchants granting it (often New Christians), known as *onzeneiros* (from the 11 per cent demanded), were seen almost as scammers, and certainly as a threat to the property of indebted and often insolvent planters. Indeed, the interest rate on loans made in Amsterdam was somewhat lower, but the higher risk of investments made in Brazil must not be overlooked. Incidentally, the interest rate on loans made in the 16th and early 17th centuries to the Spanish Crown – a risky venture but still seen as profitable – ranged between 8 and 14 per cent (Álvarez Nogal 2003: 6). Among the *onzeneiros,* the first visitor of the Inquisition in Brazil mentioned the suspected heretic João Nunes Correira, who came from a New Christian family of wealthy planters and merchants. It was alleged that the loans he made threatened the fortunes of two members of Pernambuco's political elite, the Old Christians Filippe Cavalcanti and Cristóvão Lins. Both belonged to the group of the largest and most influential *senhores de engenhos,* and also had close ties with the politically dominant families of the subsequent *donatarios.* Unlike the others, Pernambuco was a hereditary captaincy. Although at the beginning of the 17th century the Crown stepped in to defend the owners of the *engenhos* against what they claimed were ruinous debts (and the seizure of part of the plantations to pay off the debt), after protests from the merchant-creditors the king withdrew this policy in 1614 (Gonçalves 2007: 49, 64f, Schwartz 1985: 195). Its continuation threatened to financially paralyse the colony, already struggling with a lack of liquidity, and a scarcity of bullion coinage resulted in reduced tax revenues.

Among the first investors in *engenhos* we find not only Portuguese. Among the pioneers was the trading house of the Antwerp-based Catholic merchant-financier Erasmus Schetz and his sons. This influential family from Hesse was close to the Fuggers and Welsers in terms of importance and financial resources.

In addition to the southern Netherlands, the network it created also covered Germany, Italy and Brazil, included both Spanish conversos and Portuguese New Christians and could count on the support of Brazilian Jesuits from the mid-16th century. We also know that, in the early 1530s, Erasmus Schetz helped a persecuted New Christian in Antwerp who had cooperated with the merchant house of Diogo Mendes, saving his property from Spanish officials (Leoni 2005: 19f). Already in the 1630s, Erasmus Schetz became first a shareholder and then the owner of an *engenho* in São Vicente called São Jorge dos Erasmos. Martim Afonso de Sousa, founder of the São Vicente capitaincy, also collaborated with Schetz, while setting a good example as royal governor by investing in the *engenho* together with his German partner. Schetz's example is followed by other German merchants, the Flemish and, at the end of the 16th century, the Dutch, who invested in the growing in importance Pernambuco and Bahia (Stols 2004: 262f, Salvador 1978: 44f, Thomas 1998: 123, Pons 1985: 249, Emmer 1993: 81, Ebert 2008: 78f).

Carefully arranged marriages consolidated the social and economic position of the great planters. The aforementioned Filippe Cavalcanti of Pernambuco was a Florentine nobleman who, through his marriage to the daughter of Jerônimo de Albuquerque, a member of the family of the second *donatario* Duarte Albuquerque Coelho, found himself among the elite of this rich capitaincy. Also through marriage, this time to the daughter of the wealthy merchant and planter Arnau de Holanda, the German Cristóvão Lins found himself in this elite. Holanda, born in Utrecht and nephew of Pope Hadrian VI, arrived in Brazil with the first *donatario* Duarte Coelho Pereira and took part in the creation of the capitaincy. Cristóvão Linsa's brother, Sibaldo, in turn entered the family of the second *donatario*. Let us add that the Lins brothers came from a family of bankers from Augsburg, while one of their relatives represented the Fuggers in Portugal. And last but not least, through the appropriately arranged marriages of his five daughters, Arnau de Holanda created in Pernambuco an almost clan-like system of political, economic and social relationships and loyalties (Gonçalves 2007: 42, 49, 64f, Ferraz 2008).

There was no shortage of New Christians among the investors in this early period, including among the owners of the first five *engenhos* that began operating in Pernambuco in the 1540s. The owner of one of the first sugar mills and plantations in this captaincy was a *judaizante,* the merchant Diogo Fernandes from the Portuguese port of Viana do Castelo. Accompanying him as a partner was a native of Madeira – also a New Christian – Pedro Álvares Madeira, who, it was claimed, knew a bit about sugar production and plantation management. However, the Camarajibe plantation (also called Santiago, after São Thiago) founded by Diogo Fernandes proved to be a risky venture. After its partial destruction by Indians in 1554, both partners went bankrupt. This was mentioned in 1555 in a letter to the king by Jerônimo de Albuquerque, a friend of the bankrupt planter, a relative of the first *donatario* and de facto governor of Pernambuco, Duarte Coelho Pereira. He emphasised, with some exaggeration, Diogo Fernandes' vast experience in sugar production and asked for support for his suddenly impoverished friend. To no avail. Diogo Fernandes' wife Branca Dias, who was still accused of 'Judaising' in Portugal in 1543, and above all his father-in-law Bento Dias de Santiago, a wealthy merchant from the Pernambucan port of Olinda, nevertheless continued the economic activity initiated by Diogo Fernandes for some time. This was possible by using their extensive contacts with planters in Pernambuco and sugar merchants in Lisbon. Branca Dias, on the other hand, created Brazil's first orphanage for girls in the following years, only to fall victim again to the Inquisition (Wiznitzer 1960: 10f, Schwartz 2004: 160. 174, Mello 1989: 7f, 122–124, also Ribenboim 2000).

After less than a century, the trade networks created by New and Old Christians, and from the beginning of the 17th century also involving Jewish merchants from Amsterdam, would already connect Asia, Europe, Africa and the New World (Boyajian 2001: 478, Roitman 2011). Streams of goods and finance emerging in one place facilitated ventures in other parts of the world. Silver, sugar, cochineal, cocoa and other New World luxury goods were transported to Europe to finance trade with India, from where pepper and other spices and textiles and silk flow to Europe, while in a further movement, through exchanges with African merchants of Indian and European textiles and iron, they provide finance for the supply of slaves transported to Latin America. Asian wares also arrive via Lisbon in exchange for sugar to Brazil, while on the Manila Galleons they reach Spanish America in exchange for silver. Also, diamonds from India and corals from the Mediterranean finance European and Atlantic trade. Established contacts and routes cut across the formal boundaries of empires, involving merchants in joint ventures across existing political and religious divides, sometimes also linking partners from warring states. This was the case for the Dutch and Portuguese, who attempted (illegally) to trade despite the resumption of hostilities after 1621.

The economic elite of the New Christians emerged in the first half of the 17th century as part and parcel of the international system of commerce and finances co-created by *La Nação*. From a number of cases, one was selected that clearly demonstrates the global reach of operations conducted by its members during this period (Boyajian 1979, 1983, 1993, 2001, Álvarez Nogal 1997, 2003, Alpert 2001: 55):

The fortune of Manuel de Paz and his stepbrother Fernando Tinoco de Carvalho, both at the head of one of the largest groups of New Christian merchants and financiers in the first half of the 17th century, grew out of Brazilian sugar.[1] In the mid-16th century, their father managed sugar mills in Pernambuco and then, with his brothers, launched his own now *engenhos*. Manuel de Paz, born in Brazil around 1581, grew up with his adoptive brother in Lisbon, where his father had moved, leaving the Brazilian plantations in the hands of family and administrators. Thanks to family colligations, both brothers were already related to at least three family clans of New Christian wealthy merchants firmly established in Asian trade, as well as commercial and financial operations in Europe and Brazil, at the threshold of their merchant careers. In the early 17th century, Manuel de Paz and Fernando Tinoco de Carvalho were already trading in Goa, acquiring proficiency in the profession of international merchant. They invested the money of their father, who died in the early 17th century, in Indian diamonds, pearls, porcelain, indigo and cotton and silk products. They also represented the banking house of the Old Christian family Tinoco in Goa, but already linked through joint ventures and marriages to the New Christians. The activities of the two brothers involved a cousin of de Paz in Goa, another foster brother in Bahia and a cousin in the port of Olinda (Pernambuco), involved, among other things, in the slave trade. One of Fernando Tinoco de Carvalho's cousins, also residing in Olinda, was involved in contraband to the Caribbean in addition to the slave trade. His other relatives also held licences to trade and transport slaves from Angola to the New World. After the death of his father, Manuel de Paz returns to Lisbon and acts as the de facto chief merchant of the family and banker in the Tinoco banking house. In the 1730s and 1740s – a time of enormous influence for the New Christian-friendly Count-Duke de Olivares – the wealth created from Brazilian sugar and Indian trade brought Manuel de Paz and his brother into the royal court of Madrid. Along with some twelve of the most prominent *homens de negócios* from Genoese and Portuguese Nova Scotian families, both were among the *asentistas*. We are talking about merchant-bankers financing, at a considerable (until then) profit, the debts of the Crown generated in trade with Asia and in the wars waged in Europe. Indeed, Manuel de Paz was the second, sometimes third, most important

---

1   The coincidence of the name with Duarte de Paz, quoted earlier, and his father 'maestro de Paz' from the Portuguese Entre-Douro-e-Minho is coincidental.

Portuguese financial partner of the Crown. He had already participated with the main Portuguese New Christians in the negotiation of the *asientos* in the 1920s, although, unlike the other partners, he tried to stay away from the political debates on the betterment of the New Christians that accompanied the financial negotiations. He also made efforts to ensure that his name was not too closely associated with the New Christian bankers. He did this so successfully that in the works of some historians he will appear as an Old Christian. Manuel de Paz was also never forced to appear before the Inquisition, although some suspicions about his allegiance to Catholicism did arise in Goa, but fortunately after he had left the colony. The network of international payments led from Madrid by Paz and other members of the Tinoco banking house was supported by a network of closer or more distant relatives living in Antwerp as New Christians, as well as in Rouen, Paris, Amsterdam, Hamburg and Venice (more or less openly as Jews). At the same time, Manuel de Paz took care not only to obtain a title of nobility (which he achieved while still in Portugal by also becoming a knight of the Order of Christ and Avis), but also to ensure that his descendants were members of the elite knightly orders, emphasising 'purity of blood', of Portuguese and Spanish Santiago. The grand masters of these orders were members of the Portuguese and Spanish royal families (sometimes monarchs directly).[2] He was not alone in these efforts. In the merchant circle, benefits of this kind were seen as an important, non-pecuniary part of the profit counted against the sums placed at the disposal of the Crown. Although the titles he obtained did not match those previously given to Genoese merchants, the social advancement achieved by the descendant of a New Christian merchant and planter in Brazil was unquestionable. His sons, in turn, consolidated the position inherited from their father by combining capital with the splendour of aristocratic titles. However, they too, like the descendants of other major New Christian merchant-bankers, paid a heavy price. During Spain's financial collapse, they lost much of the capital still lent by their fathers to the Spanish Crown under the Count-Duke de Olivares. This price – which was also increased by the difficult-to-estimate cost of breaking the solidarity of the New Christian *asentistas* after Philip IV

---

2 Wearing the *hábito* of the order was a sign of the proper genealogy and removed the threat of inquisitorial investigation. This was all the more so since, from the end of the 16th century, there was a tightening of the criteria for membership of the religious military orders (Olival 2004: 17f, Giménez Carrillo 2011).

froze their financial obligations to the Portuguese bankers in 1647 – was nevertheless considered worth paying.

The two brothers, whose history we have recounted here in detail, did not limit themselves to amassing wealth and securing a place for themselves and their descendants in the Iberian economic elite. Along with several other prominent New Christian *homens de negócios,* they also took part in risky political and financial ventures involving them in court politics during de Olivares' time. The capital mobilised in favour of the crown by the New Christians amounted to millions of cruzados. Huge sums passed through the hands of three Portuguese *asentistas,* who operated with the help of New Christian financiers in Antwerp, between 1631 and 1640, which they transferred to Spanish financial agents in Flanders, Italy, Germany or Portugal. Performing this task – the transfer of some 30 million ducats that financed the wars fought by the Spanish Habsburgs – required the ability to mobilise silver bullion and coins within Spain itself, as well as to build trust among bankers outside Spain. Its absence would have prevented deferred payment operations or the availability of short-term credit (Boyajian 1983: 71). Other New Christian merchant-bankers, who had also amassed the beginnings of their fortunes in Brazil, participated in the court politics of the independent Portugal from 1640. With mixed results. In contrast, the meltdown of Spanish finances in 1647, preceded by the forced departure of the Count-Duke de Olivares a few years earlier, also meant the economic bankruptcy of many New Christian merchant-bankers. Their continued stay in Spain also became risky. Accused of betraying Spain and supporting independent Portugal, contributing to the financial meltdown, speculating on the value of money and other wickedness, they became easy prey for the Inquisition and growing anti-Semitic sentiment. The reaction was a migration of New Christian bankers primarily to Amsterdam and Rotterdam, as well as London, Hamburg and Paris. It was not only Spanish bankers who emigrated, moreover, but also, with some delay, financiers from Antwerp, many with close ties to the court in Madrid (Israel 1990a: 397f, 434f).

However, the episode of entanglement in court politics and the consequences of the crisis in royal finances should not obscure a fundamental fact: the activities of the two brothers showed the potential of the informal networks that emerged in the 16th and first half of the 17th century. Another New Christian merchant house, Duarte Dias Henriques, counted dozens of collaborators in Antwerp, Amsterdam, Hamburg, Lisbon, Oporo, Naples, Rome, Venice, West Africa, Ciudad de México, Bahia and Pernambuco. Sugar production and marketing were linked by Dias Henriques to the Angolan slave trade and financial operations with the royal court. Jews from Amsterdam, especially global merchants together with Protestant, but also often Catholic associates and trading partners, increased the influence of the *La Nação* networks already established in the Mediterranean and Atlantic. To be sure, however, most of the networks that emerged in the 16th and first half of the 17th century were less ambitious, usually limited to a few associates and correspondents in overseas ports, and/or members of extended family. Unlike globally operating merchant houses, markets and product ranges were also limited. The increasing prevalence of ad hoc partnerships arranged to finance one or two voyages, the greater availability of credit (especially in Amsterdam), the sharing of risk, all made it possible to include small and medium-sized merchants in the network, also on the routes to Brazil.

Appealing to the imagination, therefore, the presence of a few large globally operating trading houses did not mean the emergence of a monopoly, but instead implied their dominant position. Moreover, the Portuguese trade with Brazil did not introduce a system of convoys and restrictions analogous to those in force on the *Carrera de Indias* until the mid-17th century. Despite the issuing of a royal decree in 1592, such convoys were formed only sporadically. Resistance to them from the merchants was effective. They were unwilling to pay an additional 3 per cent tax on the export and import of goods transported. Royal monopolies, such as those on the slave trade, were therefore enforced in a decentralised manner. Caravels were also still popular among the Portuguese. They were characterised by their speed and manoeuvrability – qualities important in the event of a threat, such as after the outbreak of the anti-Dutch uprising in Pernambuco in 1645. Shipowners and captains were thinking about delivering goods and making a profit, not fighting WIC ships. According to Father António Vieira's opinion submitted to King João IV, "The caravels, Sire, are schools for escaping and creating cowards out of seamen" (Costa 2000: 61, Strum 2013b: 261–273). However, the use of this particular vessel was not only a matter of security but facilitated trade open to a diverse group of investors.

As a result, the whole – composed of networks with different scales of operation and sizes of capital – represented a new quality in the Atlantic trade, which linked Portugal, Brazil, Amsterdam and West Africa. Its core element was a merchant house with different levels of activity and decision-making. The key position was occupied by a New Christian father-patriarch/head of house residing in Lisbon or Oporto, who controlled the entire family business. In the case of Amsterdam, reference is made to a Jewish father-patriarch/head of house often in charge of a trading house. In Brazil, there are sons apprenticed as merchants, often also active as plantation managers (*feitores-mor*) or owners. They are generally part of a broader group of 'larger resident commercial agents' – *agentes fixos maiores.* The vast majority of this strategically important group, whose members had considerable capital and were empowered to make autonomous decisions, were trusted New Christians from outside the family. In the group of 542 *agentes fixes maiores* analysed by a Brazilian historian, there were only 110 family members. A small group was made up of trusted Old Christians – just over 7 per cent. At another level were the 'minor mobile trade agents' – *agentes viajantes menores* – in the ports. The composition of this large group was already different: few New Christians, the vast majority being Old Christians. In contrast to the group of *agentes fixes maiores*, these mobile agents were entrusted with much less capital and provided with detailed instructions for action (Strum 2013a: 148f, 150, 157f, see also Silva 2012: 31f).

Combining such a standard structure characteristic of Atlantic trade with trade with Asia within a single merchant house was rare. It was the privilege of the richest, but even in this case one should speak with caution of a planned intercontinental integration. Certainly, however, the sum of the numerous commercial ventures of varying scales linking the Atlantic economy with Asia translated into an interdependence that is difficult to overestimate: "the continued health and survival of the Portuguese State of India (*Estado da Índia*) depended on Brazilian sugar and African slaves" (Boyajian 1983: 12). And an extremely important point: the breakdown of the religious unity of families and circle of acquaintances, characteristic of such structures – sincere and indifferent Catholics appearing alongside crypto-Jews – did not imply a weakening of trade contacts or the rejection of solidarity actions protecting the property of family and friends and ensuring access to markets. References to a common faith and tradition facilitated economic activity but were not a *sine qua non* for cooperation. This was borne out by the often-practiced interaction with Protestant or Catholic partners. Let us therefore emphasise once again: "New Christians in Iberian territories, who traded and cooperated with open Jews elsewhere, cannot automatically be rendered thereby as crypto-Jews" (Schorsch 2006: 4, 2009: 71, Roitman 2009). Nor were crypto-Jews, even those members of the Ximenes d'Aragão family who deepened their links with Catholicism in Antwerp and Florence while interacting with *judaizantes*, religiously indifferent or Amsterdam Jews.

However, before the birth of the global trade network of the two brothers, from the 1640s Brazil, alongside Mexico, became an important area of economic activity for the New Christians in Latin America. Until the middle of the century, it was still sparsely populated by the Portuguese (about 2,000 settlers and officials and 3–4,000 Black slaves) (Marques 1976: 256f). In the following decades it entered an economic boom phase. By 1580, 58,000 emigrants had arrived from Portugal, while the colonial population in that year was already estimated at 30,000 settlers (Eltis 2002: 62, Marcilio 1984: 45). Brazil was not yet a large source of supply of luxury goods. During this period, it was trade with Asia that was the jewel in the Portuguese crown.

Certainly, however, the new colony was already promising. The growing production and trade in sugar was changing the image of Brazil as a country where, a 16th-century author noted not without irony, in place of bullion, only "a red tree called 'brasil', monkeys and parrots were found" (Kula 1970: 24). In this economic expansion of the colonies, the New Christians would, from the mid-16th century, occupy an important place in two spheres: prominent, though not dominant, among the owners of sugar plantations and mills and in the production of sugar, and much more strongly emphasised in the international trade of this commodity, both in the Atlantic and in Europe. At the same time, they would be quite special actors:

> The New Christians who migrated to Brazil–who forged through virgin territory, captured Indians, and came into conflict with the Jesuits–were men of a radically different mindset from the Ashkenazim Jews or the Sephardic Christian converts who spread across the Netherlands, France, and Italy. Highly assimilated and distanced for over a century from Jewish culture, their adventurous and violent lifestyle was markedly different from that of Jews in other parts of the world.
>
> NOVINSKY 2001b: 218

This description of Brazilian New Christians makes it easier to understand the presence of some of them among the *bandeirantes*. This fact, contrary to the stereotype of the Jew, was not accepted by many. Among them was also the co-founder of Brazilian historiography, Capistrano de Abreu, otherwise far from negatively assessing the role of the XNs in Brazilian and Portuguese history. A Jew could not be a *bandeirante*, he argued, "not [of] that fiber" (quoted in Schwartz 1997: XXVIII).

Let us therefore begin with production.

The accelerated growth of the plantation economy in Brazil can only be spoken of from the 1570s. By 1570, plantations were being experimented with along almost the entire coast settled by the Portuguese, from Pernambuco in the north to São Vicente in the south. The first shipment of sugar from Brazil probably reached Portugal as early as 1526, while the commissioning of the first *engenho* in São Vicente dates to 1532–33 (Salvador 1976: 238, Wiznitzer 1960: 10). However, due to the destruction caused by the Indians, these were often short-lived ventures. Also contributing to instability were frequent attacks by the French, interested in Brazilian timber and the lack until the late 1640s of a stable and reasonably effective colonial administration. Despite these unfavourable circumstances, by 1545 there were already 14 *engenhos* operating along the Brazilian coast, including six in Espírito Santo and two in São Vicente. In Bahia, in the Recôncavo area, and in Pernambuco, soon to be the main centres of the sugar economy, only three plantations were established during this period (Diégues Júnior 2006: 15). According to other estimates, in 1545 there were 20 sugar mills active or under construction (Augeron and Vidal 2007: 38). In the following years, the number of plantations in Pernambuco would increase to at least five.

The emerging *engenhos* were generally small-scale ventures, had outdated technologies and struggled to provide a stable Indian workforce. Some were established as investments by royal officials (such as the *donatarios* Afonso de Souza and later Duarte Coelho Pereira) and a small number of aristocrats (generally acting through intermediaries). In the following decades, religious orders and charitable institutions also began to invest in *engenhos*. However, most plantations, except the largest and those located on the best land, were the ventures of settlers who came from low status groups in Portuguese society at the time (including impoverished nobles). Merchants who combined trade with production were active – in the 1680s they accounted for a third of the owners of *engenhos* (Schwartz 1985: 265). Another important episode in the development of the sugar economy was the import from Madeira in 1535 and 1542 by Duarte Coelho Pereira of New Christian foremen familiar with the technology and organisation of sugar production.

By 1570, the number of *engenhos* is already estimated at 60, including 23 in Pernambuco and 18 in Bahia, although information about 70 plantations also appears (Schwartz 1985: 165, Boyajian 2001: 474, Kula 1970: 33). By 1583, there was almost a doubling of the number of plantations to 115, including 66 in Pernambuco and 36 in Bahia. Gabriel Soares de Sousa, a planter and explorer of the Brazilian interior, in his manuscript *Tratado descritivo do Brasil*, prepared in 1587, gives in around 1584–85 the number of 40 *engenhos* (including four under construction) for Bahia, producing a total of 120,000 arrobas of sugar (over 1,700 tons) per year. Incidentally, a similar amount of sugar was produced in the mid-16th century by mills on the island of São Tomé (Schwartz 2010: 82, Małowist 1976: 172). After less than two more decades, by 1600 the number of *engenhos* was already estimated at 190–200 throughout Brazil, while in 1629, one year before the second – this time successful – Dutch invasion, there were 346 *engenhos* in operation, including 90 in Pernambuco, 80 in Bahia and 60 in the fast-growing capital of Rio de Janeiro. However, it is difficult to be precise here. According to other data, as early as 1623 there were 137 *engenhos* operating in Pernambuco, including Paraiba and Itamaracá (yet other researchers write of 121 plantations in 1630) (Schwartz 1985: 165, Barret, Schwartz 1975: 540, Silva 2012: 80). In Bahia and Rio de Janeiro, on the other hand, there is no doubt that the development of the plantation economy would accelerate after the Dutch occupation of Pernambuco. The exclusion of the production of the *engenhos* there from the Brazilian sugar trade for almost a quarter of a century was a strong stimulus for the development of plantations in other capitals.

The figures for sugar production in Bahia in 1584–85 given by Soares de Sousa referred to the initial phase of the sugar boom. A quarter of a century later, in 1610, the 63 plantations in Bahia were already supplying approx. 4,500 tonnes of sugar per year. In Pernambuco almost two decades earlier, in 1591, an equivalent number of more efficient *engenhos* were reportedly producing around 5 600 tonnes. Sugar production in Brazil as a whole rose to over 14,000 tonnes in 1624, with a clearly dominant share of *engenhos* from Pernambuco (8,000 tonnes) and a slightly lower share of plantations from Bahia, and this did not change substantially until 1637 (Schwartz 1985: 168). According to other estimates, the production of 346 sugar mills amounted in 1629 to 22,425 tonnes, which would mean almost a doubling of sugar production in Brazil between 1624 and 1629 (Ebert 2008: 152). Such a sharp increase in production, however, appears to be partly the result of some researchers overestimating the average production of *engenhos* in 1629. The scale of such an overestimation, on the other hand, is much smaller than in Roberto Simonsen's pioneering calculations, which suggested production of around 18,000 tonnes of sugar as early as 1600 (Schwartz 1985: 531, Buescu 2011: 56–58). In any case, progress was enormous. There were also technical innovations. The new mill design (*engenho de tres paus*), introduced from 1612–17, made it possible to greatly reduce costs and, at least in theory, increase the profitability of both the mill itself and the plantation as a whole. However, historians point out that the average productivity of the *engenho* declined from the mid-17th century, for a variety of reasons (the emergence of less efficient small *engenhos*, price fluctuations and the barrenness of the land).

This growing production until the end of the second decade of the 17th century was accompanied by a rapid increase in European demand and prices (although fluctuations were considerable, not without the influence of illegal supplies to, for example, the English market at the end of the 16th century). Sugar produced in 1618 reached a value of 4 million cruzados on the Lisbon market. This would mean that the value of Brazilian sugar was close to that of the Dutch VOC's trade in Asia, although still less than the value of Portugal's entire Asian trade (Boyajian 2001: 474f, Ebert 2008: 174).[3] It was therefore exaggerated, but not overly fanciful for the New Christian Ambrósio Fernandes Brandão, author of *Diálogos das grandezas do Brasil* and owner of three plantations, to write in 1618 that sugar from Brazil "brings in more profit to His Majesty's Treasury, than all those East Indies". He was correctly pointing to the high cost of trade operations in Asia and the maintenance of the colonies, which reduced the net profit to the Crown. In the case of Brazil, "His Majesty does not spend from his own Treasury a single penny" to maintain that colony, "for the income from the tithes that are collected from this land is enough to support it" (quoted in Schwartz 2010: 206, 208f).

The crisis of sugar prices and production in Brazil would emerge in the 1620s largely as a consequence of the resumption of the Iberian Union's war with the Republic after 1621. This increased risks to Atlantic trade, disrupted supplies and at the same time contributed to an increase in forced sugar stocks in Brazilian ports. The relative saturation of the European market was also a problem. An upturn would not occur until the 1630s, although the European market was unstable at the time and price fluctuations in the following decades quite strong. Despite this unfavourable economic climate, it proved profitable to invest in plantations in Barbados. The larger-scale development of English and then French plantations in the Caribbean, initiated in the second half of the 17th century, would fundamentally change the situation in the Atlantic market by the end of the century:

> Between 1650 and 1710, the amount of Brazilian sugar on European markets dropped about 40 percent. (...) In the 1630s, about 80 percent of the sugar sold in London originated in Brazil. By 1670, that figure had fallen to 40 percent; and by 1690, to only 10 percent.
>
> SCHWARTZ 1985: 183

What role did the New Christians play in this almost century-long process of developing the Brazilian sugar economy? Decisive, as we often find in opinions and literature from the period, or exposed but far from dominant?

A clear-cut answer is hard to come by, although Sombart had a firmly held view on the matter when he noted "[the] predominance of Jewish influence in plantation development" (1951: 54). In contrast, Capistrano de Abreu (1997) did not see the need to emphasise their role in the development of the plantation

---

3 Sugar sales in the 1690s reached 2 million cruzados, while Asian pepper turnover reached 0.59 million (Costa Freire, Lains and Münch Miranda 2016: 83).

economy. The reason for such divergent approaches seems obvious: knowledge of the participation of New Christians in the development of sugar plantations until the mid-17th century was, and still is, fragmentary. Treating information on individual ventures involving the xns as a substitute for aggregate data is subject to a considerable margin of error. If, according to Salvador (1978: 51f), most of the *engenhos* in Espírito Santo were controlled by the New Christians at the end of the 16th century, the question arises as to whether such a finding for an already marginal sugar-producing region at that time can also be applied to Bahia and Pernambuco. This is doubtful. Although it is in these centres that we find from the end of the 16th century the extended family clans of the New Christian *senhores de engenho,* João and Diogo Nunes Correira and Diogo Lopes de Ulhoa. Incidentally, the political influence of the latter, thanks to his own wealth and that of his large family, his participation in the conquest of Sergipe (where he received a *sesmaria*) and the favour of the governor, was extremely strong. Despite the Inquisition's accumulation of 65 testimonies accusing him of various transgressions (including the crime of heresy and organising an *esnoga*), he remained beyond its reach. However, he had to wait a long time, as a descendant of the 'Hebrew nation', for the habit of the prestigious Order of Christ (Schwartz 1985: 266, 544, Novinsky 1972: 80f, Boyajian 1983: 23f, Fonséca 2007: 109). In contrast, the opinion of the *judaizantes* seeker in Bahia of the first half of the 17th century, the vicar Manoel Temudo, that "the greater part of those who populate [Bahia] are Jews", was indeed eagerly listened to (Novinsky 1972: 68), but its informative value was limited.

From the scattered information on Bahia, it would appear that between 1635 and 1645 the New Christians identified by the Inquisition made up between 10 and 20 per cent of the population of the colonial capital and Recôncavo, estimated at between 8,000 and 10,000 white inhabitants (Novinsky 1972: 67, 145, 1998: 302f). How many were 'unidentified' is difficult to say. Francisco A. Vernhagen, a classic of Brazilian historiography, reported that in around 1584 the population of Bahia numbered only 2,000 white settlers, 4,000 African slaves and 6,000 Christianised Indians. Whether this implied an over-representation of the New Christians among the white inhabitants of Bahia during this period, we do not know. José Antônio Gonsalves de Mello, on the other hand, reported that in 1593 the xns made up about 14 per cent of the 7,000 'souls' of the white population of Pernambuco. It also mentions 15 per cent (1,200 New Christians among 8,000 white inhabitants). In both cases, reference is made to people already recorded in Inquisition documents. Other sources give slightly different figures: in 1573, the white population of Pernambuco was estimated at 700 families (about 3,500 people), 3,000 soldiers (including valued 400 mounted troops) and 4,000–5,000 slaves (Mello 1989: 7,

Varnhagen 2011: 122, Ferraz 2008: 62). However, through mixed marriages, especially before the arrival of the visiting Inquisition in 1593, many planters and merchants counted among the noble families in Pernambuco were already 'tainted'. By the end of the 16th century, it was estimated that among whites already born in Pernambuco 19.76 per cent were those with 'the blood of the New Christians' (Silva 2012: 188). This was not an insignificant number, but the once mentioned figure of 5,000 *XN*s in Pernambuco under Dutch control (1630–54) (Manchester 1931: 148) was pure speculation. This phenomenon also occurred in Bahia, albeit on a smaller scale. Although the New Christians did not make up the majority of white settlers in the two capitals, their proportion among the middle classes and among the *senhores de engenho* was "high enough": in the 17th and 18th centuries, some 25–30 per cent of the white population in Brazil derived their ancestry from among *XN*s , with varying degrees of 'blood contamination'. In Paraíba, colonised from the 1670s, *XN* descendants probably accounted for as much as half of the white population at one point (Novinsky 1972: 68f, 2009b: 4).

Let us also draw our attention to the extremely important social group of *lavradores de cana* – sugar cane growers, organisationally separate from the elite owners of the *engenhos*. It was they who supplied the raw material to the mills. Many had their own land, but often leased additional land from the sugar mill owners. Such a division of labour was prevalent only in Brazil in the New World and replicated the experience of Madeira, where at the beginning of the 16th century there were 269 cane plantation owners for every 46 sugar mill owners. The composition of the *lavradores* was extremely diverse. In the 17th century, *lavradores* in Bahia included "Catholic priests, New Christian merchants, wealthy widows, and threadbare gentlemen". Significantly, membership of this group, although enjoying lower prestige than *senhores de engenho*, was seen as a prelude to social advancement because of land ownership. *Lavradores* were seen as owners of sugar mills *in spe* (Schwartz 1985: 295f, 303, Vieira 2004: 55).

However, in terms of plantation control, in Bahia, among the owners of the 41 *engenhos* operating in 1587–92, there were 12 New Christians (over 29 per cent). By contrast, according to Inquisition estimates, treated sceptically by Schwartz (1985: 265), in 1618, of the 34 plantations in operation, 20 were in the hands of suspected *XN* heretics (about 59 per cent). However, this was an astonishing estimate bearing in mind that a few years earlier, in 1610, there were already 63 plantations operating in Bahia. In any case, it can be said of the Inquisitors reporting on the situation in Brazil that "they were adept at finding what they wanted to find" (Thomas 1998: 138). The aim was to prove the thesis of the economic dominance of the *XN*s and the danger it entailed. In Pernambuco, where the number of mills increased from 23 to 121 between

1570 and 1630, 12 New Christians (about 16 per cent) were among the owners of 77 *engenhos in* 1608, while between 1609 and 1623 they owned 23 *engenhos*. According to other estimates, the number of *engenhos* in this capitaincy increased from 66 to 111 between 1609 and 1623, while 10 remained in the hands of New Christians. By the end of the 1720s, during the boom in sugar production that continued despite the difficulties in Atlantic transport caused by the war, 59 sugar plantations out of 346 in operation throughout Brazil (17 per cent) were probably in the hands of New Christians (Boyajian 2001: 475, Mello 1989: 26).

Much more detailed data on the occupations of New Christians in Bahia and Pernambuco one can find in the information gathered during two visits of the Inquisition, in 1591–1595 and 1618, respectively.[4] During the first visitation, three *senhores de engenho* and two *lavradores de cana* were identified among the 33 New Christians suspected of being Judaised in Pernambuco. On the other hand, during the second visitation, among the 54 New Christians accused in Bahia eight were owners of *engenhos* and four were owners of sugar cane plantations (according to other findings there were five *senhores de engenho* owners of eight cane plantations) (Pijning 2001: 492f, Wiznitzer 1960: 40). Between 1620 and 1660, 21 *senhores de engenho* and 9 *lavradores* (a total of 20 per cent of the suspect group) were among the 150 suspected heretic New Christians from Bahia. Assuming that many New Christian potential heretics were not included in the circle of suspects, and taking into account the suggestion that the Inquisition in the 17th century cautiously questioned the religious legitimacy of major *senhores de engenho*, even then their share as a group among elite sugar mill owners and those on the lower rung of the social ladder of *lavradores* was far from dominant (Novinsky 1972: 176, 70). In brief, it was substantial, difficult to overlook, but far from a monopoly.

Almost a century later (1700–1749), in the third most important sugar plantation region, Rio de Janeiro, 35 *senhores de engenho* and 30 *lavradores de cana* were among the 291 New Christians (men) suspected by the Inquisition. The group of suspects included members of the illustrious Vale family, settled in Rio de Janeiro since 1600. Five generations of these New Christians formed the basis of the economic prosperity of the family, which, before being decimated

---

4 From 1579, the role of de facto tribunal of the Inquisition was performed by the Bishop of Bahia assisted by the Jesuits and supported by the Visitor of the Inquisition (Azevedo 1922: 226f, Mello 1989: ixf, 170f). In subsequent years, lesser cases and the fate of suspects from the lower classes were decided by diocesan courts (thus saving the cost of transporting them to Portugal). In contrast, accused Judaisers and wealthy people whose property was subject to confiscation were generally tried in Lisbon (Novinsky 2001: 223f, 1998: 301).

by the Inquisition, owned four *engenhos* at the beginning of the 18th century,
together with sugar cane plantations, one of which was considered to be large.
As the number of sugar mills in the region in 1710 was 136, so the New Christian
owners of the *engenhos* would have made up about 26 per cent of the group of
planters. This was highly likely. According to some estimates, there were 21 New
Christians among the owners of 101 plantations in the 17th century, including
the very large ones owning more than 100 slaves. The higher, relatively, proportion of *senhores de engenho* among the suspects in the 18th century by the
Inquisition reflected quite well the different occupational structure of the
New Christians in Rio de Janeiro compared to Bahia and Pernambuco, less
focused on trade (Pijning 2001: 494, Schwartz 1985: 168, Gorenstein and Calaça
2005: 106).[5] The proportion of New Christians in the overall white population
of Rio de Janeiro was high, although it was an exaggeration to claim, as the
French traveller and merchant François Froger did, that in 1695 they made up
three-quarters of the white population of the city and its surroundings. At the
beginning of the 18th century, among the 20,000 total population of Rio de
Janeiro and the province, only the suspected and imprisoned New Christians,
numbering 1,118, accounted for about 6 per cent, while among the white and
free population, they accounted for about 24 per cent (Gorenstein and Calaça
2005: 112, 388).[6]

Overall, by the mid-17th century, the contribution of the New Christians to
the potential of the Brazilian sugar economy was at least 20 per cent (Boyajian
2001: 476). Such an estimate seems to reflect the consensus reached among
historians, although it still cannot be taken as definitive:

> Although claims in the early seventeenth century that most of the
> Brazilian engenhos were owned by New Christians were exaggerated,
> there is no doubt that New Christians played an active role in forming the
> sugar economy and were an important social element among the early

---

5   In the 17th century, the political dominance of the *senhores de engenho* in the municipal
     council (*senado da câmara*) of Salvador, the colonial capital, was unquestionable. In Bahia,
     the power elite would also include the great cattle breeders. Only in the 18th century would
     the merchant elite become part of the political elite in Bahia. By contrast, in 18th century
     Rio de Janeiro, it was not the planters but the merchants who wielded de facto political and
     economic power (Russell-Wood 2002: 136).
6   The embittered Frenchman insisted that the governor's restriction on his ability to trade in
     Rio de Janeiro was supposedly due to the vast preponderance of "Jews" in the city (Boxer
     1962: 107).

senhores de engheno. (...) a large proportion of the engenhos were in the hands of New Christians.

SCHWARTZ 1985: 266[7]

In turn, the financing of plantations controlled by the New Christians was not fundamentally different from the general practice in this regard. Thus, we are talking about substantial investments, which could only be financed from own capital in a handful of cases. The main source of capital for the planters was credit advanced by merchants. In the 16th and 17th centuries, this could sometimes mean one and the same person. Like the Old Christians, the new ones also often combined the role of merchant and plantation owner.

The example of the influential Nunes Correira family in Pernambuco and Paraiba at the end of the 16th century, with family and trade contacts in Portugal and other European countries, was admittedly – given the scale of the operations involved – not typical, but it reflected well the essence of combining both roles, including internationally. Not only were the brothers João and Diogo Nunes Correira owners of several *engenhos*, but João Nunes also belonged to the elite of Pernambucan merchants (*comerciante do grosso trato*). According to a Brazilian historian, he can be described as the 'capitalist' of the era. Diogo Nunes Correira, on the other hand, not only ruled two *engenhos* in the newly colonised Paraiba but had previously participated in the battles for this new territory. Incidentally, among those fighting the Indians, the New Christians also included the aforementioned Ambrósio Fernandes Brandão and several others. The production, internal transport and, eventually, the sale of sugar were largely carried out within the family network. Also through family contacts in Lisbon, provided by the third brother, Henrique Nunes Correira, João and Diogo Nunes were linked by common interests with Ximenes d'Aragão in Antwerp and other important trading houses. Arrested in 1592 in Bahia as a *judaizante* and accused of insulting the cross, he then found himself at the end of the year in the hands of the Lisbon Inquisition. However, he was very lucky and had influential protectors. As early as the end of January 1593 he was released from prison on bail by a decision of a commission of Inquisitors, which was later approved by the General Council of the Holy Office. The accusation made by the Visitor in Bahia was considered poorly founded. Set free, he moves to Madrid and then Seville. Here, he and other family members became involved in numerous commercial ventures and financial operations (including with the Spanish Court). It is worth mentioning that João Nunes Correira

---

7   A misunderstanding, however, was Friedman's (1998: 58) remark that by 1590 only one plantation – out of 200 in operation – was in Jewish hands.

was the uncle of João Nunes Saravia and, in a way, guided the beginnings of the commercial career of this later negotiator of cooperation between the New Christian merchant-bankers and the court (Mello 1989: Chapter 3, Gonçalves 2007: 48–50, Carrasco Vázquez 2004, also Assis 2007).

To add to this, some *engenhos* belonged to New Christian absentee owners, for whom the focus of their interests was in Portugal and Northern Europe. They left the supervision of the plantation in the hands of associates or trusted *feitores* (managers), often family members. An important addition to this phenomenon was the considerable fluidity within the group of New Christian *senhores do engenho*. Of the list of ten planters from Pernambuco who were active in 1609, only two are also found in the 1623 list. However, this is not certain information – some data on the contracts made are missing. The unknown names of the new owners could just as well have referred to members of a closer or more distant family, and the 10-year tax exemption period encouraged formal fluidity within the group of *engenhos* owners (Mello 1989: 8f, Ricardo 2006: 61f).

The less wealthy *lavradores da cana* – and these made up the majority of the New and Old Christians operating in the sugar economy – were much more dependent on merchant credit. Credit was extended not only for current expenses, but also for more serious investments, such as the purchase of slaves. And the terms of credit were often extremely exorbitant. On the other hand, slave traders were sometimes at a disadvantage when it came to the purchase of slaves by planters. In the event of an accumulation of supplies at the ports and an oversupply, it was the buyers who dictated the terms of purchase. And last but not least, although some *lavradores da cana* moved up the ladder of income and prestige through marriage and entry into wealthy New Christian families, this was not a mass phenomenon.

In the 16th century, some funds also flowed in as investments in sugar production by Flemings, Italians or from Portugal itself. This source, however, lost its importance from the third decade of the 17th century (the financing of plantations in Pernambuco during the 'Dutch Brazil' era is a separate issue). It cannot be ruled out that this was linked to the fact that the place of Portuguese-born plantation owners, who prevailed in the 16th and even in the first half of the 17th century, was increasingly taken by Brazilian-born *masombos* (the equivalent of Spanish *criollos*), also *XN* s. Their contacts with the metropolis were no longer so close. In contrast, such a phenomenon did not appear among the merchant elite in Bahia, among other places. Successors in the profession of international merchant were still largely descended from grandchildren residing in Portugal in the 18th century, while sons already born in Brazil moved up the scale of social prestige by becoming planters (Schwartz 1985: 204, Pijning 2001: 493, Flory and Smith 1978: 574–576).

Sugar merchants' credit, extended against future cane harvest or sugar production remained, therefore, for most *lavradores* and *engenhos* owners a primary source of finance. It solved the problem of money shortage to some extent. The issue of liquidity and lack of capital was constantly raised by planters and the colonial administration. They sometimes resorted, as in Rio de Janeiro in 1614, to sugar as a money equivalent, although in this case there were probably other reasons at play than just the lack of coinage. It has been suggested that sugar as a money substitute was a way of resolving the conflict between planters and merchants in a situation of sharply falling sugar prices, with a preference for the former (Lima 2012). A partial solution to this problem was the illicit influx of silver from Potosí provided by the *pelureiros*, with the help of Portuguese and Spanish merchants from Buenos Aires. However, it should be borne in mind that the operation of the plantation did not imply monetisation of all parts of its operations. The way costs were calculated took into account the fact that some of them were not expressed in money. This made it easier to overcome the barriers associated with its scarcity (Schwartz 1985: 218–229, Kula 1970: 142–151, Miller 1993: 145f). While this led to a reduction in the market's influence on the allocation of plantation resources, including weakening the incentives for technical innovation, this is a separate issue. In contrast, for young apprentices in the plantation or merchant profession, there remained the path of laboriously climbing the income ladder by accumulating capital in small transactions, sometimes investing in the purchase in Africa of a few slaves, all the while acting as a commercial agent. Combining practice in the profession with petty accumulation and a stroke of luck sometimes ensured success. And not just in theory. The New Christian *asentistas* under Philip IV, João Nunes Saravia, although related to the Nunes Correira family, which was influential in Brazil and Portugal in large numbers, was still an indigent salesman in the early 17th century. It was only João Nunes Correira's inclusion in the trade with Asia and Brazilian timber that launched his financial career (Alpert 2001: 60, Ricardo 2006: 111f). In turn, the aim of all these efforts was to enter the prestigious group of *engenhos* owners.

In contrast, the question of whether and to what extent the New Christians benefited from credit placed at the planters' disposal by monasteries, convents and charitable institutions is an unresolved issue. This also applies to the hypothesis of plantations being financed on a wider scale with capital provided from the turn of the 16th and 17th centuries by Jewish merchants from Amsterdam (Schwartz 2004b: 191f). However, it cannot be ruled out, if only in view of the intensive contacts between Brazilian New Christians and Jews in Amsterdam. Moreover, they were not limited to economic relations. A joint endeavour between 25 Jewish merchants from Amsterdam, Hamburg, Venice

and the New Christians of Pernambuco was the creation in 1615 of the charitable institution *Santa Companhia de Dotar Órfãs e Donzelas*, whose task was
to help orphans and poor maidens of the *nação portuguesa e da castelhana*,
also by providing the latter with a dowry. It was a successful initiative: the
number of merchants supporting it had risen to 78 by 1620. New Christian merchants from Portugal and Jewish merchants from the Republic also sometimes
owned or co-owned plantations. It is difficult to rule out capital transfers supporting production and trade in such a situation. At the turn of the 16th and
17th centuries, 38 New Christian merchants and merchant-planters were active
in Pernambuco – including major ones who were securing sugar supplies for
partners in Northern Europe. In turn, other *senhores de engenho* returned to
Portugal and operated there as sugar merchants (Silva 2012: 93, Koen 1970: 35,
Swetschinski 1981: 67–70, Mello 1989: 19). In any case, some authors have pointed
to the key role of Flemish and Dutch investments located in both transport and
sugar production controlled by Brazilian growers (Furtado 1971: 8f, also Prado
Jr. 1981: Chapter 4, Miller 1993: 126f).

However, the participation of the New Christians in Brazil's economic development was not limited to the control and/or management of the *engenhos*.
Crafts (*artes* or *ofícios mecânicas*) and agriculture to meet domestic demand,
as well as other professions related to the urban economy (doctors, apothecaries, soldiers, clerks, domestic servants), in addition to trade, were also an
important part of their activities. In 17th-century Bahia, 12 per cent of New
Christians were artisans, including the proletarians of the time: shoemakers,
barbers, bakers, musicians and sailors (Strum 2013b). The poet Bento Teixeira,
author of Brazil's first poem *Prosopopéia* and persecuted by the Inquisition,
would also appear among the New Christians in the late 16th and early 17th
centuries.

Complementary information on these groups can be found once again in
the data on the occupational structure of the New Christians accused by the
Inquisition. In Bahia in the 1690s, those employed in non-plantation agriculture accounted for 21 per cent of the accused group, while artisans accounted
for 8 per cent. In the following decades, the share of these groups decreased,
while that of merchants increased. In Rio de Janeiro in the first half of the
18th century, we find among the accused, respectively, more than 11 per cent of
those employed in non-plantation agriculture and about 3 per cent of artisans.
In both regions, the share of urban occupations outside of trade and handicraft had been increasing since the late 16th century (Pijning 2001: 492–494).
In many cases these were the professions of lawyer and doctor, which were formally closed to the New Christians. Studying law or medicine was difficult for
them due to the adoption of the 'purity of blood' principle by most universities

in Portugal and Spain. In contrast, there were no New Christians among the persecuted associated with cattle breeding in the interior (*sertão*). In the 17th century, livestock breeding and grazing were largely in the hands of a few powerful families, the *poderosos do sertão,* in Bahia (Russell-Wood 1992: IV137).

And finally, a small but economically important group were the New Christian tax farmers, collecting above all the *dízimos* for the benefit of the Church and the Crown. This notorious activity was also an opportunity to accumulate considerable capital. However, not always. A bad economy made tenders for the purchase of tax licenses less attractive. This was the case after the outbreak of war in Europe in 1618, and after the resumption of the war between the United Provinces and the Iberian Union in 1621. Indeed, in such situations, the total cost of the license and the expenses of tax collection may have been higher than the eventual profit (Strum 2013b). While it would be an exaggeration to speak of a monopoly of New Christians in this field, they were, as in the metropolis, well placed as tax collectors for pragmatic reasons.

Tax farming was also combined with involvement in other spheres of the economy and public life. Diversification was a condition for success as well as for security and survival. This applied both to diversification in trade and to combining trade with agricultural and/or mining activities. The New Christian Bento Dias de Santiago, already mentioned in the adventures of Diogo Fernandes, who from the mid-1670s rented the right to collect *dizimos* in Pernambuco and Bahia, was also a significant merchant and *engenho* owner. It was probably with him that the author of *Diálogos das grandezas do Brasil* began his plantation career as a *feitor da fazenda*. Overseas trade and the leasing of *dizimos* were combined at the beginning of the 17th century by the two largest sugar exporters in Pernambuco, both XN. In Paraiba it was Duarte Ximenes, who exported more than 80 tonnes of sugar a year, while in Itamaracá it was Manuel Nunes Matos, exporting around 70 tonnes. The latter emigrated in 1606 to Amsterdam, where he played a large role in the Jewish community. The partners of both merchants were, in Portugal and Antwerp, members of the Ximenes d'Aragão family and the Dias de Milão, also present in Brazil. At the beginning of the 18th century, some members of the New Christian Paredes family in Rio de Janeiro combined the ownership of *engenhos* with the profession of lawyer and important administrative positions (Mello 1989: 11, Ricardo 2006: 61f, Gorenstein and Calaça 2005: 105; Gorenstein 2005, Flory and Smith 1978: 579).

From the late 17th century, not only in Rio de Janeiro, but especially in Minas Gerais, which experienced an economic boom and a huge influx of migrants after the discovery of gold and diamonds, diversification continued to be an important principle:

New Christians who combined mining with farming and the trading of slaves with other merchandise achieved the highest economic gains. [One of them] appears as a farmer, merchant, miner, corn and bean plantation owner, and master of two sugar mills, as well as the owner of lands devoted to mineral extraction.

NOVINSKY 2001b: 220

Measured on a scale of economic importance, the activity of the New Christians in the plantation economy and in a wide range of urban professions was second only to their involvement in the Atlantic sugar trade.

Brazilian Sugar and the New Christians: Trade

Until the mid-16th century, sugar, which was traded mainly by Italians and Flemings, came largely from Madeira and the Canary Islands. Some quantities were also supplied by plantations from the Mediterranean area and from Morelos in New Spain. Hispaniola also appears as a centre of production. With the help of Genoese capital, Portuguese expertise and more than 15,000 African slaves, and taking advantage of tax relief, the Spaniards had developed large-scale production on this Caribbean island by the 1570s (Vieira 2004, Rodriguez Morel 2004, Alencastro 1993: 169). Above all, however, sugar from slave plantations on the island of São Tomé grew in importance during the century, and its distribution was largely ensured by the New Christians. This "truly terrible island", only slightly larger than Madeira, "played no small part in the emerging world economy": it would appear in the 16th century both as a model example of a plantation economy and as an important transit point for the slave trade (Małowist 1976: 169, Klein 2004: 204). If at the beginning of the 16th century it was Madeira that provided the lion's share of the sugar supply to Europe, by around 1570 this role had already definitively been taken over by São Tomé and then Brazil. Almost 70 per cent of the sugar reaching Antwerp – the main centre of the trade in the commodity – came from this island and only 15 per cent from Brazil. In the 1690s, on the other hand, the change in sources of supply was dramatic: 86 per cent of the sugar supplied to Europe was already coming from Brazilian plantations.

In turn, the distribution of sugar in Europe, also arriving in increasing quantities from Brazil, was handled until the turn of the 16th century by Flemish merchants and above all by the Portuguese (mostly *XN*s) residing in Antwerp, who were in close contact with the New Christians in the Portuguese ports. They, too, would be instrumental in marketing the incoming sugar from Brazil, and in breaking down the reserve with which European consumers approached this 'drug' in its new role as a part of a diet. Italian merchants, who controlled the distribution of Madeira's sugar, receded into the background. In 1570, at the height of Antwerp's commercial power, eight medium-sized wholesalers, as well as numerous small merchants, in addition to six major New Christian merchants, also distributed it (Stols 2004: 460–462, Pohl 1967: 372, Ebert 2003: 58). Earlier, from as early as the 1520s, an informal consortium of New Christians had taken a dominant position in this entrepôt for the distribution of Asian spices supplied from Portugal.

The devastating 'Spanish fury' when Spanish troops devastated and pil-
laged Antwerp in 1576 and their [renowned] re-occupation of the city in 1585
would severely damage its potential. The crisis would manifest itself almost
immediately in the *bulk trade*, and belatedly in the *rich trade*. The blockade of
access to the city from the sea by the Dutch Sea Beggars (*Watergeuzen*), and
later by regular troops of the Republic, contributed to the economic stagnation
and subsequent crisis of Antwerp. The city's population, estimated at 84,000
in 1583, halved in the following six years – mainly due to emigration to the
revolted provinces. Imports of sugar by Antwerp merchants declined by at
least 75 per cent between 1570–90. Some improvement was seen from the late
1590s, but this does not change the fact that the centre of the sugar trade was
already shifting to Amsterdam. There would also be changes among the New
Christian merchants, with the group dominating until 1570 giving way to the
new 50 merchants (Pohl 1967: 355, 371f, Israel 1995: 308). At the turn of the 16th
and 17th centuries, the related families of Ximenes d'Aragão and Rodrigues
d'Evora, among the richest in Antwerp, would occupy a special place in the
group of New Christian merchants.

However, the assumption of economic leadership by Amsterdam, Hamburg
and other ports took place gradually. Amsterdam's dominance of the Brazilian
sugar trade in Europe can only be spoken of from the truce of 1609–21, while
Antwerp did not lose its position as a financial centre until the mid-17th century. In this activity, the Antwerp 'Portuguese' played a key role by ensuring,
during the time of the Count-Duke de Olivares, the transfer of funds from
Madrid to the Spanish Netherlands and the warring armies. The migration of
bankers and the outflow of capital from Antwerp would begin with some delay,
until the early 1650s. On the other hand, unrelated to these developments,
there was an attempt in 1653–54 to obtain permission in Antwerp to legalise
Judaism. It was undertaken by Lopo da Fonseca Ramires (David Curiel), one
of Amsterdam's richest diamond merchants and at the same time a political
agent, successively, of Spain, Portugal and once again Spain. However, the idea
to build a 'synagogue' on the outskirts of Antwerp, which was put forward by
Lopo da Fonseca Ramires – who was in conflict with Amsterdam's Jews – was
quickly blocked by the Pope and the King of Spain. On the other hand, the orig-
inator and several other Jews obtained individual permission for the tolerated
practicing of Judaism and Jewish customs (Israel 1996: 211–215).[1]

---

1   The loyalty of this intriguing merchant and Spanish agent can only be spoken of in rela-
    tion to faith; it did not apply to the wider family, the Jewish community, the city or the
    Republic. In this respect, he was the opposite of his brother, Duarte Nunes da Costa (Jacob
    Curiel), residing in Hamburg and his son Jeronimo Nunes da Costa (Moseh Curiel). Both

Although the majority of Brazilian sugar was first transported to Portuguese ports, from the middle of the 16th century part of the production – contrary to Portuguese regulations – went directly to the ports of Northern Europe and then also to the Baltic region. Dutch and Flemish merchants were particularly active here. According to a preserved document, it is "true that on a number of occasions various ships sailing from Brazil and thereabouts, and having loaded there with sugar and brazilwood, have arrived [in Amsterdam] by-passing Portugal" (quoted in Israel 2001: 340). And even after a royal decree was issued in 1591 closing the colony's ports to foreign flags, the practice did not stop. Both restrictive regulations were accompanied by the confiscation of several hundred Dutch ships temporarily moored in Iberian ports. In 1595, the majority were released by the Spaniards after a few months as a gesture of goodwill, while in 1598 about half of the 500 ships broke out of Iberian ports or were bought back (Sluiter 1948: 170). Occasionally, as early as the 17th century, direct access to Brazilian sugar was permitted by issuing individual royal licenses to foreigners to trade with Brazil, provided the cargo was dutiable in Lisbon. However, this was not common, just as approvals for foreigners to settle in Brazil were rare during this period. Between 1609 and 1687 only 81 foreign merchants were granted permission to trade directly with Brazil, including 16 Flemings, 17 Dutch and 48 unidentified foreigners (Ebert 2008: 139f, see also Schwartz 2004b: 174). Incidentally, in 1623 permission to travel to Bahia and transport sugar was granted to a ship from Gdańsk (Danzig) – which had previously delivered cargo to Portugal – owned by subjects of the Polish king. Another ship from Gdańsk would call at Brazil in 1636, having previously taken grain to Lisbon (Schwartz 2010: 229f).

In any case, ships under the flag of the Republic sailed to Brazil quite regularly until the late 1590s. With a view to curbing the huge Dutch contraband and increasing customs revenues, restrictions limiting Dutch access to the colonies were not introduced with much enthusiasm until 1598, despite the ban from 1595. The provinces of Holland and Zeeland were even granted the right to send two convoys of twenty relatively large ships (at least 200 tonnes each) to Brazil annually via Lisbon – and on payment of the relevant fees. The pilots on these ships, however, had to be Portuguese. In 1598, before the royal permission for such trade was revoked, the arrival of 16 Dutch ships was recorded in Brazilian ports. They exported an average of about 1,000

---

loyally represented the interests of the Jewish community and the Spanish and, from 1640, the Portuguese Crown (Israel 1996: 201, Chapter 8, 1984). However, loyalty to the Portuguese throne would be difficult to reconcile from the late 1640s with the political preferences of Amsterdam's Jews.

tonnes of sugar to Europe per year during this period, which probably corresponded to at least half the production of the sugar mills in Bahia (1,700
tonnes in 1584–85) (Klooster 2003: 367f, Enthoven 20003: 26).

In this legal and illegal trade, until the beginning of the 17th century, the
primary means of transport used by the Dutch, Flemish and Germans were
hulks, merchant ships of greater tonnage than caravels, called *urcas* by the
Portuguese. Their Portuguese counterparts were the heavily armed *naus*, which
sailed mainly on the India route. While the tonnage of *urcas* varied between
200–300 tonnes, the caravel preferred by the Portuguese for the Atlantic trade
usually did not exceed 120 tonnes. Columbus's flag ship *Santa Maria* was a 100-
tonne *nau*. Interestingly, the Chinese "treasury ships" from the 15th century
belonged to a different league: "At 7,800 tons, the biggest of these ships were
three times the size of anything the British navy put afloat before the 1800s"
(Pomeranz and Topik 2013: 55). A combination of the shortage of quality wood,
inward-oriented political developments and market considerations prevented
China's sea expansion beyond its immediate neighbourhood. *Urcas* were also,
due to their smaller crew and substantially reduced construction costs, more
economical (Ebert 2008: 90f). According to the registry of the customs chamber in Recife, between 1595 and 1605 all the ships that called at the port for
sugar were of this type. According to other, though incomplete data, one hundred Dutch or Dutch-German ships appeared on the route between Portugal
and Brazil between 1587 and 1599. By 1600, it was estimated that Dutch ships
carried two-thirds of the sugar exported from Brazil. It was only in the following years that the place of the *urcas* was taken over by smaller but faster caravels sailing under the Portuguese flag (Schwartz 1985: 161, 2004b: 173f, Ebert
2003: 60). Also renewed in 1605, the ban on foreign ships entering Brazil – a
key element of the *exclusivo metropolitano* policy – was much more effectively
enforced. A ban on foreigners in the colonies was also introduced (in Spanish
American although this also applied to Portuguese, at the time subjects of
the King of Spain, but without serious practical consequences). The Flemish,
who were strongly present in the Brazilian timber trade, lost their licenses to
trade legally in this commodity at this time. Taken together, this suggests the
hypothesis that the Atlantic trade in sugar and other commodities on the route
between Brazil and Portugal passed largely into the hands of Portuguese merchants and shipowners in the early 17th century (Ebert 2008: 5f, 48). This then
would raise a challenge to the assertion conveyed for decades by historians and
economists about the uninterrupted domination of the Atlantic sugar trade –
at all its stages – by Dutch merchants and ships: "Since the Dutch controlled
transportation (including a part of that between Brazil and Portugal), as well
as refining and trade in sugar, the sugar trade was in their hands rather than in

those of the Portuguese" (Furtado 1971: 9, also Mauro 1987: 51). What proportion of the ships operating in the Atlantic under the Portuguese flag actually
belonged to the Dutch and Amsterdam's Jews is difficult to assess. It is equally
difficult to assess how many of the ships operating under the Dutch flag
between Portugal and the Republic actually belonged to Portuguese New and
Old Christians: "An unspecified number of (...) Dutch-built and operated vessels belonged wholly or in part to Portuguese merchants of Lisbon or Oporto,
who invested in such shipping through Amsterdam agents" (Boyajian 1983: 12).
In any case, among the Portuguese merchants active in the sugar trade both
on the Atlantic and on the European routes, a significant proportion were New
Christians. However, let us point out that "viewing the international sugar
trade as a Sephardic preserve is a position lacking in nuance" (Ebert 2008: 7).

The time of the New Christians in such a trade, and then also of the
Amsterdam Jews, begins at the end of the 16th century. The earlier activity in
the Portugal-Atlantic islands-Antwerp triangle was, viewed from the perspective of the second half of the 16th century, merely an introduction, a period
of gathering experience. And not without reason. In the 1580s and then in the
first half of the 17th century, a coincidence of several important circumstances
emerged that would define the role of the New Christians both in Atlantic trade
and in the economic life of Brazil and the Spanish colonies. One such a factor
was the establishment of the Iberian Union in 1581. It facilitated the entry of
the New Christians into the markets of the Spanish colonies, followed by the
gradual formation of the Jewish community in Amsterdam and the growth of
Brazilian sugar production and trade. The Dutch occupation of north-eastern
Brazil between 1630 and 1654 would be another watershed moment, involving–
in various ways – the Jews of Amsterdam and the Brazilian New Christians. The
1624 occupation of Salvador, the capital of Bahia by the WIC – an episode in the
renewed war with Spain (also with Portugal as part of the Iberian Union) after
1621 – heralded this breakthrough. Although a Portuguese-Spanish flotilla of
56 ships (some 12,500 sailors and soldiers and 1,185 guns), assembled extremely
quickly and efficiently, recapturing Salvador a year later (Schwartz 1991: 735),
the victory of the Iberian nobility did not deter the Dutch. A few years later, the
financially and militarily strengthened West India Company would strike at
Pernambuco. In this case, there would no longer be the enthusiastic support of
the Iberian aristocracy and nobility for the project of organising a new expedition and taking up arms.

The creation of the Iberian Union as a result of Spain's dictates complicated, despite Portugal's retained autonomy in overseas trade and colonial
management, the hitherto relatively easy access of the Dutch to Portuguese
and Brazilian ports. The pressure exerted by Madrid, already involved in the

fight against the rebellious Dutch provinces, was quite effective. Admittedly, this was a staggered process, but the consequences of the conflict between Spain and the United Provinces were being felt more and more acutely in Portuguese-Dutch relations as well, and this despite many attempts to enable "trading with the enemy". Incidentally, with the exception of some militarily important commodities, such attempts were not overly vigorously blocked by the States-General. The Iberian bureaucracy also acted without much enthusiasm during the clashes of the 1580s and 1590s. While war was a fact of life at that time, it was the Dutch who ensured the supply of many essential goods for Spain, Portugal and their colonies (Boxer 1965: 21f). Madrid's approach to the issue would only fundamentally change when the truce concluded twelve years earlier expired in 1621.

However, gradually imposed trade restrictions were doing their job. This does not just apply to Dutch access to Brazilian sugar or luxury goods imported by the Portuguese from Asia. The answer to the latter problem was to be the creation of the VOC. There were, as already mentioned, problems of access to the strategically important Portuguese salt for the fishermen of the Republic. No wonder then that from 1599 to 1605, for more than six years, at least 768 Dutch ships (an average of 120 per year) transported salt obtained illegally from Punta de Araya on the coast of present-day Venezuela to Amsterdam. This number also included 55 ships carrying contraband to the New World. This was a huge and risky undertaking: the quantities of salt imported from the Spanish colonies roughly matched the existing supply from Portugal. Already in the 1570s, around 130 ships were delivering salt from Portugal to the Netherlands annually. In 1605, in a campaign to cut off the Protestant heretics from the Punta de Araya deposits, Spanish ships intercepted several dozen Dutch vessels. In 1622, after the resumption of hostilities between Spain and the Republic, the Dutch had already definitively been cut off from Caribbean salt resources. Madrid's strategy in this matter was well thought out and effective. A flotilla of *zout-vaerders*, ships adapted to transport salt, returned to the Netherlands unloaded. The Dutch captured it in the following years on Tortuga and the tiny island of St. Martin (one of the Virgin Islands) – until Spain's successful armed intervention in 1633.

Being cut off from salt in the Caribbean and Portugal became one of the most important reasons for the Dutch fishing crisis. But these Dutch expeditions for salt (as well as tobacco, pearls and skins) also had an additional dimension. They had the effect, on one hand, of consolidating – despite setbacks – the presence of Dutch ships and merchants in the Caribbean and, on the other, by engaging Spain in the Caribbean Sea, of weakening the pressure from the Catholic empire on the first Protestant settlers in North America

(Sluiter 1948: 178f, Elliot 2006: 271). However, what had been an intensifying problem for Dutch merchants and fisheries in the first two decades of the 17th century, and for Dutch Atlantic trade in general, would soon prove to be an opportunity for the trade networks of New Christians. These were formed with the participation of emigrants and/or their descendants in the United Provinces. This applies in the first instance to the period of the Twelve Years' Truce from 1609 to 1621.

At the end of the 16th century, the first New Christian merchants appeared in Amsterdam, including 'Portuguese' arriving from Brazil. This migratory movement, small in number but important for overseas trade, was to some extent a response to the activities of the Inquisition. Indeed, in 1591, its first visitor – Heitor Furtado de Mendoça – arrived in Bahia. He was then active until 1595 in tracking down blasphemers, Judaising heretics and sodomites. In the 279 investigations he conducted in Pernambuco, Itamaracá and Paraiba, 118 (42.2 per cent) involved *judaizantes* (Oliveira 2012: 174, quoting records of the *Visitação*).

However, it was not the activity of the Inquisition in Portugal and Brazil that encouraged the migration of New Christians to Northern Europe, but, above all, market signals that accelerated the formation in the United Provinces of the centre of the Brazilian sugar trade (Green 2007: 171f, Klooster 2006: 132f). It would not be an exaggeration to say that the nascent Jewish community in Amsterdam was, in its first formative period, not only specialised in the trade of Brazilian sugar, but in fact formed around the trade of this commodity:

> The first Portuguese merchants to settle in Amsterdam were not immi-grants from Antwerp nor even primarily representatives of the major Antwerp Portuguese firms. They were merchants, especially from north-ern Portugal, who had been most actively engaged in the Brazilian trade. Indeed, a surprisingly large number had personally lived in Brazil shortly before settling in Holland.
>
> SWETSCHINSKI 2004: 106

In addition to sugar, other goods re-exported by Amsterdam Jews from Portugal until the resumption of hostilities after 1621 constituted the specific-ity of their trade: Brazilian timber, Asian cinnamon and diamonds from India. Overall, however, "the trade, industry and financial activity in which Dutch Sephardi Jews engaged was confined to only a few routes, products and forms of investment. Indeed, the commercial base of the community was extremely narrow in the early stages and only somewhat broader in the later seventeenth century" (Israel 1990a: 418). To a large extent, this was a consequence of the prohibitions still maintained by the guilds and municipal authorities, target-ing Jews to develop certain areas of production and trade. This also applied to the Netherlands. In the following period, until the end of the Thirty Years' War, the crisis in trade with Portugal caused by the Spanish embargo, the Jews of Amsterdam tried to break through by using Hanseatic, French or English ships; they also intensify their illegal trade, among others, through the New Christians in France. Above all, however, they engaged in trade with Morocco, and through Moroccan markets also traded with Spain (Israel 1990a: 419, 429f). The latter was encouraged by the migration of significant numbers of Portuguese New Christian bankers, merchants and artisans to Madrid and Seville, which had already begun in the early 1720s.

It should be noted, however, that if the sugar trade played a role that is difficult to overestimate in the formation of the community of 'new Jews' in Amsterdam, this claim cannot be mechanically applied to the economy of the United Provinces as a whole. The direct income from the sugar trade was an important, but certainly not the most important, source of the Republic's power. The combined value of agricultural production, fishing, weaving and ship-yards was many times greater than the value of sugar in the hands of (mainly) Amsterdam merchants. The value of woollen goods produced in Leiden alone was close to the value of the sugar shipped from Portugal to Amsterdam in 1630. Even taking into account the indirect income appearing in the broader sugar trade, albeit related to refinery operations, this commodity did not domi-nate Dutch trade. It was, however, so important that the prospect of profits in the sugar trade was one of the important factors justifying the establishment of the WIC (Ebert 2008: 174f). Similarly, it did not follow from the fact that the sugar trade played a crucial role in the formation of the Amsterdam Jewish community that all Amsterdam's trade in this commodity was under their and XNs control. They dominated, but they were not monopolists.

The 1609–1621 truce in the Iberian Union's war with the United Provinces was a key moment in the development of the network trade in Brazilian sugar in the Brazil-Portugal-Holland triangle. During this boom, the fortunes of many New Christians in Brazil and Europe grew. At the same time, the legal trade continued to be supplemented by illegal shipments from Brazil. These inten-sified in particular in the wake of the repression of 26 New Christian merchants in Oporto and Coimbra in 1618, who were working closely with partners from Amsterdam. The activity of the Inquisition supported by the royal administra-tion – seizure of Dutch ships with sugar cargoes and arrests – to some extent disorganised the trade on the Portugal-United Provinces route. However, the losses suffered by the New Christians are difficult to estimate; moreover, data on the number of contracts signed in 1618–19 to transport sugar via Oporto did not confirm the decline in activity. These data, however, leave much to be desired. Instead, it is highly likely that Oporto lost much of its commercial dynamism, closely linked to the sugar trade, after 1618 (Ebert 2008: appendix A, 67, 174, Swetschinski 2004: 114).

In any case, the Amsterdam Jews trading with their New Christian partners reported in a memorandum submitted to the Dutch admiralty the loss of revenue caused by the Inquisition of more than 539,000 guilders. The intervention of the States-General regarding the losses suffered by them and other Dutch merchants had a positive outcome (the truce period favoured the adoption of such a solution). This decision is also worth noting as the first intervention by a European government on behalf of Jewish residents and the refusal to treat them separately (and unequally). The status of the "new Jews" in the Netherlands itself was admittedly still undefined, but in their relations with a foreign government the Sephardim were treated as citizens: "the Dutch authorities came to see that the protection of Dutch Jews (...) had become a Dutch national interest" (Israel 1990a: 369.

The prospect of the impending end of the truce and the resumption of hostilities prompted the Dutch to fundamentally change their previous strategy in the Atlantic. This had hitherto consisted of placing the initiative in the hands of individual merchants and private ad hoc companies and avoiding involvement – especially financial – that could lead to occupation of territory and settlement. The main instrument of the new strategy was the West India Company, created in 1621 and modelled on the VOC. Given the military-commercial nature of the created WIC, this was a step already leading inevitably to a renewed war between the United Provinces and the Iberian powers.

The decision to set up the WIC, however, was not a surprise; a project to create such a company, prepared by the Flemish merchant and diplomat Willem Usselincx, had already been debated since 1606. However, it was only the seizure of power by "the militant Calvinist or Contra-Remonstrant party in which the southern Netherland emigrants were powerfully represented" that paved the way for a decision (Boxer 1965: 54f). This political change was accompanied by a radicalisation, in terms of overseas trade methods, of some merchant groups, especially from the province of Zeeland. The aggressive trade policy of the "new group of buccaneering entrepreneurs", who pushed for the creation of the WIC and represented the "rising popular and nationalist bourgeoisie'" (Puntoni 2012: 43f), found support precisely in the Calvinism of the Contra-Remonstrants. However, the actual activities of the Company did not begin until after 1623, when the necessary capital had been raised. The principle of its operation was only partly reflected in the note given in 1614 to *Heeren XVII* by the VOC governor of Batavia, Jan Pieterszoon Coen: "we cannot carry on trade without war nor war without trade" (quoted in Boxer 1965: 107). For the point is not only about trade. Approved in 1623 by *Heeren Negentien*, i.e. the WIC leadership, the *Groot Desseyn* (Grand Design) confirmed the plan to gain control of the Bahia sugar-plantation economy and the main slave ports in Africa. It assumed, above all, the weakening of Spanish pressure on the United Provinces by forcing Madrid to defend the overseas territory of the Iberian Union.

In February 1622, almost a year after the decision to create the WIC was taken, the Jewish merchants of Amsterdam submitted a 13-page memorandum on the matter to the States- General, responsible for conducting the Republic's foreign policy. Incidentally, Boxer (1957: 20) would later describe them as Dutch merchants. The immediate impetus for its preparation was the seizure and towing into Rotterdam of a Portuguese ship transporting sugar after the resumption of hostilities. The memorandum, registered in the archives as *Deductie over de handel met Brazilie via Portugal* and first published in 1918, "has been so often cited by historians as to achieve certainty through sheer repetition" (Ebert 2003: 49).[2] However, the importance of this document was not due to the precision of the data it cited. While expressing concerns in the *Deductie* about the creation of the WIC, its authors provided a realistic description of the way trade was carried out by Amsterdam Jews and Portuguese New Christians during the truce. Moreover, this description can also be applied to the almost 20-year period initiated in 1591 with restrictions on Dutch access to the New World, which preceded the signing of the Twelve Years' Truce in 1609.

The *Deductie's* defence of the hitherto generally peaceful methods of trade with Brazil and Portugal, and implicit criticism of the designs of the 'war party' that pushed for the creation of the WIC, was not without merit. During the truce period, trade in Brazilian sugar by Jewish and Protestant Amsterdam merchants, and mainly New Christians, reached its apogee. It proved successful despite the prohibitions maintained during this period, reinforced in 1598 and then in 1605, cutting off Dutch merchants from direct trade with the colonies. Incidentally, Antwerp also benefited from this boom. Despite the blockade and other impediments, the sugar trade increased by more than 44 per cent in the decade 1610–19 compared to the decade 1600–09; the presence of Portuguese merchants in the city was also maintained (in 1611 there were still 82 members in the Assembly of the Nation, while in 1619, due to migrations mainly to Amsterdam, there were already only 46) (Pohl 1967: 357f). In turn, the creation of the WIC and the resumption of hostilities led to a militarisation

---

2　All quotations from *Deductie* after Swetschinski (2004: 107, 110).

of Atlantic trade, a loss of previous achievements and uncertainty. These concerns, also expressed by groups of the traditional bourgeoisie of the Republic (the Sephardim were mostly part of it), were not taken into account. The successes achieved against the Portuguese in Asia prompted an uncompromising stance, while the prospect of renewed war in Europe justified a strategy of striking at the Iberian empire in the Atlantic. Confidence in the power of the Dutch navy and the mercenary troops was firmly established.

The Iberian Union's response to the uprising and the first aggressive steps of the WIC was to resume the economic war, including by cutting off the Dutch from the Iberian Peninsula. This was a serious impediment to the contacts of Amsterdam's Jewish merchants not only with the markets of Spain and Portugal, but also with parts of the Madrid-controlled markets in North Africa. The Junta de Comércio, created in 1623, played an important coordinating role in this war. In turn, the States-General took steps to limit the restrictions imposed on economic exchange with the Iberian Union – expecting reciprocity. The ban on trade therefore covered a limited number of goods (arms and ammunition, copper, sails, masts of considerable length, Dutch grain – so grain imported from the Baltic region was not affected). This attempt to continue trade despite the war, which alluded to previous experiences, failed. Also the illegal trade, using among other things Frisian ships and false documents,[3] did not fundamentally change the situation. Above all, Madrid's determination to bring the United Provinces to its knees did not lessen. The situation was aggravated between 1621 and 1646 by massive attacks by Flemish corsairs from Dunkirk (the pirate 'Algiers of the North' according to the authorities of the Republic) on Dutch ships, coordinated in part with the Spaniards. Basque corsairs also attacked Dutch ships. According to some estimates, between 1627 and 1634 alone, the Dunkirk corsairs captured and plundered 1,449 Dutch ships. Huge losses in the tens of millions of guilders were involved. At the same time, not trusting the local bureaucracy in Portuguese ports, especially in the north, in 1623 Madrid deployed its commissioners in them. Their task was to execute the ban on trade with the Dutch and to enforce seizures (Lunsford 2005: 110, Israel 1990a: 376).

The embargo of 1621–1647 "was the most sustained and elaborate of all the embargoes imposed by the Spanish crown during the Habsburg era" (Israel 1990a: 204). After 1621, until Portugal's independence in 1640, Sephardic merchants in Amsterdam also experienced a period of stagnation caused by the

---

3   Such as the aforementioned Lopo Ramirez (David Curiel), who continued to trade with Portugal in this way from Amsterdam (Israel 1996: 199f).

resumption of war. This was all the more so because the degree of their dependence on trade with the Iberian Union was much greater than that of Protestant
merchants. The situation was not saved by the large-scale contraband developed by the 'Portuguese' from Madrid, Seville, and Portuguese cities (López
Belinchón 2001). Instead, their actions became a pretext for intensifying xenophobic sentiments and accusations of 'looting' Spain. As a consequence of the
blockade, the number of accounts opened by Amsterdam Jews at Europe's
then main bank, the *Amsterdamsche Wisselbank* (Amsterdam Exchange Bank),
declined: from 114 in 1620 (9 per cent of total accounts) to 89 in 1641 (less than
6 per cent) (Israel 1990b: 379). German cities benefited, especially Hamburg,
where some of Amsterdam's Jews emigrated.

Thus, we read in the *Deductie* on the period before the resumption of hostilities that:

> This shipping and trade increased so strongly that annually more than
> ten, twelve, and fifteen ships were built and rigged out, here in [Holland],
> to carry here from Brazil annually thousands of crates of sugar, not to
> mention the brazilwood, ginger, cotton, pelts, and other goods-mostly
> via Viana and Oporto (...) in our ships, now partly in ours, under French,
> English, and Eastern names. This effort has been so successful that in the
> course of these twelve years the Portuguese caravels have been bested
> by the competency of our ships and we were able to claim half, even
> two-thirds, of this trade, thanks to the management of our factors in
> Portugal, under Portuguese names, who shared part and parcel with us
> in this trade. Although the King of Spain put several obstacles in our way
> (...) he was always deluded, as our gifts corrupted his officials; particu-
> larly in towns where the magistrature was not well disposed towards the
> Spaniards such as Viana and Oporto.

Describing the nature of the relationship with the largely New Christian merchants of the two ports, the *Deductie* authors pointed out that in order to facilitate Amsterdam's trade with Brazil in a situation where Dutch access to Iberian
ports was difficult, despite the truce.

> Many good and trustworthy Portuguese, mostly from Viana and Oporto,
> offered the merchants of [Holland] a helping hand and conducted this
> trade conjointly and in their name. Their loyalty to [Holland] was indeed
> so great that, during the war, when all our ships and goods were in their
> name and under their control, they could have-had they so desired-kept
> them for themselves and we were in no position to claim them back (...).

They made such a good record, proof, and account of the freight our ships had earned as well as of the profits of our manufactures, as if they had been our fathers and had lived amidst us. The magistrature of Viana itself shut one eye and secretly warned our associates and factors to guard them from damage by the Spaniards. Just now, three days before the end of the Truce, they decreed publicly in our favour that every Portuguese who owed us anything was to pay us promptly.

And finally, the authors' concern was the emerging threat to the interests of Amsterdam Jews and Portuguese New Christians operating in the Atlantic due to the creation of the WIC. If WIC captains began to attack ships flying the flag of Portugal and other countries in conflict with the Republic, this would paralyse trade with Brazil. After all, these ships potentially threatened by the Dutch largely transported goods of Amsterdam Jews and Portuguese New Christians to and from Brazil. This peculiarity of indirect trade was, according to the authors of the *Deductie*, not taken into account when setting up the WIC. Thus, we find in the memorandum a remark that Spain's trade with the New World, and Portugal's trade with West Africa and India, was conducted in a separate way from the trade with Brazil:

> All these routes are travelled by their own ships. Your subjects [from Holland] have not the least part in it. This shipping and trade takes place for their account only, such that when ships and cargoes are captured, brought to this country, and declared 'a fair prize', the inhabitants of this country, suffer no damage or harm. Things are very different with regards to the ships and goods travelling to Brazil, in which we are mutually and inseparably attached, commingled, and intertwined with Portuguese and they with us.

Let us mention, however, that even before the boom of the truce period, the importance of this indirect trade was taken into account in the legal system of the United Provinces and individual cities. This was reflected, among other things, in the settlements at the beginning of the 17th century in favour of the "new Jews" on the treatment of goods belonging to them, but also to their Portuguese relatives, transported on enemy ships and seized by the Dutch.[4] However, these regulations did not allay all the doubts of the Jewish merchants.

---

4 The return of goods belonging to Dutch Jews and Dutchmen was involved. Only monetary compensation was provided for the part of the cargo that belonged to families living in Portugal. In practice, compromise solutions were reached when settling disputes, taking into

And the activities of the WIC and Dutch corsairs after 1621 only confirmed their fears. Sugar and other goods belonging de facto to the New Christians and their Sephardic associates in Amsterdam, transported under a hostile (Portuguese or Spanish) flag, often became *van goede prinse*, the Dutch's due booty. In 1623, the already mentioned Diogo Nunes Belmonte was among the victims. However, interventions in such cases, addressed by Jewish merchants to the States-General, did not have the desired result (Israel 1990a: 379–381).

On the other hand, the emphasis in the *Deductie* of the unique – even dominant – position of the merchants of Oporto and Viana in the European sugar trade seems exaggerated. The same goes for the suggestion that, in the period prior to the creation of the WIC, it was the Amsterdam Jews and not their New Christian partners who played the role of *spiritus movens* and were the main actor in the Brazilian sugar trade (Swetschinski 2004: 106).

Briefly on these points.

The increase in importance of the two ports during the truce and their dependence on Brazilian sugar did not mean a decrease in the turnover of the port of Lisbon. In absolute numbers, Lisbon's commerce (measured, for example, by the number of contracts concluded) grew *pari passu* with the turnover of Oporto and Viana. The share of these three ports in the sugar trade cannot therefore be seen as a zero-sum game, especially in periods of prosperity. Rather, it is possible to speak of the formation of a partnership between the three ports, also including during the years of war with the Republic in the 1630s and 1640s. Ships calling at one port tended to call at the others as well due to the diversity of cargo (Ebert 2008: appendix A, Costa 2004: 3f). At the same time, until the resumption of hostilities in 1621, Lisbon was the undisputed leader in the sugar trade, although the combined turnover of Oporto and Viana gradually approached the level achieved by the port of Lisbon.

This issue is also relevant because of the likely majority share of Old Christian merchants in the overseas trade of the Iberian empires in general. This was particularly true of imports from Asia, although from the late 16th century the New Christians increased their share of trade with the East quite rapidly. In contrast to Lisbon, however, the merchants of Oporto and Viana participated to a limited extent only in the trade of oriental goods (Boyajian 1993: 35f). It was sugar from Brazil and cocoa, pearls and cochineal from the Caribbean that defined the economic role of the two ports and determined their strong dependence on the markets in Amsterdam, Antwerp and Hamburg. The opinion that, in

---

account only part of the value of the seized cargo (Roitman 2011: Chapter 6, Antunes and Roitman 2015).

the wider context of European trade of the early 17th century, "Oporto turns out to be the southernmost city of Northern Europe" is therefore not surprising (Barros 2005: 10). The same, moreover, can be said of Viana. Between 1535 and 1550 of the 56 ships that delivered sugar to Antwerp, 16 set off from Viana, while between 1581 and 1587 the port was the only one in Portugal to receive ships with sugar from Madeira (Vieira 2004: 71).

In contrast, the relationship that took shape in the sugar trade between the Amsterdam Jews and Dutch merchants on the one hand, and the Portuguese New Christians on the other, did not reflect the domination of the former. And such dominance was referred to in the traditional thesis, which highlighted the consequences of the rapid growth of Dutch maritime power: "Although the sugar trade was a joint Portuguese-Dutch enterprise, the Dutch were, in fact, the senior partners; they made profits on every phase of the business from shipping and credit operations to refining and distribution" (Lang 1979: 87).

Such a traditional view is no longer tenable today.

Certainly, many Dutch Jews, as well as Protestants interacting with La Nação, built fortunes in the sugar trade. The same was true, incidentally, of a thriving diaspora of Flemings who were active in Amsterdam, Lisbon, Seville and other ports in Europe, as well as in Brazil (although here, as in the Spanish colonies, they were often taken for Dutch). In the late 16th and early 17th centuries, one of the most active in the Brazilian sugar trade was the Flemish Cornelis Snellinck. He worked with many partners, including the New Christian, Manoel Rodrigues Vega (Veen 2000). According to estimates by Ebert, the gross profit margin on sugar transported from Brazil to Lisbon (after deducting transport costs) varied between 42 and 73 per cent in 1618–21, while it was still between 12 and 37 per cent after deducting the considerable brokerage and transport costs already in Europe itself (from Portuguese ports to Amsterdam). Merchants involved in trade on both routes were therefore able to make higher than average profits. And the scale of the sugar trade meant that even the low levies imposed on its importation (waaggeld) brought in substantial sums to the treasury of the Republic (Ebert 2008: 170f, Stols 2004: 266, Edel 1969: 27).

However, benefit sharing should not be confused with the issue of control. Fundamental decisions on production and trade remained in the hands of Portuguese and Brazilian merchants and planters:

> In most of their trading ventures of the late sixteenth and early seventeenth centuries, the Sephardim acted primarily on commission from their wealthier New Christian kinsmen, who owned the merchandise and earned most of the profits.
>
> BOYAJIAN 2001: 473

The same applied during the ceasefire period to the trade in the *pau-brasil* still sought after by textile manufacturers:

> Amsterdam merchants who handled imports of Brazil wood to the Dutch entrepôt in these years–Samuel Godijn and Nicholas du Gardin– were really just factors of the Lisbon *asentistas* who held the dyewood monopoly.
>
> ISRAEL 1989: 108

This was to some extent natural. The development of the sugar and Brazilian timber trade conducted through the networks created by *La Nação* and in contact with Protestant and/or Catholic merchants from Antwerp, Amsterdam, Rotterdam or Hamburg preceded by at least half a century (in the case of *pau-brasil* by almost a century) the emergence of Jewish partners in Amsterdam:

> At the end of the sixteenth century, at the time of Portuguese settlement in Amsterdam, the Portuguese diaspora constituted a truly international network, solidly ensconced in two centres in Portugal and Spain, with branches in the Portuguese and Spanish colonies, links to the two major European entrepôts of Venice and Antwerp.
>
> SWETSCHINSKI 2004: 63

The Amsterdam Jews therefore appeared in this venture not only with considerable delay, but also as new partners just looking for their place. However, they were not newcomers; on the contrary, they already had valuable experience in Atlantic trade and contacts in Antwerp, Brazil and Portugal.

The creation in 1630 of Nieuw-Holland and the provision for more than two decades of direct trade between Pernambuco and Amsterdam would fundamentally change this relationship, to the benefit of Dutch Jews. In any case, even in the run-up to the creation of 'Dutch Brazil', despite the prominent role played by Brazilian and Portuguese *XN*s, contacts with the emerging community of Amsterdam's Jews were important for the sugar trade of the time. Family ties, the exchange of information, the widening circle of cooperating merchants and access to markets were all parts of this mutually beneficial cooperation.

Despite the increasingly severe restrictions imposed by the Madrid court after 1605, trade in Brazilian sugar by the Dutch and Jews from Amsterdam and Hamburg, bypassing the Portuguese ports, continued, albeit on a very limited scale. Involved in such operations was, for example, in 1603 and the following years, the above-mentioned New Christian merchant Manoel Rodrigues

Vega, residing in Amsterdam. Previously engaged in the European grain trade, he was active in the sugar market with the help of, among others, his commercial agent in Bahia and Christian associates (including the Flemish merchant Cornelis Snellinck). A few years later, in 1610, he and his Protestant partner and later also his brother already co-owned a cane plantation and a sugar mill.[5] Informal commercial activity was developed around 1618 in collaboration with relatives in Lisbon by some Jews from Amsterdam who, according to a denunciation to the Inquisition, owned plantations in Brazil and 'other parts of the kingdom' (this probably meant the islands of Cabo Verde and São Tomé) (Salvador 1981: 30). According to confidential information coming to the Spanish Court, between 1608–18, the illegal trade of the Netherlands with Brazil via the Azores took the following form:

> in previous years ten ships had set sail from Holland each year to the Azores, each laden with merchandise worth 50,000 ducats. In the Azores, the merchandise was unloaded and transferred to *navios de registro* (authorised ships) to then be transported to Brazil. Before returning to Holland, these ten ships were loaded with sugar, brazilwood, and other products. However, duties were not paid in Portuguese ports, which thus defrauded the Spanish Crown of at least 80,000 ducats each year.
>
> APARICIO 2009: 6[6]

It was not only individual merchants who preferred to take shortcuts in the sugar trade, at the expense of Portuguese customs chambers. The authorities of certain Brazilian ports were also prepared to break the royal prohibitions from time to time by allowing – not gratuitously – sugar to be exported on Dutch ships. At the end of the 16th century, such illegal trade in Brazilian

---

5   He arrived in Rotterdam and then Amsterdam from Antwerp, to which his ancestors had emigrated from Portugal. This descendant of the New Christians is often cited as the first Sephardic to obtain Amsterdam citizenship in 1597 and even, with exaggeration, as "one of [the Jewish community] early leaders" (Baron 1973: 23). In fact, after settling in the Republic and setting up the first sugar warehouses, Rodrigues Vega maintained only loose ties with the Jewish community, while part of his family remained in Antwerp as Christians. In a word, he was an example of a "cultural commuter" (Roitman 2011: 41–43).

6   Information provided in 1618 by Luis Vaz Pimentel, a merchant working with Spanish diplomats. Earlier, on a trip to Portugal, Vaz Pimentel had been arrested by the Inquisition, had renounced Judaism under threat of torture and had publicly confessed other sins. He was released from prison and returned to the Netherlands around 1617. Residing in Rotterdam, he did not join the Jewish community, but was instead firmly embedded in a network of business contacts – involving Amsterdam Jews (Israel 1990a: 362–364, Salomon 1997).

sugar was also carried out for some time via Madeira (Israel 2001: 340f, Ebert 2003: 70, Vieira 2004: 73). The Dutch, in turn, supplied the colonies with European goods, the legal supply of which was far from sufficient. Portuguese, Dutch or English ships also illegally transported to the colonies wine and grain loaded in the ports of the Canary Islands and the Azores and especially Madeira, which had already specialised in the production of both commodities for some time. It does not seem, however, that this kind of expansion of the Dutch presence in Brazilian trade, which necessarily appalled the Spanish and Portuguese bureaucracy, would alter the fundamental relationship discussed here between Amsterdam's Jews and Portugal's New and Old Christians.

The 1605 renewed ban on the trade of Portuguese and Spanish colonies with foreign merchants, which tightened the earlier 1598 regulations, was reinforced by drastic restrictions on the presence of, among others, Dutch merchants and their commercial agents in Portuguese and Spanish ports. Particularly severe was the ban on foreign merchants staying within 12 miles of Iberian ports. All these moves quite effectively eliminated a significant proportion of Dutch ships and trade agents from Lisbon for several years. Only a few remained, including the Catholic Flemings, and at the same time there was a strong incentive for the Dutch to undertake an already extensive expansion in the Atlantic area (Sluiter 1942). Above all, however, the restrictions introduced in 1605 consolidated the position of the Portuguese (including the New Christians) and increased the importance of the indirect trade controlled by *La Nação*. Also, the truce signed in 1609 strengthened the importance of the New Christian networks in the Atlantic – functionally linked to the previously developed commerce between the United Provinces and Portugal (products of the Baltic region for Portuguese salt). While the terms of the truce liberalised European trade, providing Amsterdam merchants with access to Brazilian sugar and timber via Portuguese ports and partners, it maintained prohibitions on direct trade with the colonies. Significantly, the truce did not extend to Asia. The VOC's war with the Portuguese was not interrupted.

After 1609, indirect trade in Brazil's sugar and other raw materials almost completely displaced other forms of exchange. The direct trade of e.g., Hamburg with Brazil started to disappear in ca. 1600, while for the period after 1609 the Amsterdam notary archives indicate that "voyages from Holland to Brazil direct became very infrequent". The 12,000 tonnes of cargo capacity required to service the Brazilian sugar trade in the first half of the 17th century was provided by Portuguese investors financing the shipbuilding as well as their purchase of vessels in Europe (Israel 1989: 107, Costa Freie, Lains and Münch 2016: 93). This meant certain advantages for the Dutch shipyards. According to *Deductie*, annually "more than ten, twelve, and fifteen ships" launched in the Netherlands served – as ships bought or leased by the Portuguese – the Atlantic trade. A detailed estimate of the scale of these benefits is impossible to make. Assuming, however, that the Portuguese were purchasing a maximum of 10 ships per year, Ebert suggests that by 1621, approximately 16 per cent of the Atlantic trade was conducted by the Portuguese through ships purchased from the Dutch.

These were not the only indirect benefits reaped by the Dutch in their deal-ings with the Portuguese. Let us note that, with the help of Jewish partners in the Republic, most Portuguese ships engaged in trade with West Africa and the New World were insured in Amsterdam with Dutch underwriters. The cargo was also insured. Such an arrangement was facilitated by the widespread prac-tice – recorded for instance for the period 1614–17 – of insuring the transac-tions of Sephardic merchants from Amsterdam with Dutch assignees (Ebert 2008: 105, Silva 2011b: 22–24, Notarial Records 1978: 175f). Nor can informal arrangements allowing Portuguese merchants to exploit capital placed at their disposal by the English or the Dutch (with the tacit consent of Madrid) be ruled out (Blackburn 2010: 171).

The consolidation and strengthening of indirect trade was also accom-panied by illegal practices (such as the falsification of documents specify-ing the shipowner's flag or destination). Some contracts were of astonishing complexity that made it difficult, and sometimes impossible, to establish the 'nationality' of shipowners, the cargo carried and its suppliers and consignees (Ebert 2011). A consequence of the 1605–1620 tightening of the policy block-ing direct access to the colonies and, until 1609, also to ports on the Iberian Peninsula, was also the emergence of new corsairs attacking Portuguese and Spanish ships. Already in 1606, at least 130 Dutch corsair ships were operating in the Atlantic (Sluiter 1942: 34). In turn, a side effect of the truce signed in 1609 and the reduction in the number of ships serving the trade with Brazil was, among other things, an increase in the number of unemployed sailors in both the Netherlands and England. Some, disregarding the bans and penalties, joined the Muslim pirates on the notorious Berber Coast. As early as 1609, not only Dutch corsairs but also Dutch pirates would appear in the Atlantic. In one case – considered by the admiralty court at Maas – a Dutch captain used forged capers' documents. Five Portuguese, French and Spanish ships fell prey to him on the route from Brazil and Madeira (Lunsford 2005: 156f). Although the apogee of such attacks would come after the expiry of the truce in 1621 and would be carried out with unheard-of ferocity by WIC ships, the activity of corsairs and pirates was already complicating Portuguese Atlantic trade dur-ing this period. The maintenance of Amsterdam's leading role in the European sugar trade was, under these conditions, the result of "combining purchase with theft and confiscation" (Stols 2004: 267). These trends were exacerbated when hostilities resumed after 1621 and the Dutch (and Amsterdam Jews) were cut off from Iberian ports. The regression in economic contacts would continue until Portuguese independence.

The new impetus given to the exchanges in the Netherlands-Portugal-Brazil triangle during the truce thus led to the division of labour already signalled in the *Deductie* and which a historian today describes as follows:

> Portuguese Sephardic immigration put the Dutch Republic on solid footing for indirect trade for Brazilian goods through Portugal. This trade flourished after 1609. Legal trade between Portugal and the Dutch Republic gave the Portuguese control of the primary routes of colonial distribution, and the Dutch of secondary ones, making profits for merchants in both nations.
>
> EBERT 2003: 73

Thus, control of the main Atlantic supply route of Brazilian sugar, leading to the ports of Portugal, was from the early 17th century largely in the hands of the New Christians from the colonies and metropolises. However, it was not a monopoly: "merchants of Sephardic extraction, although well represented, were by no means the exclusive players" (Ebert 2008: 63). Certainly. Between 1620 and 1690, 81 New Christians (45 per cent of the total group) were among the 179 resident major merchants involved in overseas trade in Salvador da Bahia. They were also among the largest exporters of Brazilian sugar (Flory and Smith 1978). We have already mentioned Duarte Ximenes of Paraiba, owner of *engenho* and also collector of *dizimo* on sugar in Pernambuco, and Manuel Nunes de Matos of Itamaracá. These and other pieces of information seem to confirm the strong position of the New Christians, but at the same time, in the case of Bahia, the Old Christians predominated among the great merchants. In the metropolis, on the other hand – let us recall – the majority (70 per cent) among the great Lisbon merchant-bankers were New Christians. The proportion of *XN*s in the group as a whole was equally high in the 17th century. So, can the proportions recorded in Bahia also be applied to Pernambuco and Brazil as a whole? The answer will probably be negative: "[t]he Pernambuco sugar trade remained largely in the hands of the New Christians" (Mello 1989: 26).

However, it is still a matter of debate as to what extent the New Christians actually dominated Portuguese overseas trade. In traditional historiography, such dominance was taken for granted. In opposition to this tradition, some historians have, for several decades now, emphasised the role of the Old Christians in both the sugar trade and the Atlantic trade, which had been incorrectly, in their view, relegated to the background (Smith, L. Freire Costa, C. Ebert). The position of the Old Christian merchants was also aided by the repression of the Inquisition against the *judaizantes*. We should add that the importance of these merchants in Atlantic trade was also reinforced by the gradual process of diversification of trade carried out by the New Christians in the metropolis. Alongside sugar and Asian goods, new commodities and new markets (from outside the Iberian empires) increasingly appeared in their offerings. In any case, looking at the period from the end of the 16th century, it is possible to speak of the formation of a kind of duopoly in the sugar trade, formed by the Old and New Christians, although the strengths of the two groups as measured by access to financial resources, global commercial information and channels for the distribution of goods were unequal. However, if the Old Christians were inferior in this respect to their New Christian partners and competitors, this deficit was in turn partly neutralised by the political influence of the latter. We will return to this topic when discussing the establishment in 1649 of the *Companhia Geral para o Estado do Brasil*.

The main customer for Brazilian sugar at this time was Northern Europe. The shares of the various European centres in this trade can be estimated as follows: "Probably three-quarters of Brazilian production during the truce went to the north-western European entrepôts of Antwerp, Hamburg and Amsterdam, with Amsterdam probably taking half of the total Brazilian production" (Ebert 2011: 101). Control over the distribution of sugar in Europe, along the route between the Portuguese ports and Amsterdam or Antwerp and Hamburg, was largely in the hands of New Christians and Amsterdam Jews. In many cases, however, the partners of the latter in these profitable operations were not only Portuguese Old Christians, but also Dutch and German merchants. Let us add that between 1550 and 1630 at least 175 Flemings were also active in Portugal and its colonies, including from major Catholic merchant houses. However, their role in Atlantic trade during this period is often overlooked (Ebert 2011: 93f, also Crespo Solana 2014).

The scale of the European sugar trade was impressive, as were the profits achieved, only slightly behind the results achieved in Asia by the VOC:

in the second decade of the seventeenth century Brazilian sugar shipped from Portugal to Amsterdam may have had a gross annual value of 4,704,000 guilders (…). It is impossible to calculate actual profits, but at a margin of 14 per cent in the Dutch Republic, the sugar merchants might have gained 658,560 guilders (…) upon resale. By way of comparison, annual profits of the Dutch East India Company during the 1620s were calculated at 750,000 guilders.

EBERT 2011: 101[7]

As with the sugar trade, Italian cities, mainly Venice, and then Antwerp, initially played a leading role in sugar refining. The latter already had 28 refineries producing high-quality sugar in the 1570s. Earlier, in 1548, a ban was issued on the import of refined sugar into the city (Pohl 1967: 351). Single refineries also appear at the end of the 16th century in Portugal, England and in some German cities. In contrast, what was striking was the lack of refineries in Brazil. In the British colonies, profitable refining of the raw material was reserved for the metropolis and the same was claimed for Brazil (Russell-Wood 2002: 108), although Brazilian sugar was not refined, for lack of refineries, in the Portuguese metropolis. The lack of refineries in Brazil may therefore have been caused by other factors. It has been suggested that the high quality of Brazilian "clayed" sugar (described this way because of the technology used) was "suitable for immediate consumption", without refining (Schwartz 1985: 162, also Strum 2013b: 213). In contrast, the development of capital-intensive refineries in the Republic did not begin until the late 16th and early 17th centuries. By the middle of the 17th century Amsterdam was already the leader in this industry:

> The first refinery in Amsterdam was reported in 1597. From three refineries in 1605, the number increased to twenty-five in 1622, forty in 1650, and fifty or sixty in 1661. Each refinery could process nearly 1,500 chests [320 tonnes] per year, and could have stocks in reserve that were worth two tons of gold. At the time of the fire at the Nuyts refinery in 1660, the sugar burned was worth thee tons of gold.
>
> STOLS 2004: 273

In the second half of the century, Dutch refineries would also process some of the crude from the English colonies in the Caribbean for a while. The capacity of the yet-to-be-constructed refineries in English ports was insufficient at the time.

Until the middle of the 17th century, the increasing participation of the New Christians and Amsterdam Jews in the wholesale sugar trade did not extend to the sphere of production. In the Republic, refining and retailing had been

---

7   The similar scale of the sugar trade in Amsterdam was mentioned by Willem Usselincx when pushing for the creation of the WIC; it was also cited when discussing the plan to conquer parts of Brazil (Boxer 1957: 3, 14f).

a lucrative monopoly of Christian entrepreneurs and merchants protected by the city councils for more than half a century. Whether this was part of the guilds' policy of limiting the role of the 'Portuguese' in the domestic market, or a matter of a lack of investors among the Amsterdam Jews willing to finance capital-intensive refineries, is still an unresolved question. It is likely that both factors were at play. The first 'Portuguese' sugar refinery in Amsterdam was not established until 1655, founded by a recent emigrant from Spain, the merchant-banker Abraham (Tomé) Pereyr. Prior to this, Sephardim had invested in sugar refining in some German cities, where the restrictive regulations were less stringent. The permission granted to him and his brother only allowed wholesale trade in refined sugar. In 1666, the brothers sold the refinery to a Dutch investor for the substantial sum of around 45,000 guilders (Israel 1990a: 398). Abraham Pereyra was not the only wealthy emigrant from Spain at this time. From the late 1640s, there was an influx mainly of New Christian merchant-bankers to Amsterdam struck by the disaster of Spanish finance, politically weakened at the Madrid Court by the secession of Portugal in 1640 and the resignation of de Olivares in 1643. Persecuted or threatened with repression, they sought security and new opportunities outside the Iberian monarchies. These merchant-bankers migrating from Spain would be among the richest and most influential members of the Jewish elite in the Republic (Israel 1990a: 433f). However, it should be emphasised that, although thanks to this transfer of people and capital to the Republic, the number of refineries in the hands of Jewish investors increased after a few years, the balance sheet remained unchanged: "In comparison to the total output of all of Amsterdam's sugar refineries, that of the Portuguese Jewish ones was negligible" (Swetschinski 2004: 155).

The scale of the involvement of New Christians in production and overseas trade demonstrated in Brazil was never replicated in the Iberian colonies. This is also true of the role played by the La Nação networks in shaping the European world-economy from the late 15th century. In the New World, only a certain approximation to the Brazilian experience was the activity of the Amsterdam Jews in 'Dutch Brazil' (1630–1654) and, above all, in Dutch (after 1667) Suriname. However, let us bear in mind the scale and importance of this endeavour. Their activities in this colony will admittedly be important for the new WIC created after the bankruptcy of the old company, but without any significant impact on the region. The Sephardim active in the transit trade who settled in Curaçao and other small Caribbean islands would play a greater role during this period.

In the Spanish New World, on the other hand, members of La Nação began to appear in greater numbers from the second half of the 16th century. Nor would their presence in Ciudad de México, Acapulco, Cartagena de Indias and Lima escape the attention of the Inquisition. As early as 1570 and 1571, Inquisitorial tribunals would be established in Lima and Ciudad de México. Belatedly, in 1610, such a tribunal would begin operations in Cartagena. This was a time of increasing migration of 'Portuguese' to Spanish America and increased trade for several decades already. Both of these phenomena were accompanied by corruption linked to contraband. The memorandum prepared for the *Suprema* for the proposal to create a new tribunal pointed, among other things, to the influx of foreigners "infected with heresy" (i.e., Protestants) and "Portuguese, all of them Jews'". The appearance of the latter was also linked to the influx of *XN*s from Brazil, where the visitor of the Holy Office would begin operations in 1591. This was associated with an increase in repression and a growing sense of threat (Azevedo 1922: 233, Azopardo 1987: 233).

First, however, let us look at the still emotionally stirring part of the overseas trade that involved *La Nação* by the mid-17th century – the slave trade.

CHAPTER 9

The First Slaves: Context

At the height of Islamic expansion, the small-scale trade in the western Mediterranean was sustained to some extent by the slave trade until the 10th-11th centuries. Pagans were traded – first Germans, then Slavs. One of the most important centres of the trade was Prague, and "the powerful rulers of the new Slavic states also sold their subjects". Jewish merchants were also involved (Gieysztor 1987: 486). The main routes on the east-west axis led towards Muslim Spain, Italian cities and northern Africa. On another axis leading from north-eastern Europe to Byzantium and the Middle East, this trade was controlled by the Normans, together with the Rus. It cannot be ruled out that the northern route played a crucial role in this era (Bieżuńska-Małowist and Małowist 1987: 277–282, Toch 2013: 189).

The trade in white slaves in medieval Europe was a continuation of a tradition shaped back in the Roman empire. It did not constitute a disruption of the moral and legal norms of the time, especially since it involved barbarians. If there were any protests, it was against the practice of Christians themselves selling Christian slaves. The involvement of Jews in the Christian slaves trade aroused even more emotion. To put it simply, "slavery existed in Europe and the Muslim East throughout the Middle Ages. It was even much more widespread than it seemed to former scholars" (Bieżuńska-Małowist and Małowist 1987: 321) From the end of the 10th century, the slave trade from central, already Christian, Europe gradually died out, but not completely from the Mediterranean. The Western Balkans appeared in the following centuries as the European equivalent of the African Slave Coast controlled by the Ottoman Turks (Blackburn 2010: 54). The Venetians and Genoese took primacy among those Europeans involved in this area and were by no means limited to the pagan trade. However, the focus of the white slave trade gradually shifts towards the Black Sea steppes, Podolia and Russia. The number of those kidnapped from the end of the 15th to the middle of the 17th century mainly by the Tartars is estimated to be at least 2 million. Muslim pirates operating in North Africa, on the other hand, would become particularly active in the white slave trade in the century 1580–1680: they supplied 850,000 Europeans to the markets of Tunis, Algiers and Morocco during this period (approximately 1–1.25 million between 1530 and 1780) (Davis 2004).

From the late 15th century, however, there are fundamental changes concerning both the scale of this trade and the economic nature of slavery, as well as the 'colour' of the slaves. Already in the 15th century, African slaves appear in significant numbers in Spain and especially in Lisbon and southern Portugal. According to not very reliable data, they accounted for almost 10 per cent of the population of Lisbon (estimated at around 66–100,000 inhabitants) in the mid-16th century. Their share was estimated equally high, at more than 6–7 per cent, among the inhabitants of Seville (Thomas 1998: 129, Klein 2004: 203). Their presence in both these white *and* Christian countries was important. The institution of black slavery become normalised. The emergence of the syndrome of the 'Other', with increasingly pronounced racist connotations from the 16th century, thus preceded the development of the slave plantation economy. The black 'Other' constituted a kind of cultural argument that ruled out, on the one hand, the mass slavery of whites and, on the other, opened the way for trade in people on a scale hitherto unprecedented in the European history (Eltis 2000, 2002, Blackburn 2010, Drescher 2004). The progressive dehumanisation of the African was the rationale for transforming him in the emerging Atlantic economy into an important productive resource.

The economic consequences of the emergence of such a cultural argument will be shown by the conquest of the New World. The defender of the Indians, the Spanish Dominican Las Casas in the first half of the 16th century, and the equally passionate opponent of Indian slavery in Brazil, the Portuguese Jesuit António Vieira from the 1640s, both accepted black slavery. They saw the importation of African slaves first and foremost as a barrier against the devastating exploitation of Indians. Although Las Casas changed his views on this issue at the end of his life, his *Historia de las Indias*, where he considers black slavery as bad as the enslavement of Indians, would not be published until the 1870s. There are also modified as well as new ideological justifications for slavery and then the intercontinental slave trade. These two issues were initially treated, especially in France and the Netherlands – who were not involved in the slave trade until the early 17th century – in a different way. When, in 1596, Captain Van der Hagen of Rotterdam disembarked 130 slaves in Middelburg, the bewildered councillors, after much debate, refuse to allow a slave market to be held in the town and recommend that the Africans be freed. Especially as they had already been baptised. A similar decision was taken in 1571 by the *parlement* (appeallate court) of Bordeaux (Postma 1992a: 10, Thomas 1998: 148, Blackburn 2010: 61).[1] In any case, scruples when it came to the international slave trade were soon overcome from the 1620s. And by the beginning of the 18th century,

---

1   However, after Van der Hagen appealed to the States-General, the Africans freed at Middelburg found themselves, for the most part, as legally belonging to the captain, back on board and were transported to the West Indies as slaves (Hondius 2008: 86f).

the ports of Middelburg and Vlissingen would become bases for slave flotillas (Emmer 2006a: 15). In France, Bordeaux would serve as a slave port, second in importance after La Rochelle, from the second half of the 17th century. There would also be no shortage of slaves on French and Dutch plantations in the New World, but not in the metropolises (see Map 2). The balance sheet of the slave trade from 1500 for the next four centuries probably closed with a figure of approx. 30 million victims: more than 10 million Africans reached the Americas as slaves, while 1.5 million died on their journey across the Atlantic. In the same period, some 6 million Africans were sold to the Muslim East, 8 million were turned into slaves in Africa itself and 4 million lost their lives as slaves on the African continent (Manning 1992: 119f, Maddison 2003: 194–196).[2]

Arguments legitimising the slavery of already baptised Africans were drawn mainly from Aristotle's *Politics* (1992: 69) and his consideration of the "slave by nature" for whom "it is both just and expedient that they should serve as slaves", as well as from Genesis. From the 16th century, the curse that had haunted the descendants of Ham became particularly popular, in Elizabethan England being briefly raised in a widely known report made by Captain George Best from his voyages. Earlier, the theme had appeared in the reflections of the Jewish commentator on Scripture and advisor of kings of Portugal and Spain, Isaac Abrávanel, and would later be used also by Dutch Calvinists. Significantly, it was only in interpretations of this time that Ham and his descendants already permanently changed their skin colour, appearing as Blacks. In about the same period, it also becomes common to link the image of the devil not only with the Jew, but increasingly (and misleadingly) with the 'Ethiopian Black'. Colour and other elements already present in European discourse and perceptions of the African – paternalism, animalism, disregard or strangeness – appear as a syndrome. Certainly, however, Captain Best's contribution to such a transformation was difficult to overestimate – given the role that English Protestants were already beginning to play in the slave trade from the second half of the 17th century. However, he was not the only one to push such an interpretation (Schorsch 2009: Chapter 8, Blackburn 2010: 67–74).[3]

---

2   The figure of 8.5–10.5 million slaves transported to the New World, first reported by P. D. Curtin (1969: 85), was already questioned in the early 1970s as grossly underestimated (Rodney 1973). After several decades, Curtin's calculations were confirmed, with minor modifications, by the findings of the Trans-Atlantic Slave Trade Data Base project (TSTD2 edition).

3   Variations on the point of reference of the biblical curse and slavery have been debated for years (Whitford 2009). Some scholars emphasise the lack of a strong link between the curse and race until the Middle Ages. The emergence of such an iunctim is assumed to have appeared from between the 4th and 7th centuries while its transformation into a widely accepted dogma would not occur until the 15th to 16th centuries. At the same time, the intertwining of racism directed against Blacks and the rabbinic tradition referring to the Babylonian Talmud is contested (Goldenberg 2003, 1997).

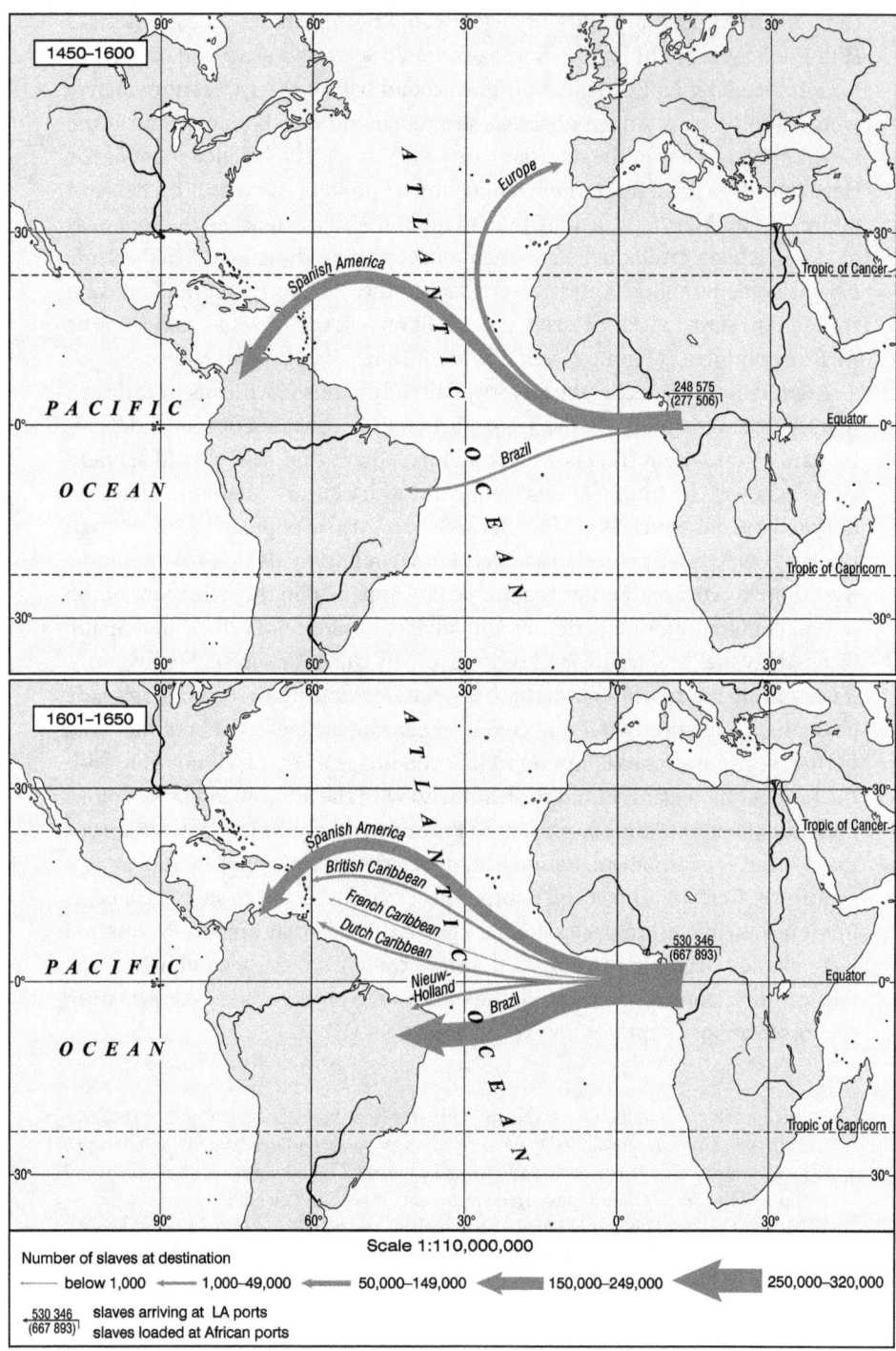

MAP 2   Atlantic slave trade, 1450–1600, 1601–1650

SOURCE: CURTIN (1969) AND TSTD2 (ELTIS AND RICHARDSON 2008) DATA

At the same time, in the Christian world, arguments drawn from Genesis went hand in hand with more pragmatic considerations. It was emphasised that in fact white merchants were not imposing slavery on Africans, but were instead taking advantage of a long tradition existing in Africa. It was argued that Africans, already as slaves, were therefore, in normal *bona fide* commercial transactions, purchased by white merchants from African chiefs and middlemen, baptised and transported across the Atlantic. The latter, argued Hugo Grotius, conquered them in local 'just wars' (Emmer 2006a: 14). And such wars justified, in turn – according to the Dutch thinker – almost every move when dealing with the defeated. Incidentally, for the Jesuits in Angola, who viewed the slave trade positively, the argument that the Portuguese were already buying slaves dispensed with the need to reach for arguments about just war (Alencastro 2013: 56).

The concept of such a war that led to the notions of 'just slavery' and 'just trade' was an essential part of the system of complex ideological (and theological) safeguards that facilitated the trade in Africans. They also enabled the sidelining of the few and inconsistently implemented Holy See documents critical of slavery (Maxwell 1975, Panzer 1996). Incidentally, in making Ham an African, in his otherwise path-breaking report Captain Best also had a practical consideration in mind: since black skin colour was, he argued, tied-up with the curse and "natural blood poisoning", rather than the effects of climate and proximity to the sun, hence crossing the equator on an ocean voyage posed no danger to whites and their children. And such concerns were not uncommon. Compared to the African, the Indian was – formally – in a much better position. This was thanks to the convergence of positions between the Church and the royal authority. The *Leyes de Burgos* of 1512 and then the *Leyes Nuevas* of 1542, which rejected Indian slavery, reflected the Crown's reluctant attitude towards the conquistadors' excessive autonomy founded on brutally enforced control over Indian labour.

Among the few voices opposing the justification of the slave trade through references to the concept of just wars was the treatise *Arte de Guerra do Mar* by Fernão de Oliveira, published in 1555. This Portuguese ex-Dominican, persecuted by the Inquisition (without any links to the *judaizantes*), was also the author of the first grammar of the Portuguese language and highly regarded treatises on navigation and shipbuilding. In *Arte de Guerra do Mar,* he argued that the "devil's trade" in slaves had by no means emerged as a fulfilment of the criteria for a just war known since the time of St Augustine and St Thomas. Such trade was instead an expression of the sinful desire for profit and power. It led to the enslavement of "peaceful free people". And regarding the argument that black slaves had been sold by their African fellow brothers, de Oliveira replied: "If there were no buyers, there would be no sellers" (Orique 2014: 107, Blackburn 2010: 120). The Dominican Domingo de Soto, alongside Francisco de Vitória, the leading representative of the 'School of Salamanca' and confessor to the emperor, two years later published his treatise *De Iustitia et Iure, libris x*, which contained critical comments on the trade in Africans and the abuse of the concept of just war (Perdices de Blas and Ramos-Gorostiza 2015).

At the same time that de Oliveira was making arguments against the trade in Africans, the ancestor of the political philosopher John Locke, the merchant and captain John Lok, could boast of London's first servant-slaves brought back from an expedition to 'Guinea'. In the Jewish world, on the other hand, where Sephardim became directly involved in the slave trade or became owners of slave plantations, the lack of congruence between the religious precepts regarding the conditional nature of slavery and the requirements of the practice was generally resolved with practical considerations in mind. This was reflected in the restrictions on the liberation of non-Jewish slaves. Like Christianity, Judaism – also alluding to the theme of the curse – was not a strong bulwark against racism and slavery or the accentuation of the separateness and inferiority of Africans. The attitude of Jews to the issue of slavery was no different from the dominant views either in antiquity and then in the Middle Ages, or during the transition to modernity initiated in the 15th-16th centuries. One can, in sum, speak of an "unquestioning acceptance of slavery among the vast majority of Jews throughout the history" and such a finding "runs contrary to acrobatic attempts by generations of scholars to interpretatively deny this reality" (Ben-Ur 2014: 38). The aforementioned Isaac Abrávanel, who belonged in Portugal and later in Spain not only to the intellectual but also to the economic elite, also listed black slaves in the list of his property (Schorsch 2004: 39). This testified to his wealth, but was not, in the eyes of contemporary Christians or co-religionists, evidence of a violation of religious principles. Let us add, however, that for Schorsch – Jewish historian who pioneered the critical tradition in studies on Jewish-Black relations in the early Atlantic era – the recent examples of scholarhip in this field are cause both of pride and concern:

> The continued rhetorical downplaying by Jewish scholars of the ugly sides of Jewish involvement in the slave system disheartens me. Very few seem willing to acknowledge in analytically significant ways, much less to focus on, the harsh, exclusionary, racialist behavior and attitudes of Jews toward blacks and mixed-race people in the Atlantic World.
>
> SCHORSCH 2019: 527

Characteristically, in a view that refers, often with exaggeration, to the tradition of slavery in Africa as a justification for the European variety of slavery, the question of the scale of the trade and the novel use of slaves on New World plantations was relegated to the background. In this regard, however, let us note the interesting hypothesis of a slavery historian, who linked the development of slave plantations in the new colonies to two factors:

> African capacity to resist ocean-borne invaders was probably one of the two key factors that determined that the sugar complex moved across the Atlantic to the Americas (...). The other factor was the willingness of some Africans to sell other Africans as slaves to Europeans.
>
> ELTIS 2002: 39

This is an interesting hypothesis, which is also related to the question discussed in the literature: to what extent was it the supply of slaves, combined with the monopoly of the metropolises on this profitable trade, that together shaped and stimulated the demand for them and accelerated the development of the slave plantation in Brazil? (Novais 1985: 102–105).

The difficulty of securing a supply of Indian labour only reinforced these tendencies. In any case, the tradition of slavery in Africa, based on a strong foundation of local custom, law and institutions (Thornton 1998: 74), does not explain the genesis of the economic institutions developed by Europeans in Brazil and subsequently in the Caribbean. The slave plantation and sugar mill and the social and racial dichotomy symbolised by the mansion (*casa-grande*) and the slave quarters (*senzala*) were unknown to African societies. In turn, by way of feedback, the demand for slaves associated with the development of these colonial institutions led to changes in the nature of slavery in Africa itself, including negative demographic changes (although their importance should not be overstated). Traditional African slavery would be transformed under new incentives into a system of slave 'export economies'. The classic examples of social imbalance and slowing, in the long term, of economic growth would become, during the heyday of the slave trade, first Upper Guinea and then Angola (Green 2011). The militarisation of African 'export economies' will also be part of this transformation process. An extreme example was Dahomey for over a century until the mid-19th century.

It is in this context that the crucial role played by the islands off the African coast must also be seen. If the earlier examples from the Mediterranean are disregarded, the slave sugar plantation was an idea put into practice from the end of the 15th century by Europeans first on Madeira and then on a larger scale on São Tomé. And the experience accumulated by the middle of the 16th century on these islands showed, on the one hand, the possibilities inherent in combining plantations with black slavery, and, on the other, ruled out, as impractical, possible projects to develop a sugar economy based on white slaves. Thus, when the need to replace the increasingly scarce Indians on the plantations in Brazil emerged at the turn of the 16th and 17th centuries, the field of choice would already be narrowed (Green 2011). In short, were it not for the new economic institutions tested on Madeira and São Tomé and the wider Atlantic context in which their development took place in the New World, settler demand for black slaves would probably have been much reduced.

And a matter of perhaps equal importance: the Christian, New Christian or Jewish attitude to the slave was expressed in the era which saw the birth of the Atlantic economy and the upheaval in European thought that paved the way for the ideas of freedom, above all in the dehumanisation of the African. The surge of the slave trade, the English Bill of Rights – a landmark achievement of the Glorious Revolution for the development of parliamentarism – and the Enlightenment went hand in hand. In the early 18th century, it would be Hume who would epitomise the unity of freedom with racism (Popkin 1992: Chapter 4). The eminent slavery scholar David Brion Davis (1966: 32f, 108) wrote about this "greatest of dualisms" in European thought. As a slave, the African was thus transformed into a *peça* (or *pieza de Indias*), a standard measure of the art of the commodity of quality. Even if not intentional, this was a reference to the Roman conception of the slave as a thing (*res*), a part of movable property (occasionally also having, according to Roman jurists, the characteristics of a 'person'). When the issue of the treatment of black slaves seized by the two warring sides in North America in 1747 and 1750 was raised during negotiations between the British and the French, the agreed approach would be to refer to the rules governing the trade in goods rather than the exchange of prisoners (Eltis 2000: 17).[4] António Vieira preaching to the slaves in Maranhão and Bahia that they are not only *peça*, but they also have a soul, was not welcomed by the planters. Also, when he said in a sermon to Africans in Bahia in 1633: "In a sugar mill you are re-living the *crucifixion* of Christ – *Imitatoribus Christi crucifixion* – because your suffering is very similar to the suffering of Our Lord on the cross and with the same passion". At the same

---

4   *Pieza de Indias* meant a healthy African aged 18–25 years. The term does not appear formally for the first time until the *asiento* of 1663; in fact, it was used in trade correspondence earlier. Terms commonly used in the 16th and first half of the 17th centuries were *esclavos* and *esclavos efectivos*. The latter referred to slaves actually delivered and was found in the *asientos* texts of 1615 and 1623 (Durán 2011: 26, Vila Vilar 1977: 188).

time, he urged the slaves to endure their fate patiently as a condition for receiving the palm of martyrdom (Russell-Wood 1968: 74, also Alden 1996: 511).

This was not, however, in the case of African slaves, a critique of slavery as an institution. Antônio Vieira shared the then common view of the salvific, evangelising mission enshrined in the fact of transporting enslaved Africans to the New World. He thus claimed that African slaves, descendants of the cursed son of Ham, uprooted from pagan Africa and baptised, were among the chosen ones. By reaching Brazil, they had already travelled halfway along the road that led to salvation and paradise (Alencastro 2006: 354f, 2013: 63–66, Blackburn 2010: 208–210).[5] *Resgate* – slave-hunting expeditions, from as early as the 1570s systematically organised by Cape Verdean and Cacheu (today Guinea-Bissau) merchants – sometimes armed, more often based on barter trade, were justified by priests, monks and laymen as the liberation of the African soul from paganism and/or the influence of Muslim heresy. Incidentally, in Brazil, *resgate,* defined as an operation to buy back or liberate Indians who had fallen into the hands of hostile tribes, was usually a way of camouflaging the de facto slavery of the unfortunates being liberated. For Antônio Vieira, on the other hand, the tragic symbiosis of sugar and the African slave, through which Brazil's wealth was created, was also evident: "Without blacks," he remarked after the Portuguese recapture of Angola occupied by the Dutch from Brazil in 1647, "there is no Pernambuco, and without Angola there are no blacks" (*Sem negros não há Pernambuco, e sem Angola não há negros*). But such voices of subdued criticism, not to mention protests against the enslavement of Africans, were rare in 16th-17th century Spain and Portugal. Likewise, moreover, in the Netherlands: since the WIC's involvement in the slave trade in the 1630s, "the list of Dutch opponents of slavery and the slave trade [is] fairly short" (Emmer 2006a: 15). All the more so because, for most citizens of the United Provinces, slavery was a matter of overseas trade, abstract and exotic when it came to contact with Africans in their own country.

This context should be kept in mind when proceeding to consider the role of the New Christians and Jews in the first phase of the Atlantic slave trade.

That the New Christians in Portugal, Brazil and the Spanish colonies, as well as those residing in the African factories, were heavily involved in the slave

---

5   An attempt by the Holy See in 1686 to criticise the slave trade showed the limitations contained in an approach that stigmatised 'unjust slavery' while endorsing 'just slavery'. Reacting to appeals from, among others, the Capuchins of the Congo and the Caribbean, the Sacra Congregatio de Propaganda Fide submitted a document to Pope Innocent XI condemning the abuse of the concept of just war in the slave trade (Gray 2010). However, this important document was ignored by Catholic and Protestant slave traders.

trade for almost a century from the mid-16th century, can hardly be doubted. *La Nação*, of which they were a part, was more or less the main actor in these ventures until the middle of the 17th century. Their participants were also, with some delay, only from the 1630s, Jews settling in the Dutch and then English colonies, and to a lesser extent in the French (due to administrative restrictions). How the balance between New and Old Christians was arranged among the Portuguese slave traders until the mid-17th century we do not know. We can only refer to the opinions of experts on the subject. It is not an isolated opinion that during the period of Spanish domination of the Atlantic system (between 1580 and 1640 jointly with Portugal), "New Christian merchants managed to gain control of a sizable, perhaps major, share of all segments of the Portuguese Atlantic slave trade" (Drescher 2001: 447). Whether, at the same time, they belonged, for the most part, to the *judaizantes,* and therefore to the crypto-Jews (Vila Vilar 1977: 94), is a matter of conjecture, probably with no chance of definitive resolution. Moreover, although Portuguese were often referred to as 'Jews' in Spanish America, this fact cannot be taken as a decisive argument in the discussion of the composition of the *negreiros* group (traders and others involved in the slave trade) or the actual religious preferences and identity of the New Christians. Domínguez Ortiz's (1971: 147) opinion that those who wished to integrate into Catholic society and forget their Jewish roots clearly outnumbered those who 'preferred to travel to the Jewish quarters (*juderias*) of northern Europe', also applies to this case. The problem arises when the strongly emphasised participation of the New Christians in the slave trade by the middle of the 17th century is transformed into a thesis of a dominant and even exclusive control exercised over it for several centuries by 'Jews' on all the main routes connecting the Americas with Africa.[6] A brief commentary is therefore necessary here.

---

6   The matter was further complicated when a volume entitled *The Secret Relationship between Blacks and Jews* was published in 1991 by the Nation of Islam, a nationalist organisation of Muslim African-Americans. The publication identified Jews as the main culprits in the Atlantic slave trade and responsible for slavery in the Americas: "Though scattered throughout the globe by political, economic and religious circumstances, [Jews] would reunite later in an unholy coalition of kidnappers and slave makers". The controversy unleashed by this hate speech-style piece had little to do with academic debate. Responding to an initiative by slavery scholars David Brion Davis and Seymour Drescher, the American Historical Association issued in January 1995 a statement unprecedented in the organisation's more than 100-year history: "The Association (...) condemns as false any statement alleging that Jews played a disproportionate role in the exploitation of slave labor or in the Atlantic slave trade". As an aside, it is important to bear in mind the apparent limitations of Jewish historiography until the end of the 20th century when it comes to race relations and slavery in the colonial era (Schorsch 2000). Just by way of example: writing about the tragic fate of Bautista

In comparison to the period beginning in the second half of the 17th century, when more than 1.7 million slaves were transported in the last two decades of the 18th century alone, this thesis is simply false. Thus, a British historian writes that "there is no sign of Jewish merchants in the biggest European slave-trade capitals when the traffic was at its height, during the eighteenth century" (Thomas 1998: 297). Among English slave traders, Jews played a secondary role, which is not surprising. This profitable and important activity for the development of the American and Caribbean colonies was controlled by Protestants. Even where initially the presence of Jews, also as planters, was evident, as in Barbados, their share of the slave supply was limited to a few percent (Friedman 1998). There is no longer any question of a significant presence of New Christians in the Portuguese slave trade. In fact, the coincidence of two facts is striking: on the one hand, after the reforms of the Marquis de Pombal, the New Christian becomes a purely historical figure; on the other hand, in this century of expansion of the slave trade, the Portuguese would retain an exposed position, second only to the English, among suppliers of African slaves, well ahead of the French and the Dutch. Also notable was the limited presence of Jews among French traders. In the *Compagnie du Sénégal*, which was for a time responsible for the lion's share of the French slave trade, Jews were absent. As competitors of Christians, they stood at a loss due to their lack of contacts among the ship captains and shipowners operating off the African coast. Thus, in the 18th century, during the period of expansion of the French overseas trade, we find only a few Jewish merchants from Bordeaux among the investors committing capital to the slave trade. In what was then the main port serving the colonial trade, the Gradis merchant house, to a lesser extent the Gradis-related Isaac and David Mendés-France of Haiti (Isaac would later settle in Bordeaux), participated in slave transactions. The Gradis, belonging to the city's elite citizens (*bourgeois*), were the only Jews among the seven largest slave traders in Bordeaux in the 18th century. In practice, this meant that between 1718–89, ten slave ships were recorded among the 221 vessels they sent to the colony. However, this scale of operation did not place the Gradis among the 25 largest French slave traders. Their elite consisted of Christian merchants from Nantes (Marzagali 2001: 276–278, 2016, Kohut 1895: 38–44, Thomas 1998: 251, Eltis and Richardson 2008: table 1.6, Friedman 1998: Chapter 6).

Peréz in Lima, Baron (1973: 311) remarked: "regrettably, we have little information about the details of his far-ranging commercial undertakings, which included agriculture, mining and probably shipping". He does not mention among his business ventures the main one – the slave trade.

By contrast, in interpretations referring to the earlier period of Portuguese domination of the slave trade, the cluster term 'Jews', sometimes supplemented by others such as 'Sephardim' or 'Hebrews', plays a key role. These terms – either used intentionally or as a result of an accepted writing manner – led to a blurring of the differences between Jews and New Christians. To the considerations already presented on the subject, let us add at this point Israel's (2009: 3) remark that in the period in question we should speak of "two distinct and in many respects broadly different networks" formed, respectively, by Sephardim mainly from the Netherlands and conversos and New Christians from the Iberian empires. When discussing slavery, it is worth bearing in mind this sharp distinction, for until the occupation of parts of north-eastern Brazil by the Dutch in 1630, the Amsterdam Jews and Sephardim elsewhere played a marginal role in the drama of the slave trade and the development of slave plantations. In practice, therefore, the terms 'Jew', 'Hebrew' or 'Sephardic' would refer, with few exceptions, only to the Portuguese, mostly New Christian *asentistas* and traders already directly organising the supply of slaves. The dominant position of the New Christians in this trade until the middle of the 17th century also raises all the aforementioned question marks about the religious and cultural identity of this group *sui generis* 100–150 years after forced Christianisation.

A partly rhetorical question comes thus to mind of whether Portuguese New Christian merchants conducted the slave trade from the mid-16th century – good as any other by the standards of the era – as 'sons of Jacob', good Christians, or simply as business people looking for profitable deals? The latter answer would seem to have come into play, especially since, leaving aside the question of the self-identification of many New Christians, it would have been difficult to distinguish any particular 'Christian' or 'Jewish' approach in the slave traders' transactions (Smith 1974, Drescher 2001). If such fundamentally different approaches were a fact, it would be difficult to explain the frequent cooperation between New and Old Christian merchants – and not only in the slave trade. Moreover, in contrast to other parts of the economy, where market modernity in the 16th, 17th and even 18th centuries only step by step supplanted tradition and non-market behaviours, the modern slave trade was from the beginning a market enterprise *par excellence*. Tradition and custom brought forth from the pre-modern economy, used for assessing the utility and rationality of actions taken, did not play a fundamental role. Instead, they became an important part of the modernity created by slavery. In the group of traffickers operating from the early 18th century from the Angolan port of Benguela, we do not find agents representing an 'impersonal capitalist rationality' or a pure rational choice approach; it was made up of *negreiros cariocas* (slave traders from Rio de Janeiro) with family ties to Creole (Luso-African) traders (Thompson 2011: 89f). This group composition and family links did not replace the market, but instead facilitated relatively safe participation in market operations. Nor was the importance placed on baptism and the prospect of salvation legitimising the slave trade, at odds with the market, profit-oriented approach to the captivated *peças*. The presence of merchants in the temple was no longer an offence igniting rebellion. It was different to some extent on the plantation: despite the profit-making orientation, "conflicts between property and paternalism" were an important feature of the plantation community (Schwartz 2004a: 4, Davis 1966: 227–230, Prado jr. 1969: 336f).

Modernity in the slave trade was thus created jointly by good Catholics and good New Christians. In the 16th and 17th centuries, the slave trade was carried out by anyone who could. On São Tomé and the Cabo Verde almost all whites and mulattoes, not excluding priests, participated in such trade. More than one royal official acted simultaneously as a factor for the traders, while in Angola he was a partner, merchant or shipowner (Salvador 1981: 13f, 74, Silva 2011b: 301, 304). Angola in particular allowed wings to spread. Its first governor, João Rodriguez Coutinho, combined the royal office with the role of *asentist*. In turn, Manuel Pereira, a member of the *Consejo de Portugal*, had established a partnership with a New Christian merchant from Lisbon before becoming governor of Angola in 1607. The latter's capital and the former's influence allowed him to develop a large-scale trade with Africans (Caldeira 2015). The involvement of some Jesuits in the Angolan slave trade is a chapter in itself. However, in the 16th century, such activity raised serious questions among some priests and friars, especially in Bahia. Not everyone shared the theses of a memorandum prepared in 1593 by the Jesuits of Angola and Brazil in defence of the slave trade, in particular the following argument: "There is no scandal in [Jesuit] priests of Angola paying their debts with slaves. Because, just as in Europe currency is coined gold and silver, and in Brazil it is sugar, in Angola and neighbouring kingdoms it is slaves" (quoted in Alencastro 2013: 58). Critics who raised the issue of the Order's and planters' 'illegal' enslavement of Indians and Africans – without explicitly attacking the institution of slavery – were, however, disavowed by the Society's visitor from Portugal; according to his view, which ultimately prevailed, the Jesuits and planters owned slaves 'legally'.[7]

---

7   Arguments justifying Jesuit involvement in the slave trade were presented by Father Baltazar
    Barreira at the turn of the 16th century. This Jesuit missionary was respectfully referred to by
    António Vieira as the 'Old Saint' (Alencastro 2013: 49–55). However, the role of the Jesuits in
    the trade of Africans should not be overestimated. In 1759, just before the dissolution of the
    order, the Jesuits owned more than 17,600 black slaves in South America, including more

It is worth bearing in mind, however, that the social prestige associated with the *negreiro* profession was low during this period. The combination of a New Christian origin with the role of a slave trader resulted in a limited social recognition, and the wealth amassed by such an individual did not resolve this problem. Gossip was sometimes enough. The admission of the famous Spanish admiral Francisco Díaz Pimienta into the Knights of the Order of Santiago in 1642 was called into question when information reached the Order that the admiral's father, who had distinguished himself at the Battle of Lepanto, was said to be of Jewish origin and, in addition, a slave trader in the Caribbean. However, after the appropriate procedures, the admiral was admitted to the Order in 1643 (Studnicki-Gizbert 2007: 65, Dominguez Ortiz 1971: 247f). Even the greatest *negreiros* were aware of such limitations. In 1604, the *asentista* Gonçalo Vaz Coutinho, who was descended from Portuguese nobility, planned to send his relative to Cartagena as factor to control slave shipments from Angola. However, the influential slave trader residing in that port, the New Christian Jorge Fernándes Gramaxo, who also acted as the factor of the first *asentistas* Gómez Reynel and João Rodríguez Coutinho (Gonçalo Vaz Coutinho's brother, who died in 1603), advised against entrusting a relative with this mission "for these trade negotiations, in this part [of the world], are not for *caballeros*". Trading in linen, wine or oil was seen as more noble (Vila Vilar 1977: 97). The exceptions were sometimes the great merchants. With one caveat, however: it would be wrong to generalise, for example, from the case of Duarte Dias Henriques, owner of an *engenho* in Pernambuco, who also traded in sugar and tobacco. In 1607–15, in Lisbon and Madrid, he signed a contract for the supply of slaves from Angola, traded in Asian spices, and in the 1620s found himself among the New Christian merchant-bankers cooperating with the royal court. Unperturbed by the Inquisition in Spain, he ended his activity as a royal *assentista* by supplying armed merchant ships bound for India with ammunition. In brief, while the *asiento* contract facilitated contacts with the Iberian elite, it was not a guarantee of social advancement, nor was it an immunity that protected against persecution. Some Portuguese *asiento* contractors found this out between 1595 and 1622.

If we leave out the elite *asentistas* and the main contractors, for the most part "Portugal's sixteenth-century slave trade (...) originated as a refuge for Jews, gypsies, exiles, and others excluded from more attractive currents of its Asian and African commerce" (Miller 1993: 126). This was also due to the

---

than 6,400 in Brazil and Maranhão, about 3,200 in Paraguay and 1,400 in Quito, and more than 5,200 in Peru (Alden 1996: 524).

(initially) marginal importance of this trade for the Portuguese economy as a whole, especially for the revenues of the crown. From the point of view of the Old Christian merchant houses and the court involved in the circulation of Indian goods, not only the slave trade but also the Atlantic trade in general was hardly an attractive proposition. Thus, on the one hand, although the presence of the New Christians, and *La Nação* more broadly, in the Atlantic trade by the end of the 16th century – including the slave trade – was already strongly accentuated, the revenue that this trade brought in was small: "the value of the slave trade to the Portuguese Crown was, through taxes per slave and so on, 280,000 cruzados, but the Eastern trade of Portugal yielded 2,000,000". At the beginning of the 16th century, the contrast was even greater: revenues from Asian spice goods reached one million cruzados, while those from the slave trade amounted to only 30,000 (Thomas 1998: 138, Marques 1976: 261).[8] (The ducat and cruzado were, with slight fluctuations, equivalent at the time). However, after only a few decades the situation in trade with Africa changed quite fundamentally. Around 1560, the value of gold exported from Elmina reached 40,000 ducats per year – a huge decline compared to 1532 when 681 kg of bullion worth around 180,000 cruzados was exported – while the trade in slaves and other goods was already yielding almost 90,000 ducats (Blackburn 2010: 116, Costa Freire, Lains and Münch Miranda 2016: 80.). These were not yet staggering sums, but the importance of the slave trade had already started to become clear.

In short, the often-repeated claim of Jewish control of the slave trade during the first one hundred and fifty years of colonisation of the New World was and is a distorting historical reality oversimplification. And this is also how we treat Salvador's (1981: xiv) thesis that "Iberian Jews were the main disposers (*detentores*) of the slave trade". The substitution of New Christians for Jews in the analysis is not a proposal for a fresh look at the trade but is instead a myth-making exercise: slavery was a matter of 'strangers', alien to Christians. Researchers who synonimise Jews and New Christians while referring to both groups as 'Jews' are reproducing the stereotypes perpetuated by the Holy Office and the bio-ethnic criteria embodied in the concept of 'blood purity'.

What is striking, on the other hand, is the mentioned limited participation of Amsterdam's Jews in this phase of the development of the slave trade. The same can be said of the Dutch Protestants. This would change after the WIC's occupation of the main Brazilian sugar-producing region in 1630, and later also

---

8   The differences in the profitability of trade in the two commodities were smaller if one takes into account the high cost of operations in Asia, as well as the expense of maintaining the colonial administration and navy (Blackburn 2010: 107f).

of important Portuguese factories in Africa (Postma 1992a: 12, 1992b: 284, 286).
Thus, a few comments on the subject.

Let us note first of all that the "apparent lack of participation" of Amsterdam
Jews in the slave trade, which would have been a consequence of religious constraints or other non-economic reasons (Boyajian 2001: 476), did not imply an
absolute absence. In the trading operations of several Jewish and Protestant
merchants in Amsterdam, the slave trade also appeared, although not in a
prominent position, as early as the beginning of the 17th century. Some of
the more enterprising Dutch captains had already been expediting to Africa
for slaves since the late 16th century. That it was possible was proved in the
1660s by John Hawkins. He was the first Englishman to deliver 300 slaves illegally from 'Guinea' to the Spanish Caribbean. Already from the 1530s, the area
of "Guinea" north of the later Cacheu was penetrated in search of slaves and
other goods by the French, with the help of *lançados*, as well as by Spaniards
from the Canary Islands. Between 1598 and 1608, the Dutch would attack
Portuguese ships and *feitorias* on São Tomé. However, the scale of their operations was small. Between 1591 and 1630, Dutch-flagged ships transported only
3,520 slaves, while corsairs in the service of the United Provinces practised
the trade in Africans from captured slave ships (Thomas 1998: 155f, Eltis and
Richardson 2008: table 1.6, Torrão 1995: 20f, 75). However, it was not only incidentally that the "new Jew" Diogo Nunes Belmonte participated in the slave
trade between 1613 and 1629. His decision to engage in this undertaking was
so at odds with attitudes and sentiments prevalent in Amsterdam that in 1615
the poet Gebrand Adriaenszoon Bredero described the slave trade, probably
with Nunes Belmonte in mind, as an "Inhumane custom! Godless rascality!
That people are being sold, to horselike slavery. In this city there are also those
who engage in that trade" (quoted in Postma 1992a: 11). In any case, this active,
wealthy merchant not only supported the founding of the first Sephardic Bet
Jacob congregation in Amsterdam in 1604, but was also a partner in many ventures of the richest Jewish merchant in the Republic at the time, Bento (Baruch)
Osorio. Whether he also benefited from his support in the slave trade, we do
not know. It was rather unlikely. The focus of Osorio's trading operations rested
between the Baltic region and Portugal and the Mediterranean. Incidentally,
sources mention more than one Dutch-Sephardic venture in Gdansk in the
16th and 17th centuries. Nunes Belmonte, on the other hand, could count in
Amsterdam on the cooperation of Manoel Carvalho, experienced in trade with
Brazil (especially as a partner providing credit), some Dutch merchants and,
above all, the New Christians in Portugal and Spain. At the same time, like
most of Amsterdam's major Protestant and Jewish merchants, Nunes Belmonte

offered a diverse range of imported goods from Africa: slaves, ivory, leather, gold, sugar and precious stones.

During this period we also find several other Jewish merchants from Amsterdam in the slave trade, Miguel de Espinosa and Pedro Gomes de Lisboa. Also mentioned is Diogo Dias (David) Querido, an important figure in the merchant community, related to Nunes Belmonte (Gottheil 1917: Chapter 8). This one, in 1611, together with other Jewish merchants, financed the presence of five large and a dozen small ships in Upper Guinea; however, there is no information confirming that their trade in the region also included – on a larger scale – slaves. What is preserved, however, is information that in 1617 a Dutch ship with a cargo of, among others, the well-known Sephardic merchant Duarte Fernandes set sail for the slave port of Ardaa in 'Guinea' (Benin). The next stage of this voyage was to be the island of São Tomé, from where – presumably with slaves – the ship would have set sail for Vera Cruz. However, it did not reach its destination. And, as in the case of Bento Osorio, the trade with Africa and the New World only complemented Duarte Fernandes' priority grain trade from the Baltic region (Mark and Silva Horta 2011: 75, Notarial Records 1978: 159, Israel 1990a: 359, 361).

Initially, the Dutch appeared in these operations mainly as shipowners and captains and as agents to insure ships and cargoes. They would only appear as slave traders from the late 1620s, initially mainly through the WIC. But even in the case of Nunes Belmonte, the contribution of the slave trade to his total commerce was small overall. Of the 45 contracts he concluded to trade with Africa by 1629, only five involved slaves. The share of such trade in the activities of other important Amsterdam Jewish merchants operating on an increasing scale in West Africa during this period was even smaller (Silva 2014: 5, 11–13, 2011b: 22, Antunes and Silva 2012: 14). Nevertheless, admittedly limited to a small group of merchants and characterised by the small scale of operations, Amsterdam's presence in the slave trade in the first three decades of the 17th century was a reality.

However, it was not only the small scale that was puzzling. In Roitman's (2009) and Green's (2007) descriptions of two separate slave trade circles that emerged in the 16th century and were largely controlled for several decades by the New Christians, it is striking that both lacked serious and sustained contact with Protestant and/or Jewish merchants from Amsterdam. The first, the southern circle, connected Angola, São Tomé, Brazil and Spain's La Plata from the 1670s. The second, established as early as the 1520s, was a northern circle that linked the Cape Verde with its mainland hinterland in Upper Guinea to the Caribbean and then, from 1574, to Cartagena, the main slave distribution hub for the Spanish New World. And it did not matter whether these New Christian slave traders were familially connected to the Jewish community of Amsterdam, as in the case of some members of the Duarte Dias Henriques merchant house active in the southern circle, or whether they were already substantially integrated into the Christian elite, as some members of the Gramaxo family active in the northern circle. It could be said that while the sugar trade acted – despite the impediments of the Spanish-Portuguese Crown – as a facilitator from the late 16th century onwards of interaction between New Christian and Jewish merchants, the slave trade played no such role. On the contrary, it was divisive. In the first half of the 17th century "a difference opened up between the Jews, who traded in hides, wax and ivory, and the crypto-Jews who, by and large, traded in slaves" (Green 2007: 175).

We find no convincing explanation of this problem so far (Boyajian 2001: 477). One can only speculate that, unlike the Portuguese New Christians, who, after the establishment of the Iberian Union, enjoyed a double monopoly in the slave trade (access to the markets of the Spanish New World and to the human resources of Africa), the inclusion of Amsterdam Jews in such a trade was outright excluded. It could not have been otherwise, given that until as late as the turn of the 16th and 17th centuries, the main recipient of slaves was the colonies of Spain's warring heretical Dutch. There were no other major markets available to Europeans. The network of 80 contacts of the Lima merchant and slave trader Manuel Bautista Pérez included, until his imprisonment by the Inquisition in 1635, Seville, Madrid, Rouen, Antwerp, Cartegena or Luanda, but not Amsterdam (Studnicki-Gizbert 2007: 99, 102). This was different in the case of sugar. The main recipient of this commodity was Northern Europe, supplied first through Antwerp, then through Protestant Amsterdam. In a way, this necessitated Madrid's de facto acquiescence to cooperation between Portuguese and Spanish merchants and also with the Dutch Jews.

Also, in contrast, in the growing deliveries of slaves to Brazil from the late 16th century from the southern circle, provided by southern merchants, the presence of New Christian trade networks was difficult to overlook. These merchants did not expect support from the Jews of Amsterdam. It was not necessary. Above all, the possible participation of Dutch Jews would not have ensured that New Christians and other members of La Nação in Angola and Brazil would have opened up new markets or created other opportunities for profitable transactions. The only thing that came into play was indirect participation, by providing access to goods that counted in trade with African merchants and rulers. In a word, the South Atlantic was a "Sephardic ocean" (Salvador 1981: 167). Moreover, after Portugal regained independence and then the expulsion of the Dutch from Angola in 1647, merchants operating in the southern circle not only retained their previous independent position vis-à-vis Amsterdam, but also attempted to eliminate the Lisbon competitors from the Angolan ventures. From the 1640s, for three decades the auctions of slave trade contracts for this region were held in Luanda. With the exception of two instances in 1654–60, all other contract holders during this period were Luanda-based merchants. The de facto independent southern circle gradually evolved into the so-called Brazilian-Angolan complex, dominated by Brazilian traders who were supported by Angolan New Christians and Luzoafricans residing in Angola (Silva 2011a: 29f, 2011b: 19f, Salvador 1978: Chapter 8 and 9, Miller 1993: 128f). The role that Angola and slaves from the region would play in the development of colonial Brazil is difficult to overestimate, but this issue is beyond the subject of our discussion (see however Alencastro 2006).

As a result, it is only from the 1630s that the Amsterdam Jews began to appear in Latin American and Caribbean markets as significant slave buyers and middlemen. By the late 1640s, however, they were primarily local resident distributors of *piezas*, a commodity supplied by the WIC, in Nieuw-Holland. From the mid-17th century, they would also take an indirect part in this trade as important shareholders in the WIC, a company they previously judged negatively. Until the 1640s, this company formally monopolised the Dutch slave trade in the Atlantic. After the relaxation of monopolistic regulations, the WIC continued to be an important player in this trade in the following decades.

Before this could happen, however, the Atlantic slave trade would be controlled for more than a century by the Portuguese, *La Nação*, a majority being New Christians. This was made possible primarily by the Portuguese monopoly of access to the human resources of West Africa. Between 1615 and 1640, the Spanish slave trade would also be in the hands of mainly New Christian *asentistas*.

CHAPTER 10

Portuguese *asientos*, Time of the New Christians

At least 51,300 slaves were thought to have been delivered to Spanish America between 1521 and 1595 (Curtin 1969: 25). But this has proved to be an underestimate. According to more recent calculations, more than 128,000 slaves were loaded in Africa onto ships bound for the Iberian colonies by 1595. It is likely that around 27–30 per cent died during the voyage, so ca. 93,000 would have reached their destination, and after taking into account earlier shipments from the 1500s-1520s, around 99,000. In the following period, between 1581 and 1640, the number of slaves loaded onto ships was estimated at 682,000, including 347,000 destined for the Spanish America. More than 528,000 (including 269,000 to Spanish America) probably reach the New World (Eltis and Richardson 2008: tables 1.2, 1.6, 1.8).[1]

The acceleration of growth was therefore obvious. The main factors driving trade were the still strongly felt labour shortage in the Spanish colonies and the demand created by the Brazilian plantations. In the 16th century, Peru became the largest buyer of slaves. Demand was also bolstered by the economies of New Spain and New Granada. Brazil as a recipient of slaves did not yet count in the mid-16th century. However, the rapid development of sugar plantations would make this Portuguese colony the main recipient of slaves around 1611. If less than 5,000 Africans arrived in Pernambuco, Bahia, and south-eastern Brazil between 1561–80, by 1611–30 there were already more than 195,000 (Eltis and Richardson 2008: table 1.3). This increase in demand was accompanied by rapidly growing supply from the late 16th century. Incentives for the more intensive use of slaves thus appeared on both sides of the market equation and both sides of the Atlantic. And this was only a prelude to the explosive growth that would happen in the following centuries. Whereas in the second half of the 16th century an average of around 4,200 slaves were sent annually to the Iberian colonies, in the half-century 1601–50 this average would reach around 12,000 'souls', and in the 18th century 65,000 (Eltis and Richardson 2008: table 1.6). The slave trade had thus already been transformed from 'craft' into 'manufacture' by the end of the 16th century and into 'modern industry'

---

1 Mortality rates of up to 30 per cent were assumed in the *asientos* of 1615 and 1623 (Durán 2011: 25). Taking into account new information on slave ship voyages, the contraband and the intra-American transfer of slaves, a more recent estimate suggests that by 1641 some 530,000 slaves had reached Spanish America alone (Borucki, Eltis and Wheat 2015: 440).

by the 18th century. However, although the scale of this trade was small in the 16th century, it would be misleading to limit ourselves to such a observation. If even by 1580 65–70 per cent of the migration to the New World was made of Europeans (Eltis 2002: 67), the presence of African slaves could no longer be ignored from the end of the 16th century. In 1570, in Ciudad de México, the number of Spaniards was estimated at 8,000, and the number of slaves and mulattoes at 9,000. In Peru, *negros esclavos y horros* (slaves and freedmen) did not go unnoticed, also during the battles against the Indian insurgents. But soon it would not be these countries but Brazil that would become a paradigmatic case of slave society (Klein 1986: 32, 36, Bakewell 2004: 334, Blackburn 2010: 143f, Ben-Ur 2014: 45f). And last but not least, the weight of different African regions in the slave supply was also changing. Until the 1570s, the majority of Africans were captured in 'Guinea', controlled by merchants from Cabo Verde and the *lançados*, while traders from São Tomé provided transit for slaves from Benin and Congo. The founding of Luanda in 1576 and the emergence of Angola as a major slave-supplying region would weaken the importance of 'Guinea'.

Compared to the 16th century, the first half of the 17th century was a time of crucial transformations: an increase in the number of slaves transported altered the demographics of some regions in the New World, and there was also a change in the organisation of Spanish trade – the transition in 1595 to the *asiento de negros*. As in the case of other *asientos*, this one also meant a "contract made for the purpose of public utility, for the administration of a public service, between the Spanish Government and private individuals" (Scelle 1910: 613). Thus one can speak about a specific public-private partnership which implied limited privatisation of the royal monopoly of the slave trade. This reform would also lead to changes in the position of New World merchants. Although the Portuguese had already played a primary role in the Spanish slave trade at the executive level in the 16th century, it is only with the transition to the new system that Portuguese *mercadores-banqueiros* would also appear among the Crown's main financial partners (*asentistas*). The reduction of their role would only occur after the break-up of the Iberian Union in 1640.

Let us consider some of these problems.

Charles V's first approvals for the transport of slaves from Africa to the Caribbean were given in 1518 (and were erroneously described as the first *asiento de negros*).[2] And not without reason. On Hispaniola and other islands,

---

2 The first *asiento de negros* can probably be spoken of in the case of the contract signed with the Welser representatives in 1528. Scelle (1910: 619–623) would refer to such a contract as

the demographic disaster caused by the exploitation of the Indians and the diseases decimating them threatened the survival of the Spanish settlers. Appeals for permission to transport Africans intensified, especially after Cardinal Regent Ximénes Cisneros imposed a ban on the shipment of black slaves from Spain in 1516, shortly before the new monarch took the throne. Describing them as "a people without honour and without faith and therefore capable of treason and [sowing] unrest", the cardinal feared a revolt by Africans (quoted in Cortés López 1989: 826). The ban on the shipment of slaves from Muslim Africa, introduced by Charles v in 1520, also provoked negative reactions. Fear of Islam being transferred to the colonies paralysed the trade. A kind of rescue operation was thus the forced transfer to Hispaniola and other islands in the 1520s of large numbers of enslaved Indians from Brazil, the coast of present-day Venezuela, Colombia and Mexico. The island of Curaçao was depopulated after 1,200 Indians were deported (Delgado Ribas 2013: 14f, Almeida Mendes 2008a: 72, Rupert 2012: 21).

The origins of the slavery of Africans in Spanish America involved the concurrent activities of Florentines, Genoese, Flemings and Germans, also collaborating Spaniards from Burgos, and to a lesser extent Spanish conversos and Portuguese New Christians. The first licences for the slave trade were thus granted in 1518 to two of Charles v's favourites and to a Fleming count, Laurent de Gouvenot (or Lorenzo Gorrevod), who was particularly close to the king (Thomas 1998: 96, Fernández Chaves and Pérez García 2016: 387f). While the consent for the first was for 400 slaves for each, the licence given to the Fleming would prove to be the solution used for more than two decades. It provided for the delivery on exclusive terms of 4,000 slaves, without paying tax. Gouvenot sold this immediately for 25,000 ducats to three Genoese merchants from Seville, who in turn successively marketed licence packages of varying sizes. The Portuguese, already experienced in the slave trade, would also participate in operations in this secondary market (Fernández Chaves and Pérez García 2016: 388f).

The Genoese who bought the licence from Gouvenot transported the first 300 slaves from São Tomé to Hispaniola as early as 1524, while in 1525 two other Italian merchants sent 145 slaves from Cabo Verde to Cuba and Hispaniola, where the brothers of one of them owned two sugar mills (Almeida Mendes 2008: 64, 72). In addition to Genoese and gradually Spanish merchants, Germans also benefited from royal privileges. The Welsers, represented in

---

an asiento general. However, the model asiento de negros would not be concluded until 1595 (Vila Vilar 1977: Chapter 1, Weindl 2008).

Seville by Heinrich Ehinger and Hieronymus Seiler (Sayller) – both of whom were also knights of the Order of Santiago – obtained in 1528, for 20,000 ducats, a licence to sell 4,000 slaves for four years until 1533. The contract with the Welsers was in fact modelled on the Gouvenot contract. Its execution, however, was not successful. This concerned both the number of slaves supplied (less than 2,500) and their physical condition. In addition, the Spanish settlers grumbled about the exorbitant prices charged for the slaves. In turn, the loan pledged by the Welser bank to Charles v granted them the right to explore and exploit using 800 slaves the 'New Andalusia' (future Venezuela). This venture too was not a success (Delgado Ribas 2013: 16, Thomas 1998: 101, Fernández Chaves and Pérez García 2016: 398f, 402). Instead, the difficulties encountered by the Welsers in effect drove increased activity on the part of Spanish merchants, primarily Andalusian conversos, although the terms of the contract with the Welsers forced them to operate mainly in the secondary market. Spanish and Portuguese contrabandists would also appear.

From the late 1530s, arrangements modelled on the Gouvenot contract gave way to a more competitive system of licences sold on behalf of the king by Seville's *Casa de Contratación*. Between 1544 and 1550, the heyday of this system, some 13,400 licences were issued to 133 buyers for the purchase and transport of slaves. More than 63 per cent of the licences were in the hands of 11 merchants and merchant groups. Despite this high degree of concentration, the licensing system did not exclude smaller contractors either. The actual number of slaves transported in the overlapping period 1541–1550 was more than 27,000 (Fernández Chaves and Pérez García 2016: 410, Cortés López 1995: 67, Eltis and Richardson 2008: table 1.2). According to a conservative estimate, between 1510 and 1599 the Crown issued licences that enabled the legal transport of more than 131,000 slaves. The cost of the licences also increased, from 2 ducats per slave in 1513, to 7 ducats in 1560. In 1561, this fee rose to around 30 ducats and would remain at this level for the rest of the century (Garcia Fuentes 1982: 6–9).[3]

The move to a licensing system facilitated the inclusion of Spaniards more widely in the slave trade and made it possible to break the previous dominance

---

3 While licences were commercial ventures, they were supplemented from the 1520s by a small number of *capitulaciónes*. The Crown allowed selected buyers to purchase between a few and a few hundred slaves with a specific objective in mind: participation in the discovery and conquest of new territory, its population and pacification, trade. Between 1520 and 1596, 75 *capitulaciónes* were issued. Data for 31 show that some 4,000 slaves were brought to the colonies under them. New Christian Luis de Carvajal, governor of Nuevo Reino de León in New Spain, obtained permission to purchase 40 slaves in 1579 (Cortés López 1989: 832, 834).

of Genoese merchants. In the 1540s, we find among the largest slave contractors Judge Gaspar de Torres with his brothers, Diego Caballero, a group of merchants consisting of Andrés de Parades, Melchior Barreto and Alonso Barrera and the brothers Gaspar and Gonzalo Jorge with the rest of the family. These names, and several others, already counted in the Spanish slave trade. They were all Andalusian conversos. The Jorge brothers maintained five ships that regularly sailed with slave shipments on the Seville-Cape Verde-New World route (Fernández Chaves and Pérez García 2016: 410, Thomas 1998: 118). The scale of their operations was significant, but they were not the dominant group of slave-trading conversos during this period. We will return to this issue in a moment.

What failed, however, was Charles V's attempt to move away from the licensing system and sign a contract whose format resembled the later *asiento general*. Such an exclusive contract was negotiated in 1552–53 with Hernando de Ochoa on behalf of the emperor by his son, later Philip II. For 184,000 ducats, de Ochoa would receive the exclusive right to supply 23,000 slaves to the New World by 1557. However, the exclusivity clause aroused protests, especially in Seville. A council of theologians convened by the emperor gave an unanimously negative opinion on the contract. This was not a criticism of the slave trade. Franciscan Alfonso de Castro, a lawyer and advisor to the emperor, defined the exclusive right, which discriminated against other merchants and was primarily intended to provide funds for the court of Charles V, as follows: "to make the law for the sole advantage of the King and not for the utility of the Kingdom would be the work of a tyrant and not of a true king". The advance of 140,000 ducats was returned to Ochoa (Delgado Ribas 2013: 16f). However, when in 1561 the price paid to the Crown per slave increased from the 7–8 ducats stipulated in the contract for Ochoa, to 30 ducats, this limited the circle of those interested in licences to large merchants.

According to some scholars, conversos and Portuguese New Christians did not play a major role as recipients of Spanish licences during the period in question (Cortés López 1995: 68f, 75). Thus, it is only mentioned that in 1556 – upon the recommendation of the Portuguese João III – Philip II granted for 55,000 ducats the ennobled New Christian Manuel Caldeira permission to export 2,000 slaves to the New World (Ventura 1999: 141–143). However, its execution, supported in Seville by the New Christian Bento Vaez, was blocked by Spanish competitors. However, according to António de Almeida Mendes (2008b: 764), contract with Caldeira "prepared the ground for the great *asientos* of the late 16th century". This is a debatable hypothesis, but certainly the activity of Caldeira, one of the leading figures in the slave trade of the time, strengthened the Portuguese (and *XN*s) position. Let us add that he was not limited to his role as a merchant trading Africans. He also served as treasurer to a Portuguese princess and also already remained firmly in the circle of Seville's economic elite. This circle also included his sons and other family members (Ventura 1999: 42–50, also Fernández Chaves and Pérez García 2012: 214f, 218, 2010). On the other hand, the Seville merchant Gaspar de Peralta, "probably a converted Jew in origins", was allowed to export 221 slaves in 1579 as compensation for part of the royal debt owed to him. This, however, was the margin of his activities. His main interests were fishing and the pearl trade. And in the activities of one of the most powerful Castilian merchants, converso Simon Ruiz, the slave trade does not appear until the second half of the 16th century, and mainly as a result of contacts with the New Christians of Oporto (Delgado Ribas 2013: 17, 19, Garcia Fuentes 1982: 33–37, Ribeiro 2011).

However, opinions minimising the role of conversos and New Christians in the Spanish slave trade during this period are not widely shared. It is emphasised that from as early as the 1520s, Portuguese and Spanish conversos formed an important centre of cooperation in the slave trade in Seville, together with *cristianos de natureza* (Old Christians). This is not surprising, as Spanish conversos probably constituted the majority of Seville's commercial elite at the beginning of the 16th century and played an essential role as lenders, but above all as merchants in the trade of agricultural products (mainly oil) and gradually in international trade (Crailsheim 2016: 76). It would therefore be incomprehensible if they excluded slaves from the field of interest. However, estimating the contribution of Spanish conversos and Portuguese *XN*s to the total slave trade is extremely difficult. In any case, in 1523 an attempt to sell 200 slaves from the Gouvenot licence taken over by the Genoese is made by the already mentioned Seville converso, judge and merchant, Gaspar de Torres. In turn, in 1536, after the expiry of the contract with the Welsers, the same Gaspar de Torres and Alonso Caballero made an offer to sign a similar contract (a supply of 4,000 slaves and immediate payment of 26,000 ducats to the crown treasury). This offer was not accepted. However, the submission of such an ambitious project by the two merchants was indicative of their good financial standing (Fernández Chaves and Pérez García 2016: 405). In 1541, Gaspar de Torres obtained, together with his brothers Diego and Alonso (Afonso), a contract to supply 300 slaves to the port of Trujillo (in present-day Honduras), for which both the bishop and the settlers, desperate for labour, had applied to the *Casa de Contratación*. Cooperation with the Portuguese was also developing. Gaspar de Torres, supported by his brothers who had been in Portugal since the 1520s, acted as an important intermediary between the Portuguese and the Spanish institutions responsible for the allocation of licences. He was, however, primarily the largest Spanish slave trader of the period. Between 1545 and 1550, he was granted permission to purchase and transport 2,317 slaves, accounting for more than 17 per cent of all licences granted in those years. In contrast, the Jorge brothers received, together with their partners, 9.7 per cent of the licences (Fernández Chaves and Pérez García 2016: 410, Ventura 1999: 39f).[4] Gaspar de Torres' brothers are also involved in the trade. Diego was in constant travel between Lisbon and Seville, while Alonso achieved a strong position at the Lisbon court. Let us also mention Gaspar de Torres' half-brother, Melchor de Torres. He resided in Santo Domingo (Española), owned three sugar mills and several smaller *trapiches*, 1,000 slaves and a hacienda, and it is he who supported the operations (sometimes illegal) of Spanish merchants, including the brothers, in the New World (Fernández Chaves and Pérez García 2012: 209–211, Rodriguez Morel 2004: 104).

The Spanish trade in Africans would also see the emergence of Lisbon merchants trading in pepper, grain and slaves, either on their own or with the help of partners. The skills in the slave trade acquired as early as the late 15th and early 16th centuries by Fernão de Noronha or João Rodrigues Mascarenhas were picked up by subsequent generations of merchants. Alonso de Torres played a particularly important role in strengthening contacts with Lisbon's merchant elite. This confidant of the Portuguese monarch in the slave trade – after his ennoblement in 1528 he was also given the *hábito* of Knight of the Order of Christ – was also, in 1529–31 and 1536–42, a high royal official and at the same time an extremely effective taxes and customs collector from Cabo Verde and 'Guinea', and later from São Tomé. The combination of these two roles was unique (unlike the roles of official and trade factor). For these and other services to the Portuguese crown, he was awarded a land grant (*carta de sesmaria*) in Bahia in 1549.[5] He continued to trade in slaves at the same time, and his representative in Seville, whose job it was to pave the way to the markets of the Spanish New World, was an Andalusian converso, also an important merchant, Alfonso Núñez.

The role played by the converts Alonso de Torres and Alfonso Núñez in establishing contacts with the Portuguese can hardly be overestimated, but they were not the only ones to collaborate with the merchants of Seville. Around the middle of the 16th century the names of Portuguese New Christians Damião

---

4   However, it would be difficult to overestimate role the Jorge brothers played in trade with the Spanish New World in the first half of the 16th century. Trade in slaves was not the most important among their ventures (Lorenzo Sanz 1979: 289–300).

5   It was Gabriel Soares de Sousa who wrote about him in 1587 in *Tratado descritivo do Brasil*, when he mentioned that on the Matoim River in Bahia "lies the famous cane plantation of Paripe. It formerly belonged to Afonso de Torres'"(quoted in Schwartz 2010: 68).

Fernandes, Luis Mendes, Pallos Dias, Emanuel and Simón Rodrigues, Manuel Caldeira were important in the Spanish trade in Africans. From the second half of the 16th century, when access to Angola was secured, one of the main roles in the slave trade would be played by the Portuguese Ximenes. According to custom office documents, between 1569 and 1579, five Portuguese merchants were among the 18 merchants who sold at least 150 slaves to the Spanish colonies; together they supplied, conservatively estimated, a third of all slaves (Thomas 1998: 117, Vila Vilar 1977: 27, Fernández Chaves and Pérez García 2016: 400f, 2012: 210, 219). In a dozen years or so, almost the entire Spanish slave trade would already be in the hands of the Portuguese, mostly XN s.

What is not in dispute, however, is the monopolistic position and crucial role played by the Portuguese in controlling the supply of slaves and ensuring their transportation from African trading posts. It mattered little whether the Spanish licence was in the hands of the House of Welser, Genoese or Castilian or Andalusian merchants. At the executive level, the Portuguese always appeared as intermediaries, agents and factors, as well as ship captains and pilots. An important place among them was occupied by the New Christians. This is well illustrated by their experience on Cabo Verde archipelago and then on the mainland – first by using a 'floating factoria' and then the fortress of Cacheu. Until the opening up of Angola these were the main centres in the Atlantic slave trade. Here and on São Tomé, the presence of New Christians, including crypto-Jews returning to the ancestral faith, was macroscopic. As late as the turn of the 16th and 17th centuries, it was almost impossible to carry out trade in the Rio de São Domingos area (north of Cacheu) without them and the *lançados*. It was in the transactions carried out in the Cacheu that the young Manuel Bautista Pérez from Peru cut his slave-trading teeth between 1612 and 1618, first as an agent of Iberian merchants, then as a minority partner with his grandfather and captain of a slave ship. The weakening of the importance of Cabo Verde and São Tomé to Angola at the end of the 16th century did not undermine the role played by the New Christians. They would appear from the beginning of the 17th century as important merchants and middlemen also in the Angolan slave trade. Luanda would in this century also become, as Cabo Verde and Cacheu had been before, an important centre for the conversion of some XN s to Judaism. Some *judaizantes*, who would appear as witnesses and victims in the great trials in Lima and Cartagena de Indias in the 1630s and 1640s, rejected Catholicism and returned to their ancestral faith precisely during their stay in West Africa (Torrão 1995: 62–64, 75, Green 2007: passim, 2015, Blackburn 2010: 142).

Attempts in the 16th century by the English, French or Flemish to break this Portuguese monopoly proved unsuccessful. On the other hand, New and Old

Christians in the metropolis and in the African trading posts expanded the scope of their activities in accordance with changes in the Atlantic economy. The trade in slaves in Elmina in exchange for African gold was from the 1520s gradually replaced by the growing number of Africans shipped to the New World. It is therefore not surprising that the slave trade procedure imposed by the Spanish bureaucracy – they had to be delivered first to Seville for inspection and customs before being transported to the American colonies – was increasingly questioned. The system guaranteeing a monopolistic position for Seville merchants and royal bureaucrats could hardly be considered effective when markets in the New World were controlled by the Spanish, while supply (access to African resources) was monopolised by the Portuguese. This contradiction was reflected on the one hand in increasing contraband and, on the other, in the more frequent approvals granted for the transport of slaves to the Spanish colonies directly from Africa. The first such consent was granted in 1525 (Almeida Mendes 2008: 759). By the 1580s, at least 67 per cent of slaves were already being shipped to the Spanish colonies directly from Africa. This was particularly true of transactions controlled by the great traders. In their case, only 5–9 per cent of slaves were transported through Seville. In addition, slave ships, largely Portuguese, were not required to travel to the Spanish New World in convoy, which undermined the effectiveness of cargo control. Portuguese merchants and captains, on the other hand, exported slaves directly from Africa with the permission of King João III from as early as the 1520s, and from 1534 such direct deliveries became systematic. It is not surprising, therefore, that in the 1580s no more than 9,600 slaves were exported through Seville, while the number of licences issued at that time was 28,667 (Garcia Fuentes 1982: 8, 20). Seville did not give way without a fight, however. The transition after 1595 to a new system of slave trade did not lead to the abolition of the obligation to first inspect cargo and levy a duty on slaves transported to the Spanish colonies in the Spanish port. In 1610 it was decided to enforce it rigorously, which would contribute to the collapse of the legal trade.

In the case of the growing supply of slaves to Brazil from the 1570s, the trade in Africans continued under licence even after the formation of the Iberian Union and the transition in Spain to the *asiento* system. The basis of the transaction was the contract (*contratos régios*) between the Portuguese merchant-bankers, *contratadores* (also called *rendeiros*), and the royal court. These in turn, using *avenças* (agreements), stipulated the relevant contracts with selected *negreiros*.[6] At the same time, we are talking about permissions

---

6   It was the *avençadores* who carried out, together with the shipowners, the captains and pilots of the ships, the minor commercial agents and their assistants and the factors, the contract,

given by Lisbon for the supply of slaves from a strictly defined African territory. Three such areas were involved: the first was 'Guinea' under the jurisdiction of the archipelago's capital Cabo Verde, together with the rival and growing centre already on the continent at Cacheu; the second was part of 'Guinea' and the Congo controlled from São Tomé; and from the 1570s, the third growing and soon to be most important area was Angola. The Portuguese *contratadores*, the counterparts of the *asentistas*, were among the economic elite. By the 1620s there would be well known merchant houses among them, mainly the New Christians Dias Henriques, Vaz de Évora, Gabriel and Gomes da Silva, the Elvas, Lamego, Ximenes families. In the following decades, new names of New Christian merchant-bankers emerged. Not only would they maintain the tradition of the slave trade, but would co-found a trading company in independent Portugal (Silva 2011 dutch: 287).

The establishment of the Iberian Union in 1580 opened Spanish America up to Portuguese merchants. The transition to the *asiento de negros* system also strengthened their position. Brazil had already been their undisputed monopoly for several decades.

The introduction of the new system in 1595, however, was not a revolution; rather, it was a tidying up of the existing regulation of the slave trade (Vila Vilar 1977: 188f), mainly with a view to increasing the Crown's revenue and relieving it of administrative responsibilities. An essential element of the new arrangement was, on the one hand, to treat the *asiento de negros* as a strategic financial decision negotiated on behalf of the Crown (similar to other *asientos*, such as those concerning army supplies or grain imports), while on the other hand, it led to an increase in the autonomy of the *asentistas*. There was a shift into their hands of decisions regarding distribution of licences among cooperating merchants, a hitherto royal prerogative of the *Casa de Contratación*. However, this formal aspect defining the position of the *asentistas* should not obscure the fundamental relationship that would be formed between them, the Crown and the *contratadores* and their collaborators operating in Africa. In a way, the *asentisa* acted as an intermediary between the Crown and the traders (Vila Vilar 1977, Newson and Minchin 2007: 19). He was powerful due to his formal powers, yet totally dependent on the Portuguese, including the XN s, who operated from the African coast in collaboration with local intermediaries. Its success or failure was also determined, as we shall see, by contrabandists.

---

took care of the transport, the cargo, the circulation of money, the completion of the formalities. Simply, they had "an essential role in the slave trade. Without them, the *contratador* would not have been able to fulfil the contract effectively" (Salvador 1981: 73).

Between 1595 and 1640, the Spanish Crown accepted five major contracts (*asientos*) for the delivery of African to the Spanish New World. This period was aptly described by Vila Vilar as the time of the "Portuguese asientos": all the *asentistas* who appeared until 1640 were Portuguese. However, from 1640 to 1651, the legal supply of slaves to the Spanish colonies ceased. This was one of the consequences of the break-up of the Iberian Union. The resumption of *asientos* after 1662 is already linked to the opening up of the Spanish slave trade to partners outside the Iberian Peninsula: Italians, English, French and Dutch (Navarrete Peláez 2015).

Between 1595 and 1640, the list of *asentistas* included:

1595–1600 Pedro Gómez Reynel

1601–1609 João Rodriguez Coutinho, then Gonçalo Vaz Coutinho

1609 Agustin Cuello (a stooge)

1610–1614 no *asiento*, working collaboration of the *Casa de Contratación* with, among others, Antônio Fernández Delvás

1615–1621 Antônio Fernández Delvás

1622 no *asiento* (bankruptcy of Antônio Fernández Delvása)

1623–1631 Miguel Rodríguez Lamego

1631–1640 Melchor Gómez Angel and Cristobal Méndez de Sousa

Were these Portuguese *asentistas* also New Christians? According to Israel (2002a: 103), during the period of the 'Portuguese asientos', all contracts were signed by the Spanish Crown "with Portuguese New Christian slave traders". Similarly, Almeida Mendes (2008: 764) argues: all the *asentistas* were "Judaised or descended from *conversos*". They were both wrong. In the system established in 1595, New Christians would not immediately be among the royal contractors. And finally, Quevedo (2008: 213) would count most of the *asentistas* among the New Christians, while being wrong about specific individuals, as discussed below.

On the first *assentista*, Pedro Gómez Reynel, we have non-conclusive information. We know that he was a wealthy Portuguese, firmly established in Seville's merchant elite, with contacts linking him to many *XN*s and Italian merchants. He was also seen as a ruthless competitor. However, there is a lack of sources that explicitly point to his Jewish roots. Slave trade historian noted cautiously that, "This first important state slaver of the new era (...) was probably a *converso*". He added that earlier, working with Rodriguez Coutinho, the later governor of Angola, Reynel "was already the king of the slave trade in Angola" (Thomas 1998: 141f). Indeed, both held licences for the slave trade from the area from 1593. Scelle (1910: 622), on the other hand, maintained that Reynel only became an *asentista* because he was Spanish.

Gómez Reynel signed the *asiento de negros* in 1595. The contract, concluded for nine years, provided for the delivery of 38,250 live slaves to the colonies designated by the Crown, nominally 4,250 per year (including 600 to La Plata). We write 'nominally' because the contract also took into account transport losses and supplementary supplies. A condition of signing the *asiento* was a downpayment of 100,000 ducats, while the cost of the nine-year rent was set at 900,000 ducats. Gómez Reynel's competitor was Antonio Nunes Caldeira, grandson of the already mentioned New Christian financier and slave trader of the time of Charles v, Manuel Caldeira. By this time, Nunes Caldeira was already linked to the Portuguese lobby in Seville and had a licence to trade slaves from the Cabo Verde and Guinea. However, he offered only 61,000 ducats for renting the monopoly (Fernández Chaves and Pérez García 2012: 219, 2010).

The contract with Gómez Reynel was never fully executed, being terminated ahead of schedule, in 1600. Over the years, this first Portuguese *assentista* supplied 25,500 slaves. His partner when it came to supplying slaves from the Congo and Angola was, among others, the New Christian Gil Fernández Ayres. The reason for breaking the contract was the emergence of (dubious) allegations of tax irregularities: Gómez Reynel was accused of selling licences to merchant-contractors at a higher price than agreed in the *asiento*, not 30 ducats per slave, but 35, 45 or even 50 ducats. However, this applied to prices obtained by Reynel from the execution of earlier contracts, before the *asiento* was signed in 1595. He was also charged with (not unreasonably) organising large-scale smuggling of slaves into the colonies. A royal lawyer from Buenos Aires accused Reynel of selling 1,828 slaves to La Plata over two years, 52 per cent above the terms of the contract. Contrabandists, who captured some of the slaves, were also a serious impediment to the contract (Schultz 2016: 28, Vila Vilar 1977: 33–37, 185, 1973: 585, Scelle 1910: 623).

The next two *assentistas* who first continued Reynel's contract, until a new *assiento* for nine years was signed in 1601, were the native brothers João Rodriguez Coutinho and Gonçalo Vaz Coutinho (it is therefore difficult to explain why Quevedo counts – erroneously, by the way – only the second among the xn s). Their contract provided for the payment of 170,000 ducats per year for the right to export 38,250 slaves. Both brothers belonged to the Order of Christ and both also held prominent positions: Rodríguez Coutinho participated in the activities of the royal *Consejo de Portugal*, while Vaz Coutinho held the office of governor of the island of São Miguel in the Azores. In 1602, João Rodriguez Coutinho was appointed governor of Angola. Together with his brother, "he was one of the few major Portuguese slave dealers of this era who were not *conversos*, and several of his brothers and sisters were monks or nuns" (Thomas 1998: 143). However, Salvador (1981: 43) notes that the "heart" of the good Christian nobles, the Coutinho brothers, was also "penetrated by Hebrew blood" when Vaz Coutinho became the son-in-law of Diogo da Veiga, a New Christian merchant from La Plata. In fact, the daughter of the merchant da Veiga was married to the grandson of Gonçalo Vaz Coutinho, who bore the same name and surname (Bonciani 2016: 170). A third brother, Manuel de Souza Coutinho, rarely mentioned, also participated in the trade carried out by the two brothers. He acted as their representative in Buenos Aires and Rio de Janeiro trading horses, slaves and silver; he also stayed, handing *asiento* matters, in Cartagena. The planned purchase of 2,500 horses in La Plata was linked to João Rodriguez Coutinho's idea of creating a cavalry troop in Angola. In contrast, neither Souza Coutinho nor any of his brothers appeared, as Cross (1978: 158) claimed, in Panama. Soon, however, Souza Coutinho broke with secular life and joined the Dominican order under the name Luis de Sousa (Ceballos 2014: 53, Bonciani 2016).

Following the death of João Rodriguez Coutinho in 1603–12,750 slaves were delivered to the American colonies during his lifetime – the *asiento* was taken over by Gonçalo Vaz Coutinho. In truth, while his brother was still alive, he was the one who ran the contract. The brother-governor was primarily interested in expanding Portuguese influence in Angola. Gonçalo Vaz Coutinho signed a new contract in 1604. His obligation to the Crown was reduced to 140,000 ducats per year, not least because of difficulties in settling the contract with his deceased brother. At the same time, the possibility of exporting slaves to La Plata, a region where the trade was largely controlled by contrabandists, was eliminated. However, the Seville Junta de Negros – the institution in charge of upholding the terms of the *asiento* led by representatives of the *Casa de Indias* and *Casa de Hacienda* – had doubts about Vaz Coutinho's execution of the contract and was also surprised by the ideas he submitted. These concerned the development, using black slaves, of a copper mine in Santiago, Cuba, and Vaz Coutinho expected extraordinary privileges and honours if his ideas were accepted. On the other hand, however, the royal bureaucracy blocked his activities for several years, making it difficult to trade licences. After five years, the contract was broken, after Vaz Coutinho had delivered 21,250 slaves (Vila Vilar 1977: 40–42, 111, 185).

In 1609, the *asiento* was signed by a certain Agustín Cuello from Salamanca. His advantage in the eyes of the decision-makers was that he was Spanish. The other candidates were not only Portuguese, but also New Christians. It turned out, however, that Cuello was in fact a stooge for the New Christian merchant Manuel Cea Brito who was farming the royal silk tax, and who had been arrested for debt (Vila Vilar 1977: 4–42f, Delgado Ribas 2013: 38).[7] In 1610–14, therefore, *Casa de Contratación* attempted to directly manage the slave trade. This was the peak of the Seville elite's mobilisation in its resistance to Portuguese expansion in the Spanish slave trade. The ultimate plan was even to eliminate the Portuguese from the *asiento* by making it compulsory for slaves to be transported out of Seville primarily by Spaniards and on Spanish ships (Vila Vilar 1977: 45).[8]

The effects of the *Casa de Contratación*'s direct management of the slave trade were lamentable, despite its collaboration – out of necessity – with Antônio Fernández Delvás, well-known in the merchant elite. Between 1612–14 the number of licences issued fell dramatically, while at the same time the renewed obligation in 1610 to transport Africans to the New World via Seville paralysed legal transactions (Vila Vilar 1977: 47). Seville's elites eventually capitulated in 1615. 'Portuguese *asientos*' passed into the hands of the New Christian *mercadores-banqueiros*. This was also the first step on the road leading to their prominent place among the Crown's main lenders in the next decade.

Antônio Fernández Delvás emerged as the first New Christian *asentista* to hold the contract for slave trade. His earlier efforts were blocked by the *Consulado* of Seville in 1609 after the machinations with the stooge substituted by Cea Brito were exposed (Scelle 1910: 623). For the next quarter of a century, the Spanish slave trade – both when it came to financial dealings with the court and the execution of *asiento* in Africa and the Atlantic – would remain under the control of the New Christians (although it is uncertain whether the *asentistas* in 1631–40 were converts). The time of the 'Portuguese asientos' became the time of the Portuguese New Christians. Once their strong presence in the trade with Brazil is taken into account, one can speak of the concentration in their hands of most of the Atlantic trade in Africans.

Let us return for a moment to the Portuguese slave trade. As mentioned earlier, even before renting the Spanish *asiento* and becoming governor of Angola, João Rodriguez Coutinho had already held a Portuguese contract for the Angolan slave trade since 1593. The transition in Spain to the *asiento* system

---

7 Portuguese Manuel Cea Brito had already emerged as a contender for the *asiento* following the death of João Rodriguez Coutinho. Imprisonment was, it seems, only an episode in his life. In the following decade, he is again a prominent merchant and tax farmer and customs collector in Seville and then an investor in Madrid (Cañas Pelayo 2016: 281).

8 This was a breakneck idea if one considers that in the 1580s, the small Portuguese merchant fleet numbered 304 ships, while the Spanish fleet numbered 650 ships (Costa Freire, Lains and Münch Miranda 2016: 93). In the decade 1561–70, Spanish-flagged ships transported less than 46 per cent of slaves to the colonies (Eltis and Richardson 2008: table 1.6).

did not invalidate the licences issued in Lisbon for the supply of slaves from specific regions of Africa. Spain could decide on the number of slaves formally imported into its colonies, but could not dictate the conditions regarding the suppliers and purchase of slaves from West Africa. As the Brazilian market grew in importance, independent of the Spanish *asiento*, the Portuguese position in the Atlantic slave trade strengthened. In any case, licences for the supply of slaves from Africa were issued by the Portuguese crown prior to the Iberian Union, and were also issued in Lisbon during its time. The decision was taken after 1581 on the basis of the opinion of the *Consejo de Portugal* (its members were exclusively Portuguese).

Most of the *asentistas* acted at the same time as Portuguese *contratadores* monopolising supplies from Angola, among other places. The case of João Rodriguez Coutinho was not an isolated one. Also Gómez Reynel, as an *asentista,* benefited from a licence granted in 1593 to trade in slaves from Angola. The same was true of Antônio Fernández Delvás, who combined *asiento* with a Portuguese contract to supply slaves from Angola and Upper Guinea, as well as another *asentista,* Miguel Rodríguez Lamego (Silva 2011: 228, 288, 290). It was not only *asentistas* that could be Portuguese *contratadors* at the same time. There were also combinations of the role of an *asiento* subcontractor with that of Portuguese *contratador*, or subcontractor in Spanish and Portuguese contracts.

Antônio Fernández Delvás held the *asiento de negros* between 1615 and 1621. The signing of a contract with this important merchant-banker was facilitated both by family connections, the favours (not disinterested) shown to the New Christian elite by Philip III's influential minister, the Prince de Lerma, and the growing presence of wealthy 'Portuguese' in Madrid and Seville (although he himself only extremely rarely moved from Portugal). Antônio Fernández Delvás was not nouveau riche, just looking to make a place for himself as an indigent *negreiro*. He came from one of the richest New Christian families, whose members had already been active in overseas trade and with links to the court for at least two generations. This wealthy merchant "connected by blood with nearly all the major slave dealers of the Spanish-Portuguese empire", was himself the largest slave trader at the time. However, kinship was not limited to the families of slave traders only. His family connections included members of the elite Ximenes d'Aragão, Rodrigues d'Evora, Veiga and Coronel families. Son and daughter marriages ensured close ties to the families of the Lisbon banker Heitor Mendes de Brito and the influential *arbitrarista* and merchant Duarte Gomes Solis (Thomas 1998: 297, Hutz 2014: 182). Although the slave trade dominated Fernández Delvás' activities from a certain point in time, his network of business contacts, established while he was still trading in Asian spices, also extended to Asia and major centres of European trade. In these regions slaves – important in the Atlantic economy – gave way to other commodities.

Fernández Delvés' contract stipulated, for an annual payment of 115,000 ducats, the right to export 40,000 slaves from Africa over eight years and deliver 3,500 *esclavos efectivos* annually (1,500 slaves were assumed to die on the journey) to Cartagena and Vera Cruz. In fact, he delivered 24,500 slaves over seven years. At the same time, the right to sell 150 slaves a year in the La Plata region was restored, albeit only a symbolic number, and in 1616 Delvas' Portuguese contracts for the purchase of slaves from Angola and Cabo Verde were confirmed. The supply of slaves via these islands had already been in the hands of a member of his family from 1615. Thus, "one man controlled the entire legal [Iberian] slave trade" (Vila Vilar 1977: 48–50, 185, Silva 2011: 228). The conditions imposed on Fernández Delvás for the execution of the contract were quite restrictive, including the obligation to transport slaves through Seville. This was the only substantial concession obtained by the Seville merchants: limiting the role of Lisbon as the main port for slave ships.[9] It is not surprising, therefore, that this powerful merchant was not only a royal *asentista*, but at the same time an organiser of the smuggling of slaves and other goods on a huge scale. All the more so given that it was at this time that the scale of the slave trade reached proportions hitherto unknown. The Spaniards and Portuguese exported more than 91,000 slaves from Africa in 1601–10, while in the following decade 1611–1620, including the Delvás contract, it was 148,000 (Eltin and Richardson 2008: table 1.6). Such a change in scale must have led to the disorganisation of legal traffic, paralysis of the institutions controlling the trade and an increase in contraband. The eminent Spanish historian even writes of the bankruptcy of the *asiento* as a system of trade. This is all the more so given that between 1618 and 1624 probably more than a quarter of the slaves were supplied to Spanish America by contrabandists (Vila Vilar 1977: 50, also Green 2007: 185).

Wealth, kinship and connections at the Madrid court did not protect Antônio Fernández Delvás from arrest. Imprisoned in 1621, he soon died of a leprosy-like illness. That the public-private partnership was a risky venture was illustrated at this time also by merchant-financiers involved in tax-farming in Africa. Failing contract holders "were ultimately stripped of their contracts, imprisoned, and deprived of assets pledged as collateral, with neither ever able to join another public-private partnership with the Crown" (Pereira 2019: 64).

---

9 Between 1595 and 1615, 263 slave ships departed from Lisbon while 47 departed from Spanish ports (no information is available on 195) (Vila Vilar 1973: 563).

Anyhow, before Delvás's arrest, the *Consejo de Indias* stated that the contract signed with him could not be fulfilled due to the scale of the mismanagement, while he himself declared bankruptcy. This only precipitated arrest. At the same time, Fernández Delvás proudly and probably truthfully claimed that he had not lost a penny on his business dealings. The tax arrears from the Spanish *asiento* and the Angolan contract were a loss to the Crown, but did not represent a loss to his private wealth. The execution of the *asiento* was taken over – despite the appointment of a formal contract administrator – by his wife, Elena Rodrigues (Roiz) Solis, already involved in her husband's commercial operations. In 1622, she even tried to get the contract renewed, but to her disappointment the *asiento* was taken over by another New Christian merchant-banker, Miguel Rodríguez Lamego. His competitors were the aforementioned João Nunes Saravia and Duarte Dias Henriques, in the following years important holders of other royal contracts.

Little is known about Fernández Delvás's relationship with Portuguese crypto-Jews. He himself was never suspected of being *judaizante*. The information that he was a New Christian married to a New Christian woman and related to many New Christians, and that "his brother-in-law (...) was arrested by the Inquisition in Cartagena" (Hutz 2008: 81), does not illuminate the issue. All of this is true, yet all that can be said about Delvása himself is that he belonged "to a numerous group of New Christians whose true confession is difficult to determine" (Vila Vilar 1977: 113). One of many cases illustrating both the phenomenon of Jewish converts as a group *sui generis* and the birth of a modern individualism that did not, however, radically dissociate itself from community ties.

Information on further *asentistas* is very scarce. We know little about Miguel Rodríguez Lamego and his family. One of its members, Antonio Mendes Lamego, received a Portuguese licence to trade Africans from Angola and the island of São Tomé even before the new slave trade system was established. His brother Antonio Rodríguez Lamego, in turn, was active in Rouen and participated in 1623 in the disputes that divided the 'Portuguese' there. Unlike the Rouenian supporters of full integration with the Christians, who were represented by the three Fonscea brothers, from a "family of New Christians and sincere converts", "men of wealth and influence", Antonio Rodríguez Lamego, "a well-known Judaizer from Rouen", represented those who wanted stronger links with Judaism. Unable to bring him before a tribunal, the Spanish Inquisition condemned him in 1635 to be burned *in effigie* (Silva 2011: 288, Carrasco Vázquez 2004: 265, 291). Miguel Rodríguez Lamego himself was "a typical Jew (*sic*) enriched by the slave trade, closely associated with fellow Jews in northern Europe, and a friend and relative of the great bankers" (Vila Vilar 1977: 113, 96f).[10]

During the selection process of the new *asentista*, the Rouen Portuguese, despite fierce internal disputes, successfully supported Miguel Rodríguez Lamego's candidacy in Madrid. Although he did not have a good reputation among the other merchants (he was called *el malo* – 'the bad one'), according to one influential member of the Junta de Negros, of the several candidates who competed for the contract, Miguel Rodríguez Lamego was considered the most reliable (Vila Vilar 1977: 96f, 113, Alpert 2001: 63f). The contract for eight years at a cost of 120,000 ducats per year provided for the delivery of 40,000 slaves (including 28,000 *esclavos efectivos*). Compared to its predecessors, historians point out, the contract signed with Rodríguez Lamego was the first not to be broken, and was carried out without bankruptcies, breakdowns or forced interruptions. This was an achievement in view of the war with the United Provinces that resumed in 1621 and the considerable losses and difficulties caused to Atlantic shipping by the Dutch fleet and corsairs. We should add that during the negotiations of the terms of the *asiento,* Seville's monopoly on the forced clearance of ships with licensed slave cargoes in the city harbour was finally broken. In the year that Rodríguez Lamego signed the contract (1623), the Lisbon port again cleared the majority of slave ships bound for the Spanish colonies.

Like his predecessors, Rodríguez Lamego was also accused of being deeply involved in illegal slave deliveries. This involved, in particular, the abuse of the *arribadas forçosas* procedure – the enforced arrival of ships at ports not previously designated in the voyage permit due to imminent danger. Contraband was made possible by the transformation of this procedure, sanctioned by law and tradition, into "malicious entries" (*arribadas maliciosas*). Cartagena de Indias and Buenos Aires in particular were the preferred ports. With the consent of the local authorities and usually after an unofficial (but lawful) visit of the trade factor to the ship preceding the boarding of the royal officials, the unregistered and unclassified slave cargo would 'disappear' or – after informal arrangements – be declared illegal and (temporarily) requisitioned. In the second case, the slaves were put up for public auction and sold to a substituted partner for a pre-agreed price. The buyer was sometimes the contrabandist himself. In the second decade of the 17th century, the price of a slave at such pre-arranged auctions in Buenos Aires did not exceed 170 pesos, while the market

---

10   The document allowing Miguel Rodríguez Lamego to stay in Madrid was accompanied by the remark that he came from "the nation of the new Christians" (Salvador 1981: 138).

price at the port at that time was 300 pesos, and 500 pesos in Potosí. More often than not, however, it was not the entire shipment that was requisitioned, but the surplus of illegally transported slaves. In the case of these *esclavos descaminados*, a high duty was not paid, after paying off officials. Using the royal *cédula de manifestaciones*, once the surplus was declared, only the tax – which was lower than the duty – was paid. The latter procedure was still possible at the beginning of the 17th century, then abolished and renewed after the Fernández Delvás contract (Scelle 1910: 625, Vila Vilar 1977: 51, 78, 113, 164, Wolff 1964: 176, Rodriguez 1956: 177, Navarrete Peláez 2007: 173). Incidentally, *el contrabando* and *descaminado* are sometimes treated interchangeably, although the former describes the introduction of prohibited goods, while the latter describes tax evasion. In practice, both terms referred to a similar category of phenomena. And finally, in some cases, contraband and "malicious entries" took place using the legal opportunities provided by the transportation of children younger than seven years old. Their sale was exempt from tax (Castilla Palma 2016).

All we know about the last *asentistas* from 1631–1640, Melchor Gómez Angel and Cristobal Méndez de Sousa, is that they were Portuguese. Both were offered an extension of the *asiento* for another six years in 1640 and moved to Lisbon a few months later after the victorious anti-Spanish revolt in Portugal. The terms of their 1631 contract took into account the disorganisation of trade caused by the continuing war with the United Provinces, and the subsequent seizure by the Dutch of the main Portuguese *feitorias* in Africa. It therefore provided for a reduced payment of 95,000 ducats and the supply of 22,500 slaves, i.e. 2,500 *esclavos efectivos* per year (it was assumed that 1,000 Africans would die on the voyage). The signing of the contract with Gómez Angel and Méndez de Sousa was accompanied by the monarch's agreement to an additional (and exceptional) transport of 1,500 slaves to the La Plata region by a Genoese merchant between 1631–35. And, as with other *asentistas* who organised trade with the help of close family and distant relatives, Cristobal Méndez de Sousa's two brothers acted as his factors in Cartagena and Vera Cruz. In contrast, "no information is available regarding their religion", although, as Vila Vilar adds, it can be assumed that "like their predecessors, they were more or less connected to the crypto-Jewish groups that dominated the fianancial world at the time" (Vila Vilar 1977: 78, 115, also Hutz 2008: 83, Salvador 1981: 139). This guesswork, however, cannot be taken as s substitute for exact information on the origins and/or religion of the two *asentistas*.

After all, the time of the Portuguese in the slave trade was not limited to the *asentistas* or, in the case of Portuguese contracts, the largest *contratadores*. Other important merchants also played a role as *agentes fixos maiores* acting on behalf of the *asentistas*. In this group, the New Christians occupied a prominent place. We have already mentioned one, Jorge Fernandes Gramaxo, who built up his position as the factor of the first *asentistas* and, from 1614, also as the commercial agent of Ximenes d'Aragao. His importance was not only due to the position he reached in Cartagena by combining the legal and illegal trade in slaves, pearls and other goods with the ownership of plantations, *trapiches* and real estate or by performing the tasks of official trade factor. These activities were accompanied by public engagement, such as involvement in the defence of the coast of New Granada against the attacks of Francis Drake in 1595 (he would purchase and arm two frigates). His friendship with the colonial officials and the bishops of Cartagena and Popayán also was a factor. However, the role he played was determined by a network of connections that ensured his supply of information, international contacts and Africans. Jorge Fernandes Gramaxo's brother, Luis Fernandes, was a merchant in Lisbon who arranged contracts for the supply of slaves to Cartagena from Cabo Verde, while Jorge Fernandes Gramaxo's nephew, bearing the same name, acted as a merchant on the main island of the archipelago. It was not without reason that he and his like-minded agents of the *asentistas* and Portuguese *contratadores* were seen on Cabo Verde as competitors of the local traders. In competition with the networks of Gramaxo, Dias Henriques and others, merchants from the archipelago, including the New Christians, stood no chance. In contrast, another son of Luis Fernandes, Antonio Nunes Gramaxo, resided in Seville. It was his responsibility to manage the slave ships that operated along the Guinean coast, as well as trade with the New World. He was supported by one of the Crown's leading financiers and negotiators, the ennobled New Christian Duarte Brandón Suárez (previously active in Brazil). And finally, let us note that family and commercial contacts also linked Jorge Fernandes Gramaxo (the elder) and his relatives to Amsterdam and Sephardic merchants (Green 2007: 151–153, Vila Vilar 1979: 166f, Navarrete Peláez 2009: 46f, Studnicki-Gizbert 2007: 85, Boyajian 1993: 143, 218, Álvarez Nogal 1997: 94f).

Fernández Delvás's factor in Cartagena was his son and then brother-in-law. However, at least as important a role was played in the commercial operations of this *asentista* by other collaborating merchants, Duarte Dias Henriques and Diogo da Veiga. The commercial and financial operations of both, when it came to slaves, mainly covered the South Atlantic area – Angola, Brazil and Buenos Aires. The former has already been mentioned. Let us only add that, without the close cooperation of both Fernández Delvás and Dias Henriques – who were contractors in the Angolan slave trade – a considerable legal and illegal supply of slaves to Buenos Aires would have been impossible (Silva 2012: 158). Diogo da Veiga, on the other hand, played an important role in Buenos Aires and La Plata in the first two decades of the 17th century, combining economic activity with involvement in local politics.

Let us also mention the example of the slave trade in the first circle, where the New and Old Christians were shareholders in a medium scale joint venture. The otherwise understandable focus on the activity of the *asentistas,* however, relegates the medium-sized *negreiros* to the background. They "do not appear in the major institutional records of monopolistic slave trading companies or large merchant houses" (Hicks 2017: 276). In fact, it was they who were the "small powerful engines [creating] the Atlantic economic space" (Torrão 1997: 114). Collaboration between these small and medium shareholders was based on a profit- and risk-sharing arrangement that was a variant of *societas maris*, already practised in the Middle Ages under different names by Italian merchants. This institution was incorporated in the second half of the 16th century into the Portuguese legal system. In most general terms it "reflected the transition (...) to a partnership with bilateral contribution of capital" (Weber 2003: 68, also Hicks 2017: 280–283). In the case quoted below, the contributions of the shareholders to the single venture carried out between 1628 and 1631 were, respectively, the capital of one and the labour (including the willingness to undertake a risky ocean voyage) and smaller capital contribution of the other.

Thus, we have two, very different, Lisbon merchants: António Fernandes Landim, who came from the indigent Old Christians, and the wealthy New Christian Francisco Dias Mendes de Brito. The former was without serious contacts in Lisbon's merchant milieu, had, however, as captain and shipowner, experience in voyages to Africa, contacts in Cacheu and negotiating skills. The latter, related to the influential Duarte Dias Henriques and firmly embedded in the *negreiros* milieu, was in turn "the paradigmatic representative of Lisbon's merchant elite" (Torrão 1997: 96). The partners' ship set sail for Upper Guinea in 1628 with Fernandes Landim as captain. The capital put up by the two merchants and loans enabled the purchase of 344 slaves in Cacheu and the recruitment of additional crew. After a voyage of one and a half months, the transport of 480 slaves (the surplus were 'passengers', i.e. slaves of the governor, Cacheu factors and other persons important to the partners) reached Cartagena de Indias (Torrão 1997: 108). After the sale of the ship and the slaves – in Cacheu, 50–60,000 réis were paid for one, while in Cartegena, more than 102,000 réis were obtained – and the repayment of loans and other costs, quite a large profit remained in the hands of the partners.

In the concerted action of the New and Old Christian merchants, religion, family ties and group loyalties were defined within the wider context of the community of interests of the Portuguese who made up *La Nação*. We do not know, writes a Portuguese researcher, whether the partners were united by ties of affection, friendship, professionalism or whether fortuitous circumstances came into play. Certainly, however, the interaction was made possible by "solid relationships of mutual trust" (Torrão 1997: 94, 2013). It is important to keep this example in mind when discussing the place of New Christians in the slave trade during the period of the 'Portuguese *asientos*'. Without interaction with the *cristãos-antiguos,* handling the increasing scale of the Atlantic slave trade would have been impossible.

When, from the second half of the 17th century, the number of slaves imported into the New World began to increase exponentially, the New Christians would soon find themselves on the margins of this specific trade. Powerful Dutch, English and French competitors appeared. However, the significance of this factor should not be overestimated. Although the New Christians stopped playing a crucial role – in fact they disappeared from this trade – the *cristãos-antiguos* of Portugal and Brazil, both white and *mulato*, maintained amidst fierce competition a strategically important position in the international slave market in the 18th century. Ships under the Portuguese flag transported between 1751 and 1800 mainly to Brazil slighty over 1.2 million slaves, whereas the vessels carrying the Union Jack brought to the New World around 1.59 million Africans (Eltis and Robinson 2008: table 1.6).

CHAPTER 11

In Spanish America: from Buenos Aires to the Stake

In Brazil, the New Christians were among the pioneers contributing to the colony's economy. It was only at the end of the 16th century that there was noticeable Portuguese activity in Spanish America, although their earlier influx had already caused concern among colonial officials and the Church. Although the New Christians would not make up the majority of Portuguese migrants arriving from the 1580s (Hoberman 1977: 498), activity within *La Nação* translated into a strengthening of their influence in particular parts of the Spanish empire. The Iberian Union was, from an economic point of view, beneficial to *La Nação* for four decades until the resumption of war with the Republic. Gaining control of the slave trade was accompanied by easier access to Spanish America, as well as an expansion of trade with Asia. Restrictions again enforced in the 1590s by Spanish rivals were of little use (Schwartz 1968: 37, 43). The Portuguese historian therefore writes: "Thousands of Portuguese (…) had gradually settled down in Mexico, Peru, and La Plata, their merchants and capital playing an important economic role" (Marques 1976: 324). Indeed, in some important places, like the Potosí mining centre, their presence was strongly accentuated: "When Portugal recovered its independence in 1640 and the Spanish autorities hastily investigated the Portuguese at Potosí, it was found that twenty of the sixty Portuguese listed were very wealthy and that one of them (…) had built up a fortune of two million pesos" (Hanke 1961: 23). At the same time, they were resented and looked at with suspicion because of their wealth, contacts and questionable genealogy.

The peak of the influx of New Christians into Spanish America occurred in the first three decades of the 17th century. Illegal migrants, although treated as aliens despite the Iberian Union,[1] formed an urban population of several thousand in the first half of the 17th century in Peru, New Spain, Cartagena and La Plata. In Brazil, the number of *XN*s also reached the thousands in the early 17th century. A change in the laws, negotiated from 1598, which had hitherto

---

1   In the first decades of the colonisation of Peru, the strangers, in the eyes of the Castilians, were Catalans, Basques and Portuguese, the latter being seen as "the least foreign" (Lockhartt 1968: 129). Between 1500 and 1650, only 389 Portuguese were formally allowed to settle in the Spanish New World (Studnicki-Gizbert 2007: 44). In Cartagena de Indias around 1630, among the foreigners residing in the port, mostly Portuguese, only 6 per cent (11) had permission to stay (Vila Vilar 1979: 156).

restricted their rights, including the right to move within the Spanish empire, was a major contributor to this mobility of the 'Portuguese'.

In 1601, Philip III's decree allowed converts to move freely in the Iberian Peninsula and, under certain conditions, to travel outside, including to the Iberian colonies. The promulgation of this decree cost the New Christians 300,000 cruzados as a contribution to the Crown treasury. The declaration of the third amnesty in 1605 with the approval of Pope Clement VIII (the previous ones had been granted in 1533 and 1577) was also of importance. Opposition from the Archbishops of Braga, Lisbon and Evora, the Portuguese Inquisition and the influential Lisbon city council, which prolonged the decision-making process, had been overcome (Marques 1993). The amnesty resulted in a pardon for suspects in the empire and allowed the release of 410 *judaizantes* from peninsular prisons. As a condition of this, the New Christians had to pay a huge contribution of 1.7 million cruzados (equivalent to about 66 tonnes of silver) within a few years.[2] Emigrants in western Europe were also encouraged to return. Without much effect. However, 75 New Christians from Rouen who returned to Spain were arrested by the Inquisition after a change in the political situation and convicted in 1609 (Alpert 2001: 64). In turn, the order issued in 1606 to remove all Portuguese and other foreigners from Buenos Aires and La Plata was ignored, despite the efforts of the governor Hernando Arias de Saavedra ("Hernandarias"). The Bishop of Rio da Plata stood up for the Portuguese artisans and merchants, skilfully reinterpreting the royal law (Ceballos 2007: 158). In 1610, the restrictions on *XN*s movement to the colonies were renewed – a condition of any travel approval was confirmation of payment of the relevant amount as part of a contribution imposed in 1605. The effectiveness of this regulation was limited. It seems that the Crown too, especially when it came to the Portuguese presence in Peru, was cautious until the 1630s about projects aimed at expelling them or significantly restricting their activities. All other reasons aside, an important factor considered was the prospect of royal court cooperation with the New Christians (Cross 1978).

All this made life difficult for the *XN*s , but the effective impact on the New Christians would come later, in the 1630s and 1640s. They were foreshadowed

---

2   For those residing in the Iberian Peninsula, the amnesty would expire in 1606, while for those residing in the colonies it would expire a year later. At the start of the amnesty negotiations, an amount of 620,000 cruzados was mentioned, later raised to 800,000 plus 200,000 to be distributed among the 'most important ministers'. As part of the final agreement, Spanish and Portuguese high court officials received gifts totalling 100,000 cruzados, including 50,000 for the Prince de Lerma (Saraiva 2001: 139f., Graizbord 2004: 22–24, Azevedo 1922: 162). According to Pulido Serrano (2006: 351–365), the total value of these gifts was much higher.

by the actions of the Inquisition in Portugal, which in the second and third decades resulted in acceleration of migrations to Spain, seen at the time as a place of relatively safe asylum. Compared to the decade 1610–1619, when Inquisition tribunals convicted 865 people in Portugal, in the following decade, 1620–1629, the number of victims increased to 2,833 and remained at a similar level until 1639. In Coimbra alone, more than 460 defendants were forced to participate in *autos-da-fé* between 1629 and 1631. In 1627 and 1630, on the other hand, several hundred people were released from the prisons of the Inquisition due to amnesties (Swetschinski 2004: 69 table 2.2, Lea 1907: 273f). One of the most notorious cases in this rising wave of persecution in Portugal was the ongoing trials between 1619 and 1624 of suspected members of the confraternity founded at the University of Coimbra by professor and dean António Hómem. Coming from a family of New Christians, this authority in canon law was first accused of 'sodomy'. The charge was later changed, and he was convicted of preaching heresy (he "became a believer in the Law of Moses, considering it beautiful and truthful") and burned at the stake. The canons and nuns who collaborated with him were counted among the *XN*s only 'partially' and treated more leniently. However, the shock these repressions provoked resulted in a dramatic increase in xenophobic attitudes and behaviours among faculty and Old Christian students, and beyond Coimbra (Baron 1973: pp. 237–240, Stuczynski 2014: 51f, Marcocci and Paiva 2013: 166–168). According to probably incomplete information gathered by the Portuguese Holy Office envoy for the Crown, between 1619 and 1627 the Portuguese Inquisition accused 231 people of heresy, including 15 priests, 44 nuns, 15 theologians (including two professors), 11 bachelors, 20 lawyers and 20 doctors (Azevedo 1922: 185).

These activities of the Portuguese Inquisition were contrasted with the lessening of repression in Spain and the Spanish empire. The activity of the Peruvian Inquisition in exposing and punishing *judaizantes,* which had been on the rise between 1595 and 1605, was greatly reduced in the following two decades after the declaration of the amnesty (Cross 1978: 158). All these changes from the end of the 16th century were associated with the *valido* of Philip III, the Duke de Lerma, described by contemporaries as the "one who ruled the king and all Spain" (Sobieski 1833: 117, 96). It was thanks to his support that there was an opening to the Portuguese and the possibility of their participation already in the first *asiento de negros*. This favourite of the king was aware that Portuguese control of the slave supply meant that resistance by the Seville merchants could not be effective. The next step was also to take up contacts, in the course of negotiating the amnesty declared in 1605, with the New Christian *mercadores-banqueiros*. Earlier, the Duke de Lerma had given his support to a project to amend the 'purity of blood' regulations submitted by the Dominican Agustino Salucio. He also played a leading role in arranging the truce between Spain and the United Provinces. However, the corruption and financial machinations in which Duke de Lerma participated, as well as the inconsistency of his opening policy towards the XNs, overshadowed this aspect of his activities. On the other hand, to the satisfaction of the Church and the people, the Duke de Lerma was instrumental in the expulsion in 1609–1614 of hundreds of thousands of *moriscos*. Anyhow, anticipating trouble, he secured for himself the cardinal's hat (and immunity) from the hands of Pope Paul V shortly before his removal from the Court in 1618.

The continuation of the opening policy, but on a larger scale, would be followed from the 1620s by the Count-Duke de Olivares, who played a part in the fall of the Duke de Lerma. It is during his reign that further moves to soften the attitude towards the XNs appeared. Among other things, from 1628, New Christians' travel to the Spanish colonies and Spain itself was already permitted (the price of such a decision was 80,000 ducats).[3] Their influx to Madrid and Seville would therefore be accompanied by a growing stream of Portuguese migrants to the New World. However, it is – in the current state of research – impossible to determine the proportion between New and Old Christians among the latter. Arguably, the picture that emerges from the files of the great trials in Lima, Cartagena de Indias and Ciudad de México, in which hundreds *judaizantes* were convicted, is to some extent distorted, if only because of the omission of a considerable number of New Christians and conversos never recorded in the investigations. In any case, in Lima and Cartagena, the 'Portuguese' acted as formidable competitors not only to the Spanish Old Christians, but often also to the already well-settled Spanish conversos. In Mexico, on the other hand, such a strongly accentuated predominance of the 'Portuguese' did not appear, especially when referring to the merchant elite controlling the *consulado* of the capital. However, one should take into account that between 1601 and 1635, i.e during the period relatively free from persecution of New Christians, at least one-quarter of important wholesalers in Mexico "shipped to known *conversos* in Seville", and probably "there were more *conversos* or semi-*conversos*

---

3 At an assembly of Portuguese bishops and their advisors convened by King Philip IV in 1628, these representatives of the church set out a position on the future of the New Christians. It boiled down to one thing – "the thorough expulsion of the whole race". In the event that this proved impossible, the bishops demanded restrictions on mixed marriages and the elimination of converts from trades and commerce. They also called for a ban on transactions between converts and the royal treasury. None of these demands were implemented, while to the last the king "answered rather curtly that it was none of their business" (Lea 1907: 276f). A year earlier, an agreement had been made between the Crown and a group of New Christian bankers on a loan to the royal treasury and access to the *asientos*.

among merchant guild members than can be shown" (Hoberman 1977: 495, 1991: 21). Thus, Spanish conversos also appeared among the defendants in the trials of 1642–1646. One in particular was the powerful merchant and financier Simón Váez Sevilla. Nevertheless, in Mexico too, the majority of victims were 'Portuguese'. It is estimated that among those suspected of Judaising, 73 per cent had grandparents from Portugal (Hordes 2005: 33f). At the same time, accusations of heresy were accompanied in all the great trials by suspicions of treason against Spain: in favour of the Dutch, as in Lima and Cartagena de Indias, or in favour of a newly independent Portugal from 1640, as in Ciudad de México.

However, before the change of policy that resulted (depending on the region) in the marginalisation of the 'Portuguese' or their total elimination, one can speak of the half-century expansion of *La Nação* in the centres of the Spanish New World. In its shadow, the economy of peripheral La Plata was also taking shape, with the participation of a number of 'Portuguese'. It was to them that the royal regulation of 1602, often quoted by historians, referred, stating that these newcomers, the *judaizantes*, "are uncertain when it comes to our Holy Catholic Faith", and tightened controls (Lewin 1987: 40f). However, the creation of the tribunal of the Inquisition in Cartagena in 1610 – intended as a move to relieve the burden on the Lima Holy Office and to impede the transfer of 'Portuguese' to the Viceroyalty of Peru – had an unplanned effect: it contributed to turning peripheral Buenos Aires into a centre for the transit of 'Portuguese' to Upper Peru and other parts of the Viceroyalty. Another regulation from 1603 spoke of the need to control the influx of Portuguese priests and religious, many suspected of being Judaised (Böhm 1998: 48, 51, Dominguez Ortiz 1971: 137f). A few comments on these issues is in order here.

At the end of the 16th century, a new continental trade route was being created with the participation of the 'Portuguese' and against the intentions of the metropolis, which will connect the Brazilian ports, Buenos Aires, Cordova, Tucumán, and the mining centre of Potosí (Rodriguez 1956: 172f). Its creation was intertwined with the contradictions of Madrid's policies towards the different parts of the empire, which were difficult to unravel. An Argentine historian writes:

> The main objective of the metropolitan authorities was to control and exploit the mining industry of Upper Peru. The priority was to preserve the trade monopoly of Lima and Seville, with which this main objective was linked. Thus, the exclusion of Buenos Aires from the regular sea routes appeared as an understandable consequence of imperial logic. [It was recognised, however, that ensuring the security of Upper Peru required] maintaining a populous centre in the Rio de la Plata and defending this flank of the empire against the temptations of the Brazilian Portuguese.

In turn, fulfilling this condition implied developing commercial activity in La Plata [including transfers of] precious metals from the 'protected' region, from Potosí and its mines.

MOUTOUKIAS 1988: 221[4]

The combination of a Peru-centered royal mining and trade monopoly that marginalised La Plata on one hand, and the need for defence of this peripheral region that required reinforcement (and new resources) on the other, was untenable. The solution to this dilemma was smuggling from the late 16th century onwards. It is also the answer to other problems. One has in mind here the more than fivefold increase between 1570 and 1604 in silver production in Potosí (Fisher 1997: 97). This fostered local demand, but its satisfaction was hampered by the royal trade monopoly. The bureaucratic machinery sustaining it "cried out for simplification; and if Spanish officials and merchants would not attempt it, creoles were glad to do it for them. The final simplification of [the monopoly trade] was to stop using it altogether, and to buy from, and sell to, contraband traders" (Bakewell 2004: 239).

Francisco de Vitória, from a family of Portuguese New Christians, played a pioneering role in initiating the trade linking Potosi and La Plata with Rio de Janeiro and Bahia. Reference is also made to the Governor of Rio de Janeiro Salvador Correia de Sá (the elder), who, according to the Viceroy of Portugal, was "the first (...) to pave this route" (Salvador 1978: 58–62, on bishop de Vitória see Helmer 1953, Canabrava 1984: 82–88, Israel 1990a: 334). Or more precisely, he blazed part of it, on the stretch between Rio de Janeiro and the *cidade de Boynos-Ayres*.

The importance of this approximately 2,100 km route was determined by geography. It took more than two months to travel the *Camino Real* from Buenos Aires via Cordova, Tucumán, Jujuy to Potosí via a route that was largely carriage driven (*camino llano*). In contrast, the journey from Lima over a similar distance, over difficult Andean trails, was twice as long. Under these conditions, the royal monopoly imposed on supplying La Plata and other parts of the Viceroyalty of Peru exclusively through Cartagena and Lima, and only with goods shipped from Seville, was increasingly contested. According to an Argentine historian, "[t]he economic struggle in the colonial era was a clash between the Rio de la Plata route, forbidden by law, and other routes artificially

---

4 Madrid's concern about Portuguese ambitions in the La Plata region had a history. As early as 1531, the nervous reaction of Spain's ambassador to the royal court in Lisbon over the expedition to Brazil of Martim Afonso de Sousa with several hundred settlers was recorded. Their task was colonisation, which would reach south to La Plata (Norton 2007: 188).

maintained". The price of goods brought to Potosí from Buenos Aires was several times lower than the price for goods brought from Lima (Gollan 1940: 79). At the same time, the *peruleiros* participating in the smuggling were making huge profits. In 1596, when trade on this illicit route was only just gaining momentum, one Portuguese reported with excitement that a *peruleiro* had purchased goods in Brazil for a substantial amount of 15,000–20,000 ducats at a time and that from 500 ducats invested, 5,000 was accrued in three months (Boxer 1973: 89f, 112–115).

Above all, Bishop de Vitória was an extremely colourful character. A young merchant from Lima, he was ordained in 1560 and subsequently sent by the Dominican Order to Madrid and Rome. The contacts he made proved extremely useful. Pope Gregory XIII consecrated him bishop of the new diocese of Tucumán, which he took over in 1582. His enemies – in particular the provincial governor, who was in conflict with the prelate – claimed that de Vitória's residence was more of a "factoria" than a place to stay for a bishop, and that he himself led the life of "not so much a prelate as a merchant". Vitória, in turn, sometimes suggested an affinity with the second general of the Society of Jesus, converso Diego Laínez Gomez de León. Thus, Bishop de Vitória would serve the cause of the Church and colonisation if only by paving the way for the Jesuits to enter Tucumán, while also being a co-founder of the *contrabando ejemplar* system in La Plata. This term was used to describe the collaboration of big smugglers with royal and municipal officials in organising large-scale contraband. This phenomenon, which began at the time of Bishop de Vitória, would already gain importance as a consolidated system in the first two decades of the 17th century.

Smuggling as a response to the growing demand of Potosí and the whole of Upper Peru and neighbouring provinces is one thing. Contraband also became one of the important mechanisms for Brazil's trade with the Spanish colony. It was fostered by the prohibitions on trade with La Plata imposed repeatedly by Madrid from 1593 in order to defend the trade monopoly of the *consulado* of Seville and, from 1613, the *consulado* established in Lima. Faced with the threat of economic disaster, limited trade with Brazil on small ships was at one point allowed. This move to liberalise contacts, however, was constantly accompanied by smuggling. This is not surprising. There was a shortage of everything in La Plata. According to a popular saying, a horseshoe imported from Europe cost more than a horse, while poverty – "poor devils without a shirt to their backs" – was, according to a 1599 account, striking (Rock 1987: 25). A desperate attempt to close the trade with Brazil and Potosí and to bring the situation under control by imposing a (short-lived) ban on the use of money in Buenos Aires in 1623 was unsuccessful. Although the customs house established in 1623 in Cordova began to generate some revenue and also strengthened the control of the local elite over the trade route from La Plata to Potosí, it was not able to eliminate illegal trade. Instead, it contributed to a more than fourfold reduction in registered imports going through Buenos Aires (Canabrava 1984: 171).

Above all, slave shipments went from Buenos Aires, directed to Potosí, but also to Chile. Buyers were also merchants and *encomenderos* on the route to the mining centre. Indigenous products were also delivered to Upper Peru from La Plata, Paraguay and Tucumán: yerba mate, cattle, hides, cereals and maize, cotton and wool products, tens of thousands of mules and horses. With the purchase of slaves, Bishop de Vitória began working with the Brazilians in Bahia and Rio de Janeiro in 1585. It was, in his view, a fully legal transaction. The formation of the Iberian Union, he argued, removed barriers to contact between the colonies of the two powers. In any case, the importation of slaves was formally authorised by the *Audiencia* Charcas. Six Jesuits and 150 slaves embarked in Brazil on the first ship ordered by the bishop alongside goods of considerable value. The clerics representing the bishop had to purchase an additional ship. However, the cargo did not reach its destination in its entirety: on the way back, the ships encountered an English pirate. Only 40–60 slaves eventually reached Tucumán. Bishop de Vitória's subsequent actions, until he was recalled from Tucumán in 1589 and sent back, unchallenged, to Europe, were more successful. This was probably helped by his friendship with Rio de Janeiro's governor Salvador Correira de Sá "O Velho", although the transactions were no longer fully legal. Also, the silver bullion with which he paid came from a suspicious source. After the bishop's first transaction, there were accusations in reports sent to Madrid that he had used silver without paying the *quinta real*. To his merit, however, was that he blazed a new trail and showed the advantages of trading with Brazil (Wolff 1964: 172f).[5]

These opportunities were not wasted. However, the way in which they were made use of – the flourishing of contraband – aroused resistance among those who, tied to local closed economies in Paraguay and in La Plata, were unable to join the activities of the new trade route. From the beginning of the 17th century, most slave ships called at Buenos Aires under the pretext of *arribada forçosa* or under a simplified procedure. When there was a total

---

5   The bishop was assisted by his brother Diego Pérez de Acosta, who had been trading in Peru for years. Accused by the Lima Inquisition as a 'judío, hereje, apóstata, contumaz, obstinado y endurecido en sus errores', he fled to Italy and then already as a Jew moved to Safed (Medina 1945: 144). In 1602, another bishop of Tucumán would also participate in the illegal slave trade, while some religious orders would set up parabanks to facilitate the accumulation of surpluses from, among other things, *contrabando ejemplar* (Crespi 2000).

ban on transporting slaves to La Plata between 1603 and 1615, 8,000 slaves reached Buenos Aires. In 1621, of the 16 ships with slaves from Brazil and Luanda that called at Buenos Aires, only three carried cargoes with the permission of Seville's *Casa de Contratación*. The governor of Buenos Aires reportedly received between 10,000 and 12,000 pesos for each slave ship received at the port at that time, which did not seem an exorbitant amount (Vila Vilar 1973: 587, Torre Revello 1958: 122f, Boxer 1973: 94). From Luanda and other African ports, some luxury goods carried from Asia were also illegally smuggled into La Plata. There was a rapid increase in this type of operation in the decade 1610–1620: the prices obtained in Lima were several times higher than those offered in Lisbon. Contraband from Europe also appeared. In 1611 alone, 15 Dutch and English ships called at Buenos Aires with unregistered cargo. Through Manila and Acapulco, along the 'Philippine route', lower-quality textiles from China also begin to reach Lima and then also Buenos Aires from the late 16th century (Boxer 1973: 92, Fisher 1997: 70, Romano 1992: 195, Klooster 2009a: 152, Bonialian 2016).

The scale of these operations that made up the *contrabando ejemplar* is evidenced by data on La Plata's trade balance. According to rather conservative estimates, between 1616 and 1625 the average annual import to Buenos Aires reached 800,000 pesos, while the average annual export of La Plata was estimated at only 36,000. This huge deficit was financed by the illicit silver trade. It represented, conservatively, 15 per cent of Potosí's total annual production (Cross 1978). *Contrabando ejemplar* was, however, more than simply criminal. In the system of royal monopoly, it was a violation of the restrictions imposed by the Crown, a way of exploiting loopholes in the law with the support not only of individual officials, but also, indirectly, of the royal treasury (which derived part of its revenue from punitive levies). Lawful and lawbreaking actions were not seen as mutually exclusive; on the contrary, they formed a system founded on a "logic of extraordinary solutions" (*extralegalidade*), whose aim was to promote economic activity seen as synonymous with the 'public good' (Moutoukias 1988: 216, 219f, also Perusset Veras 2007: 177f, Ceballos 2016).

In all these operations from the end of the 16th to the second half of the 17th century we find the 'Portuguese', both those settling permanently and *peruleiros* on a constant journey between Brazil and Upper Peru and Chile.[6] Among the settlers were also 'Portuguese' from Brazil wishing to avoid contact

---

6   The Spanish term *peruleros* referred to another group of middlemen acting on behalf of Limean merchants. They were present in Seville ensuring that goods of interest to their Limean counterparts were on the ships sailing in the annual convoy to the New World.

with the successive Inquisition visitors who appeared in the colony in 1618–19 and in 1627. In 1619, eight ships with Brazilian 'Portuguese' arrived in Buenos Aires – formally they had been embarked as 'servants' of the Spaniards and therefore as persons who could be in the territory of the Spanish colony without special permission. Although 40 were sent back to Brazil, most stayed in La Plata (Lea 1922: 421f). While participating in the contraband, the 'Portuguese' were at the same time not outside the system as a reserve or 'safety valve'. They were, like Spanish merchants and officials, an integral part of the *contrabando ejemplar* (Ceballos 2016). To what extent the *XN* s controlled this trade is impossible to determine today. Reports sent to Madrid during the system's heyday between 1618 and 1623 emphasised, often with exaggeration, their dominance. According to the assessment of the Spanish historian Guillermo Céspedes del Castillo, paradoxically, however, it was the Sephardic exiles who "became the driving force and vanguard [in the attack posing] the greatest threat to the Spanish monopoly in the Indies" (quoted in Puente Brunke 2013: 98).

By the mid-17th century, Buenos Aires can even be seen as a Portuguese trading post on the route to Peru (Lockhart and Schwartz 1983: 273). In 1622, the Portuguese constituted, according to the findings of the Argentine historian Ricardo Lafuente Machain in 1931, 25 per cent (300 people) of the total population of Buenos Aires. This estimate has been subject to criticism, although is still often quoted. Other researchers indicate that of the approximately 500 Portuguese who passed through the La Plata region between 1580 and 1640, mainly on their journey to Peru, 211 settled permanently in Buenos Aires, while in 1643, 370 Portuguese (18.5 per cent) were among the city's 2,000 inhabitants. Many were included in the elite group of *vecinos* (permanent residents with full rights). In the absence of more precise information, it is now assumed that in the first half of the 17th century, 15–18 per cent of the inhabitants of Buenos Aires were Portuguese. They constituted the majority of the foreigners residing in the city (in 1619, among 50 foreigners, 46 were Portuguese) (Ventura 2004, Ceballos 2007: 157, Schultz 2016: 25, 29). On the route to Potosí, the situation was similar: in Tucumán there were 28 Portuguese among the 100 Europeans, while in Jujuy the Portuguese outnumbered the Spanish.

A key and partly symbolic role in the *contrabando ejemplar* was played by the aforementioned Diogo da Veiga as the first on the list of the 26 largest slave traders in Buenos Aires, and Juan de Vergara as the third. About the former, a Brazilian researcher wrote that "Diogo da Vega and his comilitoni established

---

Unlike the *peruleiros* of Brazil and La Plata, the *peruleros* did not challenge the monopoly, rather they sought to share in the benefits associated with it (an example being the efforts to import books) (Rueda Ramírez 2014).

a real trade monopoly in the port of Buenos Aires" (Canabrava 1984: 125, Gelman 1987: passim, Vila Vilar 1977: 122). Da Veiga, born in Madeira, came from a family of New Christian bankers. He acted primarily as a factor of the Coutinho brothers and then of Fernández Delvás. He was also a commercial agent and representative of Duarte Dias Henriques, who held the contract for the Angolan slave trade. By 1601, da Veiga had already settled permanently in Buenos Aires. In 1610, as a landowner and permanent resident, he obtained full citizenship of the city and became a *vecino* (Ceballos 2007: 146). Fate was to tie him to the Seville-born Juan de Vergara, a young merchant active in Potosí and, from 1604, already in Buenos Aires. These ties were subsequently strengthened by Diogo da Veiga's marriage to de Vergara's sister. After a short time, Vergara became deputy governor of Hernandarias and was also given the honorary title of treasurer of the Holy Office.

Hernando Arias de Saavedra, who hailed from the Paraguayan *encomenderos*, was making efforts to curb contraband. By combating it, he wished to meet not only the expectations of the royal court, but also the demands of the *beneméritos* group with which he was associated. In this way, he "went down in history as the main opponent of contraband in the port of Buenos Aires, but at the same time there were suggestions that this was not just due to idealism. The governor's vast fortune was amassed also by seizing (by the way, legally) one third of the value of the contraband that was uncovered (Crespi 2000). He was only half successful. While 215 slaves arrived in Buenos Aires on average per year during his first governorship between 1602 and 1608, only 30 did so under his predecessor between 1596 and 1597. Under the next governor (1609–1614), more than 441 slaves were already landing in the port on average per year, while during Hernandarias' subsequent reign between 1615 and 1616 the average reached 492 slaves per year (Crespi 2000: table 1). Estimates of the total number of slaves delivered to Buenos Aires between 1601 and 1615 were, and still are, highly variable. According to official reports, 10,920 Africans landed at the port, while Hernandarias – accusing da Veiga and Vergara – claimed that in 1615 alone they both brought in 4,000 slaves illegally, while the historian writes about the delivery of 22,000 slaves (mostly illegally) (Torre Revello 1958: 124, Vila Vilar 1977: 208f). At the same time, it was during Hernandarias's rule between 1602 and 1608 that the rival group of *confederados* was consolidated, backed by a rapidly expanding group of merchants already primarily associated with Buenos Aires. The merchants from Cordova, Tucumán and Chile, who were still dominant in the city's economy at the turn of the 16th century, receded into the background. The consolidation of the *confederados* would take place in the next decade. Among its leaders and also organisers of contraband, we find Juan de Vergara, who had already broken with the governor. He was now joining forces with Diogo da Veiga.

Describing the details of the conflict between the two groups and Hernandarias and Vergara is not necessary here. Let us merely note that, despite the brief arrest in 1615 of de Vergara, da Veiga and high royal officials who headed the contrabandists, Hernandarias did not achieve much. Perhaps his greatest success was the seizure of Diogo da Veiga's financial books. These showed the scale of his commercial operations and revealed a network of contacts covering almost the entire Iberian New World (and a list of beneficiaries of corrupt loans). By contrast, de Vergara as leader of the *confederados,* competed with the *beneméritos* for power in Buenos Aires. Thanks to a change in the law, which – from 1610 – also allowed people to take up a seat in the *cabildo* by purchasing a position, Vergara bought the seats of the permanent members of the institution for himself and five members of his family and relatives in 1617. Together with da Veiga, they gained control of the *cabildo*. Following the establishment of the independent *gobernación* Rio de La Plata by the king in 1617 and the change of governor in 1618, the *contrabando ejemplar* entered a boom phase at the end of the second decade of the 17th century. Under Governor Diego de Gongóra (1618–1623), repression also ceased. Furthermore, the royal court accepted the explanations of the accused by former governor Hernandarias. This strengthened the position of the *confederados*. Of the 15 major slave traders hailing mostly from Buenos Aires, seven held positions in the colonial administration (Gelman 1987: 94). According to conservative official estimates, there was a doubling of the average annual slave supply, to 987 people.

In 1626, Diogo da Veiga was in Spain as a representative of Buenos Aires. But as early as 1627, a royal commission sent to the *Audiencia* Charcas reported financial crimes committed by him and in 1630 he was arrested. Bail and a fine paid ensured his release from Madrid prison after two years. In contrast, the descendants of this New Christian merchant, who exerted an overwhelming influence on the region's economy for more than two decades, can be found among the *gobernación's* elite. Veiga's partner, Juan de Vergara, remained in Buenos Aires as a wealthy and influential member of the *cabildo*. However, this aged former contrabandist and leader of the *confederados* was constantly hassled by the *gobernación* authorities because of his past activities (Torre Revello 1958).

Although Diogo da Veiga did not find peace towards the end of his life, the involvement of the 'Portuguese' in the economy of Buenos Aires and La Plata did not end in disaster. In the course of establishing a trade route that would prove to be one of the most important in the colonial world of the 17th century, the 'Portuguese' merchant's fate was permanently linked to the region after he become not only a citizen but also a landowner. Of the 22 major slave traders in the first half of the 17th century, 16 became hacienda owners, while 13 also combined this with ownership of *estancias* (Gelman 1987: 101f). At the same time, the inquisitorial tribunal, the galleys, exile and the stake – the main instruments in the fight against Judaising heretics and competitors in the metropolis and in Peru, Mexico and New Granada – were replaced in Buenos Aires by mixed marriages and compromise between the hitherto warring elites. Between 1600 and 1650, most of the spouses of the 140 Portuguese *vecinos* were daughters of Spaniards and creoles descended from a group of *conquistadores* and *descendantes de conquistadores*. "Structural assimilation" was therefore a reflection of the far advanced integration of the "Portuguese" since the 1620s. It also confirmed Father António Vieira's view that it was not persecution but mixed marriage and openness to New Christians that would weaken the influence of Judaism (Saraiva 2001: 133, 135). The political expression of this type of assimilation was the gradual easing of previous conflicts between *beneméritos* and *confederados*. One can even speak of the beginning of a process of elite formation representing a synthesis of both groups (Saguier 1985a: 47, Gelman 1987, Perusset Veras 2005).

We should add that after the break-up of the Iberian Union, the situation of the Portuguese worsened. The more than 200 Portuguese merchants and sailors temporarily present in La Plata were treated with particular suspicion. Even some *vecinos* were expelled, although artisans valuable to the province were protected. After the end of the persecution period, there was a return to "structural assimilation" (Ceballos 2014: passim). In Brazil, too, Portuguese independence provoked violent reactions against the Spaniards present in the colony and the 'traitors' who sided with Spain. This resulted in the loss of Duarte Dias Henriques' *engenho* in Pernambuco. He had settled years before in Madrid and remained loyal to the Spanish crown (Silva 2012: 106). However, in the case of the Brazilian colony, the next step would not be assimilation, but the resumption of repression in the early 18th century.

The fate of the 'Portuguese' and conversos in Peru and Mexico was different. Their participation in overseas trade was also expressed differently. While the activities of the Buenos Aires and La Plata merchants were dominated by the slave and silver trade, in the case of the New Christians and conversos in other regions of Spanish America – the exception being Cartagena de Indias – such narrowly focused trade was rare. This was also true in Peru, where the most prominent figure among the 'Portuguese' was Manuel Bautista Pérez. This powerful slave trader was not limited to this role, however. The range of goods he traded was much more diversified. First place in Peru's commerce in the first half of the 17th century would have to be given to wines and textiles, not slaves. The silver trade was regulated separately. This differentiation was also reflected in the trade networks of Bautista Pérez's correspondents and partners. He had the most intensive contacts with both slave-trading centres (Luanda and Cartagena) and those offering other wares (Ciudad de México, Seville and Lisbon) (Studnicki-Gizbert 2007: 98–100). In the case of Simón Váez Sevilla, on the other hand, the Mexican counterpart of Bautista Pérez in terms of the place he occupied among the New Christian merchants, one cannot speak of dependence on the slave trade at all. This unique commodity was only one part of his diversified supply of goods that included wares from China, Europe and the Spanish metropolis, ranging from silk and satin to carded linen, as well as pearls, precious stones, indigo and cacao (Quiroz 1985: 413, Hordes 2005: 43). Like other merchants in Mexico, Váez Sevilla was interested in a limited, and even at one point forbidden, regional trade that linked – via Acapulco – China and India with New Spain and the viceroyalty of Peru. The slave trade did not play a significant role in this exchange.

In contrast to the earlier, limited, activity of the Inquisition in Peru against the 'Portuguese', the repression initiated in the mid-1630s under the banner of uncovering *complicidad grande*, ended in disaster for them. According to a Portuguese historian, "both the local Spanish settlers and the Inquisition as a body started persecuting the Portuguese, under the cover of Judaism and other pretexts. By 1635 the Portuguese community in Peru had been practically destroyed" (Marques 1976: 324). But the period preceding the amnesty of 1605 would not be a time of peace either: in 1595, four 'Portuguese' were among the five apostates burnt at the stake. This "bloody work affords a foretaste of what was to come": in 1600, 14 'Portuguese' were condemned, two of them to the stake, while in 1605, of the 17 *judaizantes* convicted, three were actually burned, while six were burned *in effigie* (Lea 1922: 420f). The scale of the repression, culminating in 1639 with the great *auto de fé*, was indeed unparalleled by the previous practice of the tribunal in Peru. By mid-1636 alone, 81 people had been arrested, while the arrest of a further 80 had been halted due to lack of space in the Inquisition's secret prison. In *auto de fé*, 61 *judaizantes* were sentenced to various punishments, while Manuel Bautista Pérez (without the grace of the garrote) was burned at the stake alongside 10 others, as was the unfortunate Francisco Maldonado de Silva, held in prison for 13 years. The former was sentenced to the stake for refusing to admit his guilt, the latter as a declared adherent of Judaism (Lea 1922: 423f, 427). He was encouraged to break with Catholicism, he claimed, by his reading of the Bishop of Burgos Pablo de Santa Maria's old pamphlet against Judaism and conversos (as we know, until 1391 the bishop had been Rabbi Solomon ha-Lewi). But the role played by the

'Portuguese' in the colony's trade was also increasingly questioned by Spanish competitors. This was, it seems, one of the main elements of a complex combination that led to the launch of a spiral of repression.

In 1636, after the first arrests had already been made, the Peruvian inquisitors wrote in a letter to the *Suprema*: "They have made themselves masters of commerce. The Merchant's Street is almost theirs (...).The Spaniard who has not a Portuguese as a business partner has limited chances for success" (quoted in Cross 1978: 151). According to information provided to the Lima Tribunal, the Portuguese monopolised almost everything in Lima, "from gold brocade to sack cloth, from diamonds to cumin seeds". At the same time, a high official of the Charcas *audiencia* signalled his concern: "numerous Hebrews have already arrived and others are continuing their journey [to the province]". The letter to the *Suprema* also reads that the Portuguese often carried out mutually credited non-cash operations, which made it possible to purchase a major proportion of the cargo arriving at the port of Callao (Lewin 1987: 115f, see also Silverblatt 2000: 530). All the more so because they were reliable as borrowers. The capital amassed by the major Portuguese merchants made it possible to start negotiations for the lease of the royal customs chamber in 1634. This also had a symbolic dimension. In Potosí, on the other hand, in 1640, among the 60 Portuguese identified, 20 were counted as very rich merchants and entrepreneurs. According to not very reliable estimates, the confiscations which hit the Portuguese in the 1630s yielded 4 million pesos (the confiscated property of Manuel Bautista Pérez was valued at half a million). With these wealthy arrested merchants in mind, the view that the 'Portuguese' were the "rulers (*dueños*) of Peruvian commerce" started to appear at this time (Hanke 1961: 15, 23).[7]

However, the structure of the group brought before the tribunal was specific and different from that which characterised the Portuguese as a whole. What was striking about those arrested was the strongly marked presence of the merchant elite. Of the 59 victims of the great *auto de fé*, about whom more detailed information was preserved, 27 were rich merchants (about 46 per cent), including one very rich Manuel Bautista Perez, 17 of the accused could be categorised as medium-sized merchants, while 15 were small merchants

---

7   Almost from the beginning of colonisation, Lima and Potosí were internationalized, a kind of "a melting pot for Europeans" (Lockhart 1968: 134). The 286 foreigners residing in the late 16th and early 17th centuries in both centres would include Portuguese (117), Corsicans (57), merchants and artisans from Genoa and Venice (53), Greeks (32), as well as Chinese and Indians. The richest merchant in Lima at the time was a Corsican from the Mañara family, related to the internationally known Corzo merchants (Bradley 2001: 658, Otte 1999).

(Quiroz 1985: 414f). It is not surprising, therefore, that the consequences of the arrest of dozens of large merchants in 1635 threatened the economy of Lima and the region. Under pressure from Spanish merchants and entrepreneurs struck by the arrests not only of contractors but often of debtors, the tribunal took extraordinary measures: it appointed a kind of 'defender' to handle disputes related to commercial contracts, debt repayments, etc., twice a week, while also participating in investigations into accusations of Judaisation. The scale of the problem was enormous. It was estimated that the accumulated debt of the arrestees amounted to 800,000 pesos from commercial operations alone, which was, it was claimed, the equivalent to the entire capital in circulation in Lima at the time (Lea 1922: 425f).

An interesting and different picture emerges from the innovative research conducted by a Peruvian researcher on a group of 196 Portuguese in Lima between 1570 and 1680 (Sullón Barreto 2015). First of all, the selection of this group was not determined by information from the Inquisition's archives, where only 'criminals' or 'suspects' appear. While merchants, although not the richest, accounted for more than 44.65 per cent of the group, in second place are those 'Portuguese' who were associated, most generally, with the ocean and shipping (captains, shipowners, pilots, petty officers, sailors, ship's boys, etc.). They make up 16.98 per cent of the group. In third place, we find craftsmen – 12.58 per cent. The remainder are associated with agriculture, the church, serve in the militia, are barbers and medics etc. Although the majority in this sample were descendants of XNs, only five appeared in the field of interest of the Inquisition (without major consequences). One of them was cleared of the charge of Judaic heresy and, according to custom, rode on a white horse through the streets of the city with victory palms in hand (Sullón Barreto 2015: 72, 131f).[8] Unlike those tried by the tribunal in 1639, the members of this group cannot be described, for the most part, as being associated with Judaism.

The consequences of the *complicidad grande* discovered in 1635 affected Portuguese suspected of heresy, while at the same time the actual or alleged apostates brought before the tribunal also represented, according to the Inquisitors, a political threat to the Spanish colony. When a Portuguese

---

8 We have divergent information about the number of Portuguese residing in Peru at that time. Liebman (1971: 178) mentions 1,000, while in 1642 the colonial authorities estimated their number in Lima and Callao at 500, which would have represented 1.83 per cent of the total population in the region (Sullón Barreto 2015: 62f.) In contrast, in 1646, when the Viceroy of Peru demanded that all Portuguese leave Peru, more than 6,000 would be allowed to stay after paying 200,000 pesos (Palma 1863: 13).

historian writes about repression "under the pretext of Judaism", he is not alone in this. Ricardo Palma, the distinguished Peruvian essayist and politician of the second half of the 19th century, wrote of *complicidad grande* as the alleged cause of the repression unleashed by the Inquisition: "It was a political pretext and a religious pretext" (1894: 40).

The question arises, however, as to what extent one can really abstract from the New Christian status and 'contamination' of the repressed merchants. For the authors of the quoted letter to the *Suprema* or the anonymous informants, the matter was obvious: "Portuguese" was synonymous with a suspected XN apostasy, and this applied to practically everyone. It seems that only a thin, sometimes even invisible, line separated the treatment of Inquisitorial repression as religious staffage concealing a fierce competitive struggle (and the financial needs of the tribunal), from the genuine concern of those responsible for the fate of the Catholic church and faith with the influx of Judaising heretics. This issue is also linked to the way in which important characteristics intended to define the group of 'Portuguese' present in Peru (already lumped together as *judaizantes*) were conceptualised. Religious coherence ensured by references to Judaism and the clandestine cultivation of Jewish traditions, the desire to preserve otherness, endogamy and solidarity in action are distinctive features frequently used in the description of the 'Portuguese'.

Such a cluster reinforced the image of the New Christians as an aggressive group hostile to the church and the faith. Only a short distance separated the folk imagery of the Portuguese convert from the threatening accusation before the tribunal of the Inquisition. It was not without irony that Ricardo Palma (1893: 71) quoted the folk tale of Manuel Bautista Pérez, who, like Pilate, allowed the *judaizantes* gathered at his residence to desecrate the cross "with fury". However, the image of the New Christians as enemies of the church was a gross oversimplification, while in the case of the nearly 200-strong group cited in Sullón Barreto's study, it was downright contradictory. Moreover, in none of the dimensions mentioned above did the Portuguese constitute a clearly defined group. Treating links with Jewish tradition, even selectively, as a dominant group characteristic is neither convincing nor legitimate. Among the Portuguese in Lima, one could find knights of the elite Order of Christ, *familiares* and those aspiring to positions in the Holy Office, as well as those already 'tainted' not only with Jewish but also African blood (Sullón Barreto 2015: 71, 68, also Schaposchnik 2015: 120f).

The group that stood before the Inquisition tribunal was treated both as Portuguese enemies of the sacred faith and as a strategic political threat to the interests of the Spanish crown. The conspiracy of co-religionists was merging into one with an anti-Spanish conspiracy. A few comments, therefore, on the second topic.

Attempts made in the 1620s by the Dutch WIC to attack Spanish possessions in Chile and Peru failed, but were not forgotten. While the accusation of an anti-Spanish conspiracy was not considered in detail during the trial, nor was it proven, at the same time the issue appeared frequently in other Inquisition documents. The mood of uncertainty, even hysteria, was exacerbated by information coming from Brazil. The occupation of Pernambuco by the WIC in 1630 was seen as a threatening harbinger of a wider anti-Spanish offensive. In Madrid, it was suspected that the Dutch target was not so much the sugar of Brazil as the silver of Peru (Boxer 1957: 23). In particular, any information indicating contacts with the Republic became 'evidence' for the inquisitors. Great importance was attached, for example, to the *Cofradía de los Judíos de Holanda,* established in Amsterdam.[9] This benevolent brotherhood appears in documents as a dangerous weapon used against Spain. One of the defendants, in his testimony in 1636, described the *Cofradía* as a deeply secretive organisation whose members were prepared to die for the faith. Another defendant testified during his trial in 1639 that he had sent 8,000 ducats to Brazil for "a company of the Dutch against his Majesty [the King of Spain]". Company here meant *Cofradía de los Judíos,* not the WIC. Finally, let us still mention the documents sent in 1640 by the tribunals of Lima and Cartagena de Indias, which indicated contacts between Judaising New Christians in the colonies and 'synagogues' in the Netherlands and the Levant, and the transfer of information and money. All this, it was claimed, to support the Dutch and Turks in their fight against Spain (Klooster 2006: 188f, Adler 1909: 46f).

All this information gathered in the course of the inquisitorial investigations did not constitute convincing evidence to confirm the existence of an anti-Spanish conspiracy. The eminent historian S.B. Liebman was, it seems, off target in seeking a conspiratorial logic by linking events as disparate as the economic activity of the Jews, their trade networks and international contacts, the place they occupied in Amsterdam, Brazil, Rio de la Plata, Paraguay, Tucumán and Peru, the ripening of the revolt in Portugal, or the revolt in Evora in the 1630s. In the latter, he noted in particular collaboration between

---

9   The purpose of this brotherhood was to ransom Jewish slaves from the hands of Muslims, to support Jewish communities in Jerusalem, Safed, Hebron and Tiberias, and to create a fund to support new Jewish migrants in the Republic (Liebman 1971: 187–189). In contrast, Klooster (2006: 135) describes the *Cofradía* of the 1630s as a local clandestine initiative in Cartagena. One witness to the inquisition spoke of members of this port *Cofradía* self-taxing themselves with 300 pesos per year per person; these funds were sent to Jews in Amsterdam.

Cardinal Richelieu and the New Christians (Liebman 1971: 186f). One should add that the plan to attack Buenos Aires in 1642 from within the WIC-occupied part of Brazil was never executed. Information about a 'panic in the [West] Indies' caused by Dutch activity is no substitute for more reliable (and missing) testimony about the conspiracy. Ricardo Palma (1894: 40), on the other hand, was clearly reserved about the hypothesis of such an anti-Spanish conspiracy. Pointing out that "I do not know the sources", he suggested that "[t]he real crime [of the convicts] and the six thousand Portuguese residing in the country (...) was that they had become great owners (*grandes capitalistas*) by idle effort". Simplifications aside, it is this motive that seems to have been one of the main driving forces behind the repression of the time of *complicidad grande*.

On a smaller scale than in Peru, but in direct relation to the Peruvian investigation, the charge of *complicidad grande*, also arose in Cartagena de Indias. The overseas trade of the port and the region was dominated by foreigners, mostly Portuguese. From the end of the 16th century, Cartagena would become one of the important commercial hubs of Spanish America and, in the case of slaves, a major distribution centre. Between 1595 and 1640, the era of the 'Portuguese *asientos*', this port city received more than half of the more than 268,000 slaves transported to Spanish America (Vila Vilar 1977: 226).

Thanks to a report prepared in 1630 by a royal commission appointed to investigate the presence of foreigners in the port and the province, we have fairly detailed information on this subject (Vila Vilar 1979: 155–173, Restrepo 2011: passim). Of the 184 foreigners, more than 79 per cent were Portuguese (154). Also appearing were Italians (13), French (7), Flemish (2), as well as a Pole, a Scot and a Jew. The Portuguese were outnumbered by New Christians. According to the commission's findings, the foreigners arrived in Cartagena mostly illegally, mainly on slave ships (77 people) or as soldiers and sailors (39 people). The latter did not have to apply for a special permit to go to the colony. Considering that around 1620 the number of Spaniards in Cartagena de Indias was estimated at 500 people, and the total number of *vecinos* in 1630 at around 1,500 (Lea 1922: 462), the number of foreigners quoted in the report only confirmed the port's role as a hub for overseas trade. At the same time, the Commission determined from data on half of these 184 people, that the dominant group was made up of merchants (18), slave traders (12) and sailors (15), followed by medics (5) and shopkeepers and innkeepers (5). This occupational structure implied great wealth disparities and indicated that the foreigners settled in Cartagena were not, for the most part, part of the economic elite. The numerous small itinerant traders (*mercachifles*) and artisans could for sure not be included. "The poor and destitute are many", reported a royal official in 1630 about the situation of the Portuguese in New Granada (Ruiz Rivera 2002: 29f).

The scale of the wealth among foreigners was represented by the already mentioned families of Jorge Fernándes Gramaxo and Luis Gómez Barreto. The latter, a Portuguese-born *XN*, had been in Angola for some time and had been a member of the Cartagena de Indias *cabildo* for several years from 1607. Both belonged to a small group of great merchants (and *negreiros*) who had their own frigates, contacts in Africa, Portugal and the United Provinces, and an extensive network of connections in the region. This group would also include Diaz de Paz Pinto, Luis Franco, Diego López Fonseca, Juan Rodríguez Mesa and Luis Lemos. Most would stand before an Inquisitorial tribunal a dozen years later. Only the nephew of the late Jorge Fernándes Gramaxo, Antonio Nunes Gramaxo, escaped such a fate. Before this happened, however, the capital and contacts of the members of this narrow group enabled trade not only in slaves but also in a wider range of products. The pearl trade, dominated in Cartagena and Rio de la Hecha by Gramaxo and another New Christian, involved both Bautista Pérez from Lima and the powerful Simón Váez Sevilla from Ciudad de México. Fonseca Enríquez himself was also actively trading goods imported from China with the help of Mexican partners. Wealthy New Christians would also appear in other parts of the Nuevo Reino de Granada: the Santa Marta y Rio de la Hacha, Antioquia and Popayán areas. However, almost 70 per cent of all Portuguese would settle in Cartagena, including most of those who were to be accused or suspected Judaisers (Navarrete Peláez 2009: 34, Restrepo 2011: appendix).

However, the economic importance of the Portuguese merchants in Cartagena and the province as a whole was determined by a specific 'monoculture' – the slave trade. All the more so as the city's domestic economy was minuscule. The overseas trade not only created Cartagena de Indias but was a condition for the economic vitality of the port. The surge in the slave trade would come at a time when the royal monopoly was held by Antônio Fernández Delvás, while his son and then brother-in-law acted as the main factors in Cartagena. Just as in Buenos Aires, we can also speak of the emergence of the *contrabando ejemplar* phenomenon in Cartagena. In this complex game, in which the monopoly of the Crown was countered by local elites with a specifically defined 'public good' and a desire to increase the 'welfare of the colony', royal officials, military officers, priests and major Portuguese slave traders (mostly *XN*s) worked together (Navarrete Peláez 2007: 162–164, 170). The future governor of Cartagena informed in 1637 that each slave trader probably had to spend 14,000 pesos in bribes to more than 30 officials and guards before unloading a single ship. Other information indicated that the governor received bribes of at least 30,000 pesos a year for agreeing to the illegal unloading of a slave ship. Linking this phenomenon until the 1620s to the commercial operations of Fernández Delvás was not unreasonable. Beginning his practice as a *negreiro,* the young Manuel Bautista Pérez was angered by the size of bribes demanded in Cartagena, fulminating that Fernández Delvás "had 2,000 'thieves' working for him and that one João Batista Pinto was 'the worst pirate in the world'" (Newson and Minchin 2007: 145f). According to the royal inspector's report, 413 slaves arrived legally in Cartagena in 1618–20, while more than 4,081 were contraband. Also in 1620–21 almost half of the slaves delivered to Cartagena were contraband (Ruiz Rivera 2002: 30f, 34f).

The *complicidad grande* discovered in Cartagena and the trials brought against mainly New Christians were, practically speaking, a continuation of the persecution initiated in Peru. Previously, trials brought against *judaizantes* were rare. In the first *auto de fé* in 1614, no heretic was convicted. In the following years, the Inquisitors' attention was focused on witchcraft and witches (especially among African slaves) and blasphemers. The first seven *judaizantes* were not convicted until 1627. In 1636, it was the documents from the Lima Inquisitorial investigation that were used to initiate the repression in Cartagena. Very quickly, incriminating material concerning 19 'Portuguese' residing in the port reached the Inquisitors in Cartagena, and the first arrests were made as early as 1636. Some 21 people were soon imprisoned in the Inquisition's secret prison (the notable merchant Paz Pinto died under torture). When, after the fall of the Count-Duke de Olivares, repression against the New Christians was initiated in Spain, mainly in Seville, the earlier contacts of Seville merchants with the XNs in Cartegana would play a role in the formulation of accusations (Lea 1922: 461, 466f, Quevedo 2008: 165f, 174–182).

Some of the great merchants brought before the tribunal in 1638 were described in reports as 'rather defiant' (*bastante maliciosos*): they refused to testify, refused to admit guilt or simulated illness. One important part of the prosecution was the subject theme of an anti-Spanish conspiracy, taken over from the Lima investigation. Thus, the New Christian merchants were accused of supporting the *Cofradía de los Judíos de Holanda* fraternity and, through it, allegedly providing assistance to the Dutch operating in the Caribbean and Brazil. This was the charge leveled against one of the main defendants, Juan Rodríguez Mesa. Despite such menacing charges, the sentences of the Cartagena tribunal were mild compared to the brutality shown by the Inquisition in Lima, and a few years later in Ciudad de México (Quevedo 2008: 159).[10] No one was burned

---

10   It was only during the second investigation, after his re-arrest in 1652, that Luis Gómez Barreto testified that he had donated some funds to the *Cofradía* in order to fight the *Reynos Católicos* (Liebman 1971: 188). In the first trial, Gómez Barreto was acquitted.

at the stake. It is likely that the close contacts of the leading New Christian merchants brought before the tribunal (including Luis Gómez Barreto, Luis and Manuel Franco) not only with high royal officials but also with members of the Cartagena Court of the Inquisition played an important role here, according to a report for the *Suprema* (Quevedo 2008: 198f). Unlike in Peru, the great New Christian merchants in Cartagena were not isolated from the world of politics in the port and the region. The transit nature of Cartagena and the strategic importance of the port for Spanish and Atlantic trade (receiving and clearing the *Flota de Indias*) somewhat facilitated and encouraged close contacts. Moreover, it was Cartagena's great merchants who participated in (and in part co-controlled) the networks of commercial contacts important also for the Spanish elite. And, finally, the merchants who stood before the tribunal accused of Judaising represented 10–15 per cent of the group of 154 Portuguese in Cartagena de Indias identified in the 1630 report (Quevedo 2008: 251–253). This was a high rate when compared with the proportion of New Christians among the Portuguese as a whole (5 per cent), but a low rate when contrasted with the widespread belief that 'Portuguese' was synonymous with 'Jew'. As in Peru, the majority of Portuguese residing in Cartagena did not become objects of interest to the Inquisitors and probably had little to do with the cultivation of Jewish traditions and dogmas of the faith.

Also in Mexico, the main and richest part of the Viceroyalty of New Spain, the activity of the New Christians and conversos was interrupted by repression between 1642 and 1649. The *auto de fé* organised in 1649, which ended several years of persecution, was, by virtue of its momentum unprecedented. Information about it was announced in advance in all the towns of the colony, encouraging the faithful to participate. It was a real *auto público general,* the opposite of the *auto particular,* which was sometimes organised without public participation. This gathering, which combined the atmosphere of a fair with the religious excitement of a crowd, and which was honoured by the presence of numerous ecclesiastical and royal dignitaries, was probably attended by 30,000 people. In this last of a series of *auto de fé* the conviction of 109 *judaizantes* was announced, and incorrigible heretics were handed over to the secular authorities, 13 of which were subsequently burnt at the stake (including one without the grace of a garrote). Some 57 of the condemned were burnt *in effigie*. As before in Lima, the guilty perished in the flames and "the mob had its spectacle" (Quevedo 2008: 189, 231f, Lea 1922: 432).

In the mid-17th century, the white population of New Spain was estimated – excluding priests and religious – at 20,000. New Christians and conversos probably accounted for 10–15 per cent of this population (in the capital in 1641, the number of Portuguese, without the division between 'Old' and

'New', was, according to Israel's estimates already quoted, 1,000–1,500). Their occupational structure was not fundamentally different from that known in the Viceroyalty of Peru. The vast majority were medium and small merchants, while among the rest one finds mine owners and suppliers to the mining region of Zacatecas, clerks, goldsmiths, tailors, shoemakers, or soap-makers (Liebman 1963: 100). According to the data collected by the Inquisition on 63 defendants in the 1640s, the 'destitute' (indebted and owning few pesos) and the 'poor' (owning between 200 and 1,000 pesos) made up 22 and 21 per cent of the group, respectively, while the 'wealthy' (property between 1,000 and 15,000 pesos) accounted for 43 per cent, and the 'rich and very rich' (property between 15,000 and 70,000 pesos) accounted for 14 per cent (nine people). Among the accused, there was only one 'millionaire', with 188,000 pesos. This was Simón Váez Sevilla, and 500,000 pesos in loans granted would have to be added to his wealth (Hordes 2005: 41, 45, Quiroz 1985: 414). The wealthy and the rich included both Portuguese and Spanish converts. What differentiated Mexican conversos and New Christians from their counterparts in Peru and Cartagena was the role of the family in maintaining social contacts and cultivating selective Judaism. In Peru, the relatively weakly integrated and diversified Portuguese community was made up primarily of single men. In the group of nearly 200 surveyed, unmarried men made up 50 per cent. In Cartagena, single men made up more than half of the foreigners residing in the port. In Mexico, on the other hand, the in-group solidarity was to large extent a function of strong family ties: "Married *conversos* outnumbered single by a ratio of three to one". These differences would be reflected in the structure of the prosecuted group: the almost total absence of women among the victims in Lima and Cartagena, while in Ciudad de México they would account for 35 per cent of the groups (Vila Vilar 1979: 157, Quevedo 2008: 201, Liebman 1975: 142, Sullón Barreto 2015: 70, Hordes 2005: 46).

Until the early 17th century, however, Mexico was a relatively safe place for conversos and incoming New Christians. In fact, so were Peru and Cartagena de Indias. According to incomplete data, 84 *judaizantes* were convicted in Mexico between 1528 and 1599, of which only 23 were tried until the establishment of a permanent tribunal in 1571.[11] The establishment of the permanent tribunal of the Inquisition did not fundamentally change the situation – in the short term. In the first *auto de fé* organised in 1574, the 74 victims were mainly bigamists (27), blasphemers (2) and Protestants (36 crew members from Sir John

---

11 According to Hordes (1982a: 26), "Between 1589 and 1596, almost two hundred individuals were tried for the crime of judaizante".

Hawkins' ship). The following year, similarly: 25 bigamists and 1 Protestant appeared among the 31 convicted. Conversos and New Christians were among the victims in 1590, especially in the *auto de fé* of 1596 (*22 judaizantes* out of 66 convicted, including Luis de Carvajal 'el Mozo' and his family). After the great *auto de fé* in 1601 and the subsequent declaration of the amnesty for *judaizantes* in the Iberian Union and colonies in 1605, for the next three decades conversos and the increasingly numerous incoming 'Portuguese' felt relatively safe. As late as 1630s, Inquisitors showed little interest in information about converts cultivating certain traditional customs and meeting in 'synagogues' in private homes. However, their "fancied security (...) was approaching its end" (Lea 1922: 205–208, 229, also Hordes 2005: 47–50, Quiroz 1985: 411).

The height of repression against the Portuguese and conversos in Mexico in the relatively short period 1642–49 was the consequence of the simultaneous emergence of several factors. Undoubtedly, the example of the trial in Lima, which ended with a great *auto de fé* and stakes, acted as a stimulus to mobilise activity and defend the foundations of the Catholic faith against Judaising heretics. News of the arrests of New Christians in Spain in the 1640s played a similar role. This religious-theological motivation was accompanied by the threat posed by the political revolution in the Iberian Peninsula – the break-up of the Iberian Union and the emergence of an independent Portugal. The co-occurrence and interdependence of religious motivations ('poisoning' by heresy) and the political 'threat' from Portugal, as highlighted by the Mexican Inquisitors (Hordes 2005: 55), is also reinforced by financial considerations – the painful financial crisis of the Mexican tribunal.

First briefly on the last point. As early as 1625, it is possible to speak of "a positive correlation between the persecution of the New Christians and the financial consolidation of the Inquisition as an effectively functioning and relatively autonomous institution" (Quiroz 1985: 41). In Mexico, it was only with the initiation of large-scale investigations and confiscations in 1642 that the tribunal's financial troubles could be resolved. Although the seizures between 1590 and 1609 had already yielded 83,500 pesos (the annual royal subsidy for the Tribunal in New Spain was 10,000 pesos, while in Cartagena it was 8,400), by 1638 the tribunal in Ciudad de México was bankrupt. In this sense, the initiation of mass repression in 1642 appeared as a salvation. The Holy Office used the "alleged Jewish conspiracy to regain power, prestige and financial standing". The funds obtained through the sequestered estates of the *judaizantes* grew as follows: in 1646 – 39,000 pesos and, the following year over 148,000. In 1649, the Inquisition Tribunal reported to the *Suprema* that over 554,000 pesos had been obtained from the confiscations. In fact, as the investigation ordered by the *Suprema* into, among other things, financial irregularities in the Mexican tribunal showed, 700,000 pesos were obtained in 1642–48 and in 1649 – at least 3 million. Thus, "the confiscation of Judaizante wealth laid a firm foundation for the Holy Office's budget in the second half of the seventeenth century" (Greenleaf 1988: 399, 402–404, 419, Lea 1922: 219, 460). In Peru, too, the confiscations accompanying the repression of 1635–1639 secured liquidity to the Lima tribunal. What the actual scale of the confiscations was is not known. According to one report, it amounted to one million pesos, with Peru's viceroy informing Madrid that the funds had "even disappeared and no one knows where they went". On the other hand, an audit carried out by the Lima Inquisition mentions a sum of more than 677,000 pesos" (Quiroz 1985: 423, Lea 1922: 347). Despite the financial crisis, however, it is unlikely that the benefits associated with the repression of the 'Portuguese' in both countries were a strong enough incentive to prompt – in the absence of other motivations – the initiation of mass persecution.

In contrast, for an historian of the converts in Mexico, the main factor that triggered the crackdown on the *judaizantes* was Portuguese independence and the fear of an anti-Spanish Portuguese conspiracy. The consequences of the restoration of the monarchy in Portugal, which would result in changes in Spain's strategic position, would appear in Mexico primarily as anti-Portuguese hysteria (Hordes 1982a, 2005, Greenleaf 1988). Such sentiments found additional fodder in rumours of an anti-Spanish revolt reportedly planned in Cartagena or in dramatic information about the massacre of Spaniards in Brazil after 1640. How strongly this conviction was encoded in the memory was evidenced, for example, by the thesis of a Mexican scholar that after 1640 "the Portuguese residing in the [Spanish] colonies openly conspired against Spain. Jews of Portuguese origin were an important factor in this conspiracy. This explains the activities of the Holy Office in 1642–49" (Rueda 1946: 121). But at the same time, this threat would emerge in a particular way. Since the majority of the Portuguese residing in Mexico were XNs, political concerns would become intertwined with religious motivations. The question of fighting the heretical 'poisoning' does not disappear; on the contrary, it constitutes an important ideological justification for the political confrontation with the Portuguese.

Such an abrupt shift to repression came as a shock, contrasting with previous tolerance and often disinterest. In this growing hysterical atmosphere, it was difficult to judge whether the Portuguese were at a disadvantage as potential political enemies or the *judaizantes*. The solution to this dilemma, and the worst possible one, was suggested by life itself: the victim became a *judaizante* persecuted as both a heretic and a Portuguese.

Referring to the situation in Mexico after Portugal's restoration of independence, the Spanish monarch wrote of the Portuguese: "I am informed that they plan to seize all the gold and silver and to embezzle my Royal Fifth". The New Spain authorities received a series of, sometimes contradictory, orders (*cédulas*) from Philip IV. One ordered the removal of all Portuguese to a distance of about 90 km from the ports and the mining region in the north, another imposed a special tax (*donativo*) on them, and yet another demanded the expulsion of all Portuguese from the colonies, blocking the entry of new ones, while forbidding the departure of the wealthy (Hordes 2005: 50f, Lea 1922: 229). For about two years, the repression orchestrated by Philip IV was tempered by the Viceroy Diego López Pacheco Cabrera y Bobadilla, Duke of Escalona, cousin of the new Portuguese monarch João IV. Sympathetic to the New Christians (he himself had Jewish roots) he had previously appointed some to high positions; he was also indebted to the great merchant-bankers (Hordes 1982a: 32f). Suspected (without foundation) of sympathising with Portuguese rebels, the Duke of Escalona was forcibly removed from office in 1642 by the Bishop of Puebla, Juan de Palafox y Mendoza, acting on behalf of Philip IV.

Over the next few months, the Bishop acted as Viceroy of New Spain, Governor of Mexico and Commander-in-Chief. The repression commenced. Almost immediately, the tribunal of the Inquisition communicated the discovery of a *complicidad grande* supposedly organised by the Portuguese with the aim of destroying the Mexican Inquisition. "It was discovered" that two New Christian boys, whose conversation had been overheard by a cleric, were considering the possibility of burning down the Tribunal building in which the inquisitors also lived" (Rueda 1946: 122). Although Bishop Palafox was probably more anti-Portuguese than anti-Jewish, in practice this amounted to repression against those accused of heresy. It was more practical to hand over the trial of the Portuguese to the Inquisition than to prove the charge of anti-Spanish conspiracy in the normal courts. Very quickly, around 100 suspected *judaizantes*, including major merchant-financiers, were imprisoned by the Inquisition. Simón Váez Sevilla was also among the first prisoners (Hordes 2005: 53f, 1982: 34).

This Portuguese-raised merchant-financier, the richest among the converts, had been in Mexico since 1618. He did not limit his activities to large-scale trade: from Goa to the Philippines, the United Provinces, Spain, Cartagena de Indias and Peru. However, like many other important New Christian merchants in Mexico, Váez Sevilla did not maintain direct trade contacts with Portugal and Brazil (Israel 1990a: 327f). At the same time, it is worth emphasising that he was firmly embedded not only in the milieu of the 'Portuguese' – for many minor merchants, artisans and freedmen he was a *patrón*. He was a member of the *consulado* of Ciudad de México, and a creditor to the Viceroy Escalona and, presumably, other high officials as well. His contacts also included officials of the Holy Office.

One needs to stress this because Simón Váez Sevilla was informed in advance of the impending disaster. This allowed him to secure some of his assets and take other important decisions. Above all, however, he saved his head thanks to his contacts among Spanish decision-makers. He lost a considerable part of his fortune (500,000 pesos) but was also luckier than his business partner in Peru Manuel Bautista Pérez had been a few years earlier. In Ciudad de México, another prominent New Christian merchant, Tomás Treviño de Sobremonte, was burnt alive at the stake (he had already faced an *auto particular* in 1625). For five years, despite being tortured, he did not admit his guilt. After the sentence was pronounced, he emphasised his Jewishness, referred with contempt to Christianity and, according to reports, demonstrated "insolente rebeldía y diabólica furia" (Kohut 1896: 62). He was aware that this meant being burned alive. A report describing the execution mentioned that even the mule on which he was to reach the place of execution "refused to carry so great a sinner"; it was necessary to bring in a "tired" and obedient horse (Rueda 1946: 138, Lea 1922: 233). Váez Sevilla, on the other hand, negotiated his release from prison after his conviction and found refuge with one of the local governors for a time. He then emigrated to Seville.

The number of victims of the four trials between 1646 and 1649 was 260, including 212 *judaizantes*, although other estimates are also given (207 victims, including 119 *judaizntes*). Several people were sentenced to the stake. After this blow, the 'Portuguese' community in Mexico never recovered. Trials organised by the Holy Office after 1649 did result in the conviction of another 300 people for almost a century and a half, but this was no longer of fundamental importance for the dwindling group of Mexican New Christians (Hordes 2005, Lea 1922: 234, Greenleaf 1988: 401, Liebman 1973: 19).

The balance sheet of the Inquisition's activities in the first half of the 17th century was decidedly negative. Between 1635 and 1649, the tribunals in Lima, Cartagena and Ciudad de México convicted a total of at least 360 people. The punishment of burning at the stake affected 96 people in Lima and Ciudad de México, the majority (71) *in effigie*. However, the group of those symbolically burnt also included those who died in prison after torture or committed suicide (10 in Ciudad de México). In Cartagena, 87 people were convicted in the 17th century, of whom 58 sentences were handed down by mid-century, mostly between 1636 and 1642 (Quevedo 2008: 203f, Navarrete Peláez 2009: 33). Some of the main suspects were treated leniently or released from custody. These data confirm – as does the absence of sentences of burning at the stake – the relative self-restraint of the Cartagena tribunal. It should be kept in mind, however, that those sentenced to the galleys in these three great trials in fact received their death sentences too – spread over time. There is no information that any of the condemned returned alive home. Also, other punishments were neither humane nor lenient, but accepted by most (Liebman 1971: 176, Lea 1922: 481). Repression during the period in question affected 'Portuguese' in Buenos Aires and La Plata to a limited extent – except for the expulsions triggered by anti-Portuguese hysteria after the break-up of the Iberian Union. The commissioners of the Lima tribunal present in the port and the province did not show any particular zeal in prosecuting heretics. A historian of the Inquisition would later write: "Fortunately for Argentina, the idea of establishing a special tribunal of the Holy Office in the country (...) was ultimately not accepted by the King" (Medina 1945: 230).

A high proportion of the 360 repressed in the main centres of Spanish America were wealthy merchants who contributed to the Atlantic and regional trade networks. The activities of the Inquisition led not only to a reduced role for the xns and, more broadly, the Portuguese, in the economic and social life of the colony. The unplanned result was a weakening of Iberian influence on the development of the overseas territories. By removing the 'Portuguese', the space was widened for the Dutch and the rising in importance English and French merchants. At the same time, the tendency towards the 'Latin Americanisation' of the colony's Creole elites and economic life was reinforced. In the case of Cartagena de Indias, a combination of repression against the powerful *negreiros* and the break-up of the Iberian Union, the collapse of slave supplies and the destruction of existing trade networks, led to the marginalisation of this port. An epidemic in 1651 only exacerbated this process. The pyres in Lima and Ciudad de México thus signalled that the New Christians and Jews, who had played a major role in co-creating the Atlantic world, were finally passing into history.

Conclusion: *tempo dos flamengos* – the Amsterdam Jews in the Nieuw-Holland

No longer New Christians, but Amsterdam Jews, would appear after 1630 in New Holland (Nieuw-Holland), as the north-eastern part of Brazil conquered by the West India Company was called. For a while they got the chance to dream about having both the "Jerusalem of the North" in Amsterdam and the *Jerusalém do Brasil* (Vainfas 2012). After the defeat of the WIC in 1654, some would make their way to the Dutch and English Caribbean and New Amsterdam, while others would seek their fortunes on the Wild Coast, in the Essequibo River area – in present-day Guyana, called 'New Zealand' by the Dutch – and on the Cayenne River (present-day French Guiana). Still others made the journey across the Netherlands to Livorno and some of them subsequently took part in the Essequibo settlement experiment. The Sephardic presence on the Wild Coast was short-lived, however, and ended in the late 1660s. In contrast, the migration of the "new Jews" to the 'second Brazil', as Suriname was often referred to, would begin somewhat later (Oppenheim 1907, Klooster 2009b: 39). To a small degree only, the situation of the Dutch Jews in these regions was linked to the fate of the New Christians in the Iberian world. After the evacuation of Pernambuco, in the peregrinations of the "new Jews" who were returning to Europe or seeking security in other parts of the New World, they were not accompanied, except by a handful, by Brazilian XNs. Decades later, when the Inquisition struck forcefully against the New Christians in Rio de Janeiro, Minas Gerais and Paraíba in the first half of the 18th century, these would remain isolated: nothing is known of their contacts with Jews in Suriname or Curaçao. In this sense, while the fate of the Amsterdam Jews in the New World was an integral part of European expansion, in the Jewish narrative it was a fragment of the history of a separate diaspora.

In the last part of our survey, we will only hint at some of the problems related to the presence of Amsterdam Jews in the Nieuw-Holland. This was an interesting and, in a sense, a turning point in the history of the Sephardim and *La Nação* and in the political and economic context in which they had hitherto operated. This was particularly true of the evolution of their previous contacts with Portugal and Spain. The break-up of the Iberian Union and the end of the Thirty Years' War were essential elements of this new context. By contrast, there is no question of a decline in the activity of the "new Jews" in the Republic or in the major Dutch-controlled routes and centres of trade. Their growing presence in the Caribbean and their participation from the end of the 17th century in the Republic's trade with the area is testimony to this. They constituted the majority of merchants operating on the Amsterdam route, although the elite in Caribbean trade were Dutch and German Protestants (Israel 2001: 339).

Explaining the strongly accentuated role of Dutch Jews in the Caribbean by references to the religious tolerance granted by the Calvinists or the extent of de facto economic freedoms they enjoyed in Dutch-controlled territories does not fully explain the problem. The attitude of the English authorities towards Jews settling in their Caribbean colonies was equally positive (Fortune 1984: 35–38, Darnell Davies 1909). It seems, therefore, that the critical variable was precisely the experience Dutch Jews gained in their dealings with Brazil, first during the Twelve Years' Truce (1609–1621) and then also during the quarter-century of the New Holland. Without it, the strong involvement of the Dutch and Jews in the Caribbean trade and economy, and later in the development of the settlement and plantation society in Suriname, would have been unthinkable (Israel 2001: 339f, Odegard 2022: 65f). The transfer of knowledge and skills was an extremely important, and unplanned, outcome of the dispersal of Jews from the New Holland in 1654. *Tempo dos flamengos*, the time of the Dutch, despite their defeat in Brazil, had not been lost.

In contrast, a clash with Portugal after its independence in 1640, despite the initial enthusiasm with which this was received in the Republic, was inevitable. It also implied a growing division between Amsterdam Jews and Portuguese New Christians and, consequently, the gradual disintegration of *La Nação*. These differences were reinforced by the Dutch expansion into Africa, which increased after 1637 and was an attempt at strengthening the plantation economy of Nieuw-Holland. As early as 1624, the WIC established Fort Nassau on the Gold Coast as a base to facilitate trade with Africa, and captured Portuguese forts at Arguin and Cabo Verde. Between 1637 and 1642, the Company took control of the main centres of the slave trade – Elmina, Luanda and São Tomé. And finally, in 1645, the Brazilian Portuguese started an insurrection (*Restauração*) in the New Holland. At the same time, after the end of the Thirty Years' War, Spain, hitherto formally closed to Dutch and Jewish merchants, becomes open to them. It was an interesting and somewhat contradictory process. Although a migration of New Christian merchant-financiers from Spain began in the late 1640s, in fear of the Inquisition and confiscations, these same people – already firmly established in the Republic – would participate in the development of trade with and through Spain. At least 20 per cent of Dutch trade with the former enemy would come under the control of Amsterdam Jews, including deliveries of African slaves from the Curaçao hub to the Spanish colonies (Israel 1990a: 435). Portugal and Brazil, on the other hand, receded into the background, although in the case of the latter, the crisis in the sugar trade – a consequence of the emergence of Caribbean competitors from as early as the late 1640s – would to some extent mitigate the rapid growth of tobacco exports. At the same time, Jews dispersed throughout the Dutch Caribbean were creating new distribution channels and establishing new contacts also with the Spanish colonies, especially in the area of present-day Venezuela and northern Colombia. While there has been a prevalent opinion that these very contacts were the most important in the activities of Jewish merchants in the Caribbean (Swetschinski 1982), the following description seems more convincing:

> by the mid eighteenth century Caribbean trade was the only significant element in Dutch Sephardi overseas commerce. Thus what had once been a trading network based overwhelmingly on Lisbon and Oporto finally ended up, after a series of dramatic oscillations and upheavals, as a system based essentially on Curaçao, Surinam and St Eustatius.
>
> ISRAEL 990: 436–446

Instead, the discussion of the example of Jewish settlement in 18th century Suriname will be limited to a few remarks. This experiment, unique in scale, founded by the "coterie of Jewish colonial entrepreneurs", was a controversial and ambiguously judged experience of both the Dutch and the Sephardim. No doubt, however, that the Jewish settlement "was the only agrarian venture that endured. It is the culmination of a story that began (...) in Brazil, the birth-place of the America's first Jewish community" (Ben-Ur 2020: 32, 34). On the other hand, with the drama of Africans forced onto a slave plantation in mind, Boxer (1965: 169) wrote: "Suriname was undeniably the black spot in the Dutch tropical empire from the humanitarian point of view", pointing to "the sadistic cruelty, pig-headed selfishness and short-sighted cupidity of successive generations of planters". However, this picture of Suriname hell taken from 18th century authors needs qualification but not justification. One should take into account that the extreme brutality shown by white planters, "was a function not of the ethnicity or religion of slave owner, not of Dutch rule, but rather of sugar production itself" (Ben-Ur 2020: 4).[1] Such an argument sounds convincing but only as an introduction to the discussion which should be focused

---

1   In 1737, at the peak of the slave economy in Suriname, 115 (over 28 per cent) of the total 401 plantations were in Jewish hands, along with tens of thousands of slaves. Most of the plantations (93) were located near Jodensavanne, the informal capital of the Jewish settlers (Vink 2010: 48). The view of the particular brutality of Jewish planters was disputed as early as 1788 by famous Jewish-Surinamese author David de Isaac Cohen Nassi (Marcus and Chyet. 1974).

on the web of relations systematically linking the plantation economy, religion and ethnicity. For Amsterdam Jews, on the other hand, the economic and social success achieved in Suriname by Jewish planters turned into a disaster from the 1770s. Although the centenary of the founding of the Jodensavanne *Beraha VeSalom* (Blessing and Peace) synagogue in 1785 would see the governor of the colony and a crowd of guests in town, the celebrations occured in a place that had already been in crisis for several years and was practically depopulated (Israel 2001: 336). We also leave out the history of Jewish presence from the second half of the 17th century in the English and French colonies in the Caribbean or in Dutch Curaçao and other Caribbean islands controlled by the United Provinces. With one exception.

The history of the Jews on the tiny island of Sint Eustatius (just 21 km²), also known as 'Statia', is worth mentioning for at least two reasons. Firstly: this microcosm was a commercial giant co-created by the "new Jews". Because of the role the island played until the 1780s in the lucrative trade with the French Caribbean and English colonies, and the wealth accumulated by its merchants, it was described as the Golden Mountain. The second reason was the famous *first salute*. Thanks to the Sint Eustatius garrison's reciprocation on 16 November 1776 of the salute of honour fired as a revolted Union ship entered the harbour, the islet made American Revolution history. It was the first Dutch possession – despite the neutrality declared by the Republic – to salute the flag of those fighting for independence, according to custom. For this "encounter with history" (Tuchman 1988, Jameson 1903), and above all for collaborating illegally in the eyes of the British with the rebellious Union, the inhabitants of Sint Eustatius would pay a heavy price in 1781, after the English occupied the island. This included Jews.

The Dutch took control of Sint Eustatius in 1636. As with Curaçao, which had been seized two years earlier, the primary motive was to gain control of the strategically located island, on the route linking Dutch New Amsterdam and Nieuw-Holland, then the Wild Coast and Suriname. Its economic importance was minor until the dawn of the 18th century. Attempts to develop tobacco, cotton and coffee cultivation on this rocky islet were doomed to fail. Change would come with the incorporation of Sint Eustatius into the Dutch trading system as an entrepôt and, from 1756, a duty-free, free port. This fact, incidentally, was noted with approval by Adam Smith. Such a move also facilitated the seizure of some of the profits from the huge contraband and its legalisation. During a debate in the House of Commons on the situation on Sint Eustatius in relation to the actions of the British fleet, Edmund Burke emphasised that the merchants of this small island "had, in the spirit of commerce, made it an

emporium for all the world; a mart, a magazine for all the nations of the earth"
(quoted in Enthoven 2012: 245f).

Slaves also appeared in the trade conducted through Sint Eustatius, in
greater numbers during two periods. The first was in the 1720s, when, following the collapse of the slave trade on Curaçao, the island took over much of
the transit by supplying slaves to the French and Spanish colonies. The second
period was in the 1770s, when slaves were mainly directed to the French colonies, St Domingue, Guadeloupe and Martinique. The British colonies in North
America were also important recipients, and for almost the entire 18th century,
Suriname.[2] However, the fortunes of the island's merchants depended on trade
in a much wider range of goods, which were supplied legally and illegally by
the Dutch, English, French, Spanish and others. At the height of Sint Eustatius'
development in the 1770s, Caribbean sugar above all was traded. Its annual production on the island was just £600,000, while exports amounted to £24 million.
The transit trade also consisted of 9 million pounds of coffee, 13 million pounds
of tobacco and about 2.5 million pounds of other goods (skins, rum, indigo,
cocoa, cotton and syrup). Cargo weighting a total of approximately 48.5 million
pounds was carried in 1779 by 3,551 ships (Arbell 2002: 179, 180f). A significant
proportion of the flotilla of small ships that handled Curaçao's trade with the
ports of the Spanish colonies came under Jewish control (Israel 2001: 338).

The first Jews appeared on Sint Eustatius in 1660, but it was not until the
18th century that there was a more visible Jewish presence. The majority
were Sephardim moving from the Netherlands, the Caribbean and also from
New York and Newport. In 1722, there were five Jewish families (20–22 persons)
living on Sint Eustatius, representing 5–5.5 per cent of the white population
(423). By comparison: on Curaçao 125 Jewish families settled in 1702. In 1781,
the number of Jews living on the island was 350–400. If we assume that Sint
Eustatius was inhabited in 1779 by 3,205 people, including 1,574 whites, the Jews
would have represented 22–25 per cent of the white population (Enthoven
2012: 247, Rupert 2012: 95).[3] Their presence was therefore striking, especially

---

2　Between 1720 and 1779, more than 26,000 slaves were sold through Sint Eustatius. In a simi-
　　lar period, just over 17,500 were transported from Curaçao. Curaçao's role as a major transit
　　port for the slave trade would fall during the resumed *asientos* (with or under Dutch con-
　　trol): between 1662 and 1716 some 66,000 slaves were exported by transit (Postma 1992b: 287,
　　293, 295).

3　According to other estimates, the white population of the island was 883 in 1781, but already
　　2,375 in 1790 (Jordaan and Wilson 2014: 278, 290f). Alongside the Sephardim, Ashkenazi Jews
　　(from Germany and Bohemian lands) also appeared at some point. By the mid-18th century,
　　they probably accounted for 25 per cent of the island's Jewish population. Contacts between
　　the two groups were decidedly conflictual (Arbell 2002: 174, Böhm 1992: 220).

among merchants and shipowners, but, let us stress, far from dominant. In the island's truly cosmopolitan merchant community, the English (from the colonies) and the French were prominent. Among the 47 merchants trading with the French East Indies, Sint Eustatius' main partner, only four Jewish merchants (8.5 per cent) appeared (Enthoven 2012: 274).

The English seizure of the island shortly after the outbreak of the fourth British-Dutch war in December 1780 ended in disaster. *First salute*, but above all the involvement of the island's merchants in the large-scale supply of gunpowder, ammunition and weapons to the rebels from the 13 colonies was seen as justification for retaliation. These in turn went far beyond the norms of the 'law of nations'. Admiral George Rodney, in command of the British fleet, stunned by the wealth of the island's stores and appalled by the attitude of British merchants complicit with the Dutch, made no secret of his intentions:

> This island has long been an asylum for men guilty of every crime, and a receptacle for the outcast of every nation (...). We thought that this nest of smugglers, adventurers, betrayers of their country, and rebels to their king, had no right to expect a capitulation, or to be treated as a respectable people; their atrocious deeds deserve none, and they ought to have known that the just vengeance of an injured empire, though slow, is sure.
>
> quoted in JAMESON 1903: 702

The Admiral – an otherwise good commander but also an indebted husband and father – mixed Britain's strategic interests with anti-Jewish phobias, hatred of British merchants disloyal to the Crown and a desire to obtain a generous reward from the King for property confiscated on the island, on behalf of the Crown. The orders given to him envisaged the destruction of the harbour warehouses, especially war material for the Union, and a swift departure to face the hostile French fleet (Jameson 1903, Abbattista 2008). It did not go to plan.

The plunder lasted three months and the Admiral's actions prompted Edmund Burke to request that the House of Commons set up a committee to look into the matter. A majority of the House rejected the motion of the Whig politician (Abbattista 2008). All movable and immovable property of Jewish merchants was looted, leaving French merchants alone (for fear of possible reprisals) and treating English, Dutch, Spanish merchants and even those hailing from the rebellious Union more leniently. Their personal belongings were not seized. The value of the 150–200 ships confiscated (either moored in port or already at sea but within range of Rodney's fleet), cargo and stored goods reached the enormous sum of £3 million. It can be assumed that these losses were mainly suffered by English (including American) merchants, the Dutch, and the Jews. The latter were deprived not only of goods but also of personal belongings. Clothes were ripped apart in search of money and valuables, and graves in the Jewish cemetery were also dug up. At the same time, 101 male Jews were arrested for several days. After the majority had been released, 31 were treated as dangerous – the *poor Jews of St. Eustatius* as Edmund Burke put it – and deported to the nearby British island of St. Kitts. Such particularly brutal treatment was shown by the Admiral only in case of the Jews. The value of the looted property (in money and jewellery, furniture, bank pledges, etc.) reached £4 million (Klooster 2014: 35). In total, therefore, the Admiral and his men looted goods worth a total of £7 million.[4] Some of it was sold at a quick auction to merchants and colonists from other nearby British islands, most of it was loaded onto 34 ships and sent by convoy to Britain. Eight reached their destination. Most fell prey to the French fleet (Enthoven 2012: 273).

The shift of the main streams of Dutch trade towards the Caribbean – the emergence of Sint Eustatius as an entrepôt was part of this process – was to some extent a consequence of the failure of Nieuw-Holland (see Map 3). The presence of Amsterdam Jews in this experiment in 1630–1654, however, was not limited to participation in trade and the plantation economy. Their activity was an integral part of Dutch expansion, which they did not initiate, nor, initially were they great supporters of, especially when it came to the establishment of the WIC and the militarisation of trade. An equally important part of their presence in the New Holland was their attempt to establish, in opposition to the ideological monopoly of the Catholic Church, a space of relative tolerance. To the Iberian variant of political theology, which implied division and discrimination, they wanted to contrast the experience – carried over from the United Provinces – of the difficult formation of cooperative relations between Christians and Jews. In Jewish historiography, Nieuw-Holland will thus go down in history not so much as an economic experiment, but above all as the place where the first synagogues in the New World were legally erected and where, with the help (but also under the watchful eye) of the Amsterdam Jewish community, a numerically significant congregation would be established, and where the *hahamim* (rabbis) respected in Amsterdam, Isaac Aboab da Fonseca and Moses Raphaelde Aguilar, were present. A journey to the colony was also announced by Menasseh ben Israel. A few remarks, therefore, on the Nieuw-Holland's experiment.

---

4 After taking into account changes in the purchasing power of the pound, the equivalent amount would have been over £1.66 billion in 1998. Own calculation based on Twigger (1999: 11 table 1).

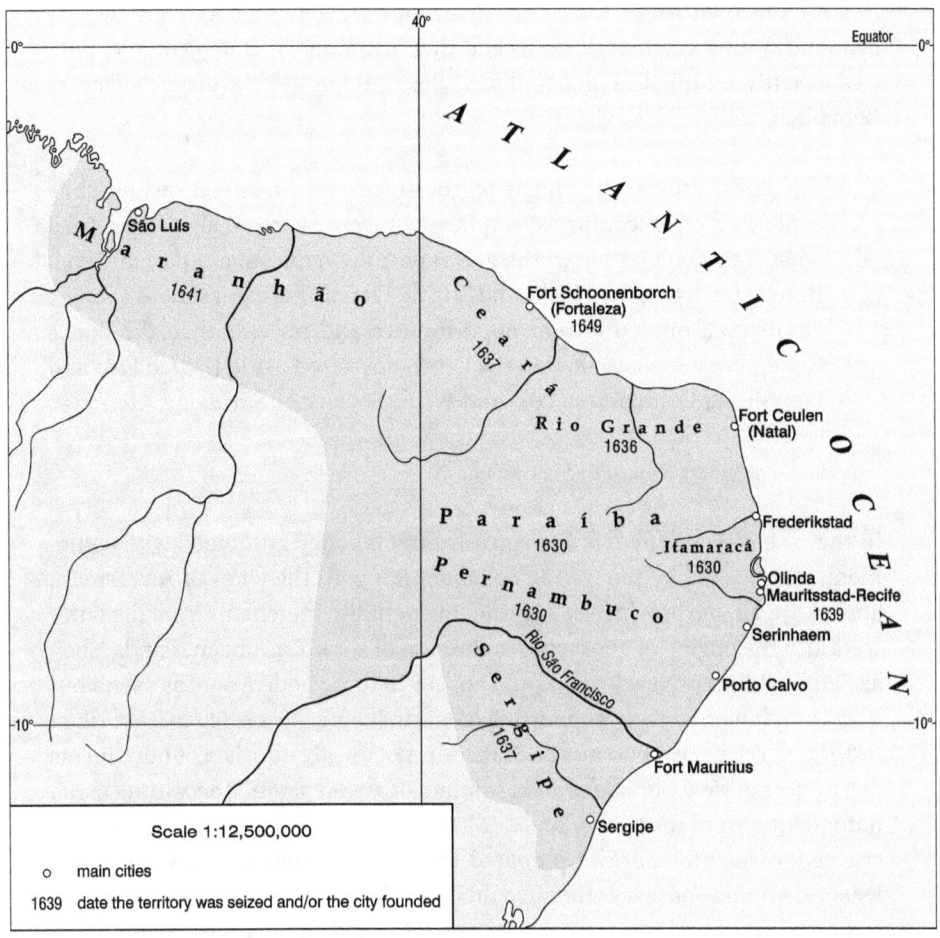

MAP 3   Nieuw-Holland, 1630–1654

SOURCE: ADAPTED FROM THE MAP IN H. HETTEMA JR., GROOTE HISTORISCHE
SCHOOLATLAS, ZWOLLE: W.E.J. TJEENK WILLINK (WIKIMEDIA COMMONS)

Trade contacts and conflicts between Portugal and its Brazilian colony and
the United Provinces led to two events in the 17th century that were intercon-
nected yet distinctly different when it came to the main actors. The common
denominator of the policies that led to the WIC's occupation of Pernambuco
in 1630 and the settlement of Amsterdam's Jews in Suriname from the 1660s
was the acceptance of colonisation as important target of Dutch expansion.
We are talking about a fundamental change, as occupation of territory and settlement had hitherto been rejected as a strategic option. Trade through other
countries' colonies was considered more advantageous, and operations in Asia

in VOC-controlled areas, forced by circumstances, were seen as a one-off der-
ogation (Pijning 2006: 232). Let us add that historians of Dutch colonial policies recently returned to and confimed this opinion held in the 17th century
Republic:

> the gains attained by Dutch partnerships and firms worldwide while
> exploiting other countries' empires (...) were far more significant than
> what they could attain in the geographically reduced and partially cha-
> rtered Dutch empire. That is, the British, French, Portuguese, and Spanish
> empires all offered greater opportunities and rewards than the States
> General or cooperation with the Dutch chartered world (Dutch East and
> West India Companies (VOC and WIC), Society of Suriname, etc.) ever
> could.
> ANTUNES AND NEGRÓN 2022: 19

In the case of Pernambuco, an aggressive trade policy, combined with settlement, was pushed by the WIC in collaboration with the elites of Amsterdam
and, above all, the province of Zeeland. Incidentally, merchants from the latter
were also the engine of expansion in the case of some Caribbean islands (such
as Sint Eustatius). "New Jews" would appear in these endeavours as useful but
only complementary and supporting co-participants. According to a Brazilian
historian, "the decision to invade Brazil was not an adventurism of buccaneers
or a project of New Christians and Jews, but an action planned according to the
natural interest of the Netherlands" (Mello 1989: 207). By contrast, in an extensive report for the *Suprema* prepared in 1634, the repentant New Christian
Esteban Ares de Fonseca elaborated on the conspiratorial vision of Jewish control of the WIC and the pre-eminent role of Jews in preparing the attack on
Brazil in 1624 and 1630 and their involvement in other wicked projects (Adler
1909, Kaplan 1994: 27f). Concurrently with the experiment in Brazil – already
in its declining phase – was the initiative of Amsterdam-based João de Yllan,
a wealthy Sephardic merchant who planned to initiate Jewish settlement in
Curaçao. Yllan, who is said to have been in Brazil on business in the early 1640s,
persuaded 12 Jewish families (about 50 people) to participate in the (unsuccessful) project in 1651 (Loker 1983: 22).

In the case of Suriname, under already different circumstances, it was the
Amsterdam Jews supported by Jewish refugees from the failed 'Dutch Brazil'
who would become an equal partner with the Dutch in colonising the territory.
Perhaps the most striking difference would be the status of the Jewish colonists. In the New Holland, it was essential to establish new rules favouring religious tolerance and the equality of Jews in economic activities in a Protestant

environment not very conducive to such pursuits. In Suriname, on the other hand, it was not so much the question of tolerance as of Jewish de facto autonomy within the framework of the already unquestioned rights concerning freedom of religion, and unfettered economic activity. Jodensavanne, founded by Jews, would even be described by some researchers as the capital of a "pseudo-state" or "ministate" (Vink 2010: 72, Ben-Ur 2020: 31).[5]

The first, however, was the New Holland in the part of Brazil occupied by the WIC in 1630. Along with the Dutch Calvinists also came – with some delay – the Amsterdam Jews. Bruno Feitler succinctly described *tempo dos flamengos*, an experiment that lasted almost a quarter of a century, as an interesting paradox: "a Catholic territory inhabited by New Christians, where Judaism was permitted, and which was subject to Calvinist rule" (Feitler 2009: 125). The defeat of the WIC was also a defeat for the "new Jews". They left Recife in 1654 along with the Dutch. The price of the Dutch presence, however, would be paid by the Brazilian New Christians – seen in toto (wrongly) as allies of the Company and traitors to the cause of Portuguese Brazil. As early as 1624, with the Dutch occupation of the capital Bahia, and the victorious operation of joint Portuguese-Spanish forces liberating the city, a handy dichotomy would emerge: "If the [Iberian] nobility were the heroes of the Bahian victory, the Jews were its villains. The mythology of the fall and recapture of Salvador quickly established two 'truths' fundamental to an explanation of these events in which social groups took expected and symbolic roles; the loyalty and valor of the nobility and the treason of the and the treason of the 'people of the Hebrew nation' (*gente da nacao hebreia*)". This widespread myth, which obscured, for example the behaviour of one Brazilian leader in Bahia who was loyal to the Dutch, although also later the leader of the anti-Dutch resistance, was useful for many reasons (Schwartz 1991: 750). In 1630, in turn, this myth provided a convenient explanation for the relative ease with which the Dutch occupied Pernambuco. And Portuguese independence in 1640 and the subsequent outbreak of an uprising in 1645 in the New Holland created a new and complicated situation for the Jews and the New Christians. One of the consequences would be an open schism in *La Nacao*.

According to the calculations of Wiznitzer (1954, 1960: 128–130), in 1645, the year of the outbreak of the anti-Dutch uprising, Nieuw-Holland had a population of 12,703, including 3,583 Indians and 2,671 black slaves. Almost half of the

---

5   In Suriname, both the British and then from 1667, the Dutch, guaranteed a number of freedoms and liberties for the Jews, which were first enshrined in 1657 in the contract for the Essequibo settlement project. These rights went far beyond those guaranteed to the "new Jews" in the Republic itself, as well as in the Nieuw-Holland (Klooster 2010–2011).

white population of 6,449 people were officers and soldiers and family members of WIC officials (3,550 people). A group of 1,450 Amsterdam Jews made up 22.5 per cent of the white population. At the threshold of the surrender in 1654, there were still 650 Jews in Recife. By contrast, according to a revised estimate proposed by Emmanuel (1962: 41), there were 1,000 Jews in Dutch Brazil in 1645, and in 1654, 600.[6]

These estimates indicate that the WIC's hopes for large-scale Dutch migration did not materialise. The social base for the settlement experiment in Brazil proved limited overall: Nieuw-Holland raised excitation mainly among the merchants of Zeeland and *Heeren XIX* hoping to replicate the financial success of the VOC, and Amsterdam Jews. The relatively small demographic potential of the Republic also played a role, although given the scale of migration from Portugal during this period, this factor can hardly be considered decisive. As a result, Protestants and "new Jews" moved into the New Holland in almost equal numbers, with the former lacking, according to the colony's Governor General, Count Johan Maurits van Nassau-Siegen (hereafter: Johan Maurits), "capitalists or settlers", people who could afford to buy slaves. Plans still envisaged in 1636 for the migration of 1,000–3,000 Dutch peasants – the sine qua non condition of the settlement project – were not realised (Wätjen 1921: 240, Pijning 2006: 220, Boxer 1957: 132, 145, Schwartz 2010: 242). Between 1580 and 1640, 2,000 Dutch and 110,000 Portuguese emigrated to the New World (Eltis 2004: 9).

The Amsterdam Jews who appeared together with the Dutch were neither co-founders of the WIC nor enthusiastic supporters of the policy of combining trade with war. We have already mentioned that, in the view of many Jewish merchants trading with Brazil during the truce period (1609–1621), the WIC posed a threat to traditional and less confrontational forms of Atlantic commerce. This was especially true for the 27 largest merchants, who controlled more than 30 per cent of the Dutch sugar trade. Also, in the province of Holland and its centre in Amsterdam, Calvinist merchants were sceptical about the project to create a WIC. This prolonged the process of raising the necessary capital by the company (Emmer 2001: 511, Pijning 2006: 211). In this

---

6   Mello (1989: 282), on the other hand, reports that in 1649 there were 344 Jews in New Holland. By contrast, the list of the Jewish economic elite given by Emmanuel (1962) included 109 names in 1654. Together with their families, this group probably numbered around 400 people. According to Mello, the number of Jews in the Dutch colony quoted by Wiznitzer would almost equal the number of Sephardim in Amsterdam, which he considers unlikely. Wiznitzer's estimates are accepted by Israel (2001: 342) and Boxer (1957: 133f). In contrast, G. Böhm (1992: 67–69) accepts Mello's calculations. For other estimates, see Falbel (2008: 110).

respect, the views of the Amsterdam Jews were also close to the ideas of the WIC's initiator, Willem Usselincx (Wätjen 1921: 29–34). Framing his project, he did not regard settlement in the future colonies and the possibility of trade as an activity subordinated to the requirements of the war already waged for decades against the Spaniards. Thus, as Boxer (1957: 15f) aptly observes, Usselincx "never explained how Dutch colonies could be founded in tropical America without fighting Spain".

Disagreements on this issue were closed by the WIC's conquest of Pernambuco and then other areas of northeastern Brazil. However, it is worth recalling these differences of opinion, because in 1634, the legend of the 'Jewish WIC' appears in the aforementioned report for the *Suprema*. According to the already mentioned New Christian informant of the Inquisition, "The West India Company, which is a Brazilian company and composed of pirates, is governed entirely by Jews of Amsterdam, for all the rich ones give their money for the said company". He further added that it was "the Jews of Amsterdam [who] were responsible for the capture of Pernambuco". This informant did not fail to add that the earlier 1624 attack of the WIC fleet on Bahia was planned by two Jews (including one living in the Republic) (Adler 1909: 48–50).[7] Note, therefore, that 18 Amsterdam Jews "are recorded in (...) incomplete list to have subscribed for 36,100 guilders of the required 7,108,000 guilders of [WIC's] original capital", raised not without difficulty between 1621 and 1623. This represented 0.5 per cent of the Company's total capital. By 1656, the share of Jewish merchants would rise to 4 per cent, and in 1671, just before the liquidation of the WIC, it would reach 10 per cent. Among the privileged shareholders, and therefore those entitled to apply for a seat on the board of directors, there was only one Jewish merchant – Bento (Baruch) Osorio (Baron 1973: 44, Mello 1989: 207–209). It is therefore difficult to accept the figures quoted as evidence of the dominance of Jews in the newly formed Company. Boxer (1957: 10) was fully justified in harshly criticising those historians who have repeated this fallacy after "ignorant and prejudiced Iberian writers".

The participation of the "new Jews" in the economy of Nieuw-Holland largely reflected preferences (and skills) formed in the Republic and transferred to Brazil. In short, in contrast to the Brazilian New Christians, present in significant numbers among the owners of *engenhos*, the involvement of Amsterdam Jews in sugar production was limited. In 1639, 166 *engenhos* were

---

7 Unlike Lea (1907: 282), who saw a grain of truth in Ares de Fonseca's revelations, Boxer (1957: 36), described his account as a "cock-and-bull story told to the Inquisition (...) and which the Inquisitors themselves disbelieved as they made no attempt to follow up the matter".

counted in Nieuw-Holland, of which 120 were operational, the remaining 46, *fogo morto*, needed repair. A year earlier, Governor Johan Maurits reported that there were 150 *engenhos* in the occupied territory, of which 51 were out of production. According to Christopher Arciszewski, a Polish Calvinist and colonel in the service of the WIC, the occupation of Brazil was a devastating operation for both sides: the destruction caused by WIC mercenaries, as well as by Brazilian marauders, was followed by more, perpetrated by the *moradores* (Portuguese settlers) who resisted the Dutch between 1630 and 1637. The destruction of sugar mills was accompanied by the setting of sugar cane fields on fire and the dispersal and/or robbing of slaves. In contrast, under Johan Maurits (1637–1644) there was a time of relative stability and development for the New Holland. But even during this period, sugar production rarely reached half of its pre-1630 level. After a relative stabilisation, about 60 per cent of the *engenhos* remained in the hands of the Portuguese (how many were XN among them we do not know), 32 per cent became the property of the Dutch, while 10, i.e. 8 per cent, was controlled by the Amsterdam Jews (Wätjen 1921: 268f, Wiznitzer 1960: 29f. Schwartz 2004b: 166f, Łopatecki 2016, Maurits 2010: 260f). Such a relatively modest share of Jews in the ownership of sugar plantations was reflected also in the estimates of investments they made into the Nieuw-Holland's economy. From around 3.45 million guilders only 9 per cent was invested in *engenhos* and cane fields (Odegard 2022: 55). As an aside, the sum total of their investments was quite substantial – one should remember that the WIC was capitalised at 7.1 million guilders.

The ownership structure of the *engenhos* that were acquired during the governor's 1637 auction of property abandoned by the Portuguese and seized by the WIC was also similar. Of the 44 *engenhos* sold, with a total value of over 1.7 million florins, 21 were in the hands of 23 Dutchmen, 17 were acquired by 14 Portuguese (including planters), while six were bought by four Amsterdam Jews. In practice, the Portuguese share was much higher and their influence on the plantation economy stronger (Mello 1989: 225). However, the information (Wätjen 1921: 267) that two thirds of the plantations auctioned had been taken over by 'Portuguese Jews' was not confirmed. Between 1637 and 1645, it was not uncommon for Dutch new owners to resell *engenhos* to Portuguese, who were less threatened by marauders and *moradores* attacking Dutch plantations. Plantations remaining in Dutch hands were often managed by the Portuguese (Boxer 1957: 144). Among the purchasers were also Jews, although it is not clear whether these were Amsterdam Jews or New Christians. However, according to the recent research, the role of Dutch investors and owners should not be underestimated – 43 sugar mills were in their hand. When it came to sugar production, therefore, Jews played a secondary role in this key economic field. Most *engenhos* remained in the hands of the Portuguese. Their advantage, when it came to the know-how necessary to manage the plantations, was obvious. The social status of the *engenho* owner, emphasised by the Portuguese (the 'noble profession' of sugar producers), was also an important factor, in turn underestimated by the Dutch, who preferred the city and the urban economy (Pijning 2006: 224, 230). Incidentally, contrary to the opinion of some historians, Jorge Homem de Pinto, the largest Brazilian planter in the New Holland, and owner of 9 *engenhos* in Paraíba, was neither Jewish nor *XN* (Wiznitzer 1960: 68f, Mello 1989: 236). On the other hand, in a group of 11 prominent Jewish planters, the leading position was held by Duarte Saraiva (David Senior Coronel), owner of 8 *engenhos,* and Pedro Lopes de Vera owning 5 *engenhos* (Ribemboim 2000: 150–159).

The focus of activity of the Amsterdam Jews – concentrated in the cities, mainly in Recife – was the financing of sugar and other trades, brokerage (*corretores*), tax collection and slave trading. In addition to merchants, medics and lawyers, we also see artisans (Böhm 1992: 71–83). There were also new developments that broadened the scope of their economic activities compared to the situation in the Republic: "Jews were (...) allowed to own shops and engage in general retail trade. The result was the emergence of a new kind of Sephardic Jewish society, one based on a wide range of trade and finance linked to tropical agriculture and a slave economy" (Israel and Schwartz 2007: 27). Jewish merchants were also beneficiaries of the changes that reduced the Company's monopolistic privileges in 1638. In particular, there was a liberalisation of the sugar trade. The bulk of this commodity was exported by private 'free merchants' (*vrijluden*), albeit only on WIC ships. According to an estimate from the period, the Company exported between 1637 and 1644 over 502,000 arrobas of sugar worth over 7.6 million florins, while private 'free merchants' exported over 1.55 million arrobas worth over 20.3 million florins (Boxer 1957: 148). Much of these private exports passed through the hands of Jewish merchants. For example, on two ships that transported sugar in 1641 and 1643 respectively, Jewish merchants owned 34–44 per cent of the cargo. Let us also mention that the Sephardim occupied an almost monopolistic position in the tax collection. In 1635–1645, between 54 and 100 per cent of the contracts for tax farming were concluded by "new Jews". The exception was in 1641, when their share fell to 10 per cent. The majority of contracts (66 per cent) were then in the hands of the trusted Nieuw-Holland municipal councillor and tax collector João Fernandes Vieira, the indebted owner of five *engenhos*. It was he who would appear in 1645 at the head of the Pernambucan insurrection and become, according to the commander of the Portuguese troops, the father of victory, "the first cause of the happiness which the crown of Portugal enjoys"

(Wiznitzer 1960: 70–72, Mello 1989: 232, 271, Boxer 1957: 122, 162, 243f, 273–276, 299f, Kellenbenz 1964: 53–56).

By contrast, in the slave trade system created by the Dutch, the "new Jews" were not suppliers, but important – though not the only – distributors of African slaves brought by the WIC. The restriction of the Company's monopoly in 1638 did not apply to several commodities whose supply it still controlled: slaves, arms and war materials and *pau-brasil*. According to more recent findings, between 1636 and 1645, 26,000 slaves were imported into Nieuw-Holland, worth some 7.6 million florins (assuming an average price of 291 florins per slave).[8] By 1642, most of them were taken from Upper Guinea and then from Dutch-occupied Angola. After the outbreak of the Pernambucan insurrection, the slave trade gradually disappeared, with only 785 Africans imported in 1651 (Postma 1992b: 286). According to the Company's documents, the share of Jewish merchants in the purchase of slaves imported by WIC fluctuated in 1637–1644 between 8 and 63 per cent. Between 1640 and 1644, at the height of the influx of slaves into the New Holland, the Jews controlled 38 to 63 per cent of this trade. Also, *senhores de engenho, lavradores*, Dutch and Portuguese merchants participated in slave purchases. However, because of the Jewish merchants, slave auctions were not held on the Sabbath and during Jewish holidays (Wiznitzer 1960: 72f, Mello 1989: 233). And, according to recent findings, Count Maurits was also an active participant in the slave transaction:

> There is in fact strong evidence (...) that indicate that Johan Maurits profited personally from the trade in enslaved Africans and dabbled in slavesmuggle ventures as well. (...) This should not be surprising. In a colonial society in which slaves were both an important form of capital, credit and social prestige, the personal involvement of a governor-general in the trade and sale of enslaved people is in accordance with the standards of the time.
>
> MONTEIRO AND ODEGARD 2020: 32

Nominally, the slave trade was profitable, both for the WIC and for Jewish and other traders. The company would buy a slave for around 93 guilders, sell in Recife for 300–400, which would suggest a fairly substantial profit margin (even after deducting transport costs and a risk margin). In reality, although formally the slave buyer owed payment within 6–12 months, delays in settling

8   Also quoted were 12–75 florins as the purchase price of a slave in Africa and 200–800 florins as the selling price in Recife (depending on the sex, age and physical condition of the African) (Boxer 1957: 139).

debts were longer and rampant; usually sugar was paid and sometimes the debt was uncollectible. In addition to the arrears of slave bills, unpaid loans made to purchase the *engenhos* auctioned in 1637 and subsequent years were also involved. The takeover by the WIC under Johan Maurits of some of the now unmanageable planters' debts did not solve the problem. As a result, by 1645 the Company's accumulated debts had reached 14 million guilders, of which 4.5 million were uncollected dues from planters (Pijning 2006: 228, Emmer 2006a: 19f). It became impossible to continue to finance the existing and still growing deficit by increasing the WIC debt.

Heeren XIX's response was to make the sale of slaves for cash compulsory. The result was the transformation of the Jews into the main intermediaries between the WIC and the planters. The "new Jews'" knowledge of Dutch and Portuguese made it immeasurably easier to carry out such operations. The private capital of the Jews and their families in Amsterdam thus appears as a solution to the deficit of a public institution like the WIC. This partly explains, according to the historian, the far-reaching tolerance of the Jews and the extension of their religious and economic freedoms, even if, as some contemporaries claimed, Johan Maurits himself was not particularly favourably disposed towards them. On the other hand, there is no doubt that the Jews had a decidedly positive attitude towards the governor (they expressed this in a letter to *Heeren XIX* from 1642). Briefly, the attitude of the colonial authorities towards the Jews was "a consequence of even obvious necessity" (Israel and Schwartz 2007: 24f).[9]

"New Jews", having cash and credit at their disposal, purchased slaves from the Company at a relatively low price and then sold them to the planters at an already much higher price. In this case, however, they also had to accept payment in instalments or in sugar. Such operations, however, due to the considerable risk, translated into high interest rates on loans. Some 36–48 per cent per year were demanded by Dutch lenders and a similar level was expected by Jewish intermediaries, who were in turn accused of usury by Dutch merchants (Boxer 1957: 139, 173). For the Jewish investors such enforced credit

---

9   Johan Maurits expressed his attitude towards the Jews in a report of 1638: professing Judaism, the Jews "in no way would (…) wish or be able to go back to being under Spanish control. On the contrary, they would strive to maintain and defend this State [Nieuw-Holland]" (Maurits 2010: 239). In a further report from 1642, he reiterates that "in times of need [the Jews] will stand faithfully by the Dutch flag" (quoted in Wätjen 1921: 230f, 234). In contrast, according to Pastor Vicente Joaquim Soler of Recife, who wrote that the Jews "ruin the traffic, suck the blood of the people, frustrate and violate the Company", the governor's attitude towards Jews was decidedly negative (Groesen 2017: 116, Haefeli 2014: 143).

and Dutch competitiors' attacks were a deadly serious problem. According to recent estimates, from around 3.45 million guilders invested by the "new Jews" in Nieuw-Holland, 51 per cent was personal loans, mainly for the purchase of slaves, followed by urban real estate and mortgages on land and finally sugar mills (Odegard 2022: 55). Let us add that the bankruptcies of some Jewish merchants and brokers were accompanied by the emergence also of huge fortunes in the hands of a narrow elite. In the background of these fortunes remained the not-so-wealthy "new Jews" and the Jewish paupers who made up the majority of Amsterdam's Sephardic migrants (Mello 1989: 285). After the loss of the New Holland, the States-General made claims to the Portuguese for the lost property of the WIC and private investors, amounting to 11.4 million guilders, of which private claims were estimated at 7.5 million. Some 63 Jewish claims (of 157 overall) came to 2.36 million guilders (the sum of 4.45 million guilders is also quoted) (Odegard 2022: 53–55). Following earlier estimates by a Jewish scholar, the losses suffered by more than 100 Dutch Jews amounted to about 2.8 million guilders, with five of them making claims totalling more than 1.14 million guilders (Emmanuel 1962: 50, 57). However, taking into account the debt owned to the Dutch and Jews, there is no doubt that the Portuguese elites paralleled the Jews in wealth. The already mentioned Homem de Pinto owed the WIC more than 1 million florins (almost 25 per cent of the debt of all planters), while the future leader of the insurrection Fernandes Vieira owed more than 320,000 (Boxer 1957: 274).

The price of the strongly accentuated presence of the Amsterdam Jews in the trade and finances of the New Holland was a growing conflict with Dutch competitors and the ministers (*predikanten*) of the Reformed church. The confluence of religious and economic motivations was strong enough to speak of the emergence of an anti-Jewish syndrome, which, left to its own devices, could threaten the principles of relative tolerance and the policy of equality declared in the colonial regulations. The presence of Jews as Jews and their desire to obtain a wide margin of freedom aroused, not surprisingly, resistance and scorn among Portuguese Catholics. According to Johan Maurits' report, the Sephardim themselves, by their behaviour, also aggravated the problem in their relations with the Calvinist "reformed community and their ministers". This included prayers and religious rituals (including singing and dancing), which became public events and irritated the Dutch. The closure of the *Kahal Zur Israel* (Rock of Israel) synagogue in Recife for a short time in 1638 enabled a compromise to be reached (Maurits 2010: 238f, Levy 2013: 128). However, as time went on, tensions over the issue eased enough for the Nieuw-Holland to become the site of not only two synagogues, but also the organisation of an intense Jewish religious life (the second synagogue, *Magen Abraham* – Shield of Abraham, was built in Mauritsstad, connected to Recife by a bridge). In any case, practising tolerance was a complicated process: many Dutch in the colony were "less liberal than their laws" (Kohut 1895: 7). We should add that these anti-Jewish sentiments were accompanied by discriminatory moves against Lutherans, Anabaptists, and Mennonites. However, the discrimination against the former is surprising, as there were many German Lutherans among the mercenary soldiers of the WIC. In contrast, Presbyterians and Anglicans would enjoy full rights (Haefeli 2014: 129f).

However, the main blow was reserved for the Catholic Church, although the enmity demonstrated by the Reformed church towards the Jews matched the intensity of the hostility towards the Catholics. The *predikaten* in particular – there were nineteen in all plus two apprentices, assisted by poorly educated laymen – displayed an almost hateful viciousness in all debates concerning the possibility of relaxing the restrictions on the Catholic Church. They were not isolated among the Dutch on this issue. Decisions planned as early as 1629, before the invasion of Pernambuco, which led in the first years of the New Holland to the removal of the Jesuits (but not the Franciscans, Carmelites and Benedictines), the prohibition of processions and the contact of diocesan priests with bishops in Portuguese Brazil, were met with fairly wide support. New priests could only come, if at all, from Europe. Services were restricted to private homes (Mello 1958, Pijning 2006, Bem 2007: 126). Although all these repressions can be seen as relatively moderate and far from a 'policy of the stake' and an attempt to eradicate Catholicism from the colonies, the Portuguese *moradores* took them in a different, more critical, way. They were, after all, along with the slaves, the vast majority in the territory occupied by the WIC.[10] In response to the demands put forward by the *moradores* in 1640, some changes were made in 1641 to weaken the previous restrictions (including the permission to hold services in churches). But these concessions, supported by Johan Maurits, were seen by many Portuguese Catholics as repression, not liberalisation. Compromise was becoming impossible. The outbreak of the anti-Dutch uprising, in which religious motivations would play an extremely important role, would only confirm such attitudes. And at the same time, the governor's departure from office in 1644 was accompanied by numerous expressions of regret also from *moradores* (Boxer 1957: 114, 156f).

The main clash between Jewish merchants, brokers and lenders and Dutch Calvinists and rivals would still take place under Johan Maurits: the conflict

---

10   Circa 1640, the population of New Holland was probably around 90,000, including 30,000 Portuguese, 30,000 African slaves and 16,000 Indians. The number of Dutch, Jews and other Europeans was estimated at 13,500 (Bem 2007: 129).

would culminate in 1641. However, between 1638 and 1640, Calvinist merchants were already submitting petitions addressed to the WIC demanding increased migration of 'good Christians', as well as a ban on mixed marriages or Jewish participation in auctions of seized Portuguese property. The result of the Calvinists' (but also the Catholics') scorn of the aforementioned 'public scandals', which included overly demonstrative Jewish rituals, which were difficult for the authorities to ignore, would result in the 1638 ban on processions and other activities outside the confines of closed houses of worship. Discreet Jewish ceremonies were allowed (Wiznitzer 1960: 74f).

Signed in the summer of 1641 by 66 Dutch, French and English merchants from Recife, the memorandum addressed to the authorities of the Republic was in fact a synthesis of all the prejudices, envy of competitors and the impossibility of accepting equal treatment for Jews in business. The pragmatic policy towards Jews of the WIC and the Governor was seen as detrimental to the interests of 'honest Christian' merchants. The tone of the memorandum was not so much harsh as downright confrontational and extremely anti-Jewish. Offended by the presence of Jews, the religious sensibilities of Christian merchants went hand in hand with the indignation of a threatened economic competitor. The company and the authorities were accused of being unsupportive of Christians, and the signatories did not understand why, despite examples in other countries where Jews had to wear distinctive red hats or yellow patches on their chests, this useful regulation was not being introduced in the colony. Concluding that almost all the trade, especially in sugar, was in the hands of the Jews, they asked why retail trade had also been placed in their hands. The Jews' knowledge of Portuguese, which facilitated their contacts with the Brazilian elite and merchants and thus increased their competitive advantage, also appeared as a pretext for the accusations (Chargas 2009: 70f). We also read:

> After all, it is known to everyone by what methods the sons of Judah operate. They lie, cheat, use false weights and measures (...). With their usury practices and systematic exploitation of Christian planters, they have become a veritable plague on Brazilian soil (...). Brazil belongs to us Christians, not to the damned children of Israel, who disgrace day after day the most holy name of Jesus Christ (...). We don't need any Israelites here, we Christians are able to do exactly what they do. And the Company will not lose a penny if Brazil is freed from the Jews. Of course, as long as rich people come to New Holland!
>
> quoted in WÄTJEN 1921: 231f

Governor Johan Maurits, according to the method of "masterful passivity" he practised, skilfully manoeuvred between the conflicting parties, trying above all to appease the radical Calvinists. His main aim, however, was to smooth over the conflict with the Portuguese; these shared fully the views of the heretical Calvinists on the issue of the Jews.[11] This was, however, a short-lived success. The *Heeren XIX,* on the other hand, addressed this outbreak of hatred, lamentations and demands for the marginalisation of the Jews without emotion. They continued to organise emigrations of Amsterdam Jews. The discriminatory moves contained in the 1642 ordinance "concerning Jews and Papists in matters of religion" were limited to, among other things, a ban on the construction of new synagogues, a ban on mixed Jewish-Christian unions, a prohibition on Jews uttering the holy name of Christ, and the adoption of a regulation that Jews could make up at most one third of all brokers appointed by the colony's authorities, and that fraud in trade was prohibited (Vainfas 2012: 236f, Wiznitzer 1960: 91, Mello 1989: 260f).

The pragmatism demonstrated by the Governor and the position taken by *Heeren XIX* helped to calm the mood somewhat, but the actions taken could only limit the destructive consequences of the dispute (such as the killings or the punishment of Jews for 'blasphemy'), but could not eliminate the fierce economic competition. The actions of the Governor and *Heeren XIX,* on the other hand, undoubtedly contributed to consolidating the support of the Amsterdam Jews and in the colony for the United Provinces. After the outbreak of the uprising, when the Dutch would be pushed quite quickly on the defensive in land warfare, the loyal position of the "new Jews" towards the Republic would be reaffirmed forcefully. In 1642, Johan Maurits could still wonder how the Jews would behave "if the King of Portugal allowed them to practise their religion" (Wätjen 1921: 234), while the answer came in the difficult year of 1645. In a memorial addressed by Amsterdam *parnasim* to the States-General, sent via city's mayors, concerning the Jews in the Republic and Brazil, we read that

> when the first ambassador of the present King of Portugal came to these countries, it was said to us in his name that he brought with him full powers from his king to grant various privileges and favors to the Jewish Nation, by this means seeking to persuade them to return to his countries and Kingdom (from where they had come). Thereupon the [Jewish]

---

11   In the close circle around Johan Maurits appeared the monk Manuel Calado do Salvador. In 1645, he took the side of the rebels. He gained fame as the author of an account of the first year of the war, and of his time working with the governor (Mello 1954). Father Calado's anti-Semitism was downright spontaneous.

Nation gave as their answer, that they knew as their sovereign no one else
but their High Mightinesses [States-General], and if he had something to
propose in this respect, he had to speak to them [their High Mightinesses]
EMMANUEL 1955: 38f

In response, the States-General, recognising the "loyalty and courage" shown
by the Jews in Brazil, assured that their discrimination would not be tolerated: Jews in the colony "shall be protected and sheltered in the same way as
the other inhabitants of the United Netherlands themselves". It was not without reason that the *parnasim* in Amsterdam called this document the *Patente
onrossa* (Charter of Honour), while historians have seen in it the first declaration of equality in the Americas (Emmanuel 1955: 38f, 43f).

In contrast, the Brazilian New Christians' cooperation with the Dutch
in both 1624 and 1630–1654 was much more complex. After Portugal's independence in 1640, it seemed that the question of Nieuw-Holland would not
complicate their situation, especially as Lisbon had declared its willingness to
make a far-reaching compromise on the Dutch presence in Brazil for a number
of reasons. Whether it was sincere is another matter. In the difficult years for
Portugal of 1647–1648, there was even consideration in Lisbon of the possibility, if not of buying back the New Holland (the price of 28 million florins
dictated by the Republic was, however, abstract) then of formally ceding it to
the Republic and paying the debts of the *moradores* owed to the WIC. On the
other hand, however, the earlier aggressive actions of the Dutch in West Africa
and the occupation of Maranhão in Brazil in 1641 posed a threat to strategic
Portuguese interests (Boxer 1957: 192). The resolution of this problem occurred
in Brazil itself. Brazilian *moradores* from the New Holland – a leadership role
played among them by planters indebted to and/or in conflict with the WIC –
substituted for the royal court in the decision-making process. The extent to
which this occurred with the king's discreet consent is a matter of debate.
According to the leaders of the insurrection, their decision to start fighting was
not coordinated with Lisbon. The insurrection thus clarified the relationship
between the colony and the metropolis, while at the same time placing the
Amsterdam Jews on the one hand, and the New Christians in Portugal and
Brazil on the other, in a conflictual situation. Indeed, the very appearance of
the Dutch in Brazil in1624 and 1630 complicated relations within *La Nação*.

The interaction of Amsterdam Jews with the WIC from the moment the
decision was taken to attack the Portuguese colony was, in a way, a matter of
course. A sense of loyalty – just to underline this factor – bound them to the
Republic, its institutions, laws and policies. The international nature of commercial operations and financial transactions became increasingly intertwined

with an emerging sense of Dutch patriotism. In the case of the Brazilian New Christians, attitudes towards the Dutch and their actions in the colony were much more varied (Vainfas 2007: 18–21). Historians note that in Pernambuco under WIC control, Brazilian New Christians by no means opted in toto for Judaism and the Dutch:

> Not all New Christians in [Dutch] Brazil (...) viewed the arrival of the Dutch as a liberation. Many took the opportunity to officially integrate into the local Jewish community, while others did so only after feeling pressure from the official Jews. Others preferred to stay Catholic even while they continued to practice Jewish rites. Yet another group of New Christians remained faithful Catholics and kept a safe distance from the newly established synagogue and its members.
>
> FEITLER 2009: 125f

The divergence of attitudes was therefore clear, and the previous relationship with the Portuguese colony was not seen as unequivocally negative. This was all the more so because the New Christians who converted to Judaism encountered relative discrimination in the Dutch colony (probably not without the influence of Jews from the Netherlands): they were "relegated to the position of second-class Jews. Insecure Jews. Colonial Jews" (Vainfas 2012: 184–186). The *XN*'s adherence to Catholicism also implied loyalty to the crown, from 1640 Portuguese again. Described by Novinsky *o homem dividido* – the New Christian representing a split consciousness – was probably equally loyal. However, it should be borne in mind that attachment to the Catholic faith did not prevent some of the Old Christians from siding with the Dutch, both in 1624 and after 1630. In any case, when we speak of the collaboration of Brazilian *XN* s with the Dutch, we are speaking in all probability of the attitudes, choices and actions of a minority. Cecil Roth therefore went far too far when he wrote that the war in Brazil "resolved itself almost into the struggle between Spaniards and Portuguese on one hand and an alliance between Marranos and the Dutch on the other". His other assertion was unfounded: "When in the second decade of the seventeenth century the Dutch began their attempt to conquer [Brazil], the local New Christians eagerly espoused their cause" (Roth 1959: 285). In fact, in Bahia, which remained beyond Dutch control, but where attempts were made to reach the *XN* s with a view to reconversion to Judaism, the involvement of the New Christians in the defence of the *capitanía* went far beyond 'proportional participation'. Both Old and New Christians were on the side of the Dutch attacking Bahia, although the number of the latter was "incomparably smaller than [those fighting] on the side of the Portuguese". An investigation by the aforementioned tracker of *judaizantes*, the vicar Manoel Temudo of Bahia, showed that only six New Christians appeared among the 22 people accused of collaborating with the Dutch in 1624. An investigation by the Bishop of Salvador between 1635 and 1637 yielded even more surprising results: collaboration with the Dutch in Paraíba was charged against 80 people, including 8 priests, 24 New Christians and 48 Old Christians (Novinsky 1972: 135f, 122–124, 128, Israel and Schwartz 2007: 49). Anyhow, in 1624 "four-fifths of the conversos in Bahia wanted nothing to do with the Dutch invaders and fled to the countryside with the rest of the population" (Groesen 2011: 173). We should add that when, at the behest of the governor of the New Holland, Johan Maurits, WIC troops attacked Bahia in 1638 – unsuccessfully, by the way – the Dutch would not be supported by the New Christians.

From the perspective of Jewish historiography at the turn of the 20th century, the cooperation of the New Christians with the Dutch was assessed positively. The choice between a Republic that ensured, even if selectively, religious freedoms, civil rights and economic freedom and a Catholic colony that sustained discrimination and allowed only exceptionally – in individual cases – social advancement, seemed to historians such as H. Graetz, G. A. Kohut or C. Roth obvious. Those who sided with the Republic "as advisors and warriors", informers and pilots on ships, made the right choice. The defence of Recife already in the final phase of the war is described as follows: when "the garrison of Recife, exhausted by famine, was on the point of surrendering unconditionally, the Jews encouraged the governor to brave resistance. A fanatical war of race and religion between the Portuguese and the Dutch devastated fair Brazil, and a famine ensued. The Jews vied with the Dutch in suffering and bravery" (Graetz 1894: 693f, also Kohut 1895: 12, 14). At the same time it was also taken for granted that the information provided by the New Christians and the "new Jews" familiar with Brazil made possible the unhindered approach of Dutch ships to the ports of Bahia in 1624 and Recife in 1630. As a matter of fact, when preparing an assault on Bahia in 1624, the WIC commanders were briefed about the approaches to the harbour and important details concerning fortifications by a Dutch merchant. A certain Dierick Ruiters, captured in Brazil and imprisoned for two-and-a-half years, escaped in 1620 and returned to the Republic. The "accuracy of [his] intelligence was unsurpassed" (Groesen 2017: 35–37). However, the mood prevailing in Spain at the time made it easier to accept the assertion that:

> Jews were considered responsible for the fall of Brazil to the Dutch in the early seventeenth century. (...) A Castilian grandee did not hesitate to claim that Pernambuco had been lost in 1630 'through the Jews'. This

was the decade when, partly in reaction against Olivares's patronage of Portuguese converso financiers, anti-Semitic sentiment was rampant in Madrid.

KAMEN 2003: 344[12]

The insurrection in Pernambuco fundamentally changed the situation and introduced new points of reference. Not only did it overlap with the crisis of Dutch policy towards the New Holland, subsequently aggravated by the outbreak of the first Anglo-Dutch war in 1652, but it even imposed, especially on the New Christians, the need to choose between loyalty to the Portuguese crown and the Brazilian colony, and 'betrayal', i.e. collaboration with the Dutch. The strength of the uprising – we are leaving aside its military aspects here – was the rapid establishment of cooperation, even if of a tactical nature, between white Pernambucan *moradores* and refugees in Bahia, groups of African slaves and mulattoes and Indians. Incidentally, the Dutch policy towards Indians proved, after some successes in the first years of the New Holland, to be a failure (Meuwese 2012), while the black slaves were to remain where they were – as plantation slaves.[13] The lack of strong support from the Portuguese metropolis during the first phase of the uprising encouraged such local processes. The actions of the insurgents, such as accepting the participation of African slaves led into battle by a black commander, were subsequently confirmed by the crown. And at the same time, an independent Portugal, which had been fighting with Spain for survival since 1640, could not antagonise the Dutch.

---

12   In the already quoted 1645 *Parnassim* appeal, only the aid given by the Jews to the Dutch in 1644 is mentioned: thanks to their contacts, they passed on information about a pending insurrection. In response as *Parnassim* stressed, the Portuguese declared "no quarters would be given to our Nation" (Emmanuel 1955: 39). However, it is ironic that the New Christian who delivered such revelations to the *Suprema* in 1634 turned out to be an authority for some historians. The strong objections of Boxer and Novinsky as to the reliability of this informer were ignored. What is more, his revelations, especially concerning the Dutch attack of 1624, were not corroborated by Portuguese reports and other documents of the period. If such did appear, it was by Spanish authors (Falbel 2008: 108–110, Schwartz 1991: 752, 758, Groesen 2011: 175).

13   The 1637 expedition to Africa organised by Johan Maurits to cut off the Portuguese from the slave supply included many Indians, while in 1642 at Maranhão it was the Indians who, together with the Portuguese, attacked the Dutch who were trying to turn them into slaves (Meuwese 2012, Boxer 1957: 84, 146, Pijning 2006: 218). In turn, the indifferent attitude towards black slaves backfired during the battles against the *moradores*. The Portuguese were supported by troops of mulattoes and black slaves who were mobilised by the promise of liberation and salvation. These troops numbered more than 400 soldiers, i.e. 20 per cent of the total insurgents in Pernambuco (Mattos 2008: 10).

The alliance with the Republic in Europe was therefore maintained despite the war in the Atlantic. Under these conditions, therefore, the insurrection appeared as a demonstration not only of the solidarity of the Pernambucan people, but also, as a Brazilian nationalist historiography would argue, of political regionalism (Pijning 2006: 230). Its glue was the Catholic faith, hostility towards Protestants and Jews, the close association of the *moradores* elite with the sugar economy, and the rejection of the dictates of the Dutch. This last factor was often combined with a fear of reprisals over the planters' unpaid debts. Thus during the prolonged negotiations that followed the defeat of Nieuw-Holland, the Portuguese accepted in principle the demand for financial recompensation for Dutch losses:

> The Crown was in fact providing cover (...) for the former debtors and new owners of real estate and enslaved workers in Brazil. The compensation was thus a way to legalize their seizure of properties and legally absolve them of their debts. Paying the Dutch was a way to reward those who had partaken in the revolt.
>
> ODEGARD 2022: 49

It is also unsurprising that hostility to the Jews was particularly dramatically demonstrated:"in the struggle against the Catholic Portuguese, the Jews, like the Dutch, risked a military defeat, but unlike [the Dutch] in the event of falling into their hands they risked their lives" (Mello 1989: 296, also Wätjen 1921: 235, Vainfas 2012: 187f). The regionalism taking shape during the insurrection had to be by definition radical and exclusionary.

Brazil's New Christians opted for the crown. This is not surprising. Only a few *XN*s chose to return to the Jewish religion, while some reconverted and returned to Catholicism (Feitler 2011: 211, 214). The majority, about whom historians were silent until half a century ago (Novinsky 1971: 498f), made the choice by retaining their previous status. And the rapid seizure of the *várzea*, i.e. the area of Pernambuco under the sugar plantations, by the insurgents and the pushing of the Dutch to the defensive, as well as the announcements of revenge against the New Christian 'traitors', were strong incentives to accelerate decision-making. Thus, we do not find New Christians, except for a handful, among the evacuees from Recife in 1654:

> the majority of the Brazilian immigrants were the descendants of (...) Portuguese Jews from Amsterdam who had settled in Dutch Brazil. If large-scale conversions of New Christians back to Judaism took place in Brazil, their echo in these Amsterdam statistics is undetectable
>
> SWETSCHINSKI 2004: 84

The distance separating the "new Jews" returning to Europe and the Brazilian New Christians was already evident. The weakening of the Republic's economic ties with Brazil in the following years would only exacerbate this process. *La Nação* was thus entering a phase of decomposition. And Brazil itself became, after the victorious war against the Calvinists and Jews, an "even more thoroughly Roman Catholic" country; the narrow margin of de facto tolerance for the New Christians and the few Protestants that existed in the colony before 1630 was eliminated (Haefeli 2014: 130f).

The decomposition of *La Nação* was also reinforced by the confluence of factors that would emerge in Portugal: "the revolt of the planters in Netherlands Brazil marked the parting of the ways politically between the Dutch Sephardim and the New Christian merchant elite of Lisbon" (Israel 1996: 158). It is likely that this divergence was determined not so much by the insurrection itself as by the consequences of Portuguese independence. The new monarchy would almost immediately find itself between the hammer of war with Spain and the anvil of the Republic. The Dutch rejected the possibility of withdrawing from Brazil and ending the attacks that had been renewed since 1645 with a view to crippling Portuguese trade with Brazil. By the end of the 1640s, in the final phase of the negotiations that would then culminate in 1648 in the peace treaties ending the Thirty Years' War, Portugal was – except for the support of a France weakened by internal conflicts – isolated. It was also boycotted for almost 30 years by the popes, who favoured Spain, which only recognised an independent Portugal in 1668. Even relations with England were strained, for João IV made no secret of his sympathies for the defeated royalists. That one of the consequences of this confluence of events would be a split in *La Nação* was not initially realised. This was evidenced by the formation of a Portuguese trading company.

However, prior to the promulgation of the royal decree (*alvará*) creating the *Companhia Geral para o Estado do Brasil* (hereafter: *Companhia*) in March 1649, the new king was taking big steps, firstly to regain control of Angola, a strategically important Brazilian colony, and, secondly to ward off the danger threatening Bahia from the Dutch. Maintaining control over Brazil was, at the time, a condition for Portugal's survival. Without the revenue from the trade in sugar and other commodities of the colony, the financial survival of the metropolis was impossible. However, taking action in both directions meant a risky confrontation with the powerful Dutch fleet. The Portuguese were unaware that the Republic was paralysed by disputes between elites concerning its future colonial policy (Pijning 2006: 202). Defying the Dutch also required capital to quickly rebuild the Portuguese fleet. And this was in short supply.

In both cases, the solution to the lack of funds came from the Portuguese New Christians. At the request of the Jesuit Antônio Vieira, a friend of his from their time together in Bahia in 1641, and the richest New Christian banker in Lisbon, Duarte da Silva, supported by other prominent *XN*s, rapidly collected 300,000 cruzados as a loan to the king. The capital raised by the New Christians would enable two tasks to be accomplished. The first was to create a fléet to block the Dutch access to Bahia. At the end of 1647, the fleet built with the New Christians' capital, consisting of 15 ships transporting 462 nobles and 2,350 soldiers, set sail for Bahia. It fulfilled its preventive mission: the WIC decided not to frontally attack the *capitanía*. The second task was to finance an expedition to recapture Luanda from the Dutch and to rescue the Portuguese besieged in the Angolan interiors. The squadron, under the command of Salvador Correia de Sá e Benevides, navigated towards Rio de Janeiro to sail towards Angola after gathering a larger force there – 15 ships transporting 2,000 soldiers. In the autumn of 1648, Luanda was recaptured, although the Dutch still remained deeply entrenched for decades to come on the Gold Coast. Thus, "[t]he Portuguese colonial empire had been saved from collapse by the money raised from New-Christian friends by Padre Antonio Vieira–a singular if patriotic combination of Jews and Jesuits" (Boxer 1949: 481).

These examples already suggested that, in the Dutch-Portuguese clash in Brazil, many influential New Christians in Portugal on the one hand, and the Amsterdam Jews on the other, found themselves on opposite sides. The former (co-)financed the war effort of the Portuguese Crown, the latter loyally supported the Dutch and the WIC. The consequence would be a split and the formation of separate loyalties. In Portugal itself, this division within *La Nação* was complicated by the clash between the Portuguese raison d'etat and the Inquisition; for the latter was constantly on the lookout for *judaizantes* (and opportunities for confiscation). The co-creator of success in Bahia and Angola, Duarte da Silva, found himself in the hands of the Inquisition as early as December 1647. The Holy Office had its opinion on the king's use of the capital of suspected *XN*s. This was also true of other plans being developed by the king's advisers and the monarch himself (Azevedo 1922: 266). While Duarte da Silva would spend five years in the prison of the Holy Office, the verdict sentencing him to exile to Brazil was not carried out. After the death of João IV in 1656, "the Inquisition not only resumed confiscation but proceeded to collect the arrears since 1649. Altogether, Padre Vieira tells us, about 1680, they had gathered in up to that time some twenty-five million, of which not more than half a million cruzados reached the royal treasury" (Lea 1907: 282).

However, the successes achieved in Bahia and Angola were not the end of the problems. While the immediate danger threatening Portuguese Brazil was averted, Dutch efforts to cut Portugal off from the colony's resources intensified. Between 1647 and 1648, corsairs acting as the *Zeewsche kaper-directie* (Zeeland Caper Board) intercepted a large proportion (220) of Portuguese ships transporting sugar to the metropolis, but also ships supplying arms and ammunition from Portugal to insurgents and Portuguese troops. Without the sugar revenue funding, among other things, the support for the insurrection, and without the supply of arms, the *Restauração* had no chance. It is at this point that a new solution emerged: the creation of the *Companhia*.

The dominant interpetation of the history of this company in Portuguese and Jewish historiography over the decades, taken from Azevedo, has placed the Jesuit Antônio Vieira as the initiator (as early as 1644) and the New Christians as its main shareholders (Boxer 1949, Wiznitzer 1960). Before pointing out some flaws in this interpretation, we need to note a few undisputed facts.

The *Companhia* was conceived, following the model of the WIC, as an instrument of war, and its main task was to protect shipments of sugar and other goods from Brazil and the supply of European goods to the colonies. By royal decree it was given a monopoly on the export of wine, flour, olive oil and cod to the colonies, with the right to dictate the price (the slave trade was regulated separately). These privileges aroused resistance in Brazil for obvious reasons (Fonséca 2007: 114f). In turn, the compensation for the protection of Brazilian exports was the right to impose a tax on every crate of sugar, bale of cotton or sack of hides exported. The company also obtained a monopoly of the export of *pau-brasil*. The method of raising capital, as outlined by Father Vieira, assumed that its suppliers would not only be the Lisbon *XN*s, but also the New Christians scattered in Europe and the Jews of the Republic. He therefore assumed that *La Nação* as a whole would come forward in a venture aimed mainly at the Dutch and intended at defence of Portuguese interests. This was an unrealistic assumption; it referred to conditions that were already history. At the same time, in order to create an incentive for Jewish and New Christian – but also other – potential shareholders, a law was proposed that would exclude the possibility of confiscating the capital of Portuguese and foreign shareholders. It would have been included in a royal decree (*alvará*) signed before the *Companhia* was established. This would have applied even to those who were guilty of "heresy, apostasy and Judaism" or resided in countries at war with Portugal. Such a provision clearly struck at the interests of the Holy Office. So much for the traditional narrative (Boxer 1949, 1957, Smith 1974: 237f).

Critics of the traditional view have argued that the presentation of the history of the *Companhia* as a joint venture between Jesuit and New Christians, and as an institution fully controlled by the latter, is one-sided. A few remarks on this subject, therefore.

Independently of Antônio Vieira, the need for a strong trading company had also already been voiced at the Lisbon court by others. The experience of the VOC, the WIC or the English companies was widely known. In this sense, tying the idea of establishing a *Companhia* exclusively to Antônio Vieira was and is a simplification (Costa 2004: 1–3, Smith 1974: 252–254). Instead, it is significant that one of the factors inhibiting the use of these examples in Portugal was the firmly established tradition of free trade with Brazil and the dominance of transport using small caravels. Even before the promulgation of the act establishing the *Companhia*, João IV issued an order in 1648 prohibiting, with a lag of three years, the use of ships of less than 350 tonnes in trade with Brazil (Boxer 1957: 206–208).

A particularly complicated problem was that of capital shortage. On this issue, the fundamental role played by Father Vieira and the New Christians is not in doubt. The differences, compared to the traditional narrative, concern two things. Firstly, the group of 19 (originally 16) merchant-bankers who collectively made up the *Junta do Comércio* in charge of the *Companhia* was diverse: although it was composed mostly of New Christians (11), the proportion of Old Christians was significant (8, including 5 *familiares*) (Smith 1974: 240). Their presence was due to their interest in the benefits usually associated with participation in a monopolistic trade. Another important stimulus was the provision pushed by Antônio Vieira, in defiance of the Inquisition, providing immunity to protect shareholder capital. English merchants participating in Portuguese trade also took a similar position. The assurances of immunity protecting investors from arbitrary decisions therefore did not arise solely because of the interests of XN s. *Alvará* in this case reflected the joint combined interests of Old and New Christians and foreign merchants in protecting property rights. Moreover, it has been suggested that *alvará* protected all New Christians, not just shareholders in *Companhia,* from confiscation (Costa 2004: 5, 2000, Smith 1974: 253f). Secondly, although the capital of *Companhia* was largely contributed by all the major New Christian merchant-bankers in Lisbon, the total share of the seven largest families (including the arrested Duarte da Silva) amounted to just over 18 per cent. There is no information about the shareholders who contributed the majority of capital (Smith 1974: 239).

In contrast, the seminal contributions by Smith and Freite Costa did not address the collapse of Father Antônio Vieira's project in the part concerning the participation of New Christians from outside Portugal and Amsterdam Jews in the *Companhia.* The arrest in 1647 by the Inquisition of Duarte da Silva was a shock reminiscent of a *panica a Bolsa* (stock market panic) in Portugal, the Republic and elsewhere (Azevedo 1922: 265–267). This powerful merchant was, as it were, a guarantor of the credibility of Lisbon. Antônio Vieira, who held talks with Jews and New Christians in the Republic and France on behalf of the king, encountered a refusal to cooperate after Duarte da Silva's arrest. In the early 1640s, whilst a reborn Portugal was fighting Spain, Lisbon could count on the co-operation of the Sephardim in Europe: "Both in Portugal and abroad (...) Jewish capital helped the cause of independence and helped itself in fruitful operations. Loans granted by Jewish companies bought ships, ammunition, and soldiers for defence" (Marques 1976: 350, also Israel 1996: 158f). Now, only Portuguese New and Old Christians made up the company's capital. The king's hastening of the decision to create the *Companhia* signalled that he regarded the actions of the Inquisition, supported by a pope hostile to the new dynasty, as detrimental to the Portuguese raison d'état. But among the Portuguese *XN*s, too, collecting the needed capital was going badly. Many did not believe the crown and feared the Inquisition. The accumulated capital of 1.25 million cruzados was only part of the planned amount. Ultimately, the *Companhia* was to have 36 ships to protect two convoys annually on the Atlantic route. At the joint request of the Old and New Christians, shareholders in the *Companhia,* a compulsory taxation of all Portuguese New Christians was introduced in 1650. Anyhow, the actions of the *Companhia*'s ships proved effective: after 1649, the WIC greatly reduced its attacks on Portuguese convoys and in 1654 the *Compahnia* took part in recapturing Recife (Costa 2004: 4, 8, 2000: 54). The Jews of Amsterdam were no longer an issue. *La Nação* was passing into history.

By a decision of the Portuguese commander, Francisco Barreto de Meneses, the surrender of the Dutch in January 1654 took place under honourable conditions. There was also no record of robbery or violence against the inhabitants of Recife. The Dutch commanders even obtained the right to export certain quantities of *pau-brasil* as a symbolic repayment of debts incurred by the *moradores*. The Republic welcomed them less kindly. Following the surrender conditions, Amsterdam Jews were treated on a par with the Dutch Calvinists. However, the Brazilian and other *XN*s were treated differently. In case of any delay in providing the ships for transportation to the Republic, the extended term of departure would apply only to Protestants (and Amsterdam Jews) and never baptised Jews. The Portuguese commander announced that "the Jews who have been Christians, these being subject to the Holy Inquisition wherein I cannot interfere". If they wanted to save themselves, they had to leave Recife within a previously set deadline of three months. Only a few Brazilian *XN*s decided to take this step. At the same time, there is no information about their persecution in Brazil immediately after 1654 (Wiznitzer 1960: 140f., Boxer 1957: 241–243). The crackdown on Brazilian New Christians, mainly in Minas Gerais, Rio de Janeiro and Paraíba, would come a few decades later, with disastrous effects.

The Amsterdam Jews mostly returned to Europe, while 23 began the long journey north. At the beginning of September 1654 they arrived, "poor and healthy", in New York, then Dutch New Amsterdam. There they were greeted by three Ashkenazi Jews who had arrived a dozen days earlier from Amsterdam (Hershkowitz, 2005, 1–3). This was the beginning of the history of an already different diaspora, with by now no closer ties to the *La Nação* formed in the 16th-17th centuries.

References

Abbattista, Guido. 2008. "Edmund Burke, the Atlantic American War and the 'Poor Jews of St. Eustatius'," *Cyber Review of Modern Historiography (Cromohs)* No. 13.

Abreu, João Capistrano de. 1922. Editor, *Primera Visitação do Santo Officio ás partes do Brasil. Confissões da Bahia 1591–92*, São Paulo: Homenagem de Paulo Prado.

Abreu, João Capistrano de., 1997. *Chapters of Brazil's Colonial History, 1500–1800*, New York: Oxford University Press.

Abulafia, David. S.H. 1987. "Asia, Africa and the Trade of Medieval Europe," in: Michael Moissey Postan and Edward Miller, eds. *The Cambridge Economic History of Europe* Vol. II: *Trade and Industry in the Middle Ages*, Cambridge: Cambridge University Press (2nd edition).

Abu-Lughod, Janet L. 1989. *Before European Hegemony: the World System A. D. 1250–1350*, New York and Oxford: Oxford University Press.

Addison, Joseph. 1761. *The Works of the Late Right Honorable Joseph Addison, Esq*, Vol. the 3rd, Birmingham: Printed by John Baskerville, for J. and R. Tonson.

Adler, Cyrus. 1909. "A Contemporary Memorial Relating to Damages to Spanish Interests in America Done by Jews of Holland (1634)," *Publications of the Americal Jewish Historical Society* No. 17.

Aguado de los Reyes, Jesús. 2005. "El apogeo de los Judios Portugueses en la Sevilla americanista," *Cadernos de Estudos Sefarditas* No. 5.

Albert, Bat-sheva. 1990. "Isidore of Seville: His Attitude Towards Judaism and His Impact on Early Medieval Canon Law," *The Jewish Quarterly Review* Vol. 80, No. 3–4.

Alden, Dauril. 1996. *The Making of an Enterprise. The Society of Jesus in Portugal, Its Empire, and Beyond, 1540–1750*, Stanford: Stanford University Press.

Alden, Dauril. 2003. "Some Reflections on Antonio Vieira: Seventeenth-Century Troubleshooter and Troublemaker," *Luso-Brazilian Review* Vol. 40, No. 1.

Alencastro, Luiz Felipe de. 1993. "The Apprenticeship of Colonization", in: Barbara L. Solow, ed., *Slavery and the Rise of the Atlantic System*, New York: Cambridge University.

Alencastro, Luiz Felipe de. 2006. "Le versant brésilien de l'Atlantique-Sud: 1550–1850," *Annales. Histoire, Sciences Sociales* Vol. 61, No. 2.

Alencastro, Luiz Felipe de. 2013. "Portuguese Missionaries and Early Modern Antislavery and Proslavery Thought." in: Joseph M. Fradera and Christopher Schmidt-Nowara, eds., *Slavery and Antislavery in Spain's Atlantic Empire*, New York and Oxford: Berghahn Books.

Alessandrini, Nunziatella and Susana Bastos Mateus. 2015. "Italianos e cristãos-novos entre Lisboa e o império português em finais do século XVI: vinculos e parcerias comerciais." *Ammentu. Bollettino Storico e Archivistico del Mediterraneo e delle Americhe* No. 7.

Almeida, A.A. Marques de. 1997. "O Zangão e o Mel. Uma métafora sobre a diáspora sefardita e a formação das elites financeiras na Europa (séculos XV a XVII)," *Oceanos* No. 29.

Almeida Mendes, António de. 2008a. "The Foundations of the System: a Reassessment of the Slave Trade to the Spanish Americas in the Sixteenth and Seventeenth Centuries," in: David Eltis and David Richardson, eds., *Extending the Frontiers: Essays in the New Transatlantic Slave Trade Database*, New Haven and London: Yale University Press.

Almeida Mendes, António de. 2008b. "Les réseaux de la traite ibérique dans l'Atlantique nord (1440–1640)," *Annales. Histoire, Sciences Sociales* Vol. 63.

Alpert, Michael. 2001. *Crypto-Judaism and the Spanish Inquisition*, Houndmills: Palgrave.

Álvarez Nogal, Carlos. 1997. *Los banqueros de Felipe IV y los metales preciosos americanos (1621–1665)*, Banco de España Estudios de Historia Económica No. 36, Madrid.

Álvarez Nogal, Carlos. 2003. *The Role of Institutions to Solve Sovereign Debt Problem: the Spanish Monarchy's Credit (1516–1665)*, Economic History and Institutions Department Working Paper 03–08, Universidad Carlos III de Madrid, Getafe, February.

Antunes, Cátia and Filipa Ribeiro da Silva. 2011. "Cross-cultural Entrepreneurship in the Atlantic: Africans, Dutch and Sephardic Jews in Western Africa, 1580–1774," *Itinerario* Vol. 35, Issue 1.

Antunes, Cátia and Filipa Ribeiro da Silva. 2012. "Amsterdam Merchants in the Slave Trade and African Commerce, 1580s–1670s," *Tijdschrift voor Sociale en Economische Geschiedenis* Vol. 9, No. 4.

Antunes, Cátia and Filipa Ribeiro da Silva. 2015. "Portuguese Jews in Amsterdam: an Insight on Entrepreneurial Behaviour in the Dutch Republic," in: Adrian Jarvis and Robert Lee, eds., *Trade, Migration and Urban Networks in Port Cities c. 1640–1940*, Liverpool: Liverpool University Press.

Antunes, Cátia and Filipa Ribeiro da Silva, and Jessica Vance Roitman. 2015. "A War of Words: Sephardi Merchants, (Inter)national Incidents, and Litigation in the Dutch Republic, 1580–1640," *Jewish Culture and History* Vol. 16, No. 1.

Antunes, Cátia and Filipa Ribeiro da Silva, and Jessica Vance Roitman, and Ramona Negrón. 2022. "The Dutch Republic and the Spanish Slave Trade, 1580–1690," *Tijdschrift voor Sociale en Economische Geschiedenis* Vol. 19, No. 2.

Aparicio, Ángel Alloza. 2009. "Portuguese Contraband and the Closure of the Iberian Markets, 1621–1640. The Economic Roots of an Anti-Habsburg Feeling," *e-Journal of Portuguese History* Vol. 7 No. 2.

Arbell, Mordechai. 2002. *The Jewish Nation of the Caribbean: the Spanish-Portuguese Jewish Settlements in the Caribbean and the Guianas*, Jerusalem: Gefen Publishing House.

Aristotle. 1992. *Politics*, London: Penguin Books.

Assis, Angelo Adriano Faria de. 2004. *Macabéias da Colônia: criptojudaísmo feminino na Bahia – Séculos XVI–XVII*, Instituto de Ciências Humanas e Filosofia, Universidade Federal Fluminense, Niterói (PhD dissertation).

Assis, Angelo Adriano Faria de. 2007. "Os infortúnios e heresias do cristão-novo Diogo Nunes, senhor de engenho na Paraíba quinhentista nas malhas de Inquisição," *Revista Eletrônica de História de Brasil* Vol. 9, No. 2.

Aufderheide, Patricia. 1973. "True Confessions: the Inquisition and Social Attitudes in Brazil at the turn of the XVII Century," *Luso-Brazilian Review* Vol. 10, No. 2.

Augeron, Mickaël and Laurent Vidal. 2007. "Creating Colonial Brazil: the First Donatory Captaincies, or the System of Private Exclusivity (1534–1549)," in: Louis H. Roper and Bertrand Van Ruymbeke, eds., *Constructing Early Modern Empires: Proprietary Ventures in the Atlantic World, 1500–1750*, Leiden and Boston: Brill.

Austen, Ralph A. and Woodruff D. Smith. 1992. "Private Tooth Decay as Public Economic Virtue: the Slave-Sugar Triangle, Consumerism, and European Industrialization," in: Joseph E. Inikori and Stanley L. Engerman, eds., *The Atlantic Slave Trade. Effects on Economies, Societies, and Peoples in Africa, the Americas, and Europe*, Durham and London: Duke University Press.

Avni, Haim. 1992. *Judios en América: cinco siglos de historia*, Madrid: MAPFRE.

Azevedo, João Lúcio de. 1922. *História dos Christãos Novos Portugueses*, Lisboa: Livraria Clássica Editora.

Azopardo, Ildefonso Gutiérrez. 1987. "El comercio y mercado de negros esclavos en Cartagena de Indias (1533–1850)," *Quinto centenario* Vol. 12.

Bakewell, Peter. 1988. *Silver and Entrepreneurship in Seventeenth-Century Potosí. The Life and Times of Antonio López de Quiroga*, Albuquerque: University of New Mexico Press.

Bakewell, Peter, 2004. *A History of Latin America: c.1450 to the Present*, Oxford: Blackwell Publishing (2nd edition).

Bałaban, Majer. 1925. *Historja i literatura żydowska ze szczególnym uwzględnieniem historji Żydów w Polsce* Vols. II, Lwów–Warszawa–Kraków: Wydawnictwo Zakładu Narodowego imienia Ossolińskich (2nd. revised and enlarged edition).

Baroja, Julio Caro. 2000. *Los judíos en la España Moderna y Contemporánea*, T. 1, Madrid: Ediciones Istmo.

Baron, Salo Wittmayer. 1928. "Ghetto and Emancipation: Shall We Revise the Traditional View?," *The Menorah Journal* Vol. 14, No. 6 (June).

Baron, Salo Wittmayer. 1967. *A Social and Religious History of the Jews: Late Middle Ages and Era of European Expansion 1200–1650*, Vol. XII: *Economic Catalyst*, New York: Columbia University Press (2nd edition, revised and enlarged).

Baron, Salo Wittmayer. 1973. *A Social and Religious History of the Jews: Late Middle Ages and Era of European Expansion 1200–1650*, Vol. XV: *Resettlement and Exploration*, New York: Columbia University Press (2nd edition, revised and enlarged).

Barrett, Ward J. and Stuart B. Schwartz. 1975. "Comparación entre das economías azucareras coloniales: Morelos, México y Bahía, Brasil," in: Enrique Florescano, ed., *Haciendas, latifundios y plantaciones en América Latina*, México: Siglo XXI Editores.

Barros, Amândio Jorge Morais. 2005. "Oporto: the Building of a Maritime Space in the Early Modern Period," *e-Journal of Portuguese History* Vol. 3, No. 1.

Bem, Kazimierz. 2007. "'Boża sadzonka przesadzona': Holenderski Kościół Reformowany w holenderskich koloniach w Afryce i Amerykach w XVII wieku," in *Odrodzenie i Reformacja w Polsce* T. LI.

Benbassa, Esther. 1999. *Jews of France: a History from Antiquity to the Present*, Princeton: Princeton University Press.

Ben-Shalom, Ram. 2009. "The Typology of the Converso in Isaac Abravanel's Biblical Exegesis," *Jewish History* Vol. 23, No. 3.

Ben-Ur, Aviva. 2014. "Atlantic Jewish History: a Conceptual Reorientation," in: Arthur Kiron, ed., *Constellations of Atlantic Jewish History, 1555–1890: The Arnold and Deanne Kaplan Collection of Early American Judaica*, Philadelphia: University of Pennsylvania Libraries.

Ben-Ur, Aviva, 2020. *Jewish Autonomy in a Slave Society: Suriname in the Atlantic World, 1651–1825*, Philadelphia: University of Pennsylvania Press.

Bernfeld, Tirtsah Levie. 2002. "Financing Poor Relief in the Spanish–Portuguese Jewish Community in Amsterdam in the Seventeenth and Eighteenth Centuries," in: Jonathan I. Israel and Reinier Salvedra, eds., *Dutch Jewry. Its History and Secular Culture (1500–2000)*, Leiden–Boston–Köln: Brill.

Bernfeld, Tirtsah Levie. 2011. "Sephardic Women in Holland's Golden Age," in: Julia R. Lieberman, ed., *Sephardic Family Life in the Early Modern Diaspora*, Lebanon, NH: Brandeis University and University Press of New England.

Bethell, Leslie. 1984. Ed., *The Cambridge History of Latin America* Vol. I and II: *Colonial Latin America*, Cambridge: Cambridge University Press.

Bieżuńska-Małowist, Iza and Marian Małowist. 1987. *Niewolnictwo*, Warszawa: Czytelnik.

Birnbaum, Marianna D. 2003. *The Long Journey of Gracia Mendes*, Budapest: Central European University Press.

Blackburn, Robin. 2010. *The Making of New World Slavery: from the Baroque to the Modern, 1492–1800*, London and New York: Verso.

Bodian, Miriam. 1999. *Hebrews of the Portuguese Nation: Conversos and Community in Early Modern Amsterdam*, Bloomington and Indianapolis: Indiana University Press.

Bodian, Miriam. 2007. *Dying in the Law of Moses: Crypto-Jewish Martyrdom in the Iberian World*, Bloomington and Indianapolis: Indiana University Press.

Bodian, Miriam. 2008. "Hebrews of the Portuguese Nation: the Ambiguous Boundaries of Self-Definition," *Jewish Social Studies: History, Culture, Society* Vol. 15, No. 1.

Böhm, Günter. 1963. *Nuevos antecedentes para una historia de los judíos en Chile colonial*, Santiago: Editorial Universitaria S.A.

Böhm, Günter. 1992. *Los sefardíes en los dominios holandeses de América del Sur y del Caribe, 1630–1750*, Frankfurt am Main: Vervuert Verlag.

Böhm, Günter. 1998. "Los 'Portugueses' en el Nuevo Mundo," *Cuaderno Judaico*, No. 23.

Böhm, Günter. 2001. "Crypto-Jews and New Christians in Colonial Peru and Chile," in: Paolo Bernardini and Norman Fiering, eds., *The Jews and the Expansion of Europe to the West, 1450–1800*, New York and Oxford: Berghahn Books.

Bogaciovas, Marcelo Meira Amaral. 2006. *Tribulações do povo de Israel na São Paulo colonial*, Universidade de São Paulo, Departamento de História, São Paulo (M.A. thesis).

Bonciani, Rodrigo Faustinoni. 2016. "Os irmãos Coutinho na Atlântico: escravidão, governo e ascensão social no tempo da monarquia hispánica," *Revista Latino-Americana de Estudos Avançados* Vol. 1, No. 1.

Bonialian, Mariano. 2016. "La 'ropa de la China' desde Filipinas hasta Buenos Aires. Circulación, consumo, lucha corporativa, 1580–1620," *Revista de Indias* Vol. LXXVI, No. 268.

Borucki, Alex, David Eltis and David Wheat. 2015. "Atlantic History and the Slave Trade to Spanish America," *The American Historical Review* Vol. 120, No. 2.

Boxer, Charles R. 1949. "Padre António Vieira, S.J., and the Institution of the Brazil Company in 1640," *The Hispanic American Historical Review* Vol. 29, No. 4.

Boxer, Charles R. 1957. *The Dutch in Brazil, 1624–1654*, Oxford: Oxford University Press.

Boxer, Charles R. 1962. *The Golden Age of Brazil, 1695–1750. Growing Pains of the Colonial Society*, Berkeley and Los Angeles: University of California Press.

Boxer, Charles R. 1973. *Salvador de Sá e a luta pelo Brasil e Angola, 1602–1689*, São Paulo: Companhia Editora Nacional.

Boxer, Charles R. 1965. *The Dutch Seaborne Empire, 1600–1800*, London: Hutchinson.

Boyajian, James C. 1979. "The New Christians Reconsidered: Evidence from Lisbon's Portuguese Bankers,1497–1647," *Studia Rosenthaliana* Vol. 13, No. 2.

Boyajian, James C. 1983. *Portuguese Bankers at the Court of Spain, 1626–1650*, New Brunswick, NJ: Rutgers University Press.

Boyajian, James C. 1993. *Portuguese Trade in Asia under the Habsburgs, 1580–1640*, Baltimore and London: The Johns Hopkins University Press.

Boyajian, James C. 2001. "New Christians and Jews in the Sugar Trade, 1550–1750: Two Centuries of Development of the Atlantic Economy," in: Paolo Bernardini and

Norman Fiering, eds., *The Jews and the Expansion of Europe to the West, 1450–1800*, New York and Oxford: Berghahn Books.

Bradbury, Scott. 2006. "The Jews of Spain, c. 235–638," in: Steven T. Katz, ed., *The Cambridge History of Judaism* Vol. IV: *the Late Roman–Rabbinic Period*, Cambridge: Cambridge University Press.

Bradley, Peter T. 2001. "El Perú y el mundo exterior. Extranjeros, enemigos y herejes (Siglos XVI–XVII)," *Revista de Indias* Vol. LXI, Núm. 223.

Braudel, Fernand. 1995. *The Mediterranean and the Mediterranean World in the Age of Philip II*, Berkeley–Los Angeles–London: University of California Press.

Braudel, Fernand. 1982. *Civilisation and Capitalism,15th–18th Century*, Vol. II: *the Wheels of Commerce*, London: William Collins Sons & Co.

Brenner, Robert. 2003. *Merchants and Revolution. Commercial Change, Political Conflict, and London's Overseas Traders, 1550–1653*, London: Verso.

Brentano, Lujo. 1916. *Anfänge des modernen Kapitalismus*, Verlag der K.B. Akademie der Wissenschaften, München.

Brunelle, Gayle K. 2003. "Migration and Religious Identity: the Portuguese of Seventeenth-Century Rouen," *Journal of Early Modern History* Vol. 7, Nos. 3–4.

Buescu, Mircea. 2011. *Historia econômica do Brasil. Leitura básica*, Salvador: Centro de Documentação do Pensamiento Brasileiro.

Bulmer-Thomas, Victor, John H. Coatsworth and Robert Cortés Conde. 2006. Eds., *Cambridge Economic History of Latin America* Vol. 1: *the Colonial Era and the Short Nineteenth Century*, Cambridge: Cambridge University Press.

Byron, George Gordon. 1837. *Don Juan in Sixteen Cantos, with Notes*, Halifax: Milner and Sowerby.

Caldeira, Arlindo Manuel. 2015. "Angola and the Seventeeth-Century South Atlantic Slave Trade," in: Filipa Ribeiro da Silva and David Richardson, ed., *Networks and Trans-cultural Exchange: Slave Trading in the South Atlantic, 1590–1867*, Leiden and Boston: Brill.

Canabrava, Alice Piffer. 1984. *O comércio português no Rio da Prata (1580–1640)*, Belo Horizonte: Editora Itatiaia (oryg. 1942).

Cañas Pelayo and Marcos Rafael. 2016. "El acceso de los judeoconversos portugueses a los cabildos municipales andaluces. Un primer acercamiento," *Mediterranea – ricerche storiche* T. 13.

Cardim, Pedro. 2004. "O governo e a administração do Brasil sob os Habsburgo e os primeiros Bragança," *Hispania* Vol. LXIV No. 1.

Carmagnani, Marcello. 2011. *The Other West: Latin America from Invasion to Globalization*, Berkeley: University of California Press.

Carrasco Vázquez, Jesús Antonio. 2004. *La minoria judeoconversa en la época del Comte Duque de Olivares. Auge y Ocaso de Juan Núñez Saravia (1585–1639)*, Faculdad de

Filosofía y Letras, Departamento de Historia II, Universidad de Alcalá, Madrid (PhD dissertation).

Carrasco Vázquez, Jesús Antonio. 2005. *El relevante papel económico de los conversos portugueses en la privanza del Duque de Lerma (1600–1606)*, Comunicación presentada al XXV Encontro de APHES, Évora, 18–19 November.

Casado Alonso, Hilario. 1997. "De la judería a la grandeza de España. La trayectoria de la familia de mercaderes de los Bernuy (siglos XIV–XIX)," *Boletín de la Institución Fernán González* (Burgos) Año 76, No. 215.

Castilla Palma, Norma Angélica. 2016. "Las estrategias del contrabando de esclavos en Nueva España: arribadas maliciosas y demasía con bambos y muleques; el caso del navío "Monserrat y San Antonio", 1636," *Relaciones. Estudios de historia y sociedad* Vol. XXXVII, Núm. 145.

Ceballos, Rodrigo. 2007. *Arribadas Portuguesas: a participação luso-brasileira na constituição social de Buenos Aires (c. 1580–1650)*, Departamento de Historia do Instituto de Ciências Humanas e Filosofia, Universidade Federal Fluminense, Rio de Janeiro (PhD dissertation).

Ceballos, Rodrigo. 2014. "Os vecinos lusitanos na restauração portuguesa: um estudo das redes sociais na Buenos Aires sescentista," *MÉTIS: história & cultura* Vol. 12 No. 25.

Ceballos, Rodrigo. 2016. "Da União à Restauração: considerações sobre o comércio, a administração e os lusitanos na Buenos Aires seiscentista," *Revista Escuela de História* Vol. 15, No. 2.

Chargas, E.C.R.B. das. 2009. "O clima de intolerância religiosa en Pernambuco," in: Helena Lewin, ed., *Judaismo e modernidade: suas múltiplas inter-relações*, Rio de Janeiro: Centro Edelstein de Pesquisas Sociais (online).

Clayton, Lawrence A. 2012. *Bartolomé de Las Casas: a Biography*, New York: Cambridge University Press.

Coates, Timothy J. 2001. *Convicts and Orphans. Forced and State-sponsored Colonizers in the Portuguese Empire, 1550–1755*, Stanford: Stanford University Press.

Coelho, António Borges. 1995. "O mercantilista Duarte Gomes Solis: análises e modelos dirigidos ao governo filipino," *ARQUIPÉLAGO. História* (2a série) Vol. 1, No. 1.

Cohen, Martin A. 1992. "The Sephardic Phenomenon: a Reappraisal," *American Jewish Archives* Vol. 44, No. 1.

Cohen, Robert. 1991. *Jews in Another Environment: Surinam in the Second Half of the Eighteenth Century*, Leiden: Brill.

Columbus, Christopher. 1893. *Journal of Christopher Columbus (during his first voyage, 1492–93), and Documents Relating to the Voyages of John Cabot and Gaspar Corte Real*, edited and translated by Clements R. Markham, London: Hakluyt Society.

Contreras, Jaime. 1996. "Domínguez Ortiz y la historiografía sobre judeoconversos," *Manuscrits. Revista d'Història Moderna* No. 14.

Cortés López, José Luis. 1989. "El esclavo negro, colonizador de América, a tráves de las capitulaciones de Indias del siglo XVI," *Studia Historica. Historia Moderna* No. 7.

Cortés López, José Luis. 1995. "1544–1550: el período más prolífico en la exportación de esclavos durante el s. XVI," *Espacio, Tiempo y Forma,* Serie IV. *Historia Moderna* No. 8.

Costa, Leonor Freire. 2000. "Pernambuco e a Companhia Geral do Comércio do Brasil," *Penélope* No. 23.

Costa, Leonor Freire. 2004. "Merchant Groups in the 17th-century Brazilian Sugar Trade: Reappraising Old Topics with New Research Insights," *e-Journal of Portuguese History* Vol. 2 No. 1.

Costa, Leonor Freire. and Pedro Lains and Susana Münch Miranda. 2016. *An Economic History of Portugal, 1143–2010,* Cambridge: Cambridge University Press.

Costigan, Lúcia Helena. 2010. *Through Cracks in the Wall: Modern Inquisitions and New Christian Letrados in the Iberian Atlantic World,* Leiden and Boston: Brill.

Crailsheim, Eberhard. 2016. *The Spanish Connection: French and Flemish Merchant Networks in Seville (1570–1650),* Köln–Weimar–Wien: Böhlau Verlag.

Crespi, Liliana. 2000. "Contrabando de esclavos en el puerto de Buenos Aires durante el siglo XVII. Complicidad de los funcionarios reales," Desmemorias. Revista de Historia Vol. 7, No. 26.

Crespo Solana, Ana. 2014. "Diasporas and the Integration of 'Merchant Colonies:' Flemish and Dutch Networks in Early Modern Spain," *Le Verger: Revue en ligne – Bouquet Histoire* No. 5, January.

Cross, Harry E. 1978. "Commerce and Orthodoxy: a Spanish Response to Portuguese Commercial Penetration in the Viceroyalty of Peru, 1580–1640," *The Americas* Vol. 35, No. 2.

Curtin, Philip D. 1969. *The Atlantic Slave Trade: a Census,* Madison, Wisconsin: The University of Wisconsin Press.

Curtin, Philip D. 1990. *The Rise and Fall of the Plantation Complex. Essays in Atlantic History,* Cambridge: Cambridge University Press.

Dale, Alfred William Winterslow. 1882. *The Synod of Elvira and Christian Life in the Fourth Century. A Historical Essay,* London: Macmillan and Co.

Davis, David Brion. 1966. *The Problem of Slavery in Western Culture,* Ithaca, N.Y.: Cornell University Press.

Davis, Nicholas Darnell. 1909. "Notes on the History of the Jews in Barbados," *Publications of the American Jewish Historical Society* No. 18.

Davis, Ralph. 1973. *The Rise of the Atlantic Economies,* London: Weidenfeld and Nicholson.

Davis, Robert C. 2004. *Christian Slaves, Muslim Masters. White Slavery in the Mediterranean, the Barbary Coast, and Italy, 1500–1800,* New York: Palgrave/Macmillan.

Delgado Ribas, Josep M. 2013. "The Slave Trade in the Spanish Empire (1501–1808): The Shift from Periphery to Center," in: Joseph M. Fradera and Christopher Schmidt-Nowara, eds., *Slavery and Antislavery in Spain's Atlantic Empire*, New York and Oxford: Berghahn Books.

Diago Hernando, Máximo. 2014. "El ascenso de los judeoconversos al amparo de la alta nobleza en Castilla después de 1492: el caso de Almazán," *Sefarad* Vol. 74, No. 1.

Diégues Júnior, Manuel. 2006. *O engenho de açuar no Nordeste*, Maceío: EDUFAL.

Domínguez Ortiz, Antonio. 1971. *Los judeoconversos en España y América*, Madrid: Ediciones Istmo.

Domínguez Ortiz, Antonio. 1999. "Réplica amistosa a Benzion Netanyahu," *Revista de la Inquisición* No. 8.

Drescher, Seymour. 2001. "Jews and New Christians in the Atlantic Slave Trade," in: Paolo Bernardini and Norman Fiering, eds., *The Jews and the Expansion of Europe to the West, 1450–1800*, New York and Oxford: Berghahn Books.

Drescher, Seymour. 2004. "White Atlantic? The Choice for African Slave Labor in the Plantation Americas," in: David Eltis, Frank D. Lewis and Kenneth L. Sokoloff, eds., *Slavery in the Development of the Americas*, New York: Cambridge University Press.

Dubin, Lois. 2006. "Introduction: Port Jews in the Atlantic World," *Jewish History* Vol. 20, No. 2.

Durán, Reyes Fernández. 2011. *La corona española y el tráfico de negros: del monopolio al libre comercio*, Madrid: Ecobook–Editorial Economista.

Dutra, Francis A. 2003. "The Vieira Family and th Order of Christ," *Luso-Brazilian Review* Vol. 40, No. 1.

Ebert, Christopher. 2003. "Dutch Trade with Brazil before the Dutch West India Company, 1587–1623," in: Johannes Postma and Victor Enthoven, eds., *Riches from Atlantic Commerce: Dutch Transatlantic Trade and Shipping, 1585–1817*, Leiden and Boston: Brill.

Ebert, Christopher. 2008. *Between Empires. Brazilian Sugar in the Early Atlantic Economy, 1550–1630*, Leiden and Boston: Brill.

Ebert, Christopher. 2011. "Early Modern Atlantic Trade and the Development of Maritime Insurance to 1630," *Past and Present* No. 213.

Edel, Matthew. 1969. *The Brazilian Sugar Cycle of the Seventeenth Century and the Rise of West Indian Competition*, "Caribbean Studies" Vol. 9, No. 1.

Elkin, Judith Laikin. 2014. *The Jews of Latin America*, Boulder: Lynne Rienner Publishers.

Elliott, John H. 2006. *Empires of the Atlantic World: Britain and Spain in America, 1492–1830*, New Haven and London: Yale University Press.

Eltis, David. 2000. *The Rise of African Slavery in the Americas*, New York: Cambridge University Press.

Eltis, David. 2002. "Free and Coerced Migrations from the Old World to the New," in: David Eltis, ed., *Coerced and Free Migration: Global Perspectives*, Stanford: Stanford University Press.

Eltis, David and David Richardson. 2008. "A New Assessment of the Transatlantic Slave Trade," in: David Eltis, David Richardson, ed., *Extending the Frontiers: Essays in the New Transatlantic Slave Trade Database*, New Haven and London: Yale University Press.

Emmanuel, Isaac S. 1955. "New Light on Early American Jewry. Fortunes and Misfortunes of the Jews in Brazil (1630–1654)," *American Jewish Archives*, Vol. 7 No.1.

Emmanuel, Isaac S. 1962. "Seventeenth-Century Brazilian Jewry: a Critical Review," *American Jewish Archives* Vol. 14, No. 1.

Emmer, Peter C. 1993. "The Dutch and the Making of the Second Atlantic System," in: Barbara L. Solow, ed., *Slavery and the Rise of the Atlantic System*, New York: Cambridge University Press.

Emmer, Peter C. 2001. "The Jewish Moment and the Two Expansion Systems in the Atlantic, 1580–1650," in: Paolo Bernardini and Norman Fiering, ed., *The Jews and the Expansion of Europe to the West, 1450–1800*, New York and Oxford: Berghahn Books.

Emmer, Peter C. 2003. "The First Global War: The Dutch versus Iberia in Asia, Africa and the New World, 1590–1609," e-*Journal of Portuguese History* Vol. 1 No. 1.

Emmer, Peter C. 2006a. *The Dutch Slave Trade, 1500–1850*, New York and Oxford: Berghahn Books.

Emmer, Peter C. 2006b. "The Dutch and the Atlantic Challenge, 1600–1800," in: Peter C. Emmer, O. Pétré-Grenouilleau and J.V. Roitman, ed., *A Deus ex Machina Revisited. Atlantic Colonial Trade and European Economic Development*, Leiden and Boston: Brill.

Endelman, Todd M. 2002. *Jews of Modern Britain, 1650–2000*, Berkeley: University of California Press.

Engels, Marie-Christine. 1997. *Merchants, Interlopers, Seamen and Corsairs. The 'Flemish' Community in Livorno and Genoa (1615–1635)*, Hilversum: Uitgeverij Verloren.

Enthoven, Victor. 2003a. "Early Dutch Expansion in the Atlantic Region, 1585–1621," in: Johannes M. Postma and Victor Enthoven, ed., *Riches from Atlantic Commerce: Dutch Transatlantic Trade and Shipping, 1585–1817*, Leiden and Boston: Brill.

Enthoven, Victor. 2003b. "An Assessment of Dutch Transatlantic Commerce, 1585–1817," in: Johannes M. Postma and Victor Enthoven, ed., *Riches from Atlantic Commerce: Dutch Transatlantic Trade and Shipping, 1585–1817*, Leiden and Boston: Brill.

Enthoven, Victor. 2012. "'That Abominable Nest of Pirates.' St. Eustatius and the North Americans, 1680–1780," *Early American Studies: an Interdisciplinary Journal* Vol. 10, No. 2.

Estatuto-Sentencia. 2008. Wolf, Kenneth B. "Sentencia-Estatuto de Toledo, 1449." Medieval Texts in Translation, 2008. Web. 22 May 2009. ganilup.googlepages.com.

Falbel, Nachman. 1999. "Sobre a presença dos cristãos-novos na capitania de São Vicente e a formação da etnia paulista," *Revista USP* No. 41.

Falbel, Nachman. 2008. *Judeus no Brasil: estudos e notas*, São Paulo: Humanitas/EDUSP.

Faur, José. 1992. *In the Shadow of History. Jews and Conversos at the Dawn of Modernity*, Albany, NY: State University of New York Press.

Feitler, Bruno. 2009. "Jews and New Christians in Dutch Brazil, 1630–1654," in: Richard L. Kagan and Philip D. Morgan, eds., *Atlantic Diasporas: Jews, Conversos, and Crypto-Jews in the Age of Mercantilism, 1500–1800*, Baltimore: The Johns Hopkins University Press.

Feitler, Bruno. 2011. "Four Chapters in the History of Crypto-Judaism in Brazil: the Case of the Northeastern New Christians (17th – 21st Centuries)," *Jewish History* Vol. 25, No. 2.

Fernández Chaves, Manuel F. and Rafael M. Pérez García. 2010. "Las redes de la trata negrera: mercaderes portugueses y tráfico de esclavos en Sevilla (c. 1560–1580)," in: Aurelia Martín Casares and Margarita García Barranco, eds., *La esclavitud negroafricana en la historia de España Siglos XVI y XVII*, Granada: Editorial Comares.

Fernández Chaves, Manuel F. and Rafael M. Pérez García. 2012. "La penetración económica portuguesa en la Sevilla del siglo XVI," *Espacio, Tiempo y Forma*, Serie IV. Historia Moderna No. 25.

Fernández Chaves, Manuel F. and Rafael M. Pérez García. 2016. "La élite mercantil judeoconversa andaluza y la articulación de la trata negrera hacia las Indias de Castilla, ca. 1518–1560," *Hispania* Vol. LXXVI, No. 253.

Ferraz, Socorro. 2008. "Sesmarías do açúcar. Sítios históricos," *Clio –Série Revista de Pesquisa Histórica* Vol. 26, No. 2.

Findlay, Ronald and Kevin H. O'Rourke. 2007. *Power and Plenty. Trade, War, and the World Economy in the Second Millennium*, Princeton; Princeton University Press.

Fischer, Lucia Frattarelli. 2011. "O processo de nobilitação dos Ximenes na Toscana," *Cadernos de Estudos Sefarditas* No. 10–11.

Fisher, John R. 1997. *The Economic Aspects of Spanish Imperialism in America, 1492–1810*, Liverpool: Liverpool University Press.

Flory, Rae and David Grant Smith. 1978. "Bahian Merchants and Planters in the Seventeenth and Early Eighteenth Centuries," *The Hispanic American Historical Review* Vol. 58, No. 4.

Foa, Anna. 2000. *The Jews of Europe after the Black Death*, Berkeley and Los Angeles: University of California Press.

Fonséca, Humberto José. 2007. "Comerciantes e cristão-novos em festa de nobre: a transgressão do ordem 'natural'," *Politeia* Vol. 7, No. 1.

Fortune, Stephen Alexander. 1984. *Merchants and Jews: the Struggle for British West Indian Commerce, 1650–1750*, Gainesville: University of Florida Press.

Friedman, Saul S. 1998. *Jews and the American Slave Trade*, New Brunswick and London: Transaction Publishers.

Furtado, Celso. 1971. *The Economic Growth of Brazil. A Survey from Colonial to Modern Times*, Berkeley and Los Angeles: University of California Press.

Garcia-Arenal, Mercedes and Gerard Wiegers. 2003. *A Man of Three Worlds: Samuel Pallache, a Moroccan Jew in Catholic and Protestant Europe*, Baltimore and London: The Johns Hopkins University Press.

García Fuentes, Lutgardo. 1982. "Licencias para la introducción de esclavos en Indias y envios desde Sevilla en el siglo XVI", *Jahrbuch für Geschichte von Staat, Wirtschaft und Gesellschaft Lateinamerikas* Vol. 19.

Gasch-Tomás, José L. 2019. *The Atlantic World and the Manila Galleons. Circulation, Market, and Consumption of Asian Goods in the Spanish Empire, 1565– 1650*, Leiden and Boston: Brill.

Gelman, Jorge Daniel. 1987. "Economia natural–economia monetaria.Los grupos dirigents de Buenos Aires a principios del Siglo XVII", *Anuario de Estudios Americanos* Vol. 44.

Gieysztor, Aleksander. 1987. "Trade and Industry in Eastern Europe before 1200," in: Michael Moissey Postan and Edward Miller, eds. *The Cambridge Economic History of Europe* Vol. II: *Trade and Industry in the Middle Ages*, Cambridge: Cambridge University Press (2nd edition).

Gil, Moshe. 2004. *Jews in Islamic Countries in the Middle Ages*, Leiden and Boston: Brill.

Giménez Carrillo, Domingo Marcos. 2011. "El oficio de linajudo. Extorsión en torno a hábitos de órdenes militares en Sevilla en el siglo XVII", *Chronica Nova* No. 37.

Gitlitz, David M. 2002. *Secrecy and Deceit: the Religion of the Crypto-Jews*, Albuquerque: University of New Mexico Press.

Go, Sabine. 2009. *Marine Insurance in the Netherlands, 1600–1870: a Comparative Institutional Approach*, Amsterdam: Aksant Academic Publishers.

Goldenberg, David M. 1997. "The Curse of Ham: a Case of Rabbinic Racism?", in: Jack Salzman and Cornel West, eds., *Struggles in the Promised Land*, New York: Oxford University Press.

Goldenberg, David M. 2003. *The Curse of Ham: Race and Slavery in Early Judaism, Christianity, and Islam*, Princeton: Princeton University Press.

Gollan, Agustin Zapata. 1940. *Caminos de America*, Santa Fe: Departamento de Estudios Etnográficos y Coloniales del Ministerio de Instrucción Publica y Fomento.

Gonçalves, Regina Célia. 2007. "Guerra e açúcar: a formação da elite política na Capitania da Paraíba (séculos XVI e XVII)", in: Carla Mary S. Oliveira and Ricardo Pinto de Medeiros, eds., *Novos olhares sobre as capitanias do Norte do Estado do Brasil*, João Pessoa: Editora Universitária/UFPB.

Gorenstein, Linda. 2005. *A Inquisição contra as mulheres: Rio de Janeiro, séculos XVII e XVIII*, São Paulo: Associação Editorial Humanitas.

Gorenstein, Linda. and Carlos Eduardo Calaça. 2005. "Na cidade e nos estaus: cristãos-novos do Rio de Janeiro (séculos XVII–XVIII)", in: Maria Luiza Tucci Carneiro and Lina Gorenstein, eds., *Ensaios sobre a intolerância: inquisição, marranismo e anti-semitismo*, São Paulo: Associação Editorial Humanitas.

Gottheil, Richard J.H. 1917. *Belmont–Belmonte Family. A Record of Four Hundred Years*, New York: Privately Printed.

Graetz, Heinrich. 1894. *History of the Jews* Vol. IV, Philadelphia: Jewish Publication Society of America.

Gray, Richard. 2010. "The Papacy and the Atlantic Slave Trade: Lourenço da Silva, the Capuchins, and the Decisions of the Holy Office", in: Laurent Dubois and Julius S. Scott, eds., *Origins of the Black Atlantic*, New York and London: Routledge.

Graizbord, David L. 2004. *Souls in Dispute: Converso Identities in Iberia and the Jewish Diaspora, 1580–1700*, Philadelphia: University of Pennsylvania Press.

Graizbord, David L. 2006. "Inquisitorial Ideology at Work in an Auto de Fe, 1680: Religion in the Context of Proto-Racism," *Journal of Early Modern History* Vol. 10, Issue 4.

Graizbord, David L. 2013. "Who and What was a Jew? Some Considerations for the Historical Study of New Christians," *Anais de História de Além-Mar* Vol. XIV.

Green, Tobias. 2007. *Masters of Difference: Creolization and the Jewish Presence in Cabo Verde, 1492–1672*, Centre of West African Studies, University of Birmingham (PhD dissertation).

Green, Tobias. 2011. "Building Slavery in the Atlantic World: Atlantic Connections and the Changing Institution of Slavery in Cabo Verde, Fiteenth-Sixteenth Centuries," *Slavery and Abolition* Vol. 32, No. 2.

Green, Tobias. 2012a. *The Rise of the Trans-Atlantic Slave Trade in Western Africa, 1300–1589*, Cambridge: Cambridge University Press.

Green, Tobias. 2012b. "Policing the Empires: a Comparative Perspective on the Institutional Trajectory of the Inquisition in the Portuguese and Spanish Overseas Territories (Sixteenth and Seventeenth Centuries)," *Hispanic Research Journal* Vol. 13 No. 1.

Green, Tobias. 2015. "The Role of the Portuguese Trading Posts in Guinea and Angola in the "Apostasy" of Crypto-Jews in the 17th Century," in: Philip J. Havik and Malyn Newitt, eds., *Creole Societies in the Portuguese Colonial Empire*, Newcastle upon Tyne: Cambridge Scholars Publishing.

Greenfeld, Liah. 2001. *The Spirit of Capitalism. Nationalism and Economic Growth*, Cambridge, Mass.: Harvard University Press.

Greenleaf, Richard E. 1988. "The Great Visitas of the Mexican Holy Office, 1645–1669," *The Americas* Vol. 44, No. 4.

Greif, Avner. 1993. "Contract Enforceability and Economic Institutions in Early Trade: the Maghribi Traders' Coalition," *The American Economic Review* Vol. 83, No. 3.

Greyerz, Kaspar von. 2008. *Religion and Culture in Early Modern Europe, 1500–1800*, New York: Oxford University Press.

Groesen, Michiel van. 2011. "Lessons Learned: the Second Dutch Conquest of Brazil and the Memory of the First," *Colonial Latin American Review* Vol. 20, No. 2.

Groesen, Michiel van. 2017. *Amsterdam's Atlantic Print Culture and the Making of Dutch Brazil,* Philadelphia: University of Pennsylvania Press.

Haefeli, Evan. 2014. "Breaking the Christian Atlantic: the Legacy of Dutch Tolerance in Brazil," in: Michiel van Groessen, ed., *The Legacy of Dutch Brazil*, New York: Cambridge University Press.

Hanke, Lewis. 1961. "The Portuguese in Spanish America, with Special Reference to the Villa Imperial de Potosi," *Revista de Historia de América* No. 51.

Hanson, Carl A. 1981. *Economy and Society in Baroque Portugal, 1668–1703*, Minneapolis: University of Minnesota Press.

Helmer, Marie. 1953. "Comércio e contrabando entre a Bahia e Potosi no Século XVI," *Revista de História* Vol. 7, No. 15.

Hering Torres, Max Sebastian. 2003. "'Limpieza de sangre': ¿Racismo en la Edad Moderna?," *Tiempos Modernos: Revista Electrónica de Historia Moderna* Vol. 4, No. 9.

Hershkowitz, Leo. 2005. "By Chance or Choice: Jews in New Amsterdam 1654," *American Jewish Archives Journal* Vol. 57, Nos. 1–2.

Herzog, Tamar. 2003. *Defining Nations: Immigrants and Citizens in Early Modern Spain and Spanish America*, New Haven and London: Yale University Press.

Hicks, Mary E. 2017. "Financing the Luso-Atlantic Slave Trade, 1500–1840," *Journal of Global Slavery* Vol. 2, Issue 3.

Hirschman, Albert O. 1970. *Exit, Voice and Loyalty. Responses to Decline in Firms, Organizations, and States*, Cambridge, Mass.: Harvard University Press.

Hoberman, Louisa Schell. 1977. "Merchants in Seventeenth-Century Mexico City: a Preliminary Portrait," *The Hispanic American Historical Review* Vol. 57, No. 3.

Hoberman, Louisa Schell. 1991. *Mexico's Merchant Elite, 1590–1660. Silver, State, and Society*, Durham and London: Duke University Press.

Hoetink, Harmannus. 1973. *Slavery and Race Relations in the Americas. An Inquiry into Their Nature and Nexus*, New York: Harper Torchbooks.

Holo, Joshua. 2009. *Byzantine Jewry in the Mediterranean Economy*, New York: Cambridge University Press.

Hondius, Dienke. 2008. "Black Africans in Seventeenth-Century Amsterdam," *Renaissance and Reformation* Vol. 31, No. 2.

Hordes, Stanley M. 1982a. "The Inquisition as Economic and Political Agent: the Campaign of the Mexican Holy Office against the Crypto-Jews in the Mid-Seventeenth Century," *The Americas* Vol. 39, No. 1.

Hordes, Stanley M. 1982b. "Historiographical Problems in the Study of the Inquisition and the Mexican Crypto-Jews in the Seventeenth Century," *American Jewish Archives* Vol. XXXIV, No. 2.

Hordes, Stanley M. 2005. *To the End of the Earth: a History of the Crypto-Jews of New Mexico*, New York: Columbia University Press.

Hühner, Leon. 1905. "Isaac de Pinto. A Noted European Publicist and Defender of Great Britain's Policy during the American Revolution," *Publications of the American Jewish Historical Society* No. 13.

Hutz, Ana. 2008. *Os cristãos novos portugueses no tráfico de escravos para América espanhola (1580–1640)*, Instituto de Economia, Universidad Estadual de Campinas, Campinas (MA thesis).

Hutz, Ana. 2014. *Homens de Nação e de Negócio: redes comerciais no Mundo Ibérico (1580–1640)*, Departamento de História, Universidade de São Paulo, São Paulo (PhD dissertation).

Huussen, Arend H. 2002. "The Legal Position of the Jews in the Dutch Republic c. 1591–1796," in: Jonathan I. Israel and Reinier Salvedra, eds., *Dutch Jewry. Its History and Secular Culture (1500–2000)*, Leiden–Boston–Köln: Brill.

Ingram, Kevin. 2006. *Secret Lives, Public Lies: the Conversos and Socio-Religious Non-Conformism in the Spanish Golden Age*, University of California San Diego (PhD dissertation).

Ingram, Kevin. 2009. "Historiography, Historicity and the Conversos," in: Kevin Ingram, ed., *The Conversos and Moriscos in Late Medieval Spain and Beyond, Vol. 1: Departures and Change*, Leiden and Boston: Brill.

Israel, Jonathan I. 1984. "An Amsterdam Jewish Merchant of the Golden Age: Jeronimo Nunes da Costa (1620–1697), Agent of Portugal in the Dutch Republic," *Studia Rosenthaliana* Vol. 18, No. 1.

Israel, Jonathan I. 1989. "Menasseh ben Israel and the Dutch Sephardic Colonization Movement of the Mid-Seventeenth Century (1645–1657)," in Yosef Kaplan et al., eds., *Menasseh ben Israel and his World*, Leiden: E.J. Brill, in Jonathan Schorsch, *Swimming the Christian Atlantic: Judeoconversos, Afroamericans and Amerindians in the Seventeenth Century*, Leiden: Brill 2009.

Israel, Jonathan I. 1989. *Dutch Primacy in World Trade, 1585–1740*, Oxford: Oxford University Press.

Israel, Jonathan I. 1990a. *Empires and Entrepots: The Dutch, the Spanish Monarchy and the Jews, 1585–1713*, London: The Hambledon Press.

Israel, Jonathan I. 1990b. "Dutch Sephardi Jewry, Millenarian Politics, and the Struggle for Brazil (1640–1654)," in: David J. Katz and Jonathan I. Israel, eds., *Sceptics, Millenarians and Jews*, Leiden–New York–København–Köln: E.J. Brill.

Israel, Jonathan I. 1995. *The Dutch Republic: Its Rise, Greatness, and Fall 1477–1806*, New York: Oxford University Press.

Israel, Jonathan I. 1996. *Conflicts of Empires: Spain, the Low Countries and the Struggle for World Supremacy, 1585–1713,* London: Hambledon Press.

Israel, Jonathan I. 1998. *European Jewry in the Age of Mercantilism, 1550–1750,* Oxford and Porland: The Littman Library of Jewish Civilization.

Israel, Jonathan I. 2001. "The Jews of Dutch America," in: Paolo Bernardini and Norman Fiering, eds., *The Jews and the Expansion of Europe to the West, 1450–1800,* New York and Oxford: Berghahn Books.

Israel, Jonathan I. 2002a. *Diasporas within a Diaspora: Jews, Crypto-Jews and the World Maritime Empires (1540 –1740),* Leiden–Boston–Köln: Brill.

Israel, Jonathan I. 2002b. "Introduction," in: Jonathan I. Israel and Reiner Salvedra, eds., *Dutch Jewry. Its History and Secular Culture (1500–2000),* Leiden, Boston, Koln: Brill.

Israel, Jonathan I. 2002c. "Philosophy, Commerce, and the Synagogue: Spinoza's Expulsion from the Amsterdam Portuguese Jewish Community in 1656," in: Jonathan I. Israel and Reiner Salvedra, eds., *Dutch Jewry. Its History and Secular Culture (1500–2000),* Leiden, Boston, Koln: Brill.

Israel, Jonathan I. 2009. "Jews and Crypto-Jews in the Atlantic World Systems, 1500–1800," in: Richard L. Kagan and Philip D. Morgan, eds., *Atlantic Diasporas: Jews, Conversos, and Crypto-Jews in the Age of Mercantilism, 1500–1800,* Baltimore: The Johns Hopkins University Press.

Israel, Jonathan I. and Stuart B. Schwartz. 2007. *The Expansion of Tolerance. Religion in Dutch Brazil (1624–1654),* Amsterdam: Amsterdam University Press.

Jacobs, Joseph. 1919. *Jewish Contributions to Civilization. An Estimate,* Philadelphia: The Jewish Publication Society of America.

Jameson, J. Franklin. 1903. "St. Eustatius in the American Revolution," *The American Historical Review* Vol. 8, No. 4.

Johnson, Harold B. 1999. "The Leasing of Brazil, 1502–1515: a Problem Solved?," *The Americas* Vo. 55, No. 3.

Jordaan, Han, Victor Wilson. 2014. "The Eighteenth-Century Danish, Dutch and Swedish Free Ports in the Northeastern Carribean: Continuity and Change," in: Gert Oostindie and Jessica V. Roitman, eds., *Dutch Atlantic Connections, 1680–1800. Linking Empires, Bridging Borders,* Leiden and Boston: Brill.

Kamen, Henry. 2003. *Empire: How Spain Became a World Power, 1492–1763,* New York: HarperCollins.

Kamen, Henry. 2005. *Golden Age Spain,* New York: PalgraveMacmillan.

Kaplan, Yosef. 1992. "La Diaspora Judeo-Española-Portuguesa en el siglo XVII: Tradición, Cambio y Modernización," *Manuscrits* No. 10.

Kaplan, Yosef. 1994. "Wayward New Christians and Stubborn New Jews: the Shaping of a Jewish Identity," *Jewish History* Vol. 8, No. 1–2.

Kaplan, Yosef. 1999. "An Alternative Path to Modernity: The Sephardi Jews of Amsterdam in Early Modern Times," in: James E. Force and David S. Katz, eds.,

Everything Connects: in Conference with Richard H. Popkin. Essays in His Honor, Leiden-Boston-Köln: Brill.

Kaplan, Yosef. 2001. "Gente política: the Portuguese Jews of Amsterdam vis-à-vis Dutch Society," in: Chaya Brasz and Yosef Kaplan, eds., *Dutch Jew as Perceived by Themselves and by Other*, Leiden–Boston–Köln: Brill.

Kaplan, Yosef. 2008. "Amsterdam, the Forbidden Lands, and the Dynamics of the Sephardic Diaspora," in: Yosef Kaplan, ed., *The Dutch Intersection: the Jews and the Netherlands in Modern History*, Leiden and Boston: Brill.

Karp, Jonathan. 2010. "Can Economic History Date the Inception of Jewish Modernity?," in: Gideon Reuveni and Sarah Wobick-Segev, eds., *The Economy in Jewish History: New Perspectives on the Interrelationsip between Ethnicity and Economic Life*, New York and Oxford: Berghahn Books.

Katz, Jacob. 1962. *Exclusiveness and Tolerance. Jewish-Gentile Relations in Medieval and Modern Times*, New York: Schocken Books.

Kayserling, Meyer. 1894. *Christopher Columbus and the Participation of the Jews in the Spanish and Portuguese Discoveries*, New York: Longmans, Green, and Co.

Kellenbenz, Hermann. 1964. "Einige Aspekte der frühen Wirtschafts- und Sozialgeschichte des Nordostens von Brasilien," *Jahrbuch für Geschichte von Staat, Wirtschaft und Gesellschaft Lateinamerikas* Vol. 1.

Kieniewicz, Jan. 1976. *Portugalczycy w Azji XV–XX wiek*, Wrocław: Ossolineum.

Klein, Herbert S. 1986. *African Slavery in Latin America and the Caribbean*, New York: Oxford University Press.

Klein, Herbert S. 2004. *The Atlantic Slave Trade to 1650*, in: Stuart B. Schwartz, ed., *Tropical Babylons: Sugar and the Making of the Atlantic World, 1450–1680*, Chapel Hill and London: The University of North Carolina Press.

Klener, Julien. 1998. "Introduction: Spanish Jewry at the Eve of the Expulsion," in: Luc Degueker and Werner Verbeke, eds., *The Expulsion of the Jews and Their Migration to the Southern Low Countries (15th–16th C.)*, Louvain: Leuven University Press.

Klooster, Wim. 1997. "Contraband Trade by Curaçao's Jews with Countries of Idolatry, 1660–1800," *Studia Rosenthaliana* Vol. 31, No. 1–2.

Klooster, Wim. 2001. "Sephardic Migration and the Growth of European Long-Distance Trade," *Studia Rosenthaliana* Vol. 35, No. 2.

Klooster, Wim. 2003. "An Overview of Dutch Trade with the Americas, 1600–1800," in: Johannes M. Postma and Victor Enthoven, eds., *Riches from Atlantic Commerce: Dutch Transatlantic Trade and Shipping, 1585–1817*, Leiden and Boston: Brill.

Klooster, Wim. 2006. "Communities of Port Jews and Their Contacts in the Dutch Atlantic World," *Jewish History* Vol. 20, No. 2.

Klooster, Wim. 2009a. "Inter-Imperial Smuggling in the Americas, 1600–1800," in: Bernard Bailyn and Patricia L. Denault, eds., *Soundings in Atlantic History*.

Latent Structures and Intellectual Currents, 1500–1830, Cambridge, MA: Harvard University Press.

Klooster, Wim. 2009b. "Networks of Colonial Entrepreneurs: the Founders of the Jewish Settlements in Dutch America, 1650s and 1660s," in: Richard L. Kagan and Philip D. Morgan, eds., *Atlantic Diasporas: Jews, Conversos, and Crypto-Jews in the Age of Mercantilism, 1500–1800*, Baltimore: The Johns Hopkins University Press.

Klooster, Wim. 2010–2011. "The Essequibo Liberties: The Link between Jewish Brazil and Jewish Suriname," *Studia Rosenthaliana* Vol. 42–43.

Klooster, Wim. 2014. "Curaçao as a Transit Center to the Spanish Main and the French West Indies," in: Gert Oostindie and Jessica V. Roitman, eds., *Dutch Atlantic Connections, 1680–1800. Linking Empires, Bridging Borders*, Leiden and Boston: Brill.

Kochanowicz, Jacek. 2006. *Backwardness and Modernization. Poland and Eastern Europe in the 16th–20th Century*, Aldershot: Ashgate Publishing Ltd.

Koen, E.M. 1970. "The Earliest Sources Relating to the Portuguese Jews in the Municipal Archives of Amsterdam up to 1620," *Studia Rosenthaliana* Vol. 4, No. 1.

Kohut, George Alexander. 1895. *Sketches of Jewish Loyalty, Bravery and Patriotism in the South American Colonies and the West Indies*, Philadelphia: Levytype Company.

Kohut, George Alexander. 1896. "Jewish Martyrs of the Inquisition in South America," *Publications of the American Jewish Historical Society* No. 4.

Kubiaczyk, Filip. 2012. "Idea Hiszpanii w projekcie politycznym Ferdynanda Katolickiego," in: Filip Kubiaczyk and Katarzyna Mirgos, eds., *Hiszpania – mit czy rzeczywistość?*, Poznań: Wydawnictwo Poznańskiego Towarzystwa Przyjaciół Nauk.

Kula, Marcin. 1970. *Początki czarnego niewolnictwa w Brazylii. Okres gospodarki cukrowej XVI–XVII w.*, Wrocław: Ossolineum.

Kula, Marcin. 1987. *Historia Brazylii*, Wrocław: Ossolineum.

Kula, Witold. 1983. *Historia, zacofanie, rozwój*, Warszawa: Czytelnik.

Kuliszer, Józef, *Powszechna historia gospodarcza średniowiecza i czasów nowożytnych*, T. 1, Warszawa: KiW 1962.

Ladero Quesada, Miguel Ángel. 1992. "Actividades de Luis de Santángel en la corte de Castilla," *Historia. Instituciones. Documentos*, No. 19.

Lang, James. 1979. *Portuguese Brazil: the King's Plantation*, New York: Academic Press.

Lea, Henry Charles. 1906–1907. *A History of the Inquisition of Spain* Vol. 1 and 3, New York: The Macmillan Company 1906–1907.

Lea, Henry Charles. 1922. *The Inquisition in the Spanish Dependencies*, New York: The Macmillan Company.

Lelewel, Joachim. 1858. *Polska. Dzieje i rzeczy jej*, Tom 1, Poznań: Nakładem J.K. Żupańskiego.

Leon, Abram. 1950. *The Jewish Question. A Marxist Interpretation*, Mexico: Ediciones Pioneras (retrieved from Marxist.org).

Leoni, Aron di Leone. 2005. *The Hebrew Portuguese Nations in Antwerp and London at the Time of Charles V and Henry VIII. New Documents and Interpretations*, Jersey City, NJ: KTAV Publishing House, Inc.

Levi, Joseph Abraham. 2005. "Portugal Meets Italy: the Sephardic Communities of the Diaspora on Italian Soil (1496–1600)," *Cadernos de Estudos Sefarditas*, No. 5.

Levine Melammed, Renée. 2004. *A Question of Identity: Iberian Conversos in Historical Perspective*, New York: Oxford University Press.

Levy, Daniela. 2013. *Anti-Jewish "Propaganda" in Brazil under Dutch Occupation*, in: Charles Asher Small, ed., *Global Antisemitism: A Crisis of Modernity* Vol. III, New York: Institute for the Study of Global Antisemitism and Policy.

Lévy, Joseph J., Yolande Cohen. 1992. *Itinéraires sépharades, 1492–1992*, Paris: Jacques Grancher.

Lewin, Boleslao. 1962. *La inquisición en Hispanoamérica: Judios, Protestantes y Patriotas*, Buenos Aires: Editorial Proyección.

Lewin, Boleslao. 1980. *Los judios bajo la Inquisición en Hispanoamérica*, Buenos Aires: Editorial Dédalo.

Lewin, Boleslao. 1987. *Los criptojudios: un fenomeno religioso y social*, Buenos Aires: Editorial Milá.

Liebman, Seymour. 1963. "The Jews of Colonial Mexico," *The Hispanic American Historical Review* Vol. 43, No. 1.

Liebman, Seymour. 1971. "The Great Conspiracy in Peru," *The Americas* Vol. 28 No. 2.

Liebman, Seymour. 1973. "The Great Conspiracy in New Mexico," *The Americas* Vol. 30, No. 1.

Liebman, Seymour. 1975. "Sephardic Ethnicity in the Spanish New World Colonies," *Jewish Social Studies* Vol. 37, No. 2.

Liebman, Seymour. 1984. *Requiem por los olvidados. Los judíos españoles en América, 1493–1825*, Madrid: Altalena Editores.

Lima, Fernando Carlos G.C. 2012. "A 'escassez de numerário' e a adoção do açúcar como moeda no Brasil colonial," *Revista Econômica* Vol. 14, No. 1.

Lockhart, James and Stuart B. Schwartz. 1983. *Early Latin America: A History of Colonial Spanish America and Brazil*, Cambridge: Cambridge University Press.

Lockhart, James and Stuart B. Schwartz. 1968. *Spanish Peru, 1532–1560. A Colonial Society*, Madison, Wisconsin: The University of Wisconsin Press.

Loker, Zwi. 1983. "Juan de Yllan, Merchant Adventurer and Colonial Promotor. New Evidence," *Studia Rosenthaliana* Vol. 17, No. 1.

López Belinchón, Bernardo José. 2001. "'Sacar la sustancia al reino'. Comercio, contrabando y conversos portugueses, 1621–1640," *Hispania* Vol. LXI, No. 3.

Lorenzo Sanz, Eufemio. 1979. *Comercio de España con América en la época de Felipe II.* Tomo I: *Los mercaderes y el trafico indiano*, Valladolid: Servicio de Publicaciones de la Diputación Provincial de Valladolid.

Lunsford, Virginia West. 2005. *Piracy and Privateering in the Golden Age Netherlands*, New York: Palgrave/Macmillan.

Luxán Melendez, Santiago de. 1993. "A colónia portuguesa de Sevilha. Uma ameaça entre a Restauração portuguesa e a conjura de Medina Sidónia?," *Penélope* No. 9/10.

Łopatecki, Karol. 2016. "Ofensywa holenderskiej Kompanii Zachodnioindyjskiej w Brazylii w latach 1634–1636," *Zeszyty Naukowe Uniwersytetu Jagiellońskiego. Prace Historyczne* T. 143, z. 4.

Maddison, Angus. 2001. *The World Economy: A Millennial Perspective*, Paris: OECD.

Maddison, Angus. 2003. *The World Economy: Historical Statistics*, Paris: OECD.

Maia, Angela Maria Vieira. 1995. *À sombra do medo: Cristãos velhos e cristãos novos nas capitanias açúcar*, Rio de Janeiro: Oficina Cadernos de Poesia, in Jonathan Schorsch, *Swimming the Christian Atlantic: Judeoconversos, Afroamericans and Amerindians in the Seventeenth Century*, Leiden: Brill 2009.

Maldavky, Aliocha. 2000. "Itinéraires des nouveaux chrétiens à Lima. Le procès de Manuel Bautista Pérez et la 'grande complicité' (1635–1639)," *Caravelle* No. 74.

Małowist, Marian. 1969. *Europa a Afryka Zachodnia w dobie wczesnej ekspansji kolonialnej*, Warszawa: PWN.

Małowist, Marian. 1976. *Konkwistadorzy*, Warszawa: PIW.

Małowist, Marian. 2010. *Western Europe, Eastern Europe and World Development, 13th–18th Centuries. Collection of Essays of Marian Małowist*, edited by Jean Batou and Henryk Szlajfer, Leiden and Boston: Brill.

Manchester, Alan K. 1931. "The Rise of the Brazilian Aristocracy," *The Hispanic American Historical Review* Vol. 11, No. 2.

Mandeville, Bernard. 1724. *The Fable of the Bees or Private Vices, Public Benefits*, London: J. Tonson (3rd edition).

Manning, Patrick. 1992. "The Slave Trade: the Formal Demography of a Global System," in: Joseph E. Inikori and Stanley L. Engerman, eds., *The Atlantic Slave Trade. Effects on Economies, Societies, and Peoples in Africa, the Americas, and Europe*, Durham and London: Duke University Press.

Marcílio, Maria Luiza. 1984. "The Population of Colonial Brazil," in: Leslie Bethell, ed., *The Cambridge History of Latin America* Vol. 2: *Colonial Latin America*, Cambridge: Cambridge University Press.

Marcocci, Giuseppe, José Pedro Paiva. 2013. *História da inquisição portuguesa (1536–1821)*, Lisboa: A Esfera dos Livras.

Marcus, Jacob R., Stanley F. Chyet. 1974. Eds., *Historical Essay on the Colony of Surinam 1788*, New York and Cincinnati: American Jewish Archives and KTAV Publishing House.

Mark, Peter, José da Silva Horta. 2011. *The Forgotten Diaspora. Jewish Communities in West Africa and the Making of the Atlantic World*, New York: Cambridge University Press.

Marques, António Henrique de Oliveira. 1976. *History of Portugal,* Vol.1, New York: Columbia University Press.

Marques, José. 1993. "Filipe III de Espanha (II de Portugal) e a inquisição portuguesa face ao projecto do 3.º perdão geral para os cristãos-novos portugueses," *Revista da Faculdade de Letras. Historia* (II série) Vol. x.

Martins, Jorge. 2008. "A emancipação dos Judeus em Portugal," *Cadernos de Estudos Sefarditas* No. 8.

Maryks, Robert Aleksander. 2009. *Jesuit Order as a Synagogue of Jews: Jesuits of Jewish Ancestry and Purity-of-Blood Laws in the Early Society of Jesus,* Leiden and Boston: Brill.

Marzagalli, Silvia. 2001. "Atlantic Trade and Sephardim Merchants in Eighteend-Century France: the Case of Bordeaux," in: Paolo Bernardini and Norman Fiering, eds., *The Jews and the Expansion of Europe to the West, 1450–1800,* New York and Oxford: Berghahn Books.

Marzagalli, Silvia. 2016. *The Atlantic World between Markets and State in 18th-century France: the Sephardim Firm Gradis in Bordeaux,* Economic History Society Annual Conference, Robinson College, University of Cambridge, 1–3 April.

Mateus, Bastos Susana and James W. Nelson Novoa. 2008. "The Case of the New Christians of Lamego as an Example of Resistance against Portuguese Inquisition in Sixteenth Century Portugal," *Hispania Judaica Bulletin* Vo. 6.

Mateus, Bastos Susana, James W. Nelson Novoa and Paulo Mendes Pinto. 2011. "Beatriz de Luna – Grácia Nasci – Grácia Beneviste, 'A Senhora'," *Cadernos de Estudos Sefarditas* No. 10/11.

Mattos, Hebe. 2008. "'Black Troops' and Hierarchies of Color in the Portuguese Atlantic World: the Case of Henrique Dias and His Black Regiment," *Luso-Brazilian Review* Vol. 45, No. 1.

Maurits, Johan. 2010. "A Brief Report on the State That Is Composed of the Four Conquered Capitaincies, Pernambuco, Itamaracá, Paraíba, and Rio Grande, Situated in the North of Brazil," in: Stuart B. Schwartz, ed., *Early Brazil: a Documentary Collection to 1700,* New York: Cambridge University Press (oryg. 1638).

Mauro, Frédéric. 1987. "Political and Economic Structure of Empire, 1580–1750," in: Leslie Bethell, ed., *Colonial Brazil,* Cambridge: Cambridge University Press.

Maxwell, John Francis. 1975. *Slavery and the Catholic Church: the History of Catholic Teaching Concerning the Moral Legitimacy of the Institution of Slavery,* Chichester and London: Barry Rose Publisher.

Medina, José Toribio. 1945. *La inquisición en el Rio de la Plata. El tribunal de Santo oficio de la inquisición en las provincias del Plata,* Buenos Aires: Editorial Huarpes S.A.

Mello, José Antônio Gonsalves de. 1954. *Frei Manuel Calado do Salvador. Religioso da Ordem de São Paulo, pregador apostólico por sua santidade, cronista la Restauração,* Recife: Universidad de Recife.

Mello, José Antônio Gonsalves de. 1958. "The Dutch Calvinists and Religious Toleration in Portuguese America," *The Americas* Vol. 14, No. 4.

Mello, José Antônio Gonsalves de. 1989. *Gente da Nação: cristãos-novos e judeus em Pernambuco 1542–1654,* Recife: Fundação Joaquim Nabuco, Editora. Massangana.

Menasseh ben Israel. 1901. *Menasseh ben Israel's Mission to Oliver Cromwell,* London: Macmillan & Co.

Metcalf, Alida C. 1999. "Millenarian Slaves? The Santidade de Jaguaripe and Slave Resistance in the Americas," *The American Historical Review* Vol. 104, No. 5.

Metcalf, Alida C. 2005. *Go-Betweens and the Colonization of Brazil: 1500–1600,* Austin: University of Texas Press.

Metz, Allan. 1992. "'Those of the Hebrew Nation': the Sephardic Experience in Colonial Latin America," *American Jewish Archives* Vol. 44, No. 1.

Meuwese, Mark. 2012. *Brothers in Arms, Partners in Trade. Dutch-Indigenous Alliances in the Atlantic World, 1595–1674,* Leiden and Boston: Brill.

Miller, Joseph C. 1993. "A Marginal Institution on the Margin of the Atlantic System: the Portuguese Southern Atlantic Slave Trade in the Eighteenth Century," in: Barbara L. Solow, ed., *Slavery and the Rise of the Atlantic System,* New York: Cambridge University Press.

Mörner, Magnus. 1975. "La hacienda hispanoamericana: examen de las investigaciones y debates recientes," in: Enrique Florescano, ed., *Haciendas, latifundios y plantaciones en América Latina,* México: Siglo XXI Editores.

Mörner, Magnus. 2002. "Changing Attitudes: Early Spanish Immigrants in the New World," *Jahrbuch für Geschichte von Staat, Wirtschaft und Gesellschaft Lateinamerika* Vol. 39.

Molas Ribalta, Pere. 1987. "Instituciones y Comercio en la España de Olivares," *Studia Historica: Historia Moderna* No. 5.

Monteiro, Carolina and Erik Odegard. 2020. "Slavery at the Court of the 'Humanist Prince': Reexamining Johan Maurits van Nassau-Siegen and his Role in Slavery, Slave Trade and Slave-smuggling in Dutch Brazil," *Journal of Early American History* Vol. 10, Issue 1.

Moutoukias, Zacarias. 1988. "Burocracia, contrabando y autotransformacion de las elites Buenos Aires en el Siglo XVII," *Anuario del IEHS* Vol. 3.

Muller, Jerry Z. 2010. *Capitalism and the Jews,* Princeton: Princeton University Press.

Munck, Thomas. 1990. *Seventeenth Century Europe. State, Conflict and the Social Order in Europe 1598–1700,* New York: St. Martin's Press.

Munro, John. 2008. "Price Revolution," in: Steven N. Durlauf, Lawrence E. Blume, eds., *The New Palgrave Dictionary of Economics,* Vol. 6, London and New York: Palgrave Macmillan.

Myers, D.N. 1998. *Of Marranos and Memory: Yosef Hayim Yerushalmi and the Writing of Jewish History,* in: E. Carlebach, J.M. Efron i D.N. Myers, eds., *Jewish History and*

Jewish Memory. Essays in Honor of Yosef Hayim Yerushalmi, Hanover, NH: Brandeis University Press.

Nation of Islam. 1991. *The Secret Relationship between Blacks and Jews* Vol. 1, Prepared by the Historical Research Department the Nation of Islam, Boston.

Nater, Laura. 2006. "Colonial Tobacco: Key Commodity of the Spanish Empire, 1500–1800," in: Steven Topik, Carlos Marichal and Zephyr Frank, eds., *From Silver to Cocaine: Latin American Commodity Chains and the Building of the World Economy, 1500–2000*, Durham and London: Duke University Press.

Navarrete Peláez, María Cristina. 2002. "Judeo-conversos en la Audiencia del Nuevo Reino de Granada, siglos XVI y XVII," *Historia Crítica* No. 23.

Navarrete Peláez, María Cristina. 2007. "De las 'malas entradas' y las estrategias del 'buen pasaje': el contrabando de esclavos en el Caribe neograndino, 1550–1690," *Historia Crítica* No. 34.

Navarrete Peláez, María Cristina. 2009. *Judeoconversos en el mundo colonial neogranadino Siglos XVI y XVII*, Instituto Colombiano de Antropología e Historia–ICANH Area de Historia Colonial, Bogotá, Diciembre (mimeo).

Navarrete Peláez, María Cristina. 2015. "Los años inciertos del comercio esclavista a los reinos de Indias: 1640–1680," *Historia y Espacio* No. 45.

Netanyahu, Benzion. 1995. *The Origins of the Inquisition in Fifteenth Century Spain*, New York: Random House.

Netanyahu, Benzion. 1999. *The Marranos of Spain. From the Late 14th to the Early XVIth Century, According to Contemporary Hebrew Sources*, Ithaca and London: Cornell University Press (3rd edition, updated and expanded).

Newson, Linda A. 2006. *The Demographic Impact of Colonization*, in: Victor Bulmer-Thomas, John H. Coatsworth, Robert Cortés Conde, eds., *The Cambridge Economic History of Latin America* Vol. 1: *the Colonial Era and the Short Nineteenth Century*, Cambridge: Cambridge University Press.

Newson, Linda A. and Susie Minchin. 2007. *From Capture to Sale. The Portuguese Slave Trade to Spanish South America in the Early Seventeenth Century*, Leiden and Boston: Brill.

Nirenberg, David. 2002. "Mass Conversion and Genealogical Mentalities: Jews and Christians in Fifteenth-Century Spain," *Past and Present* No. 174.

Norton, Luiz. 2007. "A Colonização Portuguesa do Brasil (1500–1550)," *Revista de Historia de América* Num. 138.

Notarial Records. 1978. "Notarial Records Relating to the Portuguese Jews in Amsterdam up to 1639," *Studia Rosenthaliana* Vol. 12, No. 1–2.

Novais, Fernando A. 1985. *Portugal e Brasil na Crise do Antigo Sistema Colonial (1777–1808)*, São Paulo: Editora Hucitec.

Novinsky, Anita Waingort. 1971. "A pesquisa histórica sôbre a cristão-nôvo no Brasil," *Revista de História* Vol. 43, No. 88.

Novinsky, Anita Waingort. 1972. *Cristãos novos na Bahia*, São Paulo: Editora da Universidade de São Paulo/Editôra Perspectiva.

Novinsky, Anita Waingort. 1987. "Jewish Roots of Brazil," in: J. Elkin and G. Merkx, eds., *The Jewish Presence in Latin America*, Boston: Allen & Unwin.

Novinsky, Anita Waingort. 1991. "Padre Antônio Vieira, a inquisição e os judeus," *Novos Estudos* No. 29.

Novinsky, Anita Waingort. 1998. "A inquisição portuguesa a luz de novos estudos," *Revista de la Inquisición* No. 7.

Novinsky, Anita Waingort. 2001a. "Os cristãos-novos no Brasil colonial: reflexões sobre a questão do marranismo," *Tempo* Nr 11.

Novinsky, Anita Waingort. 2001b. "Marranos and the Inquisition: on the Gold Route in Minas Gerais, Brazil," in: Paolo Bernardini and Norman Fiering, eds., *The Jews and the Expansion of Europe to the West, 1450–1800*, New York and Oxford: Berghahn Books.

Novinsky, Anita Waingort. 2006. "The Myth of the Marrano Names," *Revue des Études Juives* Vol.165.

Novinsky, Anita Waingort. 2009a. "Brazilian Marranism," in: M. Avrum Ehrlich, ed., *Encyclopedia of the Jewish Diaspora. Origins, Experiments, and Culture*, Santa Barbara, CA: ABC–CLIO, LLC.

Novinsky, Anita Waingort. 2009b. "O legado do judaísmo à civilização brasileira," in: Helena Lewin, ed., *Identidade e cidadania: como se expressa o judaísmo brasileiro*, Rio de Janeiro: Centro Edelstein de Pesquisas Sociais (online).

Novoa, James W. Nelson. 2007. "The Departure of Duarte de Paz from Rome in the Light of Documents from the Vatican Secret Archive," *Cadernos de Estudos Sefarditas* No. 7.

Novoa, James W. Nelson. 2008. "Documents from the Secret Vatican Archives Regarding the History of the New Christians in the Low Countries (1536–1542)," *Hispania Judaica Bulletin* Vol. 6.

Novoa, James W. Nelson. 2014. *Being the Nação in the Eternal City. New Christians Lives in Sixteenth-Century Rome*, Toronto and Peterborough: Baywolf Press/Éditions Baywolf.

Nusteling, Hubert P.H. 2002. "The Jews in the Republic of the United Provinces: Origin, Numbers and Dispersion," in: Jonathan I. Israel and Reinier Salvedra, eds., *Dutch Jewry. Its History and Secular Culture (1500–2000)*, Leiden–Boston–Köln: Brill.

Odegard, Erik. 2022. "Investing in Engenhos. Credit, Claims, and Sugar Mills in Dutch Brazil," *Tijdschrift voor Sociale en Economische Geschiedenis* Vol. 19, No. 2.

Olival, Fernando. 2004. "Structural Changes within the 16th-century Portuguese Military Orders," *e-Journal of Portuguese History* Vol. 2, No. 2.

Oliveira, Aurélio de. 2001. *Os Inacianos e as Companhias de Comércio em Portugal*, in: Amélia Polónia, ed., *Estudos em homenagem a João Francisco Marques*, T. 2, Porto: Faculdade de Letras da Universidade de Porto.

Oliveira, Halyson Rodrygo Silva de. 2012. *Mundo do medo: inquisição e cristãos-novos nos espaços coloniais. Capitanias de Pernambuco, Itamaracá e Paraiba (1593–1595)*, Centro de Ciências Humanas, Letras e Artes, Universidade Federal do Rio Grande do Norte, Natal 2012 (MA thesis).

Oliwa, Dominika. 2012. "Deepening the Catholic Faith or Spreeding Intolerance? The Sermon Delivered During an Auto-da-Fé in 17th-Century Portugal as an Example of Anti-Jewish Literature," *Scripta Judaica Cracoviensia* Vol. 10.

Olszewicz, Bolesław. 1931. "Gaspar da Gama: Żyd poznański w Indjach XVI wieku," *Kronika Miasta Poznania* T. 9, No. 3.

Oppenheim, Samuel. 1907. "An Early Jewish Colony in Western Guiana, 1658–1666, and Its Relation to the Jews in Surinam, Cayenne and Tobago," *American Jewish Historical Society* No. 16.

Orique, David Thomas. 2014. "A Comparison of the Voices of the Spanish Bartolome de Las Casas and the Portuguese Fernando Oliveira on Just War and Slavery," *e-Journal of Portuguese History* Vol. 12, No. 1.

Osterhammel, Jürgen and Niels P. Petersson. 2005. *Globalization: A Short History*, Princeton University Press: Princeton.

Otte, Enrique. 1999. "La red comercial de los Corzo en la expansion atlántica," *Jahrbuch für Geschichte Lateinamerikas* Vol. 36.

Palma, Ricardo. 1863. *Anales de la inquisición de Lima (estudio histórico)*, Lima: Tipografía de Aurelio Alfaro.

Palma, Ricardo. 1893. *Tradiciones peruanas. Tomo I*, Barcelona: Montaner y Simón, Editores.

Palma, Ricardo. 1894. *Tradiciones peruanas. Tomo III*, Barcelona: Montaner y Simón, Editores.

Panzer, Joel S. 1996. "The Popes and Slavery," *Homiletic and Pastoral Review*, December.

Parthesius, Robert. 2010. *Dutch Ships in Tropical Waters. The Development of the Dutch East India Company (VOC) Shipping Network in Asia, 1595–1660*, Amsterdam: Amsterdam University Press.

Perdices de Blas, Luis, José Luis Ramos-Gorostiza. 2015. "Slavery and the Slave Trade in Spanish Economic Thought, Sixteenth to Eighteenth Centuries," *History of Economic Ideas* Vol. XXIII, No. 2.

Pereira, Edgar. 2019. "The Ordeals of Colonial Contracting: Reactions to and Repercussions of Two Failed State-Private Ventures in Habsburg Portugal (1622–1628)," *Itinerario* Vol. 43, No. 1.

Pérez, Pedro Guibovich. 1991. "La cultura libresca de un converso procesado por la Inquisición de Lima," *Revista Historias* Vol. 36.

Perusset Veras, Macarena. 2005. "Élite y comercio en el temprano siglo XVII rioplatense," *Fronteras de la Historia* Núm. 10.

Perusset Veras, Macarena. 2007. "Comportamientos al margen de la ley: contrabando y sociedad en Buenos Aires en el siglo XVII," *Historia Crítica* No. 33.

Pétré-Grenouilleau, Olivier. 2009. "Maritime Powers, Colonial Powers: The Role of Migration (c. 1492–1792)," in: Wim Klooster, ed., *Migration, Trade, and Slavery in an Expanding World. Essays in Honor of Pieter Emmer,* Leiden and Boston: Bill.

Pieroni, Geraldo. 2001. "Outcasts from the Kingdom: The Inquisition and the Banishment of New Christians to Brazil," in: Paolo Bernardini and Norman Fiering, eds., *The Jews and the Expansion of Europe to the West, 1450–1800,* New York and Oxford: Berghahn Books.

Pietschmann, Horst. 2010. "The Spanish Atlantic in an Age of Transition, 1648–1700," *Jahrbuch für Geschichte Lateinamerikas* Vol. 47.

Pijning, Ernst. 2001. "New Christians as Sugar Cultivators and Traders in the Portuguese Atlantic, 1450–1800," in: Paolo Bernardini and Norman Fiering, eds., *The Jews and the Expansion of Europe to the West, 1450–1800,* New York and Oxford: Berghahn Books.

Pijning, Ernst. 2006. "'Idealism and Power': the Dutch West India Company in the Brazil Trade (1630–1654)," in: Allan I. Macinnes and Arthur H. Williamson, eds., *Shaping the Stuart World, 1603–1714: the Atlantic Connection,* Leiden: Brill.

Pinto, Isaac de. 1762. *Apologie pour la Nation Juive ou Réflexions Critiques,* Amsterdam: J. Jaubest.

Pirenne, Henri. 1914. "The Stages in the Social History of Capitalism," *The American Historical Review* Vol. 19, No. 3.

Pirenne, Henri. 1937. *Economic and Social History of Medieval Europe,* New York: Harcourt, Brace and Company.

Pirenne, Henri. 2001. *Mohammed and Charlemagne,* Mineola, New York: Dover Publications.

Pohl, Hans. 1967. "Die Zuckereinfuhr nach Antwerpen durch portugiesche Kaufleute während des 80Jährigen Krieges," *Jahrbuch für Geschichte von Staat, Wirtschaft und Gesellschaft Lateinamerika* Vol. 4.

Pomeranz, Kenneth, Steven Topik. 2013. *The World That Trade Created: Society, Culture, and the World Economy, 1400 to the Present,* Armonk, NY: M.E. Sharpe.

Pons, Frank Moya. 1985. "Sugar in Brazil: Its Early Developments and International Connections in the XVI and XVII Centuries," *Ciência & Trópico* Vol. 13, No. 2.

Popkin, Richard. H. 1992. *The Third Force in Seventeenth-Century Thought,* Leiden: Brill.

Postma, Johannes M. 1992a. *The Dutch in the Atlantic Slave Trade, 1600–1815,* New York: Cambridge University Press.

Postma, Johannes M. 1992b. "The Dispersal of African Slaves in the West by Dutch Slave Traders, 1630–1803," in: Joseph E. Inikori and Stanley L. Engerman, eds., *The Atlantic Slave Trade. Effects on Economies, Societies, and Peoples in Africa, the Americas, and Europe,* Durham and London: Duke University Press.

Prado Jr., Caio. 1969. *The Colonial Background of Modern Brazil*, Berkeley and Los Angeles: University of California Press.

Prado Jr., Caio. 1981. *História econômica do Brasil*, São Paulo: Editora Brasiliense.

Puente Brunke, José de la. 2013. *La mirada portuguesa al Perú de los Siglos XVI y XVII*, in: *Descrição geral do reino do Peru, em particular de Lima*, Lisboa.

Pulido Serrano, Juan Ignacio. 2003. *Los Conversos en España y Portugal*, Madrid: Arco/Libros.

Pulido Serrano, Juan Ignacio. 2006. "Las negociaciones con las cristianos nuevos en tiempos de Filipe III a la luz de algunos documentos inéditos (1598–1607)," *Sefarad* Vol. 66, No. 2.

Pulido Serrano, Juan Ignacio. 2011. "Plural Identities: the Portuguese New Christians," *Jewish History* Vol. 25, No. 2.

Puntoni, Pedro. 2012. "No tempo dos flamengos: memória e imaginação," in: Hugo Coelho Vieira et al., eds., *Brasil Holandês. História, memória e patrimônio compartilhado*, São Paulo: Alameda.

Quevedo, Ricardo Escobar. 2008. *Inquisición y judaizantes en América española (Siglos XVI–XVII)*, Bogota: Editorial Universidad del Rosario.

Quiroga, Gabriela de las Mercedes and A. Nieves de Vera de Saporiti. 2009. "Génesis de una gobernación: las encomiendas de Buenos Aires (1580–1617)," *Anuario del Centro de Estudios Históricos 'Prof. Carlos S.A. Segreti'* (Córdoba) No. 9.

Quiroz, Alfonso W. 1985. "The Expropriation of Portuguese New Christians in Spanish America, 1635 -1649," *Ibero-amerikanisches Archiv* (Neue Folge) Vol. 11, No. 4.

Raminelli, Ronald. 2014. "'Los límites del honor'. Nobles y jerarquías de Brasil, Nueva España y Perú, siglos XVII y XVIII," *Revista Complutense de Historia de América* Vol. 40.

Rawlings, Helen. 2006. *The Spanish Inquisition*, Oxford: Blackwell Publishing.

Restrepo, Luis Carlos. 2011. *Los Portugueses: la trata de negros esclavos y el Tribunal de la Inquisición en la ciudad de Cartagena de Indias, siglos XVI y XVII*, Sevilla (online access).

Ribeiro, Ana Sofia Vieira. 2011. *Mechanisms and Criteria of Cooperation in Trading Networks of the First Global Age. The Case Study of Simon Ruiz Network, 1557–1597*, Faculdade de Letras, Universidade do Porto 2011 (PhD dissertation).

Ribemboim, José Alexandre. 2000. *Senhores de engenho judeus em Pernambuco colonial, 1542–1654*, Recife: 20–20 Comunicação e Editora.

Ricardo, Sílvia Carvalho. 2006. *As redes mercantis no final do século XVI e a figura do mercador João Nunes Correira*, Departamento de História da Faculdade de Filosofia, Letras e Ciências Humanas, Universidade de São Paulo, São Paulo (M.A. thesis).

Rivkin, Ellis. 1957. "The Utilization of Non-Jewish Sources for the Reconstruction of Jewish History," *The Jewish Quarterly Review* Vol. 48, No. 2.

Rivkin, Ellis. 2003. *The Unity Principle. The Shaping of Jewish History*, Springfield, NJ: Behrman House, Inc.

Rock, David. 1987. *Argentina 1516–1987: from Spanish Colonization to Alfonsín*, Berkeley and Los Angeles: University of Califonia Press.

Rodney, Walter. 1973. *How Europe Underdeveloped Africa*, London: Bogle-L'Ouverture Publications and Dar es Salaam: Tanzania Publishing House.

Rodriguez, Mario. 1956. "The Genesis of Economic Attitudes in the Rio De La Plata," *The Hispanic American Historical Review* Vol. 36, No. 2.

Rodríguez Morel, Genaro. 2004. "The Sugar Economy of Española in the Sixteenth Century," in: Stuart B. Schwartz, ed., *Tropical Babylons: Sugar and the Making of the Atlantic World, 1450–1680*, Chapel Hill and London: The University of North Carolina Press.

Roitman, Jessica Vance. 2009. "New Christians, Jews, and Amsterdam at the Crossroads of Expansion Systems," in: Wim Klooster, ed., *Migration, Trade, and Slavery in an Expanding World. Essays in Honor of Pieter Emmer*, Leiden and Boston: Brill.

Roitman, Jessica Vance. 2011. *The Same but Different? Inter-cultural Trade and the Sephardim, 1595–1640*, Leiden and Boston: Brill.

Romano, Ruggiero. 1992. *Conjonctures opposées. La "crise" du XVIIe siècle: en Europe et en Amérique ibérique*, Genève: Librairie Droz.

Roscher, Wilhelm. 1875. "Die Stellung der Juden im Mittelalter, betrachtet vom Standpunkt der allgemeine Handelspolitik," *Zeitschrift für die gesammte Staatswissenschaft*, Bd. 31, Heft 4.

Rosenblat, Angel. 1954. *La población indígena y el mestizaje en América T.II: El mestizaje y las castas colonials*, Buenos Aires: Editorial Nova.

Roth, Cecil. 1959. *A History of the Marranos*, New York and Philadelphia: Meridian Books.

Roth, Cecil. 1961. "Economic History of the Jews," *The Economic History Review* (New Series) Vol. 14, No. 1.

Roth, Norman. 2002. *Conversos, Inquisition, and the Expulsion of the Jews from Spain*, Madison, Wisconsin: The University of Wisconsin Press (2nd edition).

Rowland, Robert. 2001. "New Christian, Marrano, Jew," in: Paolo Bernardini and Norman Fiering, eds., *The Jews and the Expansion of Europe to the West, 1450–1800*, New York and Oxford: Berghahn Books.

Rueda, Julio Jimenez. 1946. *Herejias y supersticiones en la Nueva España*, Mexico: UNAM / Imprenta Universitaria.

Rueda Ramírez, Pedro. 2014. "Las redes comerciales del libro en la colonia: «peruleros» y libreros en la Carrera de Indias (1590–1620)," *Anuario de Estudios Americanos* Vol. 71, No. 2.

Ruiz Rivera, Julián Bautista. 2002. "Los portugueses y la trata negrera en Cartagena de Indias," *Temas Americanistas* Nr 15.

Rupert, Linda M. 2012. *Creolization and Contraband: Curaçao in the Early Modern Atlantic World*, Athens and London: University of Georgia Press.

Russell-Wood, Anthony J.R. 1968. *Fidalgos and Philanthropists: The Santa Casa da Misericórdia of Bahia, 1550–1755*, Berkeley and Los Angeles: University of California Press.

Russell-Wood, Anthony J.R. 1992. *Society and Government in Colonial Brazil, 1500–1822*, Aldershot: Variorum Ashgate Publishing Ltd.

Russell-Wood, Anthony J.R. 1993. *A World on the Move. The Portuguese in Africa, Asia, and America 1415–1808*, New York: St. Martin's Press.

Russell-Wood, Anthony J.R. 2002. "Centers and Peripheries in the Luso-Brazilian World, 1500–1808," in: Christine Daniels, Michael V. Kennedy, eds., *Negotiated Empires: Centers and Peripheries in the Americas, 1500–1820*, New York: Routledge.

Ryś, Grzegorz. 2023. *Chrześcijanie wobec Żydów. Od Jezusa po inkwizycję XV wieków trudnych relacji*, Kraków: Wydawnictwo WAM

Saguier, Eduardo R. 1985a. "The Social Impact of a Middleman Minority in a Divided Host Society: The Case of the Portuguese in Early Seventeenth-Century Buenos Aires," *The Hispanic American Historical Review* Vol. 65 No. 3.

Saguier, Eduardo R. 1985b. "Political Impact of Immigration and Commercial Penetration on Intra-Colonial Struggles: Buenos Aires in the Early Seventeenth Century," *Jahrbuch für Geschichte von Staat, Wirtschaft und Gesellschaft Lateinamerika* Vol. 22.

Salomon, Herman Prins and António Faleiro. 1997. "The Case of Luis Vaz Pimentel: Revelations of Early Jewish Life in Rotterdam from the Portuguese Inquisition Archives," *Studia Rosenthaliana* Vol. 31, Nos. 1–2.

Salomon, Herman Prins, António Faleiro. and Aron di Leone Leoni. 1998. "Mendes, Benveniste, de Luna, Micas, Nasci: The State of the Art (1532–1558)," *The Jewish Quarterly Review* Vol. 88, No. 3–4.

Salvador, José Gonçalves. 1976. *Os cristãos-novos: povoamento e conquista do solo brasileiro (1530–1680)*, São Paulo: Pioneira/EDUSP.

Salvador, José Gonçalves. 1978. *Os cristãos-novos e o comércio no Atlântico meridional (Com enfoque nas Capitanias do Sul 1530–1680)*, São Paulo: Livraria Pioneira Editora.

Salvador, José Gonçalves. 1981. *Os magnatas do tráfico negreiro (séculos XVI e XVII)*, São Paulo: Pioneira/EDUSP.

Sampaio, Antonio Carlos Jucá de. 2014. "Comércio, riqueza e nobreza: elites mercantis e hierarquização social no Antigo Regime português," in: João Fragoso et. al, eds., *Nas rotas do Império. Eixos mercantis, tráfico e relações social no mundo português*, Vitória: EDUFES.

Sánchez Durán, Álvaro. 2015. "Los hombres de negocios portugueses: una élite profesional en la Castilla del siglo XVII. Posibilidades de movilidad social e intermediación," *Tiempos Modernos* Vol. 8, No. 31.

Saraiva, António José. 2001. *The Marrano Factory: The Portuguese Inquisition and Its New Christians, 1536–1765* (revised and augmented by H.P. Salomon and I.S.D. Sassoon), Leiden: Brill.

Scelle, Georges. 1910. "The Slave-Trade in the Spanish Colonies of America: The Assiento," *The American Journal of International Law* Vol. 4, No. 3.

Schaposchnik, Ana. 2015. *The Lima Inquisition: The Plight of Crypto-Jews in Seventeenth-Century Peru,* Madison: The University of Wisconsin Press.

Schipper, Ignaz. 1917–1918. "Der jüdische Kapitalismus (Zur Sombart-Brentano-Kontroverse)," *Der Jude: eine Monatsschrift* Heft 1–2.

Schorsch, Jonathan. 2000. "American Jewish Historians, Colonial Jews and Blacks, and the Limits of Wissenschaft: A Critical Review," *Jewish Social Studies: History, Culture, Society* Vol. 6, No. 2.

Schorsch, Jonathan. 2004. *Jews and Blacks in the Early Modern World,* New York: Cambridge University Press.

Schorsch, Jonathan. 2005. "Jews and the Racial Imagination in the Writings of Sephardim in the Long Seventeenth Century," *Jewish History* Vol. 19, No. 1.

Schorsch, Jonathan. 2006. "Sephardic Jews in the Atlantic World: Agents and Victims of Empire (review of J.I. Israel, *Diasporas within a Diaspora*)," *H-Atlantic, H-Net Reviews,* May.

Schorsch, Jonathan. 2009. *Swimming the Christian Atlantic: Judeoconversos, Afroamericans and Amerindians in the Seventeenth Century,* Leiden: Brill.

Schorsch, Jonathan. 2019. "Revisiting Blackness, Slavery, and Jewishness in the Early Modern Sephardic Atlantic," in: Yosef Kaplan, ed., *Religious Changes and Cultural Transformations in the Early Modern Western Sephardic Communities,* Leiden and Boston: Brill.

Schulamith, C. Halevy. 2011. "Blood in the Church: The Inquisition against Hernando Alonso," *Hispanic Judaica Bulletin* No. 8.

Schultz, Kara Danielle. 2016. *'The Kingdom of Angola is not very far from here': The Rio de la Plata, Brazil, and Angola, 1580–1680,* The Graduate School of Vanderbilt University, Nashville, Tennessee, December (PhD dissertation).

Schwartz, Stuart B. 1968. "Luso-Spanish Relations in Hapsburg Brazil, 1580–1640," *The Americas* Vol. 25, No. 1.

Schwartz, Stuart B. 1985. *Sugar Plantations in the Formation of Brazilian Society: Bahia, 1550–1835,* Cambridge: Cambridge University Press.

Schwartz, Stuart B. 1989. "The Formation of a Colonial Identity in Brazil," in: Nicholas Canny and Anthony Pagden, eds., *Colonial Identity in the Atlantic World, 1500–1800,* Princeton: Princeton University Press.

Schwartz, Stuart B. 1991. "The Voyage of the Vassals: Royal Power, Noble Obligations, and Merchant Capital before the Portuguese Restoration of Independence, 1624–1640," *The American Historical Review* Vol. 96, No. 3.

Schwartz, Stuart B. 1997. "Introduction. A House Built on Sand: Capistrano de Abreu and the History of Brazil," in: J. Capistrano de Abreu, *Chapters of Brazil's Colonial History*, 1500–1800, New York: Oxford University Press.

Schwartz, Stuart B. 2004a. "Introduction," in: Stuart B. Schwartz, ed., *Tropical Babylons: Sugar and the Making of the Atlantic World, 1450–1680*, Chapel Hill and London: The University of North Carolina Press.

Schwartz, Stuart B. 2004b. "A Commonwealth within Itself: the Early Brazilian Sugar Industry, 1550–1670," in: Stuart B. Schwartz, ed., *Tropical Babylons: Sugar and the Making of the Atlantic World, 1450–1680*, Chapel Hill and London: The University of North Carolina Press.

Schwartz, Stuart B. 2010. Ed., *Early Brazil: a Documentary Collection to 1700*, New York: Cambridge University Press.

Seed, Patricia. 2001. "Jewish Scientists and the Origin of Modern Navigation," in: P. Bernardini and N. Fiering, eds., *The Jews and the Expansion of Europe to the West, 1450–1800*, New York and Oxford: Berghahn Books.

Semo, Enrique. 1973. *Historia del capitalismo en México. Los orígenes, 1521/1763*, México: Ediciones Era.

Silva, Janaína Guimarães da Fonseca. 2007. *Modos de pensar, maneiras de viver: Cristãos novos em Pernambuco no século XVI*, Centro de Filosofia e Ciências Humanas, Universidad Federal de Pernambuco, Recife (MA thesis).

Silva, Janaína Guimarães da Fonseca. 2012. *Cristãos-novos nos negócios da capitania de Pernambuco: relacionamentos, continuidades e rupturas nas redes de comércio entre os anos de 1580 e 1630*, Centro de Filosofia e Ciências Humanas, Universidade Federal de Pernambuco, Recife (PhD dissertation).

Silva, José Gentil Da. 1987. *Morskie dzieje Portugalczyków*, Gdańsk: Wydawnictwo Morskie.

Silva, Filipa Isabel Ribeiro da. 2011a. *Dutch and Portuguese in Western Africa: Empires, Merchants and the Atlantic System, 1580–1674*, Leiden and Boston: Brill.

Silva, Filipa Isabel Ribeiro da. 2011b. "Crossing Empires: Portuguese, Sephardic, and Dutch Business Networks in the Atlantic Slave Trade, 1580–1674," *The Americas* Vol. 68 No. 1.

Silva, Filipa Isabel Ribeiro da. 2014. "Portuguese Sephardi of Amsterdam and the Trade with Western Africa, 1580–1660," *Le Verger: Revue en ligne – Bouquet Histoire* No. 5.

Silverblatt, Irene. 2000. "New Christians and New World Fears in Seventeenth-Century Peru," *Comparative Studies in Society and History* Vol. 42, No. 3.

Simpson, Lesley B. 1971. *Many Mexicos*, Berkeley and Los Angeles: University of California Press (4th edition revised).

Simpson, Lesley B. 1982. *The Encomienda in New Spain. The Beginning of Spanish Mexico*, Berkeley and Los Angeles: University of California Press (revised and enlarged edition).

Sluiter, Engel. 1942. "Dutch Maritime Power and the Colonial Status Quo, 1585–1641," *Pacific Historical Review* Vol. 11, No. 1.

Sluiter, Engel. 1948. "Dutch–Spanish Rivalry in the Caribbean Area, 1594–1609," *The Hispanic American Historical Review* Vol. 28, No. 2.

Smith, Adam. 1904. *An Inquiry into the Nature and Causes of the Wealth of Nations*, Vol. 2, London: Oxford University Press.

Smith, David Grant. 1974. "Old Christian Merchants and the Formation of the Brazil Company, 1649," *The Hispanic American Historical Review* Vol. 54, No. 2.

Sobieski, Jakób. 1833. *Dwie podróże Jakóba Sobieskiego ojca Króla Jana III odbyte po krajach europejskich w latach 1607–13 i 1638*, edited by Edward Raczyński, Poznań.

Sombart, Werner. 1902. *Der moderne Kapitalismus. Erster Band: Die Genesis des Kapitalismus*, Leipzig: Verlag von Duncker & Humblot.

Sombart, Werner. 1915. *The Quintessence of Capitalism. A Study of the History and Psychology of the Modern Business Man*, London: T. Fisher Unwin.

Sombart, Werner. 1916. *Der moderne Kapitalismus. Band I: Die vorkapitalistische Wirtschaft*, München und Leipzig: Verlag von Duncker & Humblot.

Sombart, Werner. 1928. *Der moderne Kapitalismus. Dritter Band: Das Wirtschaftsleben im Zeitalter des Hochkapitalismus*, München und Leipzig: Verlag von Duncker & Humblot.

Sombart, Werner. 1937. *The New Philosophy*, Princeton: Princeton University Press.

Sombart, Werner. 1951. *The Jews and Modern Capitalism*, New York: Collier Books.

Sombart, Werner. 1967. *Luxury and Capitalism*, Ann Arbor: The Univeristy of Michigan Press.

Soria Mesa, Enrique. 2010. "Los linajudos, honor y conflicto social en la Granada del Siglo de Oro," in: Julián José Lozano Navarro and Juan Luis Castellano, eds., *Violencia y conflictividad en el universe barroco*, Granada: Ediciones Comares.

Sosnowska, Anna. 2019. *Explaining Economic Backwardness. Post-1945 Polish Historians on Eastern Europe*, Budapest: Central European University Press.

Sousa, Lúcio de. 2019. "Judaeo-Converso Merchants in the Private Trade between Macao and Manila in the Early Modern Period," *Journal of Iberian and Latin American Economic History* Vol. 38, No. 3.

Soyer, François. 2007a. *The Persecution of the Jews and Muslims of Portugal: King Manuel I and the End of Religious Tolerance (1496–7)*, Leiden: Brill.

Soyer, François. 2007b. "The Massacre of the New Christians of Lisbon in 1506: A New Eyewitness Account," *Cadernos de Estudos Sefarditas* No. 2.

Soyer, François. 2008. "King Manuel I and the Expulsion of the Castilian Conversos and Muslims from Portugal in 1497: New Perspectives," *Cadernos de Etudos Sefarditas* No. 8.

Spinoza, Benedict. 1891. *A Theologico-Political Treatise*, in: *The Chief Works of Benedict Spinoza* Vol. I, London: George Bell and Sons (revised edition).

Stern, Malcolm H. 1992. "Portuguese Sephardim in the Americas," *American Jewish Archives*, Vol. 44 No. 1.

Stols, Eddy. 2004. "The Expansion of the Sugar Market in Western Europe," in: Stuart B. Schwartz, ed., *Tropical Babylons: Sugar and the Making of the Atlantic World, 1450–1680*, Chapel Hill and London: The University of North Carolina Press.

Strum, Daniel. 2013a. "Resiliência da diáspora e expansão do mercado de agentes ultramarinos no comércio atlântico moderno: os agentes dos mercadores judeus e cristãos-novos na rota do açúcar," *Anais de História de Além-Mar* Vol. xiv.

Strum, Daniel. 2013b. *The Sugar Trade. Brazil, Portugal and the Netherlands, 1595–1630*, Stanford: Stanford University Press.

Stuczynski, Claude B. 2011. "Harmonizing Identities: the Problem of the Integration of the Portuguese Conversos in Early Modern Iberian Corporate Polities," *Jewish History* Vol. 25, No. 2.

Stuczynski, Claude B. 2014. "Negotiated Relationships: Jesuits and Portuguese Conversos – A Reassessment," in: James Bernauer and Robert Aleksander Maryks, eds., *"The Tragic Couple:" Encounters Between Jews and Jesuits*, Leiden and Boston: Brill.

Studnicki-Gizbert, Daviken. 2000. "Companies, Mercantilism and the Development of Seventeenth-Century Overseas Commerce," *Portuguese Studies* Vol. 16.

Studnicki-Gizbert, Daviken. 2002. "Interdependence and the Collective Pursuit of Profits: Portuguese Commercial Networks in the Early Modern Atlantic," in: Diogo Remada Curto and Anthony Molho, eds., *Commercial Networks in the Early Modern World*, European University Institute Working Paper HEC No. 2002/3, Florence.

Studnicki-Gizbert, Daviken. 2005. "Revisting 1640; or, How the Party of Commercial Expansion Lost to the Party of Political Conservation in Spain's Atlantic Empire, 1620–1650," in: Peter A. Coclanis, ed., *The Atlantic Economy during the Seventeenth and Eighteenth Centuries: Organization, Operation, Practice, and Personnel*, Columbia: University of South California Press.

Studnicki-Gizbert, Daviken. 2007. *A Nation Upon the Ocean See. Portugal's Atlantic Diaspora and the Crisis of the Spanish Empire, 1492–1640*, New York: Oxford University Press.

Studnicki-Gizbert, Daviken. 2009. "La Nación among the Nations: Portuguese and Other Maritime Trading Diasporas in the Atlantic, Sixteenth to Eighteenth Centuries," in: Richard L. Kagan and Philip D. Morgan, eds., *Atlantic Diasporas: Jews, Conversos, and Crypto-Jews in the Age of Mercantilism, 1500–1800*, Baltimore: The Johns Hopkins University Press.

Sullón Barreto, Gleydi. 2015. *Vasallos y extranjeros. Portugueses en la Lima virreinal, 1570–1680*, Departamento de Historia de América I, Universidad Complutense de Madrid, Madrid (PhD dissertation).

Sutcliffe, Adam. 2009. "Jewish History in an Age of Atlanticism," in: Richard L. Kagan and Philip D. Morgan, eds., *Atlantic Diasporas: Jews, Conversos, and Crypto-Jews in the Age of Mercantilism, 1500–1800*, Baltimore: The Johns Hopkins University Press.

Sweezy, Paul M. 1978. "A Critique," in: *The Transition from Feudalism to Capitalism*, London: Verso.

Swetschinski, Daniel M. 1981. "Kinship and Commerce: The Foundations of Portuguese Jewish Life in Seventeenth-century Holland," *Studia Rosenthaliana* Vol. 15, No. 1.

Swetschinski, Daniel M. 1982. "Conflict and Opportunity in "Europe's Other Sea": The Adventure of Caribbean Jewish Settlement," *American Jewish History* Vol. 72, No. 2.

Swetschinski, Daniel M. 2004. *Reluctant Cosmopolitans. The Portuguese Jews of Seventeenth-Century Amsterdam*, Oxford and Portland, Oregon: The Littman Library of Jewish Civilization.

Szlajfer, Henryk. 2010. "Żydzi Wernera Sombarta," in: Werner Sombart, *Żydzi i życie gospodarcze*, Warszawa: Wydawnictwo IFiS.

Szlajfer, Henryk. 2012. *Economic Nationalism and Globalization. Lessons from Latin America and Central Europe*, Leiden and Boston: Brill.

Tavim, José Alberto Rodrigues da Silva. 2011. "Jews in the Diaspora with Sepharad in the Mirror: Ruptures, Relations, and Forms of Identity: a Theme Examined Through Three Cases," *Jewish History* Vol. 25, No. 2.

Temkin, Samuel. 2011. *Luis de Carvajal: The Origins of Nuevo Reino de León*, Santa Fe, NM: Sunstone Press.

Thomas, Hugh. 1998. *The Slave Trade. The History of the Atlantic Slave Trade 1440–1870*, London: Papermac.

Thompson, Estevam C. 2011. "Negreiros in the South Atlantic: the Community of "Brazilian" Slave Traders in Late Eighteenth Century Benguela," *African Economic History* Vol. 39.

Thornton, John. 1998. *Africa and Africans in the Making of the Atlantic World, 1400–1800*, Cambridge: Cambridge University Press.

Toch, Michael. 2008. "Economic Activities of German Jews in the Middle Ages," in: Michael Toch in cooperation with Elisabeth Müller-Luchner, ed., *Wirtschaftsgeschichte der mittelalterlichen Juden. Fragen und Einschätzungen*, München: R. Oldenbourg Verlag.

Toch, Michael. 2013. *The Economic History of European Jews: Late Antiquity and Early Middle Ages*, Leiden and Boston: Brill.

Torrão, Maria Manuel Ferraz. 1995. "Rotas comerciais, agentes económicos, meios de pagamento," in: Maria Emília Madeira Santos, ed., *História Geral de Cabo Verde* (*1560–1650*), Vol. II, Lisboa–Praia: Instituto de Investigação Científica Tropical/ Instituto Nacional da Cultura de Cabo Verde.

Torrão, Maria Manuel Ferraz. 1997. "De Santiago para Costa la Guiné: a tranferência do centro geográfico dos negócios e a manutenção da élite comerciante. As transacções da companhia de António Fernandes Landim e de Francisco Dias Mendes de Brito (1629–1630)," *Arquipélago. História* (2ª serie) Vol. II.

Torrão, Maria Manuel Ferraz. 2013. "Os Portugueses e o trato de escravos de Cabo Verde com a América Espanhola no final do século XVI. Os contratadores do trato de Cabo Verde e a Coroa. Uma relação de conveniência numa época de oportunidades (1583–1600)," in: Pedro Cardim et al. eds., *Portugal na monarquia hispânica. Dinâmicas de integración e de conflicto*, Lisboa: CHAM Universidade Nova de Lisboa/ Universidade des Açores.

Torre Revello, José. 1958. "Un contrabandista del siglo XVII en el Río de la Plata," *Revista de Historia de América* No. 45.

Trachtenberg, Joshua. 1943. *The Devil and the Jews. The Medieval Conception of the Jew and Its Relation to the Modern Antisemitism*, New Haven: Yale University Press.

Tritle, Erika. 2015. "Anti-Judaism and a Hermeneutic of the Flesh: a Converso Debate in Fifteenth-Century Spain," *Church History and Religious Culture* Vol. 95.

Trivellato, Francesca. 2009a. "Sephardic Merchants in the Early Modern Atlantic and Beyond: Toward a Comparative Historical Approach to Business Cooperation," in: Richard L. Kagan and Philip D. Morgan, eds., *Atlantic Diasporas: Jews, Conversos, and Crypto-Jews in the Age of Mercantilism, 1500–1800*, Baltimore: The Johns Hopkins University Press.

Trivellato, Francesca. 2009b. *Familiarity of Strangers: the Sephardic Diaspora, Livorno, and Cross-Cultural Trade in the Early Modern Period*, New Haven and London: Yale University Press.

Tuchman, Barbara W. 1988. *The First Salute: a View of the American Revolution*, New York: Alfred A. Knopf.

Twigger, Robert. 1999. *Inflation: the Value of the Pound 1750–1998*, House of Commons Library Research Paper 99/20, London.

Uchmany, Eva Alexandra. 2001. "The Participation of New Christians and Crypto-Jews in the Conquest, Colonization, and Trade of Spanish America, 1521–1660," in: Paolo Bernardini and Norman Fiering, eds., *The Jews and the Expansion of Europe to the West, 1450–1800*, New York and Oxford: Berghahn Books.

Vainfas, Ronaldo. 2007. "Tipologia de desengano: cristãos-novos portugueses entre Amsterdão e o Brasil holandês," *Cadernos de Estudos Sefarditas* No. 7.

Vainfas, Ronaldo. 2012. "Jerusalém pernambucana," in: Hugo Coelho Vieira and Nara Neves Pires Galvão, Leonardo Dantes Silva, eds., *Brasil Holandês. História, memória e patrimônio compartilhado*, São Paulo: Alameda.

Varnhagen, Francisco Adolfo. 2011. *História geral do Brasil. Leitura básica*, Salvador: Centro de Documentação do Pensamiento Brasileiro.

Veen, Ernst van. 2000. *Decay or Defeat? An Inquiry into the Portuguese Decline in Asia, 1580–1645*, Research School of Asian, African and Amerindian Studies (CNWS), Leiden University.

Ventura, Maria da Graça A. Mateus. 1999. *Negreiros portugueses na rota das Índias de Castela (1541–1556)*, Lisboa: Edições Colibri/Instituto de Cultura Ibero-Atlântica.

Ventura, Maria da Graça A. Mateus. 2004. *A participação dos portugueses no comércio regional e inter-regional hispano-americano, a partir do Rio da Prata (1580–1640)*, Colóquio internacional *Território e Povoamento – A presença portuguesa na região platina*, Instituto Camões, Colonia del Sacramento, Uruguai, 23–26 March.

Vieira, Alberto. 2004. "The Sugar Economy of Madeira and the Canaries, 1450–1650," in: Stuart B. Schwartz, ed., *Tropical Babylons: Sugar and the Making of the Atlantic World, 1450–1680*, Chapel Hill and London: The University of North Carolina Press.

Vila Vilar, Enriqueta. 1973. "Los asientos portugueses y el contrabando de negros," *Anuario de Estudios Americanos* Vol. 30.

Vila Vilar, Enriqueta. 1977. *Hispanoamérica y el comercio de esclavos*, Sevilla: Escuela de Estudios Hispano-Americanos.

Vila Vilar, Enriqueta. 1979. "Extranjeros en Cartagena (1553–1630)," *Jahrbuch für Geschichte von Staat, Wirtschaft und Gesellschaft Lateinamerika* Vol. 16.

Vila Vilar, Enriqueta. 2005. "Los europeos en el comercio americano: Sevilla como plataforma," in: Renate Pieper and Peer Schmidt, eds., *Latin America and the Atlantic World/ El mundo atlántico y América Latina (1500–1850). Essays in Honor of Horst Pietschmann*, Köln–Weimar–Wien: Böhlau Verlag.

Vink, Wieke. 2010. *Creole Jews: Negotiating Community in Colonial Suriname*, Leiden: KITLV Press.

Vlessing, Odette. 1995. "The Portuguese-Jewish Merchant Community in Seventeenth-century Amsterdam," in: Clé Lesger and Leo Noordegraaf, eds., *Entrepreneurs and Entrepreneurship in Early Modern Times: Merchants and Industrialists within the Orbit of the Dutch Staple Market*, Den Haag: Stichting Hollandse Historische Reeks.

Voltaire. 1901. *The Works of Voltaire. A Contemporay Version* Vol. VI (*Philosophical Dictionary*), New York: E.R. DuMont.

Wachtel, Nathan. 2001. "Marrano Religiosity in Hispanic America in the Seventeenth Century," in: Paolo Bernardini and Norman Fiering, eds., *The Jews and the Expansion of Europe to the West, 1450–1800*, New York and Oxford: Berghahn Books.

Wachtel, Nathan. 2011. "The 'Marrano' Mercantilist Theory of Duarte Gomes Solis," *The Jewish Quarterly Review* Vol. 101, No. 2.

Wachtel, Nathan. 2013. *The Faith of Remembrance. Marrano Labyrinths*, Philadelphia: University of Pennsylvania Press.

Wadsworth, James E. 2007. *Agents of Orthodoxy: Honor, Status, and the Inquisition in Colonial Pernambuco, Brazil*, Lanham: Rowman & Littlefield Publishers.

Wätjen, Hermann. 1913. "Das Judentum und die Anfänge der modernen Kolonisation," *Vierteljahrschrift für Sozial- und Wirtschaftsgeschichte* 11. Bd., H. 3 und 4.

Wätjen, Hermann. 1921. *Das hollandische Kolonialreich in Brasilien. Ein Kapitel aus der Kolonialgeschichte des 17. Jahrhunderts*, Gotha: Verlag Friedrich Andreas Perthes A.-G.

Wallerstein, Immanuel. 1974. *The Modern World-System: Capitalist Agriculture and the Origins of the European World-Economy in the Sixteenth Century*, New York: Academic Press.

Wallerstein, Immanuel. 2011. *The Modern World-System II: Mercantilism and the Consolidation of the European World-Economy, 1650–1750*, Berkeley and Los Angeles: University of California Press.

Walton, Timothy R. 1994. *The Spanish Treasure Fleets*, Sarasota, Florida: Pineapple Press, Inc.

Weber, Max. 1974. *The Protestant Ethic and the Spirit of Capitalism*, London: Unwin University Books.

Weber, Max. 2003. *The History of Commercial Partnership in the Middle Ages*, Lanham: Rowman & Littlefield Publishers.

Wee, Herman Van der. 1971. "The Economy as a Factor in the Start of the Revolt in the Southern Netherlands," *Acta Historiae Neerlandica* Vol. V.

Weindl, Andrea. 2008. "The Asiento de Negros and International Law," *Journal of the History of International Law* Vol. 10.

Wexler, Paul. 1996. *Non-Jewish Origins of the Sephardic Jews*, Albany: State University of New York Press.

Whitford, David Mark. 2009. *The Curse of Ham in the Early Modern Era. The Bible and the Justifications for Slavery*, Farnham and Burlington: Ashgate Publishing Limited.

Wiznitzer, Arnold. 1954. "The Number of Jews in Dutch Brazil (1630–1654)," *Jewish Social Studies* Vol. 16, No. 2.

Wiznitzer, Arnold. 1960. *Jews in Colonial Brazil*, New York: Columbia University Press.

Wolf, Kenneth Baxter. 2009. "Convivencia in Medieval Spain: a Brief History of an Idea," *Religion Compass* Vol. 3 No. 1.

Wolf, Lucien. 1901. "Introduction: The Return of the Jews to England," in: *Menasseh ben Israel's Mission to Oliver Cromwell*, London: Macmillan & Co.

Wolff, Inge. 1964. "Negrosklaverei und Negerhandel in Hochperu 1545–1640," *Jahrbuch für Geschichte von Staat, Wirtschaft und Gesellschaft Lateinamerikas* Vol. 1.

Zahedieh, Nuala. 1999. "Making Mercantilism Work: London Merchants and Atlantic Trade in the Seventeenth Century," *Transactions of the Royal Historical Society* Vol. 9.

Zahedieh, Nuala. 2018. "Defying Mercantilism: Illicit Trade, Trust, and the Jamaican Sephardim, 1660–1730," *The Historical Journal* Vol. 61, No. 1.

Zając, Ewa. 2014. "Kultura intelektualna Żydów sefardyjskich w średniowiecznej Hiszpanii," *Roczniki Kulturoznawcze* T. V Nr 4.

Index

Not included due to very numerous references: Jews, Sephardim, New Christians, *XN*s, conversos, crypto-Jews, *La Nação*, Inquisition, Amsterdam, Lisbon, Portugal, Spain, the Netherlands, Brazil.